The Queen

of America

Goes to

Washington

City

Edited by

Michèle Aina Barale,

Jonathan Goldberg,

Michael Moon,

and Eve Kosofsky

Sedgwick

THE QUEEN OF AMERICA GOES TO WASHINGTON CITY

Essays on Sex and Citizenship

Lauren Berlant

Berlant talks about a new litmus test for citizenship: (private, personal action: sex, etc the trans. of the ~~prov~~ public sphere into private - or the supplanting of the public by the private.

DUKE UNIVERSITY PRESS *Durham & London 1997*

© 1997 Duke University Press
All rights reserved
Printed in the United States of America on acid-free paper ∞
Typeset in Carter and Cone Galliard by Keystone Typesetting, Inc.
Library of Congress Cataloging-in-Publication Data
appear on the last printed page of this book.

Contents

Acknowledgments

During the early 1990s I delivered sections of this book at more universities than it would be prudent to mention, and many conversations changed the ways the *Queen* now appears. Each chapter has its own set of acknowledgments: for reading large chunks or the book as a whole, I thank the Feminism and Visual Culture group at Chicago (Beth Helsinger, Laura Rigal, Martha Ward); the Center for the Critical Analysis of Contemporary Culture seminar at Rutgers (especially Neil Smith, George Levine, Tim Brennan, Jaime Hovey); and my most excellent reading group comrades at the University of Michigan (Fernando Coronil, Roger Rouse, David Scobey, Julie Skurski).

I must also thank individual friends and colleagues. Tom Stillinger was my closest interlocutor during the book's early years, and I am profoundly indebted to his wisdom, support, and sheer hard work. Ben Anderson, Mandy Berry, Geoff Eley, Beth Freeman, Jody Greene, Elaine Hadley, June Howard, Mary Poovey, Eve Sedgwick, Dana Seitler, Sasha Torres, Candace Vogler, Lisa Wedeen, and Robyn Wiegman read and talked with me about these matters at length, in critical and inspiring ways. Ethan Putterman and Suchi Gururaj provided valuable research aid; Leslie Patterson, Dana Seitler, Gwen Harrigan, Burton Avery, Satre Stulke, and Beatriz Muñoz Santiago performed some arduous clerical and creative archival acts, for which I am very grateful. I must also acknowledge Madeline Matz at the Library of Congress, whose erudition and warmth considerably enriched the making of the archive.

Many of these chapters have previously been published in some form. I thank *boundary 2* (especially Don Pease, Jonathan Arac, Paul Bové, and the great editor Meg Sachse); *Public Culture* (especially Carol Breckenridge and Arjun Appadurai); *Feminist Studies* (especially Rayna Rapp and Judy Gardiner); *American Literature* (especially Cathy Davidson and Michael Moon); Cary Nelson; and Dilip Gaonkar. I also thank Beth Freeman for (permission to include) our collaborative work, "Queer Nationality." Ken Wissoker was an inspired and *patient* editor. As were the attending editors of Series Q (Jonathan Goldberg, Michael Moon), whose feedback was acute and motivational.

Finally, the *Queen* is dedicated to four beloved people of great genius whose *liveness* gives substance to all my optimism: Michael Warner, Laura Kipnis, Katie Stewart, Roger Rouse.

The Queen

of America

Goes to

Washington

City

Introduction: The Intimate Public Sphere

Something strange has happened to citizenship. During the rise of the Reaganite right, a familial politics of the national future came to define the urgencies of the present. Now everywhere in the United States intimate things flash in people's faces: pornography, abortion, sexuality, and reproduction; marriage, personal morality, and family values. These issues do not arise as private concerns: they are key to debates about what "America" stands for, and are deemed vital to defining how citizens should act. In the process of collapsing the political and the personal into a world of public intimacy, a nation made for adult citizens has been replaced by one imagined for fetuses and children.[1] How did these changes come to be, and why?

The story can be told many ways. During this period, a cartoon version of a crisis in U.S. citizenship has become established as a standard truth. In the cartoon version of the shaken nation, a citizen is defined as a person traumatized by some aspect of life in the United States. Portraits and stories of citizen-victims — pathological, poignant, heroic, and grotesque — now permeate the political public sphere, putting on display a mass experience of economic insecurity, racial discord, class conflict, and sexual unease.

This coupling of suffering and citizenship is so startling and so moving because it reveals about national power both its impersonality and its intimacy. The experience of social hierarchy is intensely individuating, yet it also makes people public and generic: it turns them into *kinds* of people who are both attached to and underdescribed by the identities that organize them. This paradox of partial legibility is behind much of the political and personal anger that arises in scenes of misrecognition in everyday life — at work, on the street, at home, under the law, and even

2

in aesthetic experience. Yet the public rhetoric of citizen trauma has become so pervasive and competitive in the United States that it obscures basic differences among modes of identity, hierarchy, and violence. Mass national pain threatens to turn into banality, a crumbling archive of dead signs and tired plots.

This exhaustion of cultural struggle over the material and symbolic conditions of U.S. citizenship is a desired effect of conservative cultural politics, whose aim is to dilute the oppositional discourses of the historically stereotyped citizens — people of color, women, gays, and lesbians. Against these groups are pitted the complaints not of stereotyped peoples burdened by a national history but icons who have only recently lost the protections of their national iconicity — politicians who are said to have lost their "zone of privacy"; ordinary citizens who are said to feel that they have lost access to the American Dream; white and male and heterosexual people of all classes who are said to sense that they have lost the respect of their culture, and with it the freedom to feel unmarked.[2]

Indeed, today many formerly iconic citizens who used to feel undefensive and unfettered feel truly exposed and vulnerable. They feel anxious about their value to themselves, their families, their publics, and their nation. They sense that they now have *identities,* when it used to be just other people who had them.[3] These new feelings provoke many reactions. One response is to desire that the nation recommit itself to the liberal promise of a conflict-free and integrated world. Another is to forge a scandal, a scandal of ex-privilege: this can include rage at the stereotyped peoples who have appeared to change the political rules of social membership, and, with it, a desperate desire to return to an order of things deemed normal, an order of what was felt to be a general everyday intimacy that was sometimes called "the American way of life." To effect either restoration of the imagined nation, the American ex-icon denigrates the political present tense and incites nostalgia for the national world of its iconicity, setting up that lost world as a utopian horizon of political aspiration.

These narratives of traumatized identity have dramatically reshaped the dominant account of U.S. citizenship. They also show that politics by caricature can have profound effects: on the ways people perceive their own social value and the social value of "Others"; on the ways they live daily life and see their futures; and on mainstream political discourse, which exploits the national identity crises it foments to claim a popular mandate for radical shifts in norms of ideology and political practice.[4]

The Queen of America Goes to Washington City attends to the ways in which these rhetorics of a traumatized core national identity have come to describe, and thereby to make, something real. It tracks the triumph of the Reaganite view that the intimacy of citizenship is something scarce and sacred, private and proper, and only for members of families. It focuses on the ways conservative ideology has convinced a citizenry that the core context of politics should be the sphere of private life. In so doing, it develops a different story about what has happened to citizenship in both the law and daily life during the last few decades. The privatization of citizenship has involved manipulating an intricate set of relations between economic, racial, and sexual processes. This chapter begins to lay out some aspects of their relation.

Here is another way of telling the story. My first axiom is that there is no public sphere in the contemporary United States, no context of communication and debate that makes ordinary citizens feel that they have a common public culture, or influence on a state that holds itself accountable to their opinions, critical or otherwise. By "ordinary citizens" I mean ones without wealth and structural access to brokers of power. The antiwar, antiracist, and feminist agitations of the sixties denounced the hollow promises of the political pseudopublic sphere; then, a reactionary response grew dominant, which claimed that, in valuing national criticism over patriotic identification, and difference over assimilation, sixties radicals had damaged and abandoned the core of U.S. society.

A conservative coalition formed whose aim was the privatization of U.S. citizenship. One part of its project involved rerouting the critical energies of the emerging political sphere into the sentimental spaces of an amorphous opinion culture, characterized by strong patriotic identification mixed with feelings of practical political powerlessness. A number of different forces and themes converged to bring about this end: the antifederal but patriotic nationalism of Reagan Republicanism, which sought to shrink the state while intensifying identification with the utopian symbolic "nation"; a rhetorical shift from a state-based and thus political identification with nationality to a culture-based concept of the nation as a site of integrated social membership; the expansion of a mass-mediated space of opinion formation that positions citizens as isolated spectators to the publicity that claims to represent them; the marketing of nostalgic images of a normal, familial America that would define the utopian context for citizen aspiration. Much of this agenda continues beyond the Reagan years, as Clintonite liberalism strives to find a middle ground on the right.

This set of successful transformations has reinvigorated the idea of the American Dream. It would be all too easy to ridicule the Dream, and to dismiss it as the motivating false consciousness of national/capitalist culture. But the fantasy of the American Dream is an important one to learn from. A popular form of political optimism, it fuses private fortune with that of the nation: it promises that if you invest your energies in work and family-making, the nation will secure the broader social and economic conditions in which your labor can gain value and your life can be lived with dignity. It is a story that addresses the fear of being stuck or reduced to a type, a redemptive story pinning its hope on class mobility. Yet this promise is voiced in the language of unconflicted personhood: to be American, in this view, would be to inhabit a secure space liberated from identities and structures that seem to constrain what a person can do in history. For this paradoxical feeling to persist, such that a citizen of the Dream can feel firmly placed in a zone of protected value while on the move in an arc of social mobility, the vulnerability of personal existence to the instability of capitalism and the concretely unequal forms and norms of national life must be suppressed, minimized, or made to seem exceptional, not general to the population. This sets the stage for a national people imagining itself national only insofar as it feels un-marked by the effects of these national contradictions.

The fear of being saturated and scarred by the complexities of the present and thereby barred from living the "Dream" has recently pro-duced a kind of vicious yet sentimental cultural politics, a politics brim-ming over with images and faces of normal and abnormal America. In the patriotically-permeated pseudopublic sphere of the present tense, national politics does not involve starting with a view of the nation as a space of struggle violently separated by racial, sexual, and economic inequalities that cut across every imaginable kind of social location. In-stead, the dominant idea marketed by patriotic traditionalists is of a core nation whose survival depends on personal acts and identities performed in the intimate domains of the quotidian.

It is in this sense that the political public sphere has become an inti-mate public sphere. The intimate public of the U.S. present tense is radically different from the "intimate sphere" of modernity described by Jürgen Habermas. Habermas portrays the intimate sphere of the Euro-pean eighteenth century as a domestic space where persons produced the sense of their own private uniqueness, a sense of self which became a sense of citizenship only when it was abstracted and alienated in the nondomestic public sphere of liberal capitalist culture. In contrast, the intimate public sphere of the U.S. present tense renders citizenship as a condition of social membership produced by personal acts and values, especially acts originating in or directed toward the family sphere. No longer valuing personhood as something directed toward public life, contemporary nationalist ideology recognizes a public good only in a particularly constricted nation of simultaneously lived private worlds.[5]

This vision of a privatized, intimate core of national culture rings dramatic changes on the concept of the body politic, which is rarely valued as a *public*.[6] In the new nostalgia-based fantasy nation of the "American way of life," the residential enclave where "the family" lives usurps the modernist promise of the culturally vital, multiethnic city; in the new, utopian America, mass-mediated political identifications can only be rooted in traditional notions of home, family, and community. Meanwhile, the notion of a public life, from the profession of politician to non-family-based forms of political activism, has been made to seem ridiculous and even dangerous to the nation. Downsizing citizenship to a mode of voluntarism and privacy has radically changed the ways national identity is imagined, experienced, and governed in political and mass-media public spheres and in everyday life.

The Queen of America asks why it is, and how it has come to be, that a certain cluster of demonic and idealized images and narratives about sex and citizenship has come to obsess the official national public sphere. It asks why the most hopeful national pictures of "life" circulating in the public sphere are not of adults in everyday life, in public, or in politics, but rather of the most vulnerable minor or virtual citizens—fetuses, children, real and imaginary immigrants—persons that, paradoxically, cannot yet act as citizens. It asks why acts that are not civic acts, like sex, are having to bear the burden of defining proper citizenship. It asks why a conservative politics that maintains the sacredness of privacy, the virtue of the free market, and the immorality of state overregulation contradicts everything it believes when it comes to issues of intimacy. It asks why the pursuit of some less abstracted and more corporeal forms of "happiness"—through sex and through multicultural and sexual identity politics—has come to exemplify dangerous and irresponsible citizenship for some and utopian practice for others.[7] Meanwhile, it also asks to what degree liberals and the left have absorbed the conservative world view, relinquishing the fight against structural inequality for a more labile and optimistic culturalist perspective.

Each chapter to follow tracks a controversial guiding image of U.S. citizenship through the process of its privatization; and each highlights some pilgrimages to Washington, the capital space which stands in for the nation, acting as its local form. These secular pilgrimages measure the intimate distances between the nation and some of the people who seek to be miraculated by its promise. We will see that in the reactionary culture of imperiled privilege, the nation's value is figured not on behalf of an actually existing and laboring adult, but of a future American, both incipient and pre-historical: especially invested with this hope are the American fetus and the American child. What constitutes their national supericonicity is an image of an American, perhaps the last living American, not yet bruised by history: not yet caught up in the processes of secularization and sexualization; not yet caught in the confusing and exciting identity exchanges made possible by mass consumption and ethnic, racial, and sexual mixing; not yet tainted by money or war. This national icon is still tacitly white, and it still contains the blueprint for the reproductive form that assures the family and the nation its future history. This national icon is still innocent of knowledge, agency, and accountability and thus has ethical claims on the adult political agents who write laws, make culture, administer resources, control things.

But most important, the fetal/infantile person is a *stand-in* for a complicated and contradictory set of anxieties and desires about national identity. Condensed into the image/hieroglyph of the innocent or incipient American, these anxieties and desires are about whose citizenship — whose subjectivity, whose forms of intimacy and interest, whose bodies and identifications, whose heroic narratives — will direct America's future. But the abstract image of the future generated by the national culture machine also stands for a crisis in the present: what gets consolidated now as the future modal citizen provides an alibi or an inspiration for the moralized political rhetorics of the present and for reactionary legislative and juridical practice.

These questions — of sex and citizenship, of minor and full citizens, and of mass national culture — have long been concerns regarding the United States (from Tocqueville's suspicion of democracy's infantilizing effects to the infantilized masculinity of the cold war).[8] But the national nervous system has become especially animated by the right-wing cultural agenda of the Reagan revolution.[9] One effect of this revolution has been to stigmatize these long-standing anxieties as "victim politics," a phrase that deliberately suppresses the complexity, ambivalence, and incoherence of social antagonism in the everyday life of contemporary citizenship.

The right-wing cultural agenda of the Reagan revolution — a phrase that resonates throughout this book — is my name for the public discourse around citizenship and morality that a complex bloc of activists has engendered during roughly the last two decades.[10] I have suggested that it bases its affirmative rhetoric on a nationalist politics of intimacy, which it contrasts to threatening practices of nonfamilial sexuality and, by implication, other forms of racial and economic alterity. The Reagan revolution not only has suffused "the personal" with political meanings well beyond those imagined in the "sexual revolution" of the 1960s, but it has had three other important consequences. First, it has helped to create some extremely limiting frames for thinking about what properly constitutes the practice of U.S. citizenship. One famous example of this process is Peggy Noonan and George Bush's image of the American people as "a thousand points of light."[11] This brightly lit portrait of a civic army of sanctified philanthropists was meant to replace an image of the United States as a Great Society with a state-funded social safety net. It sought to substitute intentional individual goodwill for the nation-state's commitment to fostering democracy within capitalism. Practical citizenship is here figured as something available to good people with good money. Now the Christian Coalition and the Republican Party are promoting legislation to put this fantasy into institutional practice by, among other things, advocating the transfer of federal entitlement programs for the "deserving poor" to private, voluntary, "faith-based" organizations.[12]

In addition, following the Reaganite tendency to fetishize both the offensive example and the patriotic norm, the increasingly monopolistic mass media act as a national culture industry whose mission is to micromanage how any controversial event or person changes the meaning of being "American." The constant polling used by this media apparatus, which includes the solicitation of testimony on talk radio and television, along with telephone interviews, has paradoxically enabled the standards and rhetorics of citizenship to become so privatized and subjective that even privileged people can seem legitimately to claim "outsider," if not "minority," status.[13] With political ideas about the nation sacrificed to the development of feelings about it, nationality has become a zone of trauma that demands political therapy.

The third consequence of the Reaganite cultural revolution involves the way intimacy rhetoric has been employed to manage the economic crisis that separates the wealthy few from everyone else in the contemporary United States. By defining the United States as a place where normal intimacy is considered the foundation of the citizen's happiness, the right has attempted to control the ways questions of economic survival are seen as matters of citizenship. This use of intimacy is extremely complicated. First, it helps displace from sustained public scrutiny the relation between congealed corporate wealth and the shifting conditions of labor; second, it becomes a rhetorical means by which the causes of U.S. income inequality and job instability in all sectors of the economy can be personalized, rephrased in terms of individuals' capacity to respond flexibly to the new "opportunities" presented to them within an increasingly volatile global economy; third, it enables the hegemonic state-business class to promote a virulent competition between the native-born and immigrant poor. Even when economic issues are explicitly joined to institutions of intimacy — as in the current emphasis on family-oriented state entitlements for the middle classes — the "economic" foregrounds personal acts of saving and consumption over what happens in the workplace and the boardroom.[14]

As discussions of the politics of sex and bodily identity in the United States have become so fascinating and politically absorbing, a concern with the outrages of American class relations has been made to seem trite and unsexy. It is my view that a critical engagement with what ought to constitute the social privileges and obligations of citizenship must be reorganized around these questions — of national capitalism, metropolitan and rural poverty, environmental disintegration, racist thinking and ordinary concrete practice, and other banalities of national evil. Questions of intimacy, sexuality, reproduction, and the family — the concerns of this book — are properly interrelated with these questions of identity, inequality, and national existence. No doubt these issues and institutions of intimacy will continue to be central to the disposition of national life, but as separate entities they should no longer overorganize the terms of public discussion about power, ethics, and the nation.

The materialist litany that the previous paragraph just begins to recite has been made to seem orthodox, boring, facile, or an occasion for paralyzed mourning.[15] Numerous efforts have been devoted to neutralizing these issues, all of which aim to separate out consideration of the economic conditions of citizenship from questions of culture and subjectivity. It almost goes without saying that the wealth of the wealthy classes in the United States is protected by this divisive rhetoric. The suggestion that capitalism is always on the brink of failing — as the current rhetoric of downsizing and scarcity would claim — terrorizes many workers into feeling competitive with each other and into overvalorizing individual will, as though personal willpower alone would be enough to make "market democracy" deliver on its "promise." Likewise, the utopia of a color-blind and gender-consensual society has been used as an alibi to make cases of egregious inequality seem like exceptions to a national standard, rather than a structural condition. In addition, the political alliance between business culture and the Christian right enables legitimate political dissent and outrage to be recast as immorality and even blasphemy.[16] Finally, the use of intimacy as a distraction from critical engagement with a general matrix of ordinary hard hierarchy actually impairs discussions of intimacy itself, in its broader social contexts.

The hegemonic achievement of Reaganite conservatism is also evident in its effects on its adversaries on the left. For example, a growing number of scholars and activists who speak from identity movements celebrate the ways U.S. subalterns develop tactics for survival from within capitalist culture: forms of activity like gay marriage, critically-motivated acts of commodity consumption, and identity-based economic investment zones are said to make marginalized social groups more central, more legitimate and powerful in capitalist society. Yet for all the importance of survival tactics, a politics that advocates the subaltern appropriation of normative forms of the good life makes a kind of (often tacit) peace with exploitation and normativity, as well as with the other less happy and frequently less visible aspects of capitalist culture outlined above.[17]

In addition, many radical social theorists see the political deployment of intimacy crises as merely ornamental or a distraction from "real" politics. They have become alienated by the intensities of the sex and identity wars, which seem to be disconnected from more important and public questions of equity, justice, and violence in political life in general.[18] But they have been misdirected by a false distinction between the merely personal and the profoundly structural.[19] These forms of sociality too often appear to be in separate worlds of analysis and commitment, with catastrophic political consequences for critical engagement with the material conditions of citizenship.[20] It is the purpose of *The Queen of America* to challenge both the terms of the Reaganite revolution and the ways it has been opposed. Above all, it is to interfere with the intimate image of the national body that has, like a sunspot, both illuminated and blinded the world of mass politics and national fantasy in the contemporary United States.

"I Hate Your Archive": On Methodology and National Culture

Americans experience themselves as national through public sphere accounts of what is important about them: this is why the manufacture of public opinion is crucial both for producing citizens and seeing how citizens are produced.[21] Yet people are not saturated by their identity as citizens, even during political campaigns, at baseball games, or listening to talk radio. Unless the terms of their normality or membership are being actively challenged, many people claim that their national identity is an extremely minor or null modality of their everyday experience of who they are. Being American or national feels inconsequential to their ordinary survival and makes no difference when they are thinking about what it is in their intimate lives that sustains them.

In this book I am not trying to argue that citizenship is *really* the central category for people who imagine themselves primarily propped up by other identifications and axes of hope for the future. Nor am I claiming that the sum of the texts I engage equals the meaning of being American. Quite the contrary. Practices of citizenship involve both public-sphere narratives and concrete experiences of quotidian life that do not cohere or harmonize. Yet the rhetoric of citizenship does provide important definitional frames for the ways people see themselves as *public,* when they do.

At the moment, an incessant public struggle over the meaning of being a citizen of the United States encounters a widespread sense that the nation-state is an autonomous device that has little to do with the needs of ordinary people. The reactionary right's hegemonic project has been to say that it is closing this gap. Yet it is also the case that the abstracting of the U.S. state from its citizens has become more acute during the era of Reaganism. The anti-political politics of contemporary conservative culture has many paradoxical effects on citizen subjectivity, among which is the angry fading of public political agency aspirations.

Nowhere is this paradox more starkly evident than in the recent proliferation of hyperpatriotic but antifederal militia-style activity.

The patriotic intensity of the Reaganite right works against identification with government itself, especially in its federal incarnation. It makes citizenship into a category of feeling irrelevant to practices of hegemony or sociality in everyday life. We might call this antipolitical politics "national sentimentality": it is sentimental because it is a politics that abjures politics, made on behalf of a private life protected from the harsh realities of power.[22] The sense that this discussion is considered *not* to be about citizenship, that it is about using power only to create the conditions of true intimacy, has been one of the great advertising coups of the conservative campaign to turn the nation into a privatized state of feeling.

I have deliberately used the language of advertising to describe the means by which the contemporary conservative or traditional conception of national life has been advanced. Advertising makes explicit the routes by which persons might individually and collectively give a name to their desire. It does not tell the truth about desires that already exist, although it does not merely invent desires for people. But advertising helps bring to consciousness a will to happiness that transcends any particular advertisement or commodity, but which becomes authorized by them. The official public-sphere campaign to demonize radical justice movements and to make only particular kinds of national life iconic has deployed the very strategies of linking happiness to desire that advertising uses, so that politicians can say that all who hold a certain sustaining set of wishes hold the same intimate feelings about how they should be reflected in national life, whether or not people actually do make these linkages in any conscious, consistent, or coherent way. The right-wing national culture industry thus forges the very name of political desire; at this moment, the absorption of these wishes into the brand names "American Dream" and "American Way of Life" has virtually taken on the form of common sense. Throughout this book I will point to the routes by which some reactionary arguments have become prosaic. Paradoxically, once they become banal, they are at their most powerful: no longer inciting big feelings and deep rages, these claims about the world seem hardwired into what is taken for granted in collective national life.[23]

In the spring of 1994, I delivered as a lecture a chapter from this book. Afterward, a colleague said, "I really admired your thinking, but—I hate your archive." I loved this moment (I knew an anecdote was forming), but I had to know more. Was this an aggressive disciplinary question, implicitly asking me to return to the more canonical or literary texts on which I had honed my professional reading and analytic skills? Did he think it was cheating, somehow, to read closely texts that are not obviously conceptually challenging? In response to these queries he assented generally, but he also wanted me to speak more explicitly in the traditional languages and narratives of critical theory, and in particular to make explicit the ways Foucault, Benjamin, and Gramsci have enabled my understanding of national culture. (He was right about that, but apparently hadn't heard the ways other work—say, that of Eve Sedgwick, Hortense Spillers, Fredric Jameson, Michael Warner, and Judith Butler—has also made this analysis possible. But this miscue over my archive raises other questions about the politics of academic theory.)[24] This exchange also helped me to clarify the professional juncture at which I and others in cultural studies stand at the present moment:[25] because humanists traditionally get value by being intimate with the classics (literary and theoretical), those who think through popular materials and waste thought on objects that were not made for it threaten to degrade the value of intellectual life in general and the value of the humanities in particular.

In the previous paragraphs I demonstrate why a different strategy of reading can be productive for the analysis of contemporary American life. One does not find the materials of the patriotic public sphere theorizing citizenship in either beautiful or coherent ways. These materials frequently use the silliest, most banal and erratic logic imaginable to describe important things, like what constitutes intimate relations, political personhood, and national life. In this book I am conducting a counterpolitics of the silly object by focusing on some instances of it and by developing a mode of criticism and conceptualization that reads the waste materials of everyday communication in the national public sphere as pivotal documents in the construction, experience, and rhetoric of quotidian citizenship in the United States.[26] The very improvisatory ephemerality of the archive makes it worth *reading*. Its very popularity, its effects on the law and on everyday life, makes it important. Its very ordinariness requires an intensified critical engagement with what had been merely undramatically explicit.

There might, of course, be other reasons why people might hate my archive. A reader might feel that this book is not evenhanded and that it is stacked in order to be politically correct, while others have suggested that it is far too sympathetic to the kinds of utopian wishes for unconflicted normality expressed by both liberals and conservatives. One colleague asked me: "Why bother reading middlebrow nonsense like *Time* magazine and reactionary dogma like the *Contract with America,* when you could be theorizing and promoting the world-building activities evident in the pamphlets, zines, polemics, and literatures of radical or subaltern publics?" I do track both formal and informal subaltern resistance throughout the book, but I am more interested in looking at the moments of oppressive optimism in normal national culture: to see what kinds of domination are being imagined as forms of social good; what kinds of utopian desires are being tapped and translated into conservative worldviews; what means are being used to suppress the negative fallout of affirmative culture; what it might take to make linked kinds of knowledge, power, and experience no longer seem separate. I read these mainstream documents and discourses of the nation not as white noise but as powerful language, not as "mere" fiction or fantasy but as violence and desire that have material effects.

Someone might also hate my archive because it is so resolutely *national.* Increasingly, radical scholars have been demanding the end of an American Studies that places the United States and the nation form in general at the center of the history of the present tense.[27] Transnational capital and global media produce subjects and publics that are no longer organized around the politics of representation within the confines of a single state, and states increasingly ally with transnational capital in organizing processes of production that transect their borders. In addition, the combination of migration and new technologies of travel and interpersonal communication have so changed and challenged the ways national life operates that the notion of a modal person who is a citizen with one pure national affiliation and loyalty to only the place she or he currently lives markedly underdescribes the experiences and political struggles of persons across the globe.

But this does not mean that states are not still powerful political agents, or that the ideology of nationhood has become enervated, the faint howling of an archaic dream of democratic legitimation. Indeed, it is precisely under transnational conditions that the nation becomes a more intense object of concern and struggle. This is why this book focuses on the story the official national culture industry tells in the contemporary United States, a story that instates an intimate public sphere as a site of mediation in which citizens can both feel their linkage to one another through the nation and negotiate their relation to the transnational. In this way the nation form retains its centrality to definitions and possibilities of political agency. Borrowing its aura from romantic or domestic privacy, this sentimental version of the nation provides a scene in which fragments of identity are held to become whole. Part of the aim of soliciting intensified identification with the idealized nation is a highly contested project of shrinking the state and breaking down its function as a "utopia of social labor."[28] The simultaneous contraction of the state and expansion of the nation produces an incoherent set of boundary-drawing panics about the profound economic and cultural effects of transnational capitalism and immigration. Tracking the American Dream machine, for all its banality and parochialism, must thus be part of the project of describing the specificity of politics and subjectivity in a present tense that is at once national and transnational.

I try saying something different about these national objects through experimental or unusual kinds of storytelling, for I feel that I can best show how the national present has been constructed through radical recontextualization.[29] This kind of writing does not aspire merely to comment on or contextualize its object; it brings new objects into being via the textual performance. I want to make the hegemonic national icon/stereotype and the narratives that maintain the political culture they operate in look unfamiliar and uninevitable, while also shifting the ways mass politics, critical practice, identity, embodiment, and intimate political feelings can be imagined and mobilized.

This project of frame-breaking through overreading the discursive scene of the contemporary nation was first inspired by the following passage from Harriet Jacobs's *Incidents in the Life of a Slave Girl* (1861), to which I will return in chapter 6. Jacobs tells the story to show how slaves maintained optimism about political and personal freedom despite massive evidence to the contrary. Some slaves even clung to the idea of a United States that would, if it could, purify itself of its most unjust institution. Jacobs's friend reports that another slave, a literate one, has read in the newspaper some exciting news: on learning that the president tolerated a nation that trafficked in slavery, "the queen of 'Merica . . . didn't believe it, and went to Washington city to see the President about it. They quarrelled; she drew her sword upon him, and swore that he should help her to make them all free." This prompts Jacobs to observe:

That poor ignorant woman thought that America was governed by a Queen, to whom the President was subordinate. I wish the President was subordinate to Queen Justice.[30]

Jacobs shows that a great deal of language and logic circulating through the national public sphere is absurd, ignorant, and extremely consequential to the ways people understand and act within what they perceive to be the possibilities of their lives. She takes seriously this failed communication about the nation not only to show how dominated people find ways to sustain their hopefulness in a cruel world, but also to show how the kinds of invention, innovation, and improvisation her illiterate interlocutor practiced with only partial knowledge could be used radically, for the reimagination of collective political life within the nation.

The drastic redefinition of American personhood during the Reagan era has been established as common sense by being marketed as merely descriptive of what already exists, even while controversy has long been raging around its contours. This compels me to write *The Queen of America* as an iconoclastic national counterfantasy, one meant to make you pause long enough to consider how, if you are a U.S. citizen or live in the United States, the ephemera of patriotic conservative orthodoxy have become central to your public definition.

On the Heterosexuality of the Queen

In the quasi-queer film *Boys on the Side* (dir. Herbert Ross, 1995), a heterosexual man who is speaking to a lesbian about his longing for a woman they both desire says, "I think heterosexuality's going to make a comeback." His joke would be an ironic throwaway line were it not for the film's commitment to associating heterosexuality with "life" and lesbian desire with the virtue of abstinence and the tragedy of death by AIDS. (This takes some doing, since the AIDS transmitted in the film originates in a heterosexual one-night stand, but no matter.) The defining sexual event of the generation currently coming to national power in the United States was the sexual revolution, with its accompanying shift in the availability of birth control / abortion: this was a revolution, largely, in heterosexuality. While gay- and lesbian-rights movements were contemporary with the sexual revolution, the revolution that dominated the public-sphere discussion of sex and feminism was not mainly concerned with nonheterosexual forms of identity or behavior. In contrast, for the current generations entering into sexuality, the defining issue is AIDS and other forms of disease and death. The transformation in national sexual culture from thinking about sexuality in terms of lives already in progress to imagining sexuality in the shadow of deaths to be avoided registers a shift in the contours of national personhood that is widely experienced, but little narrated. This is a revolution that has forced a generation of sexual subjects to become conscious of a much larger variety of life practices, and to see that these constitute a field of choices and identifications ordinary people make.

No one coming into sexuality in contemporary America can avoid thinking about gay, lesbian, bisexual, transsexual, transgendered, or other categories of sexuality. Some might share with their parents a nostalgia for a time when sex practice seemed to flow naturally from the life-building hopes children are taught to have for the stable reproductive family and for wedding presents. These are the people for whom the desire for heterosexuality to make a "comeback" actually makes some sense. To them, a "comeback" would mean that you would not have to think about sexual preference; it would mean that only the rare and unfortunate people who have the nondominant sexuality would have to imagine it, and then keep it to themselves.

Many of us, however, experience the world as permeated by the practices and narratives of what Michael Warner has called heteronormative culture — a public culture, juridical, economic, and aesthetic, organized for the promotion of a world-saturating heterosexuality.[31] The phenomenal forms of heteronormative culture will vary as people locate themselves differently in racial, class, gender, regional, or religious contexts, contexts which mark the experience of sexualization with specific traumatic/liberatory intensity. But nowhere in the United States has heterosexuality gone into a decline or "left" in a way that makes the idea of a comeback even remotely plausible. It has been and remains culturally dominant. There is a vast culture industry constantly generating text and law on behalf of heterosexuality's preservation and extension into resistant or unincorporated domains of identification and fantasy. Take, for example, *The Crying Game* (dir. Neil Jordan, 1992), with its offer of a celibate same-sex couple in heterosexual drag as the fantasy solution to the problem of sexual and postcolonial violence. Or take sex education, which has again become controversial now that its tendency is to speak of things not conjugally heterosexual, like different sexual preferences and nonreproductive sexual practices. According to the cultural agenda of the radical right, sex education, when it happens at all, should be a great terrorist device for breaking in straight sexual subjects who fancy each other but don't have sex, as in *The Crying Game:* if not, it will be seen simply as an immoral mechanism for promoting sex.

Yet it is a sexual and political fact that heterosexual life no longer seems the only mentionable one in the United States. This is what continues to fuel a state of sexual emergency, through homophobic and racist policies in the state and federal system, along with various forms of defensiveness, rage, and nostalgia among ordinary citizens who liked it better when their sexuality could be assumed to be general for the population as a whole. Heterosexuality has never "left": it has had to become newly explicit, and people have had to become aware of the institutions, narratives, pedagogies, and social practices that support it.

The false history of ex-privileged heterosexuality—the story that it went out of fashion—tells us something important about how nationality and sexuality meet up in the official public sphere. Identity is marketed in national capitalism as a property. It is something you can purchase, or purchase a relation to. Or it is something you already own that you can express: *my* masculinity, *my* queerness, for example (this is why bisexuality has not made it fully into the sexual star system: it is hard to *express* bisexuality). Michel Foucault and scholars like Judith Butler and Jonathan Ned Katz have shown how sexuality is the modern form of self-intelligibility: I am my identity; my identity is fundamentally sexual; and my practices reflect that (and if they don't, they require submission to sexual science, self-help, or other kinds of law).[32] The account of the total correspondence between acts and identities that marked the controversy over gays in the military manifested the juridical understanding of sexuality: my perverse act expresses my perverse identity; the state has a compelling interest in protecting the family by repressing my perversion; hence, no gays in the military; and hence, no privacy protection for any non-reproductive sexual practice or identity. Insofar as the politics and the medical crisis brought into collective awareness by AIDS has made it impossible to draw an absolute public boundary between U.S. citizens and gay people, and as that increasing consciousness makes people aware of and more interested in gay, lesbian, and queer culture, it has also helped broaden the conservative rage against non-heteronormative forms of sexual activity and identity, which include all kinds of nonreproductive heterosexual activity, and sex and childbirth outside marriage.

But identity need not be simply a caption for an image of an unchanging concrete self. It is also a theory of the future, of history. This leads to the second way sexuality has met up with national fantasy. I have described the first way in the regulation of "perversion" on behalf of a heterofamilial citizenship norm. The second is in the way the generational form of the family has provided a logic of the national future. When the modal form of the citizen is called into question, when it is no longer a straight, white, reproductively inclined heterosexual but rather might be anything, any jumble of things, the logic of the national future comes into crisis.

This crisis of the national future, stimulated by sexual politics, comes at a time when America feels unsure about its value in a number of domains: in world military politics, in global economics, in ecological practice, and in the claim that the nation has a commitment to sustaining justice, democracy, and the American Dream when there seems to be less money and reliable work to go around. Along with sex-radical politics and feminism, multiculturalism and transnational capitalism and the widening social inequities that have accompanied it have called the national narrative into question. *What will the American future look like?* Suddenly no narrative seems to flow naturally from the identity people thought was their national birthright: of course, that birthright was partly protected because it was tacit. But let us think for a minute about this birthright, its corporeal norms, and the future it purported to produce.

Here is a brief story about the history of birthright citizenship in the United States, beginning with a familiar kind of long view. In the eighteenth century, the United States came into being via a democratic revolution against a geographically distant monarchial authority and an economically aggressive colonial marginality. The fantasy of a national democracy was based on principles of abstract personhood (all persons shall be formally equivalent) and its rational representation in a centralized state and federal system. The constitutional American "person" was a white male property owner: more than that, though, was unenumerated in the law.

These abstract principles of democratic nationality have always been hypocritical.[33] From the beginning, entire populations of persons were excluded from the national promise which, because it was a promise, was held out paradoxically: falsely, as a democratic reality, and legitimately, as a promise, the promise that the democratic citizenship form makes to people caught in history. The populations who were and are managed by the discipline of the promise — women, African Americans, Native Americans, immigrants, homosexuals — have long experienced simultaneously the wish to be full citizens and the violence of their partial citizenship. Of course, the rules of citizenship constantly change, both in the law and in the public sense of how persons ought to be treated, protected, and encouraged to act. But it is not false to say that over the long term some of us have been American enough to provide labor but not American enough to be sustained by the fullest resources of democratic national privilege.

During the twentieth century, however, changes in the economy and in the juridical and everyday life politics of identity have forced the birthright assumptions of U.S. nationality into a vulnerable explicitness, and this very explicitness is making the patriots of the ex-tacit nation very unhappy. In response, a virulent form of revitalized national heterosexuality has been invented, a form that is complexly white and middle class, for reasons I address throughout. I found, when circulating chapters from this book, that some readers feel I am too hard on heterosexuality. I do not mean to be coming out against it. I simply do not see why the nation has to have an official sexuality, especially one that authorizes the norm of a violent gentility; that narrows the field of legitimate political action; that supports the amputation of personal complexity into categories of simple identity; that uses cruel and mundane strategies both to promote shame for non-normative populations and to deny them state, federal, and juridical supports because they are deemed morally incompetent to their own citizenship. This is the heterosexuality I repudiate.[34]

Feminist politics has long authorized my dedication to producing new contexts for understanding the politics, economics, and everyday practices of intimacy; its conjuncture with queer and materialist theory and activism is the context for this book's project. Queer/feminist activity in and outside the academy has enticed its participants to develop new names, analytics, contexts, and institutions for politics, practices, and subjectivities. It has broadened the notion of what sexuality is beyond the public/private divide, and has challenged a notion of gender that can overorganize how to understand machineries of domination, a notion that has tended to push questions of sexuality, race, class, and ethnicity to an ever-receding horizon of what "we" feminists promise to understand "later." This kind of commitment to conjunctural practice has also challenged the forms and styles of writing, research, and representation that typically buttress professional credentials, pushing me to work rigorously beyond my expertise in ways that feel at once risky and absolutely necessary.

Yet, to use a phrase from one of my anonymous readers, this book mainly "takes the temperature of the hegemony," focusing on the pseudoapolitical citizenship rhetoric of U.S. political culture. *The Queen of America* is not a redemptive text that maps or draws what kind of utopia a revitalized citizenship form or a post-heteronormative nation would be. In this sense it is not the opposite of the Christian Coalition's *Contract*. Confronting the unpredictable effects of changes in longstanding habits of political subjectivity — how relations among the state, the law, economics, and intimacy are imagined, for example — is a necessary precondition for thinking past the scene of normativity that pervades the contemporary United States. At the same time, to create new contexts that are something other than slightly less bad versions of what exists requires committing to two kinds of work: discerning places where counterhegemonic alliances might be produced, and taking on the discomforts and risks even to "privilege" (with a small *p*) entailed by that commitment. The tactic of this book is to begin to enumerate some of these forms of risk and optimism while tracking the divisive and wishful forms of the American Way of Life, with its particularly constricted dream of vanquishing economic, cultural, and sexual unpleasantness. In this spirit *The Queen* does a diva turn on citizenship, attempting to transform it from a dead (entirely abstract) category of analysis into a live social scene that exudes sparks, has practical consequences, forces better ways of thinking about nationality, culture, politics, and personhood.

I have suggested that citizenship is a status whose definitions are always in process. It is continually being produced out of a political, rhetorical, and economic struggle over who will count as "the people" and how social membership will be measured and valued. It must, then, be seen as more than a patriotic category. In this book, citizenship provides an index for appraising domestic national life, and for witnessing the processes of valorization that make different populations differently legitimate socially and under the law. The pilgrimage to Washington D.C. that links the different citizenship scenes in this book depicts both real and conceptual distances that occupants of the United States have felt the need to traverse: not always because they want to usurp the space of national mastery, but sometimes because they seek to capture, even fleetingly, a feeling of genuine membership in the United States. In reformulating citizenship as a vital space on which diverse political demands can be made, *The Queen* seeks also to remind that despite all appearances the conservative engagement with sex is also a comprehensive politics of citizenship, one that has had practical, theoretical, and extraordinarily intimate public consequences.

As these paragraphs have suggested, *The Queen of America Goes to Washington City* has an argument, but not one developed solely in a linear way. As a whole the text does not try to prove that these examples *constitute* the sum of national culture, but that the privatized citizenship they have come to represent has been installed, in many places, as the moral foundation of national life. Disclosing what is being passed off as citizenship requires a set of complexly related essays, whose cases, arguments, and images continuously anticipate and refer back to one another. The chapters could have been arranged in several ways. The one I have chosen is as follows:

Chapter 1, "The Theory of Infantile Citizenship," takes its cue from a large number of pilgrimage-to-Washington narratives, with their intensified and polemical national pedagogies. This chapter focuses on the infantile citizen whose naive citizenship surfaces constantly as the ideal type of patriotic personhood in America, in ways that are both extremely simple and extremely complex. While the infantilized citizen of the democratic United States was predicted by Tocqueville and inhabits many patriotic pilgrimage narratives, I am claiming that there is a historical specificity to the iconicity of the current modal citizen, the child or youth on whose behalf national struggles are being waged. The central text of this chapter is an episode of *The Simpsons* titled "Mr. Lisa Goes to Washington."

Chapter 2, "Live Sex Acts," adjusts the perspective on the innocent, pre-historical infantile citizen by looking at a horror currently organized around her body: the antisex culture wars that are also and always wars over what people and practices will count as national. If chapter 1 shows how the future United States is being optimistically imagined and legislated as a home for a child-citizen protected from the violences of capitalism, class, race, and sexuality, this chapter shows how scandals around sex and sexuality are being orchestrated to locate this future nation only in private, intimate life. I address the ways conservative pressures to reroute sex away from mass culture and the public sphere and back to heterosexual bedrooms have become linked to radical feminist antipornography agitation and legislation. One important strategy for the rightwing/feminist move to privatize sex is the deployment of theories of the photographic image, which are central to the imagination of citizenship in antiporn ideology. Its main argument is that, against "live" citizenship forms that tend to deviate from the generic or "dead" norms of national personhood, homophobic conservatives and radical feminists have intensified the image of the ideal citizen as an innocent young girl or the young girl's parent, in contrast to the disgusting "adult" culture that fouls the nest of its own national privilege, valuing consumption and pleasure over family, domesticity, and other scenes of virtue.

Chapter 3, "America, 'Fat,' the Fetus," comes in two parts: "Big Babies/Fetal Citizens," and "The Cinema of the Moving Fetus." As a whole, it begins the move away from the infantile citizenship paradigm toward three complicated cases of citizenship agitation in the intimate public sphere. It takes the double story of the previous essays—about women and infants, and the politics of their different utilities in the formation of national legitimacy—and plays their citizenship politics through the problem of fetal citizenship. It also develops the insights on photographic ontology introduced in the previous chapter. Most broadly, this essay argues that the ordinary logics of infantile, female, and generic or full U.S. citizenship have undergone a radical change in the production of the fetus as a person with citizenship rights. It argues that a kind of isomorphism between domestic privacy and the ideology of public intimacy has fostered the image of fetal personhood as the icon of ideal citizenship. In addition, as privacy becomes a central scene of national political imagination, the fetus becomes a mass-media form itself, providing a tissue of logics through which notions of social connectedness and the national future are transmitted. Using the notion of a politics of scale implicit in the earlier chapters, this chapter shows how the struggle to define citizenship around the fetus has involved distorting and redistorting the size of female/fetal bodies in ways that are both important and ordinary. The texts this chapter uses, including Raymond Carver's short story, "Fat," *Look Who's Talking*, *The Silent Scream*, fetal home videos, and *I Love Lucy*, dramatize across different genres some ways that reproduction is currently conceptualized.

Chapter 4, "Queer Nationality," was cowritten with Elizabeth Freeman at a time when the activist group Queer Nation worked nationally to change the ways straight and gay people experienced the public spaces of everyday life and the ordinary trajectories of everyday identity. This chapter takes up the claim of "Live Sex Acts" that "live" cultures of American citizenship have taken on the nation in creative and complicated ways. Here we try to show the kinds of guerrilla tactics Queer Nation deployed for building subculture and claiming legitimacy in the mainstream national public sphere. We also return to the question of how to measure the different scales of citizenship formation experienced by children, lesbians, gay men, and youths. Trying to open up spaces beyond those of identity politics, this chapter contrasts the spectacles of nationality Queer Nation wielded to the negativity of metropolitan queer youth culture, which has taken up the challenge to invent forms of radical, postnational counterpublicity, especially through a vast network of queer 'zine exchanges.

Chapter 5, "The Face of America and the State of Emergency," turns to a final case of incipient citizenship: immigration to the contemporary United States. Rather than focusing on the practical workings of U.S. citizenship policy, this chapter looks at the relation between a popular culture's view of a white-based national public sphere and a national public that is made up multiculturally. Its main texts are *Forrest Gump, Time* magazine's "special issues" on immigration from 1985 and 1993 (especially in the latter's forging of a false, virtual citizen that *Time* calls "The New Face of America") and Michael Jackson's "Black or White." As I continue to argue that the face of America's typical citizen is undergoing transformations in the political public sphere in response to pressures from the live, public margins of citizenship — (im)migrants, youth, people of color, feminists, queers — I tell a particular story here about the morphing of citizenship from mass-popular representational acts into abstracted forms and spaces of intimate privacy. This is another story about what official storytelling does to designate a new face of America as the modal or model citizen; it acts out an optimistic desire to create a posthistorical future in which all acts take place in a private space of loving citizen discipline, a space in which, meanwhile, public political life is demonized, national heterosexuality is deployed for the reproduction of a racially dominant white-ish culture, and the same old violences of race, gender, and exploitation that are the nightmarish primary text of the American way of life produce justification for a radical reinvention of politics.

Finally, chapter 6: "The Queen of America Goes to Washington City: Notes on Diva Citizenship," uses the saga of Anita Hill and the narratives of Harriet Jacobs (*Incidents in the Life of a Slave Girl*) and Frances E. W. Harper (*Iola Leroy*) to tell two stories. One story is about an arduous pilgrimage to full citizenship in American law and the public sphere that African American women have had to make during the last century, a pilgrimage from sexual domination in domestic and laboring spaces where "privacy" names the privileges of the boss and his family, to public sphere renunciations of the nation for the pseudo-democratic promises it makes that still authorize these spaces of privileged exploitation. The uncanny rhyming of the women's pilgrimages over a century during which so much else has drastically changed requires a different history of the nation to be told, not from its ideal but from the grounds of hard experience. To name the form of political subjectivity this radical split between utopian and practical citizenship engenders, this chapter introduces a notion of Diva Citizenship. The second story this chapter tells is of Diva Citizenship itself, its potential for generating affect and political action in response to democratic cruelties, its limit as a kind of heroic spectacle. For if the Diva citizen achieves individually the grand scale of nationality, her or his very success also contributes to the privatization of citizenship by indicating that individual will alone might transform the public sphere and dissolve the hierarchies of exploitation that constitute the material conditions of contemporary national life.

1   The Theory of Infantile Citizenship

When Americans make the pilgrimage to Washington they are trying to grasp the nation in its totality. Yet the totality of the nation in its capital city is a jumble of historical modalities, a transitional space between local and national cultures, private and public property, archaic and living artifacts, the national history that marks the monumental landscape and the everyday life temporalities of federal and metropolitan cultures. That is to say, it is a place of national *mediation,* where a variety of nationally inflected media come into visible and sometimes incommensurate contact. As a borderland central to the nation, Washington tests the capacities of all who visit it: this test is a test of citizenship competence. Usually made with families or classmates, the trip to the capital makes pedagogy a patriotic performance, one in which the tourist "playing at being American" is called on to coordinate the multiple domains of time, space, sensation, exchange, knowledge, and power that represent the scene of what we might call "total" citizenship.[1] To live fully both the ordinariness and the sublimity of national identity, one must be capable not just of imagining, but of managing being American.

To be able to feel less fractured than the nation itself would be, indeed, a privilege. Audre Lorde tells a story of her family's one visit to Washington, in 1947.[2] Lorde's parents claimed to be making the trip to commemorate their two daughters' educational triumphs, an eighth grade and a high school graduation. The truth is, though, that Lorde's sister Phyllis was barred from accompanying her graduating class on its celebratory visit to Washington because she was African American and Washington was a southern, segregated city, not at all "national" in the juridical or the democratic sense. The Lorde family refused to acknowledge racism as the catalyst for its own private journey. Rather, patriotism was the tourists' alibi, a blinding one that enabled the parents to deny what was everywhere visible: that racism is a national system.

Lorde relates that whenever the family encountered its unfreedom to enter certain spaces of private property, no one would acknowledge the irony: that although "public" monuments like the Lincoln Memorial allow African Americans like Audre Lorde and Marian Anderson access to a space of symbolic national identification and inclusion,[3] the very ordinary arrangements of life in America, eating and sleeping, were as forbidden to the Lorde family in Washington as America itself is to those without passports. This is to say that in Washington the bar of blackness exposed contradictions between regimes of democracy and property, effectively splitting the idealized nation from the capitalist one, while each nonetheless governs the defining terms of U.S. citizenship.[4]

Still, they scheduled their visit to Washington on Independence Day. When Lorde bitterly remarks on her exile from the America that patriotism depicts, symbolized in general by the apartheid of the capital, and in particular by a waitress's refusal to let the family celebrate the nation's birthday by eating ice cream they had paid for *inside* a restaurant, she describes it as the line she steps over from childhood to something else, a different political, corporeal, sensational, and aesthetic "adulthood": "The waitress was white, and the counter was white, and the ice cream I never ate in Washington D.C. that summer I left childhood was white, and the white heat and the white pavement and the white stone monuments of my first Washington summer made me sick to my stomach."[5] Lorde's "education" in national culture provoked a nauseated unlearning of her patriotism — "Hadn't I written poems about Bataan?" she complains, while resolving, again, to write the president, to give the nation another chance to not betray her desire for it — and this unlearning, which is never complete, as it involves leaving behind the political faith of childhood, cleaves her permanently from and to the nation whose promises drew her parents to immigrate there and drew herself to identify as a child with a concept of national identity she was sure she would fulfill when she grew into an adult citizen.

This essay explores a particular national plot: the pilgrimage to Washington.[6] It focuses not on a news or a biographical event but on an episode of the popular weekly cartoon television show *The Simpsons* titled "Mr. Lisa Goes to Washington." It will also engage the other tourist/citizenship pilgrimages this episode revises, notably *Mr. Smith Goes to Washington* (dir. Frank Capra, 1939). In so doing it seeks to describe the ways the fantasy norms of the nation form simultaneously produce normative political subjectivity and create public spaces of exaggeration, irony, or ambivalence for alternative, less nationally focused, or just more critical kinds of political identification. This chapter also deals with a particular conflict about identity that is currently raging in the United States: between a patriotic view of national identity, which seeks to use identification with the ideal nation to trump or subsume all other notions of personhood, and a view that is frequently considered unpatriotic and victim-obsessed, in which citizenship talk takes as its main subject the unequal material conditions of economic, social, and political struggle and survival. That this struggle over citizenship is so often about the lives and experiences of racial, gendered, and sexual minorities and the working class means that its story will frequently seem to be solely about subaltern bodies and identities, which bear the burden of representing *desire for the nation* generally. But, as we will see, once the national body is exhumed from the crypt of abstraction and put on display, everyone's story of citizenship is vulnerable to dramatic revision.

This investigation of political subjectivity and its mediations — on the body, in the media, in the nation — introduces one other type of traditional citizen, one that complicates the story of national identity politics I have been telling. This citizen form figures a space of possibility that transcends the fractures and hierarchies of national life: I call it the infantile citizen. The infantile citizen of the United States has appeared in political writing about the nation at least since Tocqueville wrote, in *Democracy in America,* that while citizens should be encouraged to love the nation the way they do their families and their fathers, democracies can also produce a special form of tyranny that makes citizens like children, infantilized, passive, and overdependent on the "immense and tutelary power" of the state.[7] *Mr. Smith Goes to Washington* brings this form into its classic modern representation: as Jefferson Smith (James Stewart) comes to Washington to put nationalist ideology into political practice, he is called, among other things, "a drooling infant" and "an infant with little flags in his fist." The infantile citizen's ingenuousness frequently seems a bad thing, a political subjectivity based on the suppression of critical knowledge and a resulting contraction of citizenship to something smaller than agency: patriotic inclination, default social membership, or the simple possession of a normal national character. But the infantile citizen's faith in the nation, which is based on a belief in the state's commitment to representing the best interests of ordinary people, is also said to be what vitalizes a person's patriotic and practical attachment to the nation and to other citizens. Tocqueville's observation turns out to be a very complicated one about the paradoxes of political subjectivity in the United States. Central to the narrative mode of the pilgrimage to Washington, and so much other national fantasy, is a strong and enduring belief that the best of U.S. national subjectivity can be read in its childlike manifestations and in a polity that organizes its public sphere around a commitment to making a world that could sustain an idealized infantile citizen.[8]

To begin to give substance to the paradoxes, limits, and dreams encoded in this ideal citizen form, here is a synopsis of "Mr. Lisa Goes to Washington." Young Lisa Simpson wins a trip to Washington ("all expenses paid") by writing a "fiercely pro-American" patriotic essay for a contest that her father, Homer Simpson, discovers in a complimentary copy he receives of a magazine called *Reading Digest*. In Washington the family stays at the Watergate, visits a fictional national mint, encounters Barbara Bush in her White House bathtub, and comments on national monuments. Then Lisa accidently witnesses a congressman receiving a bribe (one that would precipitate the destruction of her beloved hometown national park by corporate logging interests). Enraged and embittered, she tears up her prizewinning essay about the nation form's natural beauty, and substitutes for it a new essay about how Washington truly "stinks." As a result, Lisa loses the national jingoism contest, and along with it her simply patriotic belief in the promise of the national. A Senate page witnesses her loss of faith in democracy, and calls his senator for help. Within two hours the FBI has jailed the crooked congressman, who instantly becomes a born-again Christian. On witnessing the effects of her muckraking, Lisa exclaims, "The system works!" What could she possibly mean by this? We will return to the question of systems later.

I have described the aspects of this plot that tend to be repeated in the other pilgrimage-to-Washington narratives. Someone, either a child or an innocent adult identified with children, goes to the capital. The crisis of her/his innocence/illiteracy emerges from an ambivalent encounter between America as a theoretical ideality and America as a site of practical politics, mapped onto Washington itself. Because children cannot read the codes, they disrupt the norms of the national locale: their infantile citizenship operates the way Oskar Negt and Alexander Kluge predict it would, eliciting scorn and derision from "knowing" adult citizens but also a kind of admiration from these same people, who can remember with nostalgia the time that they were "unknowing" and believed in the capacity of the nation to be practically utopian.

As it is, citizen adults have learned to "forget" or to render as impractical, naive, or childish their utopian political identifications in order to be politically happy and economically functional. Confronting the tension between utopia and history, the infantile citizen's stubborn naïveté gives her/him enormous power to unsettle, expose, and reframe the machinery of national life. Thus the potential catastrophe of all visits to Washington: Can national identification survive the practical habitation of everyday life in the national locale? Can the citizen/tourist gain the critical skills for living nationally without losing faith in the nation-state's capacity to provide the wisdom and justice it promises? Is the utopian horizon of national identity itself a paramnesia or a Žižekian "fantasy" that covers over entrenched contradictions and lacks in national culture?[9] Are naive infantile citizenship and paralyzed cynical apathy the only positions a normal or moral American can assume? How a given text answers these questions has little to do with the particular infantile citizen who generates its national crisis; it has everything to do with the contradictions threatening "adult" or "full" citizenship in the political public sphere.

The transition in Audre Lorde's life — from patriotic childhood to a less defined but powerful rage at the travesty everyday life can make of national promises for justice — marks a moment in the education of an American citizen that is typical of the personal and fictional narratives of the pilgrimage to Washington. When cinematic, literary, and televisual texts fictively represent "Washington" as "America," they theorize the conditions of political subjectivity in the United States and reflect on the popular media's ways of constructing political knowledge in a dialectic of infantile citizenship and cynical reason. They also reflect on the power of the other form that mediates the nation to itself as a durably tangible thing that already exists in nature and in history: the national body. After thinking through at more length the different scenes of the nation's mass mediation I will return to *The Simpsons,* as it prods the patriotic ideology of national identity without bursting its utopian bubble.

Technologies of Citizenship

Audre Lorde's story takes place in 1947, a particularly intense time for U.S. self-reflection on what citizenship was about. Stephen Heath argues that recent dramatic developments in global media culture have so changed the conditions of political subjectivity that the category "citizen" is now archaic. Many worthy theorists of television concur, arguing that the ruptural force of its technologies and the monopolistic tendency of its capitalization have radically transformed the material conditions and normative representations of national culture and political agency.[10] It is now a commonplace in television criticism to say that the structure of televisual experience promotes the annihilation of memory and, in particular, of historical knowledge and political self-understanding. This may be an effect of its ontology and ideology of "liveness," which encourages mass subjective absorption in the present tense through regimes of banality, distraction, interminable "flow," and periodic catastrophe or scandal; it may be an effect of the implicitness of capital in generating the aura of "free" entertainment (which makes the consumer's engagement with commercialized renderings of contemporary power, history, and identity both the problem and the critical promise of the medium); it may be an effect of the "global" images that have come to saturate the scene of consumption, soliciting consumer identifications to a postpolitical and postnational utopia of "culture" and confusing the era of the present tense with an imminent yet obscure future; or, most likely, it may be an effect of some combination of these factors.[11] But because in all areas of its mode of production television encounters, engages, and represents both the social and political routines of citizenship, and because it underscores the activity of animating and reflecting on as well as simply having a national identity, the problem of generating memory and knowledge in general becomes fraught with issues of national pedagogy, of how to represent what counts as patriotism and what counts as criticism to the public sphere.[12]

If, as I have described, the pilgrimage to Washington is already all about the activity of national pedagogy, the production of national culture, and the constitution of competent citizens, the specific role of mass mediation in the dissemination of national knowledges redoubles and loops around the formation of national identity. There is nothing archaic about citizenship — instead, its signs and cadences are changing. As Margaret Morse argues, television makes history by annexing older forms of national self-identity, cultural literacy, and leisure.[13] It does this continuously to reacclimate consumer identifications during structural transitions in national and international public spheres. In these conditions of uneven development, the work of media in redefining citizenship and framing what can legitimately be read as national becomes more, not less, central to any analysis of political identity in postmodern American culture.

This is to say that the definitional field of citizenship — denoting simple identification by a national identity category, a reflexive operation of agency and criticism, or a mode of social membership — is precisely what is under contestation, as the development of what we might call "mass nationality" changes the face of power, both in the United States and globally. Consider, for example, the escalating claims made on behalf of televised populist town halls, conservative talk radio, and elite "expert" insider-culture talk shows, that they are sites where the core nation reveals itself to itself; or track the constantly changing stream of representative men who replace each other on magazine covers because, at particular moments, they represent to the dominant media the current state of political hegemony; or follow the trajectory of the public discussion, pursued in chapter 5, about what kind of face can be said to be the "true" face of America, a game of representative naming that encodes concerns about whether the histories and struggles of people of color, especially among the U.S. working and nonworking poor, will be deemed legitimate subjects of patriotic discourse, state policy, and ordinary social life. All of these modes of publicity are normative technologies of citizenship that seek to create proper national subjects and subjectivities. Yet even as they do this, by intensifying certain social antagonisms in order to consolidate specific interest groups, all those involved in the production of mass nationality would say that their main concern is with serving citizens by bringing a truly democratic public sphere into being.

The question of how publicity mediates the form of proper nationality predates the postmodern televisual moment, and requires a much longer investigation than will happen here. Briefly, since *The Birth of a Nation* and *Mr. Smith Goes to Washington,* pilgrimage-to-Washington narratives have foregrounded the problem, place, and promise of different media in the business of making nationality and making it personal to citizens; many also show the costs of the mass media's control over the terms and scenes in which critical national identifications are produced, even while these technologies are also considered vital for any sense of a citizenship in the United States that is politically agentive.

A film like *In Country* (dir. Norman Jewison, 1989) epitomizes one kind of case in which the routes to citizenship are traced, where the central question is how to create citizens through technologies of national memory, technologies that assume an a priori distance between the nation and "the people." These are narratives about which media will enable the production of the national present tense from the materials of the past. They focus more on stable communicative objects like monuments and personal artifacts than on the apparatus of mass culture, whose effects are nonetheless everywhere (like the televisions that are always on in a room showing the standard news stories of an era) and constitute the evidence of a plot's location in a specific historical moment. In this mode of national narrative, stories of mass trauma like war or slavery are encoded in plots of familial inheritance, wherein citizens of the posttraumatic present are figured in a daughter's or a son's coming to public terms with a generational past that defines her/him and yet does not feel fully personal.

In *In Country,* Samantha Hughes (Emily Lloyd), the daughter of a deceased Vietnam veteran, finds her father's letters and diary from Vietnam, his dog tags, and pictures of his life in a kind of shoebox museum her mother keeps hidden in a room where the detritus from the cultural radicalism of the sixties is also stored. In the 1980s, this archaic material returns to sight as so much crazy colorful excess. Meanwhile, her mother has become a normal suburban housewife trying to leave the working classes and build a professional life, and the sixties and Vietnam seem almost like a dead moment, an adolescent phase the family/nation went through and survived, unlike the father.

The trauma of coming to know these personal forms of publicity makes Samantha progressively more restless, for every story she hears and reads about Vietnam is an unfinished one, still pulsating like an exposed wound long after the war is officially ended. A traumatic story is always interminable — that is what makes it traumatic. Samantha compulsively devours every text and story she can until she feels entirely impossible, bearing as her own the unconcluded tales of her grandmother, her uncle, and other Vietnam veterans (who, though survivors, are all still sexually and physically disrupted). Samantha then sees that *everyone* she knows is a Vietnam veteran: the men who are living with horrible memories and no economic or sexual prospects; the women who are desperately trying to produce normality for the men.

She wants to save all of these people from dying or becoming mere story, like her father. Her main object lesson is her uncle, Emmett Smith (Bruce Willis), a self-destroying vet who is still plagued by the war's saturation of his bodily senses, but who refuses the therapeutic reparations the postwar culture offers him, including every form of talk. At first Samantha thinks that telling the war's whole story will cure the war's trauma. Yet as she makes the rounds to elicit and tell the traumatic stories she is collecting she sees dramatic evidence that repetition just aggravates psychic wounds. *In Country* stages the image of the successful therapy Samantha finds in the figurativeness of its title: a euphemism for being in Vietnam, "in country" comes to refer to the rural South, and then to the United States. To enter the next stage of her own narrative, Samantha must break free of the local trauma circuit and make a pilgrimage to Washington, to the classic national monuments, and to the Vietnam Memorial. She takes on her trip her traumatized uncle and her dead father's elderly mother.

Once in Washington, they walk to the memorial and find the father's name. The monumental minimalism of the epitaph is stark and moving, collapsing all desperate need for story into the perfect boundedness of the name. Climbing an unstable ladder, Samantha and her grandmother trace out the letters that spell her father's name on the stone, and they can barely stay on the ladder for all the intense bodiliness their touch enkindles. Contact with the monument, though, means more than gaining deeper, if prosthetic, intimacy with the father's remains (they have more personal things like his letters, after all, to cherish back at home). The monument makes the father's life public: only the immortalizing impersonality of U.S. citizenship can bring Samantha and her family resolution, happiness, and peace. Engraved in monumental time, it is as though his physical self were only now truly dead, a name and not a living story, while in contrast his national self still lives in a state of pure and enduring value.

This infantile citizen's pilgrimage to Washington represents the ways solid contact with the nation's official media can seem to complete citizens' unfulfilled lives — and even a relation of mere seeming can make optimism look plausible, and not deluded. *In Country* and many other pilgrimage-to-Washington films argue that contact with the monumental nation can turn a citizen's infantilizing rage, anger, and crazy-making feelings of betrayal into a calm, stabilized, mature or adult subjectivity ready to "let the past go" and, with amnesiac confidence, face the prospects of the present. On the other hand, the name of the father inscribed with so many others in stone on a national monument portrays the mute historical blank that defines a large part of the collective and personal content of traumatic political memory.

In contrast to the pilgrimage-to-Washington plots that narrate surviving, remembering, memorializing, and containing the traumatic national past, there is another species of narrative that involves surviving a present moment that feels menacing. This mode of pilgrimage plot tends to use what Benedict Anderson has identified as the simultaneity-effect of paper and electronic media, whose consumption is said to produce a general sensation of constant collective citizenship.[14] In this version of the pilgrimage-to-Washington narrative, the brush with mass-mediated citizenship involves a crisis of the present tense, and casts the personal experience of national identity as an overwhelming and exciting shock to the systems of so many alienated, cynical, ignorant, or almost-dead Americans.

Examples abound of this narrative variant, which portrays citizenship through representations of overstimulated political subjectivity and intensified nationalist pedagogy.[15] The classic instance of frighteningly live nationality is *Mr. Smith Goes to Washington,* which popularized the convention of using real media personalities in a film about the present tense to authenticate the "news" being made on the spot and manipulated in the filmic plot.[16] (However, as in *In Country,* in *Mr. Smith* national monuments and personal media like hand-printed newspapers and carrier pigeons remain the sacred sites for the formation of trustworthy and intimate national identifications.) *Mr. Smith* stages its struggle over who controls the meaning of mass citizenship as a war between two newspapers: a big Hearst-like influence-peddling paper and a paper, *Boy's Stuff,* produced by young Boy Rangers and distributed to "the people" by boys pulling little wagons. But telephones, radio, and telegrams are here even more central communicative devices for the formation of the mass nation. The rapid transmission of real and false information for the purpose of rallying the "public" into active opinion-making both enables and disables the communicative contexts democracy requires, which means that the structural critique the film offers of the antiknowledge effects of U.S. patriotic ideology tends to get overwhelmed by plots about putting "good men" in the places where national power becomes concrete.[17] As for the rest of the citizens, they are taught to accept that they are, and even desire to be, "average" — that is, passive, distant, and relatively uninformed about the workings of the national machine, except in those moments where they are solicited to act nationally by giving opinions, money, blood, or votes.[18] These examples, I hope, begin to suggest why television's role in constructing the hegemony of the normative nation must be understood as a partial, not a determining, moment in a genealogy of crises about publicity, ideology, and the production of national subjects.

More than a struggle to establish a political public sphere, norms of proper national subjectivity and concepts of social membership are at stake in the problem of creating images of mass nationality. One other aspect of the ways media technologies create national subjects needs airing here, and this concerns the construction of the image archive that provides corporeal models of normal citizenship. Whenever citizenship comes to look like a question of the *body,* a number of processes are being hidden. The body's seeming obviousness distracts attention from the ways it organizes meaning, and diverts the critical gaze from publicity's role in the formation of the taxonomies that construct bodies publicly. Hortense Spillers has argued that nationalized bodies always appear to have a magical, mythical aura of meaning invulnerable to the pulsations of the historical nation.[19] The general iconicity of the national body thereby veils how historical, contingent, and incoherent body typologies are. For example, if everyone hails from some specific place and some specific people, when and why does a person become a *kind* of thing like a national ethnicity? Or when did "woman" begin to be explicitly a political category, a category designating not a body with organs, but a kind of experience-related opinion?

You may have noticed that, in the filmic examples above, the citizen whose story is in question is a man in public, a white man, the modal American. When a given symbolic national body signifies as *normal*—straight, white, middle-class, and heterosexual—hardly anyone asks critical questions about its representativeness. In mass society its iconicity is intensified by commodity culture's marketing of normal personhood as something that places you in the range of what is typical in public and yet is personally unique. Subaltern personhood, in contrast, allows for no subtlety or personal uniqueness in mass society, producing reams of national stereotypes, with all of their negative transhistoricism. It has no institutions that make available to it the privileged status of the un-marked. Thus even when subaltern style cultures are appropriated for the ornamentation of privilege and the extension of hegemonic subjectivity to new realms of sensation, technique, and cynical knowledge about power, the very availability of these borrowed practices tends to intensify the aura of incompetence and inferiority—the subalternness—of the subaltern subject. The subaltern body's peculiar burden of national surrogacy enables many stories of minoritized citizenship to be "included" in the self-justifying mirror of the official national narrative while being expatriated from citizenship's promise of quotidian practical intimacy.

Because "Mr. Lisa Goes to Washington" tells its story from that under-defined space where a stereotypically normal U.S. "family values" ideol-ogy and the struggles and social alienation of the U.S. working classes overlap, its infantile citizenship narrative forces the stratifying procedures of official national culture to become explicit. Tracking the Simpson family from the fictional Springfield, TA, to Washington, D.C., will thus require formulating a logic of national subjectivity from the bottom's diverse perspectives and, at the same time, understanding how those very perspectives become irrelevant to both the jokes and the moving anecdotes the national story tells about them.

Incompetent Citizens, Junk Knowledge, and the U.S. Working Class

The ur-infantile citizen narrative is actually the presidential autobiography. Currently, the most vital instantiation of this form appears cinematically every four years at political nominating conventions, where a candidate establishes the value of his "character" by way of an infantile citizenship-style autobiography that casts his pilgrimage to Washington as a life-structuring project that began in childhood (see also Senate confirmation testimony speeches such as the famous "bootstraps" speech of Supreme Court Justice Clarence Thomas).

In critical contrast, "Mr. Lisa Goes to Washington" shares with *Born Yesterday* (dir. George Cukor, 1950), *The Distinguished Gentleman* (dir. Jonathan Lynn, 1992), and other "Washington" narratives a rhetoric of citizenship that initially locates the utopian possibilities of national identity in the anarchic, frightening, and/or comic spectacle of someone's personal *failure* to be national. The scene of citizenship is revealed by way of events that humiliate an ordinary citizen, disclosing him/her as someone incapable of negotiating the semiotic, economic, and political conditions of his/her existence in civil society. And just as the dirty work of representing the detritus of a white, bourgeois national culture will almost inevitably go to the citizens whose shameful bodies signify a seemingly natural incapacity to leave behind the vulgar and become "cultured," the plot of "Mr. Lisa Goes to Washington" is embedded not in Lisa's story but in the gross activities of the failed proletarian father, Homer Simpson.

The show begins with Homer opening his junk mail. He is reading what the mail says and commenting sarcastically about the letters, outraged by their mistakes (for example, one is addressed to "Homer Simpsoy") and their promises of sudden wealth with no risk or labor. Yet, for all his cynical knowledge, Homer makes a gravely optimistic reading error. Rapacious and desiring to the point of senselessness, he takes a representation of a "winner's check" in a Publishers Clearing House-like contest to be a representation of real money that he has won. He goes to the bank to cash the million-dollar pseudocheck — which is covered with phrases like "void void void" and "This is not a check" — and is devastated to find the "deal," as he puts it, "queered."

Throughout the episode, Homer continues to show himself incompetent in the face of money — indeed, in a scene toward the end he makes the very same error with another check. When the eventual winner of the patriotism contest symbolically shares his prize with Lisa, a prize represented by what the young man calls an "oversized novelty check," Homer yells from the audience, "Give her the check!" and then, amidst everyone's laughter, protests whiningly, "I wasn't kidding." At every moment that money appears in the show, Homer has no understanding of it — unlike Bart, who understands and exploits to his great pleasure the ambiguity of the word "expenses" in the phrase "all expenses paid." In contrast, Homer is surprised and betrayed at his constant discovery that even in Washington money is not "free."

What Homer does do well is drool and moan and expose himself compulsively like an idiot relegated to his insipid appetites. Immediately after his humiliation by the nonnegotiable pseudocheck, he becomes, literally, the "butt" of more jokes about freedom, personhood, and money: recovering from the shock of his ineptitude with money he stands up and shows the *Simpsons* audience the top, cracked part of his partially exposed rear. This is the initial perspective from the bottom "Mr. Lisa Goes to Washington" establishes, the baseline of political incompetence. Like a bald spot or an unzipped fly, the crack of the butt winks at the cruel superior public that knows how to use money, how to distinguish between real and false checks, and how to regulate its body.[20] Homer has no capacity to think abstractly, or to think, period, as when, facing a sheaf of freshly made money, he drools on the head of a worker at the Mint, or when he self-righteously sputters, "Lousy, cheap country!" on learning that the Mint does not give out free samples.

There are many other instances in this episode of Homer's humiliation by the tacit text of bourgeois nationality. Receiving his free copy of *Reading Digest* completely changes Homer's life, as well as the life of his family. Homer becomes so excited by getting knowledge about the world on a scale he can comprehend (exciting narratives, little sound bites) that he tries sincerely to enter the public as someone with language and knowledge. But his working-class brutishness is constantly broadcast, like his butt in the earlier scene. For example, after the triumph of Lisa's essay in the "Veterans of Popular Wars" contest, a contest

judge feels suspicious of young Lisa for having written such a beautiful essay. The judge opines, "Methinks I smell the sickly scent of the daddy," and decides to interview Homer. But Homer becomes entirely aphonic, grunting in the face of her interrogation. As a result, she gives Lisa extra points for having survived descending from such a brute. Later, snorting down "free" food at the convention in Washington, Homer keeps losing language, even at moments when he sincerely wants to express the way his life has been improved by reading *Reading Digest*. Speaking to a spokeswoman for the magazine, he tries but fails to think of a word that would adequately attest to his love of the magazine's vocabulary-builder sections; then he asks for but is unable to retain the information clarifying this chain of signs: "V (very) I (important) P (person)." Why should he? for he is none of these things. With none of the social competence of a person who has knowledge about money or the world, he demonstrates what George Lipsitz has called the "infantile narcissism" of consumer self-addiction: "Who would have thought," Homer says to Lisa, "that reading or writing would pay off!"[21]

"Have . . . You Ever Run into Any Problems Because of Your Superior Ability?": Lisa Simpson, Smart Girl Citizen

When Homer "loses" the million dollars, his wife, Marge, consoles him by showing him the "free" *Reading Digest* they have received in the mail. Like Billie Dawn (Judy Holliday) learning to negotiate the topography of power through print and other national media in *Born Yesterday,* Homer becomes a quasi intellectual while he reads the magazine: he pulls the children away from a "period" film they are watching on television about the Anglo-American theft of land from Native American nations (which depicts a white preacher telling an "Indian chief" that the tribe's homeland will be more valuable if they abandon and irrigate it) and reads them a true-life adventure story; he is caught reading on the job at the nuclear power plant by Mr. Burns, who asks his assistant, "Who is that bookworm, Smithers? . . . His job description clearly specifies an illiterate!"; he reads "Quotable Notables" as a substitute for eating lunch. But when Homer reads that *Reading Digest* sponsors a patriotic essay contest for children, he loses interest in the magazine and throws it out. This is when "Mr. Lisa" takes over the plot: fishing as usual through the garbage of her family's affections to salvage some emotional capital, she becomes, as Bart says, "the pony to bet on."

Of what does Lisa's smartness and competence consist? When she first attempts the patriotic essay, she props a book in front of herself, tries dutifully to quote Ben Franklin and to narrate how a bill becomes law. When this form of quotational patriotism fails, Mr. Lisa tries another tack, and bicycles to Springfield National Park for further inspiration. In so doing she derives the authority of her interpretation from the nation's putative alliance with nature. In the theory of this alliance the United States is a domain of value untouched by history or hierarchy: the nation's priceless essence is located in what transcends the world of practical citizenship, with its history of nationally sanctioned racial, sexual, and economic exploitation. (This conjuncture of nature and nation directly cites *Mr. Smith Goes to Washington,* in which Jefferson Smith expresses his national feeling by writing legislation that would establish a national summer camp for underprivileged boys: there, the boys would be turned into infantile citizens through the "American values" that would be inculcated in them by immersion in the nation's natural order.) "America, inspire me," Lisa says to the park, and a bald eagle straight from the national seal alights in front of her. This collaboration of nature and the National Symbolic animates Lisa, who then writes passionately, not from books, but naturally, from feeling.[22] The show provides a montage of the speeches by several "patriots of tomorrow" in which Lisa's speech takes top honors.

During this little speech-making montage, the "nation" imagined by its youth is usually signified by a pastel national map marked by the kinds of local-color images that airport postcards often sport, by some regional accents, and by the homely spun-out puns and metaphors of American children.

> So burn that flag if you must! But before you do, you'd better burn a few other things! You'd better burn your shirt and your pants! Be sure to burn your TV and your car! Oh yeah, and don't forget to burn your house! Because none of those things would exist without six red stripes, seven white stripes, and a helluva lotta stars!! (Nelson Muntz, Springfield, TA, "Burn, Baby, Burn")

> Recipe for a Free Country: Mix one cup liberty, with three teaspoons of justice. Add one informed electorate. Baste well with veto power. . . . Stir in two cups of checks, sprinkle liberally with balances. (Anonymous girl, Rosemont, Minnesota, "Recipe for a Free Country")

> My back is spineless. My stomach is yellow. I am the American nonvoter. (Anonymous boy, Mobile, Alabama, "The American Non-Voter")

> Ding dong. The sound of the Liberty Bell. Ding. Freedom. Dong. Opportunity. Ding. Excellent Schools. Dong. Quality Hospitals. (Anonymous boy, Queens, New York, "Ding-Dong")

> When America was born on that hot July day in 1776, the trees in Springfield Forest were tiny saplings, trembling towards the sun, and as they were nourished by Mother Earth, so too did our fledgling nation find strength in the simple ideals of equality and justice. Who would have thought such mighty oaks or such a powerful nation could grow out of something so fragile, so pure. Thank you. (Lisa Simpson, Springfield, TA, "The Roots of Democracy")

There is a certain regularity to what counts as an infantile citizen's patriotic essay: the range of tonalities and rhetorical modes notwithstanding, fiercely patriotic citizenship always requires the deployment of analogies that represent the threat of imaginary violence to the natural body — of the biosphere, the citizen, the flag, the mappable nation. Even the feminine essay, "Recipe for a Free Country," carries the implied warning that bad citizenship and bad government are forms of bad nutrition that threaten the body politic.

Why does Lisa win? Is she simply smarter or more creative than the other kids? She wins with her essay, "The Roots of Democracy," because she uses not just analogy but a national allegory that organically links the nation's natural growth to the emergence of its political facticity. In addition, her speech is itself an allegory of infantile citizenship, for the nation grows out of "something so fragile, so pure," so young. No secular or human power has yet affected its course, and the notion of a natural course implicitly assures that the United States will extend into the infinite future. In so lushly and economically establishing the United States as a figure of "life," Lisa's intelligence is established as superior to the jingoism of ordinary Americans, all of whom the episode portrays as politically infantile, whether young or old. In front of the White House, the tourists encounter some white, middle-class adult/infantile citizens carrying protest-style placards, which proclaim, "Everything's A-OK," "No Complaints Here," and "Things are Fine." Even the ultimate contest winner, Vietnamese immigrant Trong Van Din, indulges in empty patriotic formalism, declaring, "That's why, whenever I see the Stars and Stripes, I will always be reminded of that wonderful word: flag!"

When Lisa gets to Washington, she feels supremely national, symbolic, invulnerable, intellectual. Although her superiority to other children derives simply from her capacity to sustain a metaphor, and although in Washington she pulls pranks and acts like a kid, she also seeks there an affirmation of her idealized self-image: learning early that the reason people go to national conferences is to find confirming images of their ideal selves, she asks the other finalists, "Have either of you ever run into any problems because of your superior ability?" and hugs them when they assent, saying plaintively, "Me too!"

Lisa's capacity to reflect on language and power marks her as the national Simpson in this episode. But the public surely knows that it is Bart, not Lisa, who has captured the minds and money of consumers who identify with his bratty tactical disruptions and exploitations of the bourgeois public sphere. Her already confirmed failure as a commodity outside the show surely follows her around every episode in which she imagines that she might find a place for her "superior talents" on a national scale. In this regard she is Homer's twin, not his opposite: their excesses of body and language mark them both precisely as American incompetents, citizens unfit to profit from their drives and talents in a national symbolic and capitalist system.

Trauma, Therapy, and National Fantasy: "The System Works!"

While each of the Simpsons is finding and reveling in his/her level of national (in)competence, the federal nation is itself busily corrupting the natural, symbolic, and economic forms that variously inspire the Simpson family. Scandalous national corruption is tacitly everywhere in the episode: the family stays at the Watergate; their bank advertises itself as "not a savings and loan"; Homer scoffs, "Yeah, right," at a sign in the White House bowling alley that claims Nixon bowled back-to-back three-hundred-point games there; Teddy Kennedy sits at the patriotism award ceremony looking formless and dissipated; Lisa's congressman is shown cynically exploiting her for a photo opportunity (a form of presidential mass mediation invented, of course, by Nixon).

But when Lisa witnesses the bribe that threatens to despoil Springfield National Park, the tacit knowledge of national corruption the show figures via "Nixoniana" becomes itself the explicit ground of a counternational symbolic order, produced by an enraged Lisa. The show figures the political meaning of her rage through a genealogy of aesthetic forms with which national criticism and patriotism have been traditionally organized and mediated. The transformation of consciousness, sensuality, causality, and aesthetics Lisa experiences is, again, typical of the infantile citizenship story, in which the revelation of the practical impossibility of utopian nationality produces gothic, uncanny, miraculating effects on the infantile persons whose minds are being transformed by "true," not idealized, national knowledge.

Lisa's path toward becoming a citizen with complex knowledge follows the double logic of citizenship technologies outlined in the previous section: from sentimental experiences of the nation through contact with its monumental media to political experiences of it as a massmediated, crisis-oriented site of intensified publicity. I have described how, in stage one of Lisa's political education, she immerses herself in the culture of feelings organized by the National Symbolic. Then, early in the morning of the day she is scheduled to give her patriotic speech, she visits a monument from which she can borrow another rush of national inspiration. The monument Lisa visits is fictional: it is the "Winnifred Beecher Howe" Memorial, which is said to have been raised in tribute to "an early crusader for women's rights [who] led the Floor Mop Rebellion of 1910," and who later "appeared on the highly unpopular 75 cent piece."

Howe's motto, "I Will Iron Your Sheets When You Iron Out the Inequities in Your Labor Laws," measures the absurd space of Lisa's imaginary relation to American nationality. Given the way patriotic discourse normally veils national capitalism's undemocratic effects and relegates women's value to the private sphere, it is ludicrous to think that the

44

United States would honor as an ideal citizen a female labor activist who led demonstrations against the exploitation of women's work; it is absurd to think that the nation would preserve in stone the wild ungoverned state of a working-class housewife's body in messy domestic regalia. But Lisa does not note this absurdity, which exists only for the audience: the United States in which *she* lives has a tradition of respecting class struggle, women's political efforts, and female citizenship in general. Instead, Lisa's disaffection from the nation form arises when she sees her congressman take the bribe.

Lisa is heartbroken. "How can I read my essay now, if I don't believe my own words?" To solve this soul-wrenching problem she follows fastidiously in the tradition of *Mr. Smith Goes to Washington* and *The Littlest Rebel* (dir. David Butler, 1935), and many other pilgrimage narratives, by turning to Abraham Lincoln.[23] Lisa looks up from the reflecting pool at the Lincoln Memorial and asserts that "Honest Abe" will "show me the way." Unfortunately, the Lincoln Memorial is overcrowded with Americans obsessed with the same possibility. In *Mr. Smith* the crowd mills around the monument walls as a child reads aloud the "Gettysburg Address": a montage of white people, Jews, and African Americans merge in rapt appreciation of a bygone world where a visionary man would risk making the nation into a practical utopia for all members of "the people." In "Mr. Lisa," the same crowd reappears in cartoon form, this time projecting questions to Lincoln's stony, wise, iconic face. They

range from "What can I do to make this a better country?" to "How can I make my kid brush more?" and "Would I look good with a mustache?"

Lisa, crowded out in the cacophony of national-popular need, then goes on to Jefferson's memorial; here the cartoon refers to a scene in *Born Yesterday* where Billie Dawn also visits Jefferson's memorial, seeing in his example the possibility of her own revolutionary emancipation from ignorant and degraded patriarchal working-class privacy to nation-tinged, literate middle-class romantic intimacy. Alas, Jefferson's cartoon statue

Shirley Temple (in *The Littlest Rebel*) achieves with a "living"
Lincoln what Jeff Smith and Lisa Simpson dream of as they
look at his statue: intimacy with the president's body. (Above)

yells at Lisa, resenting that his own accomplishments are comparatively
underappreciated by the ignorant American people, and she slinks away.
Resting, dejected, on the Capitol steps, Lisa has a conversion experience.
Right in front of her very eyes, federal workers in their white-collar suits
turn into pigs, their true, symbolic selves: there is a brief music video

during which she sees the federal pigs with skins engraved in the mode of dollar bills scratch each others' backs, gorge themselves at troughs over-brimming with cartoon dollar bills, and then wipe their mouths on the flag.

This mutation of the cartoon (in the style of Thomas Nast and others) places this episode of *The Simpsons* in a classic American genealogy of critical editorial cartooning, where national criticism takes the form of deeply felt sarcasm. Moreover, the gluttonous snorting of the pigs refers to Homer's own grotesque greedy excesses, thus retroactively reframing the class hierarchies and incompetence of national culture that the Simpson family embodies into what is truly repulsive, the patriarchal and economic corruption of both the National Symbolic and the U.S. federal system. The migration of U.S. grossness from the working classes to the state itself is reflected in the change Lisa forces when, the scales having fallen from her misty eyes, she changes the topic of her essay from "The Roots of Democracy" to "Cesspool on the Potomac."

But this explosion of the affect, vision, sensation, and aesthetics of normative American citizenship is followed by yet another dislocation in Lisa's experience of being national. This involves resituating her in the crisis logic that makes modern citizenship not monumental, but electric. "Mr. Lisa Goes to Washington" makes this transition in a montage sequence that takes place at the moment the Senate page beholds Lisa's loss of faith in democracy. The page telephones a senator; the FBI entraps the corrupt congressman, on videotape; the Senate meets and expels him; George Bush signs the bill; a newspaper almost instantly reports the congressman's imprisonment and conversion to a born-again conscious-ness; Lisa says, "The system works!"

As in the telephone, telegraph, newspaper, and popular-media mon-tage sequence of *Mr. Smith Goes to Washington, The Simpsons* produces na-tional criticism through a transformation of time, space, and media that involves shifting from the lexicon of patriotic monumentality and classi-cal national representation to accelerating postmodern media forms: video, microchip bugs, cameras, late-edition daily newspapers. In addi-tion, here the FBI's mastery establishes it as the guardian of America, much as in the films *Gabriel Over the White House* (dir. Gregory La Cava, 1933) and *The Pelican Brief* (dir. Alan Pakula, 1993). In contrast to the corrupt and lazy local print media of *Mr. Smith, The Simpsons,* and dozens of other pilgrimage-to-Washington films, mass-media formations are the real citizen-heroes here. Televisual technology itself becomes the representative of the "average man" who rises above his station, protected by FBI agents who seek to clean out and preserve all sorts of purity: of language (the FBI agent uses a southern drawl in his criminal guise and reverts to a television announcer's "pure" generic intonations in his "real" persona as the police), of region, and of the stream of faith that connects residents of the "mythical" Springfield, TA, to the nation that represents America in Washington.

In two minutes of television time and two hours of accelerated real time, then, the national system heals itself, the cesspool is cleaned out, and nature returns "home" to the discourse of national growth. Nothing feels complicated about this swift transformation. The performance of mass media-orchestrated political culture reveals the official or normative national culture industry to be a system of meaning in which *allegory is the aesthetic of political realism* at every moment of successful national discourse. Allegorical thinking helps to provide ways of explaining the relation between individuals' lives, the life of the collectivity, and the story of the nation form itself. But much less benign things can be said about the normative deployment of national allegory.[24] As all of the infantile citizens' patriotic essays satirically remind us, the overorganizing image or symbolic tableau emerges politically at certain points of structural crisis, helping to erase the complexities of aggregate national memory and to replace its inevitably rough edges with a magical and consoling way of thinking that can be collectively enunciated and easily manipulated, like a fetish. In this way, for example, patriotism can be equated with proper citizenship. This means that the politically invested overorganizing image is a kind of public paramnesia, a substitution for traumatic loss or unrepresentable contradiction that marks its own contingency or fictiveness while also radiating the authority of insider knowledge that all euphemisms possess. Extending from these sources of collective imagination, hegemonic allegories of the social appear to confirm inevitabilities and truths where strange combinations of structure and chaos reign behind the screen of the sign.

The competent citizen knows this about the hypocrisy of nationalist rhetoric, and learns how to read conveniently and flexibly between the lines, thus preserving both utopian national identification and cynical practical citizenship. Nothing shows this better than this episode of *The Simpsons,* which critiques the corrupt world veiled by patriotic bromides via pastiche and broad jokes rather than leaving anyone with a bad taste in her mouth. This temporalizing or narrative mode of resolving questions about the way power dominates bodies, value, exchanges, and dreams in the national public sphere is typical of the infantile citizenship genre, for narrative temporality isolates events that might also be represented as a protean system characterized by consistent violence and unevenness. As it is, when Lisa says, "The system works!" she embodies the Reaganite "patriot of tomorrow," because despite all the perverse privileged prerogative she has witnessed she continues to believe that a system exists, that "bills" motivated by democratic virtue do become law, and that a truly good nation will always emerge heroically to snuff out the bad one.

"Spitballs Are Not Free Speech"

I have described how in "Mr. Lisa," as in every fictive pilgrimage to Washington, national monuments, traditional symbolic narratives, print, radio, and television news coexist with other popular phenomena. Here the right-wing cultural agenda of the Reagan/Bush era is everywhere in the narrative, including in its recourse to sarcasm as a form of criticism and in the subtlety of the Nixon intertext, which "reminds" us, without interfering with the pleasure of the narrative, of a televisual moment when the nation thought it possible to imagine a patriotic mass-mediated *criticism*. It is not just that television histories, children's textbooks, *Reader's Digest,* FBI surveillance video, national parks, and national spaces are here brought into conjunction, constituted as the means of production of modern citizenship. It is not just that the Bushes themselves are portrayed here as benign patriarchs — for this might be coded as the text's return to the modality of wishful resolution that seems to mark the crisis of *having* national knowledge inevitably produced by the pilgrimage.

But the very multiplicity of media forms asks us to engage the genres of patriotism itself, modes of collective identification that have become the opposite of "protest" or "criticism" for a generation of youths who have been drafted to vitalize a national fantasy politics unsupported by either a utopian or a respectable domestic political agenda. The construction of a patriotic youth culture must be coded here as a postmodern nationalist mode of production. In this light, Bill Clinton's recent appearances on *Mr. Rogers' Neighborhood,* MTV, and so on involve merely one more extension of the national aura to the infant citizens of the United States, who are asked to identify with a "youthful" idealism untempered by even a loving critical distance.

This is to say that Lisa's assertion that the system works counts as even a parodic resolution to her crises of knowledge because consciousness that a system exists at all has become what counts as the ideal pedagogical outcome of contemporary American politics. Thus, in the chain that links the fetus, the wounded, the dead, and the "children" as the true American "people," the linkage is made through the attribution to normal-style citizens of a zero-sum mnemonic, a default consciousness of the nation with no imagination of agency—apart perhaps from voting, here coded as a form of consumption. In other words, the national knowledge industry has produced a specific modality of paramnesia, an incitement to forgetting that leaves simply the patriotic trace, for real and metaphorically infantilized citizens, that confirms that the nation exists and that we are in it. Television is not the cause of this substitution of the fact (that the nation exists) for the thing (political agency) but is one of many vehicles where the distilling operation takes place, and where the medium itself is installed as a necessary switchpoint between any locales and any national situation.

Let me demonstrate this by contrasting the finales of *Mr. Smith* and "Mr. Lisa." It is a crucial and curious characteristic of infantile citizenship narratives that the accumulation of plot tends to lead to an acceleration and a crisis of knowledge relieved not by modes of sustained criticism but by the quasi-amnesia of ersatz consciousness. At the end of *Mr. Smith,* Jefferson Smith is defeated by the congressional and capitalist manipulation of the law, property rights, and the media. Smith, who has been filibustering and improvising on what discursive virtue might look like in the Senate, is confronted by a wagonload of telegrams embodying a manufactured public opinion mobilized against his cause; dispirited and depleted, Smith faints on the Senate floor. His loss of spirit drives Senator Joseph Paine (Claude Rains) to attempt suicide and to confess everything. In the film's final moments, a hubbub led by Clarissa Saunders (Jean Arthur) claims victory over corruption, and the mob dances out of the chambers into, presumably, the streets. In other words, overwhelmed by joy at the victory of Smith's particular truth and virtue, the film leaves Mr. Smith lying there on the Senate floor, unconscious. It feels like a patriotic moment. But it might be interesting to speculate about what Smith would think when he awoke. Would he think the system had worked? How could he, when it totally failed, or was teeteringly maintained by the fragile conscience of one man with national power?

In contrast, it might seem that Lisa's awakening changes the condition of her citizenship. But her belief in the "system" is renewed by the shock of national power the television-style media produce for her. By the end, the waste and excess that has dominated the scene of patriotism makes her forget not just what she knew, but what she did not know. And we realize, on thinking back to her speech, that at no point did Lisa know anything about America. She could be inspired by the National Symbolic and disillusioned by the corruptions of capital; she is moved aesthetically by nature's nation and repelled by the boorish appetites of both professional and ordinary men. But not at all transformed by her experience of Washington, she merely remembers she had experiences there.

It turns out, in short, that Lisa was not that smart. What makes her fail this way? I have described how America is split into a National Symbolic and a capitalist system in "Mr. Lisa Goes to Washington." But this simple description is for infants, just as Bart's opening pedagogical punishment on the classroom blackboard, "Spitballs are not free speech," reduces the problem of protecting costly speech to a joke, a joke that once again allegorizes the conceptual problematic of freedom and its media by locating politics in a disgusting body. Likewise, the violent insult to women's citizenship this cartoon absurdity clothes in sarcasm is expressed, in the episode, by more corporeal grossness: in the afterglow of the congressman's sale of his favors to the lobbyist while standing at the foot of the woman's memorial, they look at Howe's monumental body and say, "Woof woof!" and "What a pooch!" Lisa's response to the revelation of sexism and graft is not to think of these qualities as the national system, nor to become an adult; that is, to form a critical consciousness in the place of the passive patriotism the official national culture machine seeks to inculcate. Her first response is to become abjected to America, by visiting Lincoln and soliciting his pedagogy. We have seen there, comedically, even radically, how the overidentification with national icons evacuates people's wisdom from the simplest judgments of everyday life. It is not surprising, then, that Lisa is so primed to believe what the newspaper tells her about the self-purifying system of the hegemonic nation: this is why she can have faith in the nation, "free" from the encumbrance of ambivalent knowledge.

The infantile citizen has a memory of the nation and a tactical relation to its operation. But no vision of sustained individual or collective criticism and agency accompanies the national system here. The national culture industry provides information about the United States but has no interest in producing knowledge that would change anything: in what sense is it knowledge, then? To infantilized citizens like Lisa, having at least a weak understanding of an overwhelming mountain of material seems better than nothing, and also the only thing possible. It is not surprising, in this context, that the two commercials between the opening credits of *The Simpsons* and the narrative proper—for the U.S. Army and for an episode of *In Living Color* that featured the violent heterosexualization of a gay film critic—promote the suppression of American gay identity on behalf of a national fantasy of a military life that, even after the Cold War, is more vital than ever for (re)producing national boyhood and heterosexual national manhood. It is not surprising, in this context, that I could pull the script of this episode from a "Simpsons" bulletin board on the Internet, a vast reservoir of knowledge that is said to have "revolutionized" the prospects of political agency and social integration across the nation. Just as every pilgrimage-to-Washington narrative deploys information technologies to link the abstract national to the situated local, underinformed, abjected, and idealistic citizen, so too the rhetoric of the Internet confirms its necessity at every moment for the production of the knowledge that every American needs in order to be competent to the most reduced notion of what citizenship entails.

Yet a distinguished tradition of collective popular resistance to national policy has taken the form of marches on Washington, by dispossessed workers, African Americans, gays, lesbians, queers, pro- and antichoice activists, feminists, veterans of popular and unpopular wars, for example. These collective activities invert the small-town and metropolitan spectacle of the "parade" honoring local citizens into national acts, performances of citizenship that predict votes and make metonymic "the people" whom representatives represent, but they also claim a kind of legitimate mass political voice uniquely performed outside the voting booth. On the one hand, mass political marches resist, without overcoming, the spectacular forms of identification that dominate mass national culture—through individualizing codes of celebrity, heroism, and their underside, scandal—for only in times of crisis are Americans solicited to act en masse as citizens whose private patriotic identifications are indeed *not enough* to sustain national culture at a particular moment. On the other hand, we might note as well the problem mass political movements face in translating their activities into the monumentalizing currency of national culture. In this light, we witness how an impersonation or an icon of political struggle can eclipse the movement it represents — for instance, in the image of Martin Luther King or Louis Farrakhan on the Mall; in the image of the subaltern citizen in the body of the fetus; or in the image, currently dominating national culture, of the infantile citizen, too helpless to do anything but know, without understanding, what it means that the "system" of the nation exists "freely," like "free" television itself.

2 Live Sex Acts

(Parental Advisory: Explicit Material)

I am a citizen of the United States, and in this country where I live, every year millions of pictures are being made of women with our legs spread. We are called beaver, we are called pussy, our genitals are tied up, they are pasted, makeup is put on them to make them pop out of a page at a male viewer. . . . I live in a country where if you film any act of humiliation or torture, and if the victim is a woman, the film is both entertainment and it is protected speech. Now that tells me something about being a woman in this country.
  — Andrea Dworkin[1]

I open with this passage not simply to produce in advance the resistances, ambivalences, and concords that inevitably arise when someone speaks with passion and authority about sex and identity, but also to foreground here the centrality, to any public-sphere politics of sexuality, of coming to terms with the conjunction of making love and making law, of fucking and talking, of acts and identities, of cameras and police, and of pleasure in the text and patriarchal privilege, insofar as in these couplings can be found fantasies of citizenship and longings for freedom made in the name of national culture.

I'm going to tell you a story about this, a story about citizenship in the United States. It is about live sex acts, and a book called *Live Sex Acts*, and a thing called national culture that, in reference to the United States, I mean to bring into representation here — which is hard, because the modality of national culture in the United States that I will describe exists mainly as a negative projection, an endangered species, the shadow of a fetish called normalcy, which is currently under a perceived attack by sex radicals, queers, pornographers, and pop-music culture. This perceived attack on national morals raises a number of questions. What kinds of forces in national life are being both marked and veiled by the culturally defensive demonization of atypical sexualities? And if sex and sensuality radicals were really circulating a kind of pleasure acid that could corrode the American Way of Life, what about it exactly would they be attacking?

Some vulnerable spots on the national terrain should be flagged from the very outset. The first is the national future. Because the only thing the nation form is able to assure for itself is its past, its archive of official memory, it must develop in the present ways of establishing its dominion over the future. This is one reason reproductive heterosexuality and the family always present such sensitive political issues. As the next chapter will detail, reproduction and generationality are the main vehicles by which the national future can be figured, made visible, and made personal to citizens otherwise oblivious to the claims of a history that does not seem about them individually. The anxieties surrounding the process of making people into national subjects confirm that the hegemonic form of national culture is fragile and always in the process of being defined, even when it appears as a thing with an essential character that can be taken prisoner like the soul in fierce battles between rival gangs of angels and devils.

Once it is established that national culture demands a continuous pedagogical project for making people into "private citizens" who understand their privacy to be a mirror and a source for nationality itself, it becomes equally important that the national culture industry generated a mode of political discourse in which the nation form trumps all other images of collective sociality and power. However, the content of the nation's utopian project has been complicated during the rise of the Reaganite right. One axiom of this ideology has been to destroy an image of the federal state that places its practice at the center of nation formation. The right's attempt to shrink domestic government and thereby to hack away at the hyphen between the nation and the state has required the development of new technologies of patriotism that keep the nation at the center of the public's identification while shrinking the field of what can be expected from the state.[2]

During the last twenty years as well, the sexual minorities of the United States — heterosexual women and gays and lesbians — have developed sexual publics that not only demand expanded protections from the state and the law but also challenge the practices, procedures, and contents of what counts as politics, including questioning whether the nation form as such should continue to organize utopian drives for collective social life. Additionally, using the forms of publicity that capitalist culture makes available for collective identifications, some of these sex publics have exposed contradictions in the free market economics of the right, which names nonmarital sex relations as immoral while relations of economic inequality, dangerous workplaces, and disloyalty to employees amount to business as usual, not provoking any ethical questions about the privileges only some citizens enjoy. These complex challenges, posed by a diverse set of politically embodied publics, are therefore both central to how citizenship must be thought as a question of sexuality, and convenient distractions from the conservative project of installing a sanitized image of normal culture as the nation's utopian aspiration.

One result, introduced in the last chapter, is that the national culture industry is also in the business of generating paramnesias, images that organize consciousness, not by way of explicit propaganda, but by replacing and simplifying memories people actually have with image traces of political experience about which people can have political feelings that link them to other citizens and to patriotism. This process veils, without simply suppressing knowledge of, the means by which the nation's hegemonic contradictions and contingencies are constructed, consented to, displaced, and replaced by images of normal culture that "the people" are said already to accept. In the last chapter the political fantasy of the infantile citizen was the overorganizing national image, the gratifying public paramnesia. In this chapter that place is held by an image of extremist and hypersexualized citizens recently generated in the public struggle over what will count as the core national culture. Most of the time political discourse about sex in this modality is a way of creating instant panic about the fragility of people's intimate lives; most of the time, extravagant sex is a figure for general social disorder, and not a site for serious thinking and criticism about sexuality, morality, or anything. But the relation between nationalized knowledge and amnesia is not one of mutual negation. Instead, we never really know whether the forms of intelligibility that give citizens access to political culture are monuments to false consciousness, or are the inevitable partial truths of publicly held information. Michael Taussig argues that state knowledge is a site of the full "coming together of reason and violence" that generates paradoxes of knowing and unknowing, such that ordinary pragmatic detail, goodenough comprehensions of national activity, and traumatized pseudo-knowledges together can be said to constitute the ongoing lived relations among states, national ideology, and citizens.[3] Along with drawing attention to sexuality and its place in the contemporary construction of U.S. citizenship, the sex culture wars I investigate here provide a way of exploring what different kinds of national world are brought into being by different conceptions of sex.

This chapter began as a review of some recent feminist work on pornography.[4] In it I take no position on "pornography" as such, but discuss it in terms of how, more broadly, the U.S. citizen's vulnerability and aspiration to a nationally protected identity has been orchestrated by a national culture industry that emphasizes sexuality as the fundamental index of a person's political legitimacy. In this regard the chapter refocuses the discussion of sex and representation away from the domain of the politics of sexual difference and toward the conjunction of sexuality, mass culture, and mass nationality.

In particular, I am interested in tracing some meanings of privacy, a category of law and a condition of property that constitutes a boundary between proper and improper bodies, and a horizon of aspiration vital to the imagination of what counts as legitimate U.S. citizenship. Privacy here describes, simultaneously, a theoretical space imagined by U.S. constitutional and statutory law; a scene of taxonomic violence that devolves privilege on certain actual spaces of practical life; a juridical substance that comes to be synonymous with secure domestic interiority; and a structure of protection and identity that sanctions, by analogy, other spaces that surround, secure, and frame the bodies whose acts, identities, identifications, and social value are the booty over which national culture wages its struggle to exist as a struggle to dominate sex.

Thus, this story will indeed contain graphic images, parental advisories, and magical thinking — that is to say, the usual dialectic between crassness and sublimity that has long dressed the ghosts of national culture in monumental forms, and made it available for anxious citizens who need to invoke it on behalf of stabilizing one or another perceived social norm. This story has real and fictive characters, too — John Frohnmayer, Andrea Dworkin, Tipper Gore, and some fat, queer Nazis who try to join the military — but its main players are a little girl and an adult, both Americans. The little girl stands in this chapter as a condensation of many (infantile) citizenship fantasies. It is in her name as future citizen that state and federal governments have long policed morality around sex and other transgressive representation; the psychological and political vulnerability she represents has provided a model for other struggles to transform minority experience in the United States. And it is in her name that something Other to her, called, let's say, "adult culture," has been defined and privileged in many national domains. Although not without its contradictions: we have the adult by whose name pornography is marked, as in "adult books," and, on the other hand, the adult who can join with other adults to protect the still unhistorical little girl whose citizenship, if the adults act as good parents, might pass boringly from its minority to what has been called the "zone of privacy" or national heterosexuality "adult" Americans generally seek to inhabit.

"Zone of privacy" is a technical phrase, invented in a Supreme Court opinion of 1965. It was Justice William O. Douglas's opinion in *Griswold v. Connecticut* that designated for the first time the heterosexual act of intercourse in marital bedrooms as protected by a zone of privacy into which courts must not peer and with which they must not interfere. Justice Douglas's rezoning of the bedroom into a nationally protected space of privacy allowed married citizens of Connecticut for the first time to purchase birth control. It sought to make national a relation that it says precedes the Bill of Rights. It consolidated the kind of thinking that happened when the justices recently, in *Bowers v. Hardwick,* confirmed the irreducible heterosexuality of the national bedroom, as it established once again that homosexuality has no constitutionally supported privacy protections in the United States. It could have been otherwise. Writing a memo to be circulated among Supreme Court justices, Daniel Richman, a clerk for Thurgood Marshall, sought to instruct the Court about oral and anal sex. He wrote to the justices, in capital letters, "THIS IS NOT A CASE ABOUT ONLY HOMOSEXUALS. ALL SORTS OF PEOPLE DO THIS KIND OF THING."[5] He does not name the "sorts" of people. But in almost referring to heterosexuality, that sacred national identity that happens in the neutral territory of national culture, Richman almost made the "sex" of heterosexuality imaginable, corporeal, visible, public.

Thus, I mean to oppose a story about live sex acts to a story about "dead citizenship." Dead citizenship, which haunts the shadowland of national culture, takes place in a privacy zone, and epitomizes an almost Edenic conjunction of act and identity, sacred and secular history. It involves a theory of national identity that equates identity with iconicity. It requires that I tell you a secret history of acts that are not experienced as acts, because they take place in the abstract idealized time and space of citizenship. I use the word "dead," then, in the rhetorical sense designated by the phrase "dead metaphor." A metaphor is dead when, by repetition, the unlikeness risked in the analogy the metaphor makes becomes so conventionalized as to no longer seem figural, no longer open to history: the leg of a table is the most famous dead metaphor. In the fantasy world of national culture, citizens aspire to dead identities — constitutional personhood in its public-sphere abstraction and suprahistoricity, reproductive heterosexuality in the zone of privacy. Identities not live, or in play, but dead, frozen, fixed, or at rest.

The fear of ripping away the privacy protections of heteronational culture has led to a national crisis over the political meanings of imaginable, live, and therefore transgressive sex acts, acts that take place in public either by virtue of a state optic or a subcultural style. By bringing more fully into relief the politics of securing the right to privacy in the construction of a sexuality that bears the definitional burden of national culture, I am in part telling a story about preserving a boundary between what can be done and said in public, what can be done in private but not spoken of in public, and what can, patriotically speaking, be neither done nor legitimately spoken of at all, in the United States. Thus there is nothing new about the new national anthem, "Don't Ask, Don't Tell, Don't Pursue." I am also telling a story about transformations of the body in mass national society, and thinking about a structure of political feeling that characterizes the history of national sentimentality, in which, at moments of crisis, persons violate the zones of privacy that give them privilege and protection in order to fix something social that feels threatening: they practice politics, they generate publicity, they act in public, but in the name of privacy. I mean to bring into representation these forms of citizenship structured in dominance, in scenes where adults act on behalf of the little-girl form that represents totemically and fetishistically the unhumiliated citizen.[6] She is the custodian of the promise of zones of privacy that national culture relies on for its magic and its reproduction.

Looking for Love in All the Wrong Places: Live Sex Acts in America

When John Frohnmayer made his pilgrimage to serve the National Endowment for the Arts in Washington, he was a "babe in the woods" of politics who hoped to "rekindl[e]" the "free spirit" of the nation, a spirit now endangered by television and other mass-mediated forms of alienation in the United States.[7] He initially imagined using the NEA to re-produce the nation through its localities — emphasizing not cities (which are, apparently, not localities), but the rural and provincial cultures whose neglected "vitality" might help return the mass nation to a non-mass-mediated sense of tribal intimacy. Frohnmayer's autobiography, *Leaving Town Alive: Confessions of an Arts Warrior,* describes in great detail the deep roots of the nation in aesthetic genealogies of an organic citizenry. For example, he tells of the gospel roots of rap, the spirit of fiddling in an age of "overamplified electronic music," Native American weaving, ballet, and other arts that make "no mention of homosexuality, foul words, or nudity"[8] — which, according to this logic, become phenomena of cities and of mass culture.

Yet his ambitions for cultural reformation did not protect Frohnmayer's tenure at the NEA, which was so riddled by the competition between a certain metropolitan and an uncertain national culture that he was driven out of office. The cases of the X, Y, and Z portfolios of Robert Mapplethorpe, of the NEA Four, and of *Tongues Untied* are famous examples of how sex-radical performance aesthetics were unassimilable to the homophobic and mock-populist official national culture-making machine that currently dominates Washington. But what got Frohnmayer actually fired was the NEA's support of a *literary* publication project in New York City that dragged the nation into the dirt, the waste, and the muck of sex and other gross particularities. This project, managed by a press called "the portable lower east side," produced two texts in 1991: *Live Sex Acts* and *Queer City.* The Reverend Donald Wildmon made these texts available to every member of Congress, President George Bush, and Vice President Dan Quayle. He also wrote a letter to them citing an excerpt from a poem as evidence for the virtually treasonous use of taxpayer money to support art that besmirched national culture.

My first exhibit, or, should I say, my first "inhibit," is the poem "Wild Thing," written by the poet "Sapphire" (Ramona Lofton) and published in *Queer City.* "Wild Thing" is written in the fictive voice of one of the boys whose wilding expedition in 1989 resulted in the rape and beating of the woman called "the Central Park jogger." Here is the excerpt from the poem that Wildmon sent to Congress:

I remember when
Christ sucked my dick
behind the pulpit
I was 6 years old
he made me promise
not to tell no one.[9]

I will return to this poem anon. But first, let me characterize the scandalous magazines that were the context for it. Frohnmayer describes *Queer City* accurately: "Although some of the pieces were sexual in tone and content, they were clearly meant to be artful rather than prurient."[10] *Queer City* is a collective work of local culture, positing New York as a vibrant site of global sexual identity, a multinational place where people come to traverse the streets, live the scene, have sex, write stories and poems about it, and take pictures of the people who live it with pleasure and impunity. It is an almost entirely apolitical book, except in the important sense that the title *Queer City* remaps New York by way of the spaces where queer sex takes place, such that sexual identities are generated in *public,* in a metropolitan public constituted by a culture of experience and a flourish of publicity.

In contrast, and although *Live Sex Acts* is equally situated in New York City, a marked majority of its texts explain sex in terms of the national context and the political public sphere; indeed, many of the essays in *Live Sex Acts* are explicit responses to the right-wing cultural agenda of the Reagan revolution. They demonstrate that it is not sexual identity as such that threatens America, which is liberal as long as sex aspires to iconicity or deadness, and suggest rather that the threat to national culture derives from what we might call sex acts on the live margin, sex acts that threaten because they do not aspire to the privacy protection of national culture, nor to the narrative containment of sex into one of the conventional romantic forms of modern consumer heterosexuality. This assertion of a sexual public sphere is also striking because *Live Sex Acts* closes by moving beyond a sexual performance ethic and toward other live margins. Two final segments, Krzysztof Wodiczko's "Poliscar: A Homeless Vehicle" and a portfolio of poems by patients at Creedmoor Psychiatric Hospital, explicitly seek to redefine citizenship by naming who lives on the live margins, and how.[11] They show how the waste products of America must generate a national public sphere and a civic voice. To do this, the live margin must find its own media. A radically redefined category of live sex acts here becomes a mass medium for addressing and redressing the official national culture industry.

In any case, as Frohnmayer says, the scandal these two magazines created had nothing to do with what kinds of subversive effect their small circulation might conceivably have had or aspired to, with respect either to sexual convention or national identity. He describes the uproar as an effect of bad reading. Donald Wildmon has spent much time in the last decade policing sexual subcultures. He does this by attempting to humiliate state and federal arts councils that use taxpayer money to support transgressions of norms a putative ordinary America holds sacred. To christen the national as a locale with discernible standards of propriety, he uses the logic of obscenity law, which since the 1970s has offered local zones the opportunity to specify local standards with respect to which federal law might determine the obscenity of a text.

Wildmon is unconcerned with the referential context of both the wild thing and the poem about it. This lack of concern is central to the story of the Central Park jogger: many have noted how a serious discussion of the wilding event—in terms of the politics of public spaces, of housing projects, of city parks as homes and public property, of gender, of race, of classes and underclasses, of sexuality, of mass media, and of the law— was deflected into a melodrama of the elite. Here, Wildmon seeks to make irrelevant any full exploration of the wilding poem by deploying the anti-live-sex terms of the "true" national culture he claims to represent. Already on record accusing the NEA of promoting "blasphemy" *and* "the homosexual lifestyle," Wildmon grasped the passage "Christ sucked my dick" and brought it to the attention of Jesse Helms, who shortly thereafter got Frohnmayer, whom Pat Robertson had nicknamed "Satan," fired.[12]

Frohnmayer claims to know nothing about homosexuality in the United States, and I believe he is right, though he knows something about homoeroticism. For example, in arguing against the Helms amendment[13] he suggests the difficulty of telling "whether homoeroticism differed from garden-variety eroticism, whether it applied to females as well as males, whether it would pass muster under the Fourteenth Amendment tests of rational classifications and equal protection, or whether it was illegal for two persons of the same gender to hold hands, kiss, or do something more in deep shadow."[14] Of course we know there is no deep shadow for gay sex in America: deep shadow is the protected zone of heterosexuality, or dead citizenship, and meanwhile all

64

queers have is that closet. But if Frohnmayer does not know sex law, he knows what art is and also knows that when the NEA funds works of art it effectively protects them from obscenity prosecution.[15] Thus he legitimates this poem and *Queer City* in toto by reference to the standard of what art *attempts*. If the aspiration to art makes sexual representation protected by the national imprimatur, it is the content of "Wild Thing" that secures the success of its aspiration. Frohnmayer writes:

> These lines have been taken out of context and sensationalized. The poem, in its entirety, is emotional, intense and serious. . . . [It] deals with an actual event—the violent rape of a female jogger in Central Park—and must be read in its entirety in order to receive a fair appraisal. . . . It's not meant to make us feel good. It's not meant as an apology for a violent act. And it's certainly not meant to be sacrilegious, unless pedophilia is part of religious dogma. The poem is meant to make us think and to reflect on an incredibly brutal act in an allegedly civilized society.[16]

Again, there is much to say about wilding, the wild thing, the poem about it, the song it refers to, and the wild incitement to govern expression that this unfinished event has generated, which results in the contest over national meaning and value. First of all, Wildmon reads the poem as a direct indictment of the church for its alleged implied support of homosexual child molestation. Frohnmayer contests this reading with one that focuses on the purported failure of the black family to guide youth toward disciplined obedience to patriarchal authority. In Frohnmayer's description, the fate of the white woman represents what will happen to America when undersocialized boys abused by life in the projects and failed by parents leave their degenerate natal locales. They will terrorize property, women, and the nation: they will be bad men.

Frohnmayer's version of the poem cuts out entirely the poet's image of the fun, the pleasure, indeed the death-driven *jouissance* of the wilding man, his relation to mass culture, to his own body, to his rage at white women and men, his pleasure in his mastery over language, and over the racist conventions he knows he inspires. Clearly that isn't the stuff of art or America. Most importantly, Frohnmayer parentalizes the nation by locating the virtue of art in its disclosure that the source of sexual violence and social decay (the end of American civilization) is in absent fathers and failed mothers. He ventriloquizes the poet's ventriloquized poem about wayward youth to prophesy about the future of national culture, which is in danger of collective acts of wilding. This hybrid official image—of the nation as a vicious youth, and as a formerly innocent youth betrayed by bad parenting, and as a child who might be saved by good official parents—is at the heart of contemporary citizenship policy. Here is a story about the attempt to construct a national culture that resists an aesthetic of live sex in the name of youth, heterosexuality, and the national future.

What "Adults" Do to "Little Girls": Minor Citizens in the Modern Nation

When Anthony Comstock made his pilgrimage to Washington in 1873 to show the Congress what kinds of literature, information, and advertisements about sex, contraception, and abortion were being distributed through the U.S. mails, he initiated a process of nationalizing the discipline of sexual representation in the United States in the name of protecting national culture. Comstock installed this regime of anxiety and textual terror by invoking the image of youth, and, in particular, the stipulated standard of the little girl whose morals, mind, acts, body, and identity would certainly be corrupted by contact with adult immorality.[17] Until the 1957 *Roth v. United States* and the 1964 rulings on the novel *The Tropic of Cancer* and the film *Les Amants,* the Comstockian standard of the seducible little girl reigned prominently in court decisions about the obscenity of texts; indeed, as Edward de Grazia describes in *Girls Lean Back Everywhere: The Law of Obscenity and the Assault on Genius,* this putative little girl who might come into harmful contact with unsafe sexual knowledge and thus be induced by reading into performing harmful live sex acts (at least of interpretation) has been central to defining minor and full citizenship in the United States. She has come to represent the standard from which the privileged "adult" culture of the nation has fallen. Protecting her, while privileging him, establishing therein the conditions of minor and full citizenship, has thus been a project of pornographic modernity in the United States.

To certify obscenity legally a three-pronged standard must be met. The material must appeal to a prurient interest in sex; be patently offensive to contemporary community standards; and be "utterly without redeeming social value."[18] The Roth and Miller decisions nationalized obscenity law for the first time, thus defining the adult who consumes pornography as an American in the way that the Fourteenth Amendment enfranchised

African Americans as full citizens by locating citizenship primarily in the nation and only secondarily in states. Speaking of pornography's consumers, Dworkin and MacKinnon put succinctly this conjuncture of what we might call pornographic personhood, an amalgam of nation, nurture, and sacred patriarchy: "Pornography is their Dr. Spock, their Bible, their Constitution."[19] De Grazia's history of obscenity in the United States, along with his anthology *Censorship Landmarks*, reveals how the pressure to define obscenity has all along involved a struggle to define the relative power of national, state, and local cultures to control the contact the public might have with prurient materials. For example, in *Jacobellis v. Ohio*, the Ohio case concerning *Les Amants*, Justice Brennan argued that "We recognize the legitimate and indeed exigent interest of States and localities throughout the Nation in preventing the dissemination of material deemed harmful to children. But that interest does not justify a total suppression of such material, the effect of which would be to reduce the adult population . . . to reading only what is fit for children."[20] This tendency to nationalize the obscene, the child, and the adult has been checked by the "community standards" doctrine embraced by Chief Justice Warren Burger in 1973. This doctrine empowers local police, judges, prosecutors, juries, and citizen interest groups to determine the standards of local morality from which the nation should protect them. The Burger Court thus dissolved a major blockage to promoting a conservative cultural agenda, at least from the vantage point of Supreme Court precedent; the constitutional protection of free speech against the "chilling effect" of censorship, which sought to avert the terroristic effects of political repression on speech, could be avoided by localizing the relevant "context" according to the most local community standards. Central to establishing and maintaining these standards is the figure of the vulnerable little girl, a figure for minors in general. The situation of protected minor citizenship is thus a privilege for protection from adult heterosexual exploitation that national culture confers on its youth, its little girls and boys; paradoxically, the aura of the little girl provides a rationale for protecting the heterosexual privacy zones of "adult" national culture.

Sometimes, when the little girl, the child, or youth or invoked in discussions of pornography, obscenity, or the administration of morality in U.S. mass culture, actually endangered living beings are being imagined. Frequently, however, we should understand that these disturbing figures are fetishes, effigies that condense, displace, and stand in for arguments about who "the people" are, what they can bear, and when, if ever. The purpose of this excursus into the history of obscenity law has been to recast it within an assembly of parental gestures in which adult citizens are protected as children are protected from representations of violence and sex and violent sex, for fear that those representations are in effect understood as doctrine or as documentary fantasy. Even the most liberal obscenity law concedes that children must neither see nor hear immoral sex/text acts: they must neither know them nor see them, at least until they reach that ever more unlikely moment of majority when they can freely consent to reading with a kind of full competence they must first be protected from having.

Nowhere is this infantilizing confluence of media, citizenship, and sex more apparent and symptomatically American than in the work of Andrea Dworkin, Catharine MacKinnon, and the 1986 report on obscenity popularly called the Meese commission report. Much has been written on the paradoxical effects of this collaboration between these radical feminists and the conservative cultural activity of the Republican-dominated state: Carole Vance and Edward de Grazia give scathing detailed accounts of the ideological excesses and incoherences of this collaboration, and MacKinnon and Dworkin write eloquently about why the sexual harms women experience must be mended by law.[21] I am not interested in adjudicating this debate here in its usual terms (civil rights/harm speech/antipatriarchal versus First Amendment/free speech/sex radical) — but I mean to be entering it obliquely, by examining the logics of its citizenship politics. I am interested in how it has helped to consolidate an image of the citizen as a minor, female, youthful victim who requires civil protection by the state whose adult citizens, especially adult men, seem mobilized by a sex- and capital-driven compulsion to foul their own national culture.

This story can be told in many ways. The first step of the argument by which pornography represents harm speech that fundamentally compromises women's citizenship in the United States establishes that pornography is a live sex act. It is live partly because, as the Milwaukee ordinance avows, "Pornography is what pornography *does.*" There is a sense here, shared by many textual critics (not just of pornography), that texts are muscular active persons in some sense of the legal fiction that makes corporations into persons: texts can and do impose their will on consumers, innocent or consenting.[22] Second, this notion of textual activity, of the harm pornographic texts perform as a desired direct effect on their consumers, has become intensified and made more personal by the visual character of contemporary pornography.

The optical unconscious dominates the scene of citizenship and pornographic exploitation the Meese commission report conjures. I quote at length the opening to the chapter called "The Use of Performers in Commercial Pornography." This chapter opens with a passage from André Bazin's "The Ontology of the Photographic Image": "The objective nature of photography confers on it a quality of credibility absent from all other picture-making. . . . The photographic image is the object itself, the object freed from the conditions of time and space that govern it."[23] The text glosses this representation of the image:

> The leap from "picture making" to photography was . . . the single most important event in the history of pornography: images of the human body could be captured and preserved in exact, vivid detail. As with every other visible activity, sex could now, by the miraculous power of the camera, be "freed from the conditions of time and space." 'Sex' in the abstract, of course, remains invisible to the camera; it is particular acts of sex between individual people which photographs, films, and video tapes can record.[24]

By equating the violence that photography performs on history and personhood with the citizenship harms of pornography, the commission locates the solution to sexual violence in a return to the scene and the mode of production, and indeed, in her own work, MacKinnon sees herself as a materialist feminist for this reason. This powerful view has incited a fundamental shift in the focus of assessments of pornography's effects. While social scientists are still trying to determine whether seeing violence leads to violence, and how, this antipornography view also insists on engaging with the backstory of the porn, taking its effect on performers and on the businessmen who control the condition of the performers as an important measure of its meaning. Furthermore, as we shall see, the exploitation of the pornographic performer becomes the model for the exploitation and violence to all women involved in the path of pornography's circulation.

> Unlike literature or drawing, sexually explicit photography cannot be made by one person. . . . No study of filmed pornography can thus be complete without careful attention to the circumstances under which individual people decide to appear in it, and the effects

of that appearance on their lives. Nor is this an academic or trivial exercise. The evidence before us suggests that a substantial minority of women will at some time in their lives be asked to pose for or perform in sexually-explicit materials. It appears, too, that the proportion of women receiving such requests has increased steadily over the past several decades. If our society's appetite for sexually-explicit material continues to grow, or even if it remains at current levels, the decision whether to have sex in front of a camera will confront thousands of Americans.[25]

The ordinary woman and the pornographic model will experience second-class citizenship in U.S. society, the argument goes, because sexualization constructs every woman as a potential performer of live sex acts that get photographed. The Meese commission supports this by showing how even models in pornographic films insist that "acting" in pornography is a fiction: it is sex work euphemized as acting; it is public euphemized as private and personal; it is coerced and exploitative, euphemized as consensual and part of a simple business exchange.

To find a precedent for protecting actors in pornography from experiencing in their jobs the unfreedom U.S. women experience in everyday heterosexual life, the Meese commission, MacKinnon, and Dworkin turn to the model of child pornography, both to psychologize the vulnerability of women and to justify the prosecution of all pornographers. "Perhaps the single most common feature of models is their relative, and in the vast majority of cases, absolute youth." By definition, pornographers are exploiting young girls when they pay women to perform sex acts in front of cameras. Exploiting women-as-young-girls, they are performing a class action against women's full citizenship in the U.S. public sphere.

> Pornographers promote an image of free consent because it is good for business. But most women in pornography are poor, were sexually abused as children, and have reached the end of this society's options for them, options that were biased against them as women in the first place. This alone does not make them coerced for purposes of the Ordinance; but the fact that some women may "choose" pornography from a stacked deck of life pursuits (if you call a loaded choice a choice, like the "choice" of those with brown skin to pick cabbages or the "choice" of those with black skin to clean toilets) and the fact that some women in pornography say

they made a free choice does not mean that women who are coerced into pornography are *not coerced*. Pimps roam bus stations to entrap young girls who left incestuous homes thinking nothing could be worse. . . . Young women are tricked or pressured into posing for boyfriends and told that the pictures are just "for us," only to find themselves in this month's *Hustler*. . . . Women in pornography are bound, battered, tortured, harassed, raped, and sometimes killed. . . . Children are presented as adult women; adult women are presented as children, fusing the vulnerability of a child with the sluttish eagerness to be fucked said to be natural to the female of every age.[26]

Leo Bersani has argued that the big secret about sex is that most people don't like it; but also that the fundamental transgressiveness and irrationality of sex makes its enactment a crucial opportunity to resist the dead identities of the social.[27] We see in the antipornographic polemic of MacKinnon and Dworkin a fundamental agreement with Bersani's position, although they reach antithetical conclusions: they would argue, more dramatically, that the little girl too sexualized to be a citizen has no privilege, no "adult" advantages, that would allow her to shuttle between legitimated sociality and a sexual resistance to it. Rather, she is the opposite of "someone who matters, someone with rights, a full human being, and a full citizen."[28] The sentimental logic of this antipornography argument thus links women and children to the nation in a variety of ways. In terms of the public contexts where civil rights are experienced as a matter of everyday life, women are paradoxically both the bearers of the value of privacy and always exposed and available to be killed into identity, which is to say into photography, into a sexual optic, and into heterosexuality, but not the sacred kind. Thus the cycle of pornography: it makes men child abusers who sentimentalize and degrade their objects; meanwhile, because young girls and women need to survive both materially and psychically in a culture of abuse, they become addicted to the stereotypical structure of sexual value and exploitation, forced to become either subjects in or to pornography. In this way the child's, the young girl's, vulnerability is the scene merely covered over and displaced by the older woman's pseudoautonomy; the young girl's minority is the true scene of arrested development of all American women's second-class citizenship. For this reason, this logic of infantile second-class citizenship has become both a moral dominant in the public sphere and a precedent in court prosecution of pornography.

Court prosecution of pornography found its excuse to rescue adult women from pornographic performance by taking the image of the vulnerable child performer of sex acts as the auratic truth of the adult. The Supreme Court decision in *New York v. Ferber* in 1982 for the first time extended its analysis of such material to encompass the "privacy interests" of the performers—in this case children. Filming children in the midst of explicit sexual activity harmed them not only because of the sexual abuse involved, but also because "the materials produced are a permanent record of the children's participation and the harm to the child is exacerbated by their circulation." In addition, the continued existence of a market for such materials was bound to make it more likely that children would be abused in the future, thus justifying a ban on distribution.[29] We have seen this argument before—that child abuse begets itself, that child porn begets both abuse and porn, and that these beget the damaged inner children of adult women, who therefore must be saved from the child pornography that is the truth of their submission to the sex apparatus that befouls the national culture whose privileges women have either no access to, or access to only by virtue of proximity to heterosexual genital intercourse. The stakes of this vision of juridical deliverance therefore are not just personal to some American women, but reveal fundamental conditions of national identity for all women in the United States.

Even more striking is how vital a horizon of fantasy national culture remains, even to some radicals, in its promise of corporeal safety and the privacy of deep shadow. When Dworkin asserts that women's everyday experience of sexual degradation in the United States is both a condition of their second-class citizenship and the most fundamental betrayal of them all, she also seeks to occupy the most politically privileged privacy protections of the very national sexuality whose toxic violence defines the lives of American women. Here America's promise to release its citizens from having a body to humiliate trumps the feminist or material-ist visionary politics Dworkin might have espoused, politics that would continue to imagine a female body as a citizen's body that remains vul-nerable because public and alive, engaged in the ongoing struggles of making history.

How to Raise PG Kids in an X-Rated Nation

We have seen that in Washington the nationalist aspirations to iconicity of the high arts and the ars erotica play out a wish to dissolve the body.

They reveal a desire for identity categories to be ontological, dead to history, not in any play or danger of representation, anxiety, improvisation, desire, or panic. This sentimentality suggests how fully the alarm generated around identity politics in the United States issues from a nostalgia or desire for a suprahistorical nationally secured personhood that does not look to acts of history or the body for its identifications. Recently, the education of the American into these fantasy norms of citizenship has become an obsession about pedagogy. My third inhibit in this argument about how the moral domination of live sex works in contemporary U.S. culture takes the form of a book report on Tipper Gore's *Raising PG Kids in an X-Rated Society*.[30]

It would be very easy to cite passages from this book in order to humiliate it. It is full of bad mixed metaphors, pseudoscience, and rickety thinking. But I want to take seriously its images of the citizen as a minor. The mirror that Gore looks into shows a terrible national present and foretells a frightening future for what she calls our national character. Her representation of the inner child of national culture repeats precisely the icon of feminized infantile vulnerability I have described as the scene of national anxiety in the previous two sections of this essay; she assumes as well the absolute value of the implicit, private, sacred, heterofamilial fetish of national culture. But my main interest is to trace the logic and social theory of citizen action that emerges here, which has become dominant in the contemporary U.S. public sphere, for reasons I have tried to suggest. The book's very reference to "PG kids" in its title suggests a theory of national personhood in which each person is an undeveloped film whose encounters with traumatic images and narratives might well make him or her a traumatized person who repeats the trauma the way a film repeats scenes. It suggests that a rating system for such persons might reveal their identities to each other, and protect us all from the mere repetition of violence that is the social text of the United States, an X-rated place with X-rated adult citizens begetting a generation of monsters (someone might call it "Generation X").

Raising PG Kids in an X-Rated Society opens like a slasher film, with a scene of Tipper Gore fleeing New York City to the "familiarity, love, and comfort of home" in bucolic Washington, D.C.[31] Yet she finds that the sin of the big city has invaded Washington through the infectious circuits of mass culture. At home Gore faces what she has purchased for her eleven-year-old daughter: a record, *Purple Rain,* which contains "Darling Nikki," a song that glamorizes masturbation. With MTV, Gore realizes, Prince and his ilk make sexual trouble for her daughters: "These images frightened my children; they frightened *me*!"[32] Gore then sets out on a pilgrimage from her living room, through Washington, to the nation, to defend youth from premature contact with sex. By "sex" she means the practice of violent liveness the antipornography activists above also imagine, as portrayed here in lyrics, on album covers, in rock concerts, and on MTV. Meanwhile, what she means by "youth" is similarly elastic, as the vulnerable little-girl citizen of American culture ranges in this book from age one to her early twenties, the time when, Gore admits, kids are finally competent to enter "sexual relationships."[33] However, she also uses the consumer bromide "youth of all ages" to describe the ongoing surprise, hurt, humiliation, and upset even adults experience when having unwonted encounters with all kinds of "excess," including sex, alcohol, drugs, suicide, and satanism.

Under the pressure of this youth crisis, which also generalizes to all ages and is therefore in her view a crisis of national character and national culture, Gore joined with other concerned wives of men powerful in the U.S. state apparatus to engender a counter-public sphere — via the Parents Music Resource Center (PMRC) — whose purpose is to make the profit-driven sexually suffused popular-music industry nationally accountable for terrorizing a generation of American youths through premature exposure to a world of live sex acts. Gore claims her arguments are antimarket but not anticapitalist, anti-sexual explicitness but not pro-censorship, "pro-morality" but not antisex. She notes acutely that there seems to be a lyric/narrative hierarchy in obscenity law. Although children are indeed not permitted access to adult films, books, and magazines, they are permitted access to equally explicit record covers, live-performance rock concerts and videos of songs, as well as lyrics that perform the same acts minors are not allowed to consume when they are not the market population designated by capitalists. "If no one under eighteen can buy *Penthouse* magazine," she writes, "why should children be subjected to . . . hard-core porn in the local record shop? A recent album from the Dead Kennedys band contained a graphic poster of multiple erect penises penetrating vaginas. Where's the difference? In the hands of a few warped artists, their brand of rock music has become a Trojan Horse, rolling explicit sex and violence into our homes."[34]

In addition to pointing out the intemperance of the record industry and the artists who produce what she calls "porn rock," and in addition to exposing the contradictions in the law's stated intention to protect

74

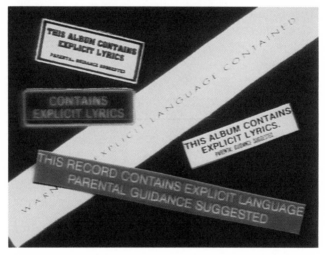

The rap/comedy group 2 Live Crew popularized and were prosecuted for promoting the sense of "live" that signifies the threat of sex and the cultural transgressions of racial and economic underclasses. From the film *Banned in the USA* (dir. Penelope Spheeris, 1990). (Above)

These labels for album covers were suggested by the PMRC to help keep unwelcome knowledge from the minds of children. The record industry has adopted them. From the film *Banned in the USA* (dir. Penelope Spheeris, 1990). (Below) children, two other issues dominate Gore's reading of the general crisis in national culture. They do not involve critiques of the immorality of capitalism and law. They involve the failure of American adults to be competent parents and a passionate argument to extend the model of infantile citizenship to nonminor U.S. citizens through an image of the adult citizen as social parent. In particular, Gore depicts the devastating effects of adults' general refusal to acknowledge the specifically limited capacities of children, such that proper boundaries between children and adults are no longer being drawn. She also testifies to the failure of the family to compensate for the escalating norms of sexual and corporeal violence in everyday life, mass culture, and the public sphere at large.

Gore turns to social scientists and psychologists to mourn the loss of childhood in America: not only in families with latchkey children whose mothers work, not only in broken families (that is, ones without fathers), but even in the 7 percent of families with intact originary parental couples, stay-at-home mothers, and fully genetically related children, parents have begun to mistake the eloquence of children for "mature reasoning powers and critical skills."[35] She argues that "anyone who attempts to debate the porn rock issue as if young people are in the same intellectual and emotional category as adults does them a terrible injustice. We need to let children be children. Children think differently from adults, and process information according to their own stages of development."[36]

If the cognitive difference between children and adults were not enough to require special adult wisdom with respect to superintending the lives of children, Gore goes on to show that the dissolution of the "smiling nuclear family," increases in family violence, spouse abuse, and child abuse, and, most dramatically, the "violent world" of life in the United States have resulted simultaneously in the saturation of children's minds with scenes of terror and the desensitization of their minds toward terror, through its transformation into pleasure and entertainment.[37] Gore argues that adults have ruined American society with their excesses, with their will to make public intimate and complicated relations, like sex, and with their negligent complacence about the violence, annihilation, exploitation, and neglect into which children are thrust daily. This sacrifice to the indulgences of U.S. adulthood is the distinguishing mark of the generation of children that currently exists. In contrast, Gore distinguishes (and, one must say, misremembers) her own generation, which we might call the generation of 1968, by its relation to two key texts: "Twist and Shout" and *I Love Lucy*.[38]

Thus when Tipper Gore places the words "Explicit material — parental advisory" on the title page of her book, we are to understand that her project is to train incompetent American adults to be parents, as a matter of civic and nationalist pedagogy. Although all Americans are youths in her view — in other words, incompetent to encounter live sex acts or any sex in public — she also desperately tries to redefine "adult" into a category of social decay more negative than any national category since the "delinquent" of the 1950s. The new virtuous category of majority is "parent." The new activist citizenship Tipper Gore imagines to express the true morality of U.S. national culture refuses the contradictions of traditional patriarchal privilege that both moralizes against and promotes the erotic terrorizing of women and children. (No sympathetic mention is made of the sexually terrorized Others on the live margins of national heterosexuality.) In every chapter Gore advises parents to think of parenting as a public profession, like being a lawyer or a politician, and she encourages what she calls "parental solidarity" groups to take the private activity of nurturing children away from mass-media-induced but home-circulated materials that promote sex and violence. She imagines a nation controlled by a local, public, community matrix of parental public spheres.[39] Above all, she characterizes this grassroots model of citizenship on behalf of the "rights" parents have to control what they and their children encounter as a model for national political agency itself. Here are the last words of the conclusion: "It's not easy being a parent these days. It's even tougher being a kid. Perhaps together we can help our society grow up."[40]

Wild Things

I was cruising, one early spring morning, the Sunday morning talk shows: *Meet the Press, This Week with David Brinkley, Face the Nation.* But along the way I ran across a couple of video events that I have not yet recovered from seeing. The first was a Jerry Falwell commercial, played during the *Old Time Gospel Hour.* In this minute-long segment he offers us the opportunity to spend four dollars engaging in citizenship acts. We might call 1-900-288-3402 in support of "the new homosexual rights agenda" soon, he said, to be signed into law by President Clinton. Or we might call 1-900-288-3401 to say that although we pray for the president, we do not support "the new homosexual rights agenda," we do not want our "children to grow up in an America where a new homosexual rights agenda" is law. He keeps repeating the phrase "new homosexual rights agenda," and posts the phone numbers on the TV screen, the background for which is a purple, and not a lavender-tinted, American flag. Next I flipped to C-SPAN, which happened — I say "happened" as though it were random — to be showing a tape of a speech given by Major Melissa Wells-Petry, sponsored by the Christian Action Network, a speech shown at least once later the same day, which I taped and watched compulsively. Major Wells-Petry, a U.S. military attorney, is giving a speech about why gays ought to be barred from the military. She describes the vast incompatibility of the nation and the gay man; she knows the law, well, colloquially. Her reason for rejecting a gay presence in the military is that when someone says, "I am a homosexual," there is "data" to support that he is "likely to engage in homosexual acts." There is no possibility that a homosexual has an identity that is not evidenced in acts. She says the courts have proven that to be homosexual is to behave as a homosexual, just as a pilot can be said to be a pilot because he flies airplanes. I have no idea if she is secretly thinking about the "cruising" altitude of planes, or about the cliché that queers are light in the loafers. In any case, she also argues that gayness is only one of many behavioral identities the army bars from service, and she names two others: in an aside, she notes that fatness makes you unfit for service; more elaborately, she recounts a case where a Nazi walked into a recruiting station and asked to enlist, but was barred from enlisting because being a Nazi makes you unfit to serve in the U.S. military. I fell into a dream that day, about *Griswold v. Connecticut* and *Roe v. Wade,* two cases I was teaching the following week. These two cases are generally thought to be crucial to the struggle to gain sex equality in the United States. *Griswold v. Connecticut* made it possible for married couples to buy birth control; *Roe v. Wade* made it possible to abort some fetuses birth control didn't prevent from being conceived. But the language about heterosexuality and pregnancy these cases promoted did nothing to shake up the normative relations of sex and nationality in modern America. In my dream, I tried to explain to someone in a supermarket how the zone of privacy established for married sex acts in *Griswold* even further enshrined heterosexual reproductive activity as the fundamental patriotic American fetish, so powerful it was entirely private, it was the only fixed sign in the national language. Indeed, I insisted on telling her, and with great painful prolixity, of Justice Harlan's

cited opinion, that "The right of privacy is not an absolute. Thus, I would not suggest that adultery, homosexuality, fornication and incest are immune from criminal enquiry, however privately practiced. . . . [But] the intimacy of husband and wife is necessarily an essential and accepted feature of the institution of marriage, an institution which the State not only must allow, but which always and in every age it has fostered and protected."[41] Then, somehow bored in my own dream, I turned my back and looked out the window, where I saw a pregnant woman wandering naked in traffic. I watched her, transfixed, for the longest time. When I awoke, I asked myself, what is the wish of the dream? I didn't know, but what flashed up instead was a line from *Roe v. Wade* that goes, "The pregnant woman cannot be isolated in her privacy."[42]

Let me review the argument: Insofar as an American thinks that the sex he or she is having is an intimate, private thing constructed within the lines of personal consent, intention, and will, he or she is having straight sex, straight sex authorized by national culture; he or she is practicing national heterosexuality, which makes the sex act dead, in the sense I have described, using a kind of metaphor that foregrounds heterosexuality's function as a sacred national fetish beyond the disturbances of history or representation, protected by a zone of privacy.

The privacy zone that projects national culture as a shadow effect of scandalous or potentially destabilizing acts of sexual alterity has a history, and I have tried to telegraph it here as a history of some live acts that counter an ideology of dead citizenship. Most important, until recently there has never been, in the United States, a public sphere organized around sex and sexuality—that is to say, a public sphere demarcated by what Geoff Eley has described as a political culture.[43] The prehistory of this moment must transform our accounts of the contemporary public sphere as well as of citizenship, nationality, acts, identities, sex, and so on. It might start with racial and gendered corporeal counterpolitics of the period after the Civil War, part of a general citizen reform movement, but also specifically around issues of property and reproduction, the two most sacrosanct areas the Constitution designates. Suffrage meant to bring these nineteenth-century primitivist categories into national modernity, and the history of national sentimentality this essay partly tells has to do with the public failure of suffrage to solve the relation between the body and the state in the United States, such that a tactical shuttling between assimilation and banishment remains central to the complicated histories of those sexed, racialized, female, underclassed subjects who can be seen animating the live margins of the U.S. scene. In any case, as the Queer Nation motto "We Are Everywhere, We Want Everything" suggests, the scandal of sexual subculture in the contemporary American context derives in part from its insistence on a noninfantilized political counterpublic that refuses to tie itself to a dead identity; that sees sexuality as a set of acts and world-building activities whose implications are always radically TBA; that seeks to undermine the patriotic ethics in which it is deemed virtuous to aspire to live in abstract America, a place where bodies do not live historically, complexly, or incoherently, guided by a putatively rational, civilized standard. The basic sex-radical tactic has been to countercorporealize at every moment, and so to de-elect the state and other social formations that have patriarchalized and parentalized national culture. This is not enough, as Michael Warner has argued.[44] But it is the beginning of a *movement,* and it's a live one.

This is to say that a radical social theory of sexual citizenship in the

United States must not aspire to reoccupy the dead identities of privacy, or name the innocence of youth as the index of adult practice and knowledge, or nationalize sexuality or sex as the central mode of self-legitimation or public identity-making. In this way it can avoid repeating the utopian identification that infantile citizenship promises, which distracts everyone from turning to the nation form and thinking about its inexhaustible energy for harnessing capitalism to death through promises of eternal identity and images of life activity. It can then avoid repeating the struggle between crassness and sentimental sublimity that defines all of our bodies in the United States; all of our live sex if we're lucky enough to have it; our dead citizenship; and our potentially undead desires to form a live relation to power, nature, sensation, and history within or outside the nation form as we know it. The risk is that peeling away the fantasies that both sustain and cover over the sexual bodies living the good life in the zone of privacy will also tear away some important protective coverings, like the fantasy of privacy itself, the way a Band-Aid covering an unhealed wound will take away part of the wound and its bit of healing with it. But such violence and failure, such an opening of the wound to air, is a foundational condition for the next steps, which, after all, remain to be taken, seen, and critiqued, though not rated with an X, a PG, or a thumbs-up — unless the thumb is related to something else, like a fist.

3 America, "Fat," the Fetus

BIG BABIES, FETAL PERSONS

Pregnancy/Citizenship

A man humiliates himself in front of his wife's family; his wife, visibly pregnant and visibly tired of her husband's greedy sentimental spectacle, retreats to the bedroom of her youth, strips down to the underwear of her maternity, and watches Super-8 films on the wall, home movies of her own childhood. The husband comes to seek forgiveness. Seeing that the wife wants not to see him, he interrupts the consolation of her cinematic memory by stepping into the filmic image itself, forcing the projector beam to shoot images of the wife's childhood family onto his crisp, white shirt. There, he demands the wife's forgiveness in the light of this second, now private, trespass on her family fantasy. Seeing that this intervention also alienates her, the husband flips around the projector, and aims these images of the wife as a playing child at her own pregnant belly. In this act the couple comes together, rapturously watching her pregnant belly, which now serves as a screen for the family pictures. She points at herself on her belly: "this is me"; she points at her sister and her father, loving her memory of their free play; she seems like the child on the belly and like the mother of the family she remembers; then, the images on the belly suddenly go blank and the couple reenters the present tense of the pregnancy. They merge oceanically in the fantasy that their child will be a boy as beautiful as the home movie images they've seen, whose spatial simultaneity on the wife's body seem almost to call him forth. In the next scene, she gives birth to a girl. The husband dies of heart failure soon after, one day on a frozen pond.

This scene, from the 1991 film *Once Around* (dir. Lasse Hallstrom), plays on the contemporary national and mass-cultural fixation on turning women into children and babies into persons through the media of photography and cinema. Against her will, the woman's body becomes a screen for projections of maternal plenitude; against her will, the distance collapses between herself as a child and herself as spectator of her own lost embodied dignity. Her pregnant belly is the screen of *unmediation* that collapses these extremes. Meanwhile, the matte technique that neutralizes the belly's roundness, such that it seems not to distort the familial images made for projection onto a flat wall, provides an image of cinema that affirms its mastery over the scene of reproduction. It is as though the pregnant body, opened up to the cinematic gaze, would reveal a developing roll of film, or a video monitor displaying an endless loop of floating fetal images. It is as though the three-dimensionality of the female body were itself a special effect, exposed as such by the presence of the fetus, which flattens out whatever corporeal excess the pregnant body shows.

Once a transgressive revelation of a woman's sacred and shameful carnality, the pictorial display of pregnancy is now an eroticized norm in American public culture.[1] And although *Once Around* dramatizes a struggle between two immigrant families over the question of whose "ethnic" style will survive in modern metropolitan America, its reliance on maternity to secure properly familial norms of intimacy and continuity makes the bodies in it national in a way that has only tangentially to do with the problem of assimilation that riddles its sentimental narrative. The wife's silence as she watches the images of herself on the wall of her childhood bedroom marks a space of a longing narrative for a world that does not yet exist, except in mirages of wish and nostalgia, for her or for American women in general. This narrative would provide an account of how what we might call "fetal motherhood," in which the mother follows the condition of the fetus, has taken over the representational space of public dignity and value that used to be reserved as a utopian promise for women.

For so long, and quite apart from the degree of civil rights U.S. women have achieved, the promise of maternal value has defined a source of power and social worth available to any woman. But the contemporary scene of fetal motherhood involves a stark shift in the social meaning of this aspect of women's historical value. To demonstrate this, we might begin at another prior manipulation of maternal legitimacy, from the U.S. nineteenth century: the slave mother's burdensome relation to the status of her child, by way of a rule that was at once central to and parodic of traditional national family values.

To "follow the condition of the mother" was the slave child's legal and experiential condition in antebellum America. But in slavery, "mother" was not a positive site of social possibility. To follow her "condition" as slave was to inherit the sheer negativity of her status, a nothingness redeemed only if she produced value for someone else, acted as her owner's productive property. By focusing solely on the maternal context of slave reproduction, white society could disavow the often violently biracial genealogy of slave children. The fictive or theoretical relation of fathers to offspring could be exploited on behalf of patriarchal property: paternal acts were turned into public nonfacts and could thereby circumvent the law's exposing gaze. This maternal line of entailment without entitlement set up the horizon of the slave child's relation to political embodiment—that is, to an obscured futurity, an unstable identity, and a negated political self-sovereignty.

To name fetal motherhood following this juridical and cultural logic marks a similar delegitimation of agency, history, and identity for the reproducing woman. In this context, the pregnant woman becomes the child to the fetus, becoming more minor and less politically represented than the fetus, which is in turn made more *national,* more central to securing the privileges of law, paternity, and other less institutional family strategies of contemporary American culture.

The wife in *Once Around* is caught between traditional rubrics of identity and an experience of a difference from herself that finds no home in any discursive field, whether domestic, ethnic, regional, or national. Her pregnant body's utility as an index of heritage, assimilation, estrangement, and change is similarly irrelevant to the available counterhegemonic discourses of "identity" in cultural studies or American culture at large. Yet, her body bears the burden of keeping these gendered, racial, class, ethnic, and national identities stable and intelligible. Pregnant and estranged from herself, the wife in *Once Around* is nonetheless an identity machine for others, producing children in the name of the future, in service to a national culture whose explicit ideology of natural personhood she is also helping to generate. It is no wonder that her pregnant silence, released into narrative, would express a desire for what she calls an "adventure" of self-understanding, an adventure she can yet barely imagine with the lexicon she has that provides her conception of change.

This essay is not about maternity. It seeks to provide tools for thinking about the image antagonism or war of distortion that has saturated public discourse about reproduction in the United States since the rise of the Reaganite right in the 1970s. It was not always the case that everyone knew what a fetus looked like. Now it is. It was not always the case that the news of someone's pregnancy would be followed by the question, will she keep it? Now it is, increasingly, and the answer to the question of "keeping it" has generated even more conventional scenes — depicting abortion, adoption, female bodily expansion, strange and ordinary family life — that register the different and unsettling narrative effects that such a profound cause can have.

In these scenes of contemporary reproduction, the fetus is definitively cast as a complete and perfect thing and/or a violently partial thing, somehow ripped away from the mother's body that should have completed it. In these scenes, the maternal body is a perfect glowing thing and/or a thing that grows large and inhumanly grotesque. Meanwhile, both women and fetuses are now said to be emotionally traumatized by the increasing instability of the contexts in which reproduction happens. But if some of these powerful images have long been available in treatises on women's threat and beauty, it is also the case that in the last twenty years manipulations of these images into a contest between the mother and the fetus have produced new contexts for their meaning, and new meanings that have penetrated without entirely saturating the experience of everyone's reproduction in everyday, ordinary life.

To engage the politics of bodily scale in the intimate public sphere requires reading conjuncturally, taking different contexts of reproduction and holding them in intimate suspension. This chapter will track and link a variety of these domains. It will involve thinking about the media of reproduction — pictures, sonograms, videos, films — and their use in producing institutions of intimacy, from the couple to the nation form itself. It will also entail uncoupling reproduction from the beautiful narrative that so often and so powerfully governs the ways women who reproduce are thought about, a narrative in which the pregnant woman is cast in advance as already a mother embarked on a life trajectory of mothering.[2] I will assume throughout that gender categories are best seen as spaces of transformation, nodal points that are supposed to produce general social intelligibility while encrusted with constantly changing noncoherent meanings. This double aspect produces a constantly changing relation between the ongoing accretion of associations these categories collect and the gratifying fantasy of fixity that the clean, iconic image of sexual difference can provide. In this chapter I mean to take on different aspects of the pregnant woman's multidimensional form — its fat, its femaleness, its fetus — to explicate its status as a national stereotype and a vehicle for the production of national culture. As a stereotype, it condenses and camouflages many forms of utopian cultural investment and many critical relations of violence and displacement.

The chapter has already divided into two. "Big Babies, Fetal Persons" begins with thinking about fat, pregnancy's least antagonizing feature: not explicitly saturated by the cultural politics of the political public sphere, fat serves as a more ordinary measure of the burden the feminine body bears for visually maintaining the pseudostability of social existence. The chapter then moves to the other end of the scale, to the image of the iconic fetus marketed by pro-life activists as something paradoxically ahistorical (human nature itself) and profoundly historical (its fate has been said to be the nation's fate). The emergence of fetal photography in contemporary U.S. culture is there addressed as another fixated context for fetality. The essay's second part, "The Moving Fetus," looks at the cinema of the fetus, and at the ways mass-cultural images of active, mobile fetuses have affected representations of citizenship — of policy, publicity, and agency, identity, and intimacy — in contemporary American culture. My main texts will be Raymond Carver's "Fat," *Life* magazine's Lennart Nilsson photos of the beginnings of life, the pro-life videos *The Silent Scream, Eclipse of Reason,* and *Let Me Live,* and the films *Look Who's Talking* and *Look Who's Talking Too.* These texts, in four different genres — postmodern minimalist literature, popular print media, political propaganda, and celebrity entertainment — all circulate narratives of change around representations of the polar embodiments of reproduction: pregnancy and fetality, or fetuses. The scale of the changes in norms of body, voice, and identity the texts represent through the pregnant/fetal image suggest some major changes that are happening in the juridical and cultural logics of American personhood. I will argue throughout that the convergence of mass culture and mass nationality has profoundly unsettled the traditional privacy protections of the privileged national body, generating a normative image of ideal citizenship as a kind of iconic superpersonhood, of which the fetus is the most perfect unbroken example.

But more than the visual politics of mass culture have changed the norms of U.S. identity production. I have suggested elsewhere some

senses in which, in America, bodies in public have embodied and organized the polar ends of political hierarchy.[3] In mass-mediated public
spheres and the spaces of everyday life, to have had a remarkable American body has meant that a person has become magical and symbolic:
perhaps in an auspicious, iconic way, as for a powerful queen or a president; perhaps in a devastating way, as when a private person is touched
by scandal and becomes public game for bodily distortion as a form of
symbolic humiliation. But not just power or scandal brings the body
into a scene of vulnerable corporeality. Every day, in ordinary, banal
ways, members of the politically distressed populations of the United
States — for example, women, queer people, people of color, and the
indecorous of any, especially lower, class — get humiliatingly named and
reduced to their stereotypic embodiment during moments of distraction
or preoccupation. This might involve a direct encounter, say, when sex-
ualizing catcalls interrupt the flow of walking on the street or working at
a job; or it might be more indirect and impersonal, as when something
randomly encountered on television happens to remind you that the
stereotype that gives you meaning in the public sphere is a despised one,
one that some people find disgusting.[4]

The emergence of fetality has retraumatized a set of already vulnerable
bodies: the body of the already vulnerable woman further unsettled by
pregnancy and now even more intensely exposed to misogyny and state
parentalism; the impoverished, the young, the often African American,
Native American, or Hispanic women who have had little access to reproductive health support apart from a scandalous history of state chi-
canery with regard to contraception;[5] the fetus vulnerable to law and to
abortion; pregnant women and fetuses alike, forced to register ideological contestations over what comprises "the good life" in America. But
the culture of national fetality also newly touches the previously privileged — because unmarked — unexceptional citizen, who identifies often,
but not always, as straight, white, male, and middle class. His new exposure to mass-mediated identity politics makes him experience himself
as suddenly embodied and therefore vulnerable. An entire culture can
come to identify with, and as, a fetus. In these ways, Americans generally
are now in a transformative moment in the scale, the normative exempla,
and the "optical unconscious" of citizenship.[6] The pregnant woman and
the fetus thus register changes in the social meanings of gender and
maternity; as they meet up in national culture they also raise questions
about intimacies, identities, politics, pictures, and public spheres.

What to Eat When You're Expecting: Fat

"My life is going to change. I feel it." — Raymond Carver, "Fat"[7]

The woman who says this is a literary character, the unnamed narrator of Raymond Carver's story "Fat." She displays, in this, the story's closing line, a remarkable union of knowledge and affect. She says that she can prophesy the future in the present, because she knows her feelings are true. How did she manage this respect for her feelings? The short answer is, she met a fat man. The fat man, through no direct agency of his own, changes her life by changing her relation to her body, her work, her domestic life, her sexuality, fantasy, and narrative. That is to say, he changes her mentally. He makes her think and fantasize about change. Yet she does not know in the abstract what the story she tells (to her friend Rita) means. She seems to sense that telling it, even telling it badly, might establish for her a point of view from which she will see the horizons of her own imminent self-expression. In other words, she tells the story to gain a space of happy estrangement from her self-identity, her given lexicon. To gain a space, or to be one? The aspiration to represent, imagine, and experience the condition of postidentity is indeed the meat of "Fat." I indulge myself here in a thick description of it.

In "Fat," two persons frustrated in their bodies meet and serve each other. We might call these persons "the fat man" and "the heterosexual woman," for these are the public embodied identities that mobilize their crises in the text, and indeed their anonymity both to each other and to the reader would suggest that their embodied exemplarity is the point of their characterization. For instance, when the fat man enters the restaurant where the narrator works as a waitress, he provides a startling "semiotic substance" for the workers there.[8] Just as they turn items of raw food into intelligibly cooked dishes, they bring him, through offscreen gossip, from mere anonymity to specific generic anonymity: "This fat man was the fattest person I have ever seen" (1); "Who's your fat friend? He's really a fatty" (2); "God, he's fat!" (3); "How is old tub-of-guts doing?" (4); "Harriet says you got a fat man from the circus out there" (5); "Sounds to me like she's sweet on fat-stuff" (5); "Some fatty" (5). In addition to this naming frenzy, the fat man's presence provokes a childhood memory for Rudy, the restaurant's cook and the narrator's lover:

> I knew a fat guy once, a couple of fat guys, really fat guys, when I
> was a kid. They were tubbies, my God. I don't remember their

names. Fat, that's the only name this one kid had. We called him Fat, the kid who lived next door to me. He was a neighbor. The other kid came along later. His name was Wobbly. Everybody called him Wobbly except the teachers. Wobbly and Fat. Wish I had their pictures. (6)

In contrast to the fat man's impassive incitement of interpretation, the waitress who narrates the story is embroiled in a fable of penetration, in a heterosexual story that marks all personal spaces for her, public and private. I mean this in contrast to reading the story as a context in which gender identity dominates as a source for understanding the narrator, for the network of gossip, teasing, commentary, and metacommentary she coordinates within the restaurant culture suggests that her function in the space is to produce an occasion for heterosexual, not "feminine," discourse. In addition to the restaurant, the waitress occupies two other places: her home, which she shares with her lover Rudy, and her girl-friend Rita's house, where she tells her friend about the complex event condensed in the fat man's appearance, and where her transition from the narrative of heterosexuality seems most likely to happen. Each of these places, marked by the centrality of kitchens and food to casual intimacy, takes on a form of the family function and displaces it into a public space. In each of these spaces the waitress's relation to the cook, Rudy, is saturated with their domestic sexuality. She describes every friend she has in the restaurant in terms of her domestic life: Margo is "the one who chases Rudy"; another worker, Joanne, elicits Rudy's "jeal-ousy" of her attention to the fat man. The waitress goes home and, after serving food to Rudy just as she has served the fat man, she has bored and alienated sex, as if the stale aftertaste of domestic pseudointimacy were, after all, inevitable; and it is clear, finally, that she and Rita are quite used to telling monotonous narratives of heterosexual alterity in the ritual confidentialities of "girl talk." The waitress herself provides a banal ob-ject of erotic traffic for everyone's commentary, just as the fat man pro-vides an anerotic spectacle that elicits communication. It is in her transi-tion from heterosexuality to some other erotic formation that a story paradoxically about *situatedness,* a politics of location, provides spectacles of transitional embodiment.

In the bowels of the restaurant, then, where erotic chatting and teas-ing distracts the workers from the boredom and alienation of earning money, in the living rooms and kitchens of domestic spaces, and in the neighborhood of childhood, where so many norms are fixed, fat excites. It elicits fresh interpretation, it permits direct commentary on the embarrassment of public embodiment, it allows conjecture about desire, it brings perversity and compulsion into an unthreatening realm of conversational play. Fat is so powerful and so social that it overwhelms the proper name of the person, whose fat takes over the space where personality usually resides.[9] Appropriately, Carver stores these experiences of postindividuality in the story's own name, "Fat," which refers not obviously to a person, but to the substance. Like a proper name, fat is always fundamentally a thing, a thing of excess. But as a thing that denotes an unquantified substance, its very fixity accrues to itself an unshakable stability of identity. (This aura of phantasmatic stability is what, I gather, distinguishes the person named Fat from his friend, the person named Wobbly, about whom we can know very little from this story and whose name thus also describes the condition of our knowledge about him. I would feel on shaky ground hazarding an opinion about Wobbly, while I feel I can grasp Fat.) It is the function of fat personhood here to signify the problem of descriptive adequacy under a regime of stereotypicality, which is also the problem of "identity" that proper names elide by their very banality. In contrast, the waitress whose encounter with the fat man leads to her attempt at narrative sees in him a body of knowledge, an opportunity for a kind of magical thinking about corporeality, sensation, scale, and change.

Like her colleagues, the waitress who serves this customer is excited by the mass of man she sees. Her excitement derives, however, not from her own pleasure in reducing the immobilized Other to his essence or substance, nor from heterosexualizing him, but from the experience of visual amazement and conversational intimacy this encounter occasions. She does not identify him but identifies *with* him, yet not in a mirroring way. For her bored friend Rita, she compulsively lists details of this man: his clothes; his "long, thick creamy fingers"; his "strange way of speaking" with its "little puffing sound[s]" and its shifting personal pronouns that shuttle between "I" and "we," as in the sentence "I think we will begin with a Caesar salad" (1); the small waves of his hand and the slight squeaking shift of his sweaty seated body (2, 3); his form so vast she interrupts her narrative to marvel at the memory — "Rita, he was big, I mean big," and "God, Rita, but those were fingers" (1, 2). In this short space of time, the waitress becomes addicted to the fat man. She hovers over him like a mother, or a lover, feeding him creamy, milky things, such as butter, sour cream, pudding, and ice cream. She is not thinking of her service as a symbolic act. She wants to think that she likes "to see a man eat and enjoy himself" (3), but when the fat man refuses her fantasy of his autocannibalistic pleasure ("'I don't know,' he says. 'I guess that's what you'd call it'" [3]), she realizes, "I know now I was after something. But I don't know what" (4). She is not thinking about herself with any clarity at all, nor participating in the kinds of speculations I have been making about what motivates her identification with the fat man's deliberate caloric and sensual excess. She has no evident capacity to interpret this encounter and to learn from her interpretation, which is why she retells it to Rita compulsively; and in this blockage, too, she is like the fat man, who admits his compulsion to rep/eat:

> I put the Special in front of the fat man and a big bowl of vanilla ice cream with chocolate syrup to the side.
> Thank you, he says.
> You are very welcome, I say — and a feeling comes over me.
> Believe it or not, he says, we have not always eaten like this.
> Me, I eat and I eat, and I can't gain, I say. I'd like to gain, I say.
> No, he says. If we had our choice, no. But there is no choice. (5)

At its most intense moments, this story represents compulsion — not at first a compulsion to narrate but rather the experience of having been *compelled* to live as a hieroglyph or a stereotype, in a body that condenses a narrative whose form seems to assure the impossibility of choosing otherwise, of being something other than a fact, a social identity, a function in a system of conventions. For the waitress, this is a narrative of heterosexual identity; for the customer, it is the story of being, simply, fat. For her, it is a narrative about self-alienation and certain corporeal insufficiency; for him, it is a narrative in which the very compulsion to desire specific things ("Caesar salad," "a bowl of soup with some extra bread and butter," "lamb chops," "[a]nd baked potato with sour cream" [1, 2]) forces him to risk insatiability, a constant inadequacy to one's own desire. Finally, the waitress's compulsion to occupy a position of instrumentality, service, and exchange — food in her mouth, penis in her vagina, food in her hand at the customer's table — meets with the fat man's need to be served, to work at remaining the object of someone's verb. The two, in short, come together on these two experiential points: that of compulsion and that of the resignation that accompanies compulsion, which is born of the knowledge that under a regime of necessary identity, "choosing" one is a mere fantasy of agency, intention, and consciousness.

But if the first trillion occasions of "I eat and I eat" produce neither pain, gain, nor any other transformational material for the waitress, this encounter affixes to the compulsion to repeat a compulsion to think differently about change, to think about becoming historical. To become historical after being for so long and so deeply at best a living stereotype is to take on the project of acting in excess to the forms of distortion you normally inhabit. In this case, the waitress's appropriation of her own capacity to produce such excess happens with all deliberate speed. When she leaves the fat man, she goes home with Rudy and appears to act in her usual way. "I put the water on to boil for tea and take a shower. . . . I pour the water in the pot, arrange the cups, the sugar bowl, carton of half and half, and take the tray in to Rudy" (5, 6). Silently, and at the same time, she has two transubstantiating fantasies. The first takes place while she prepares to serve Rudy his tea and *his* domestic milk product, half and half. As the water boils, "I put my hand on my middle and wonder what would happen if I had children and one of them turned out to look like that, so fat" (5–6). In the second fantasy the waitress describes relaxing to have sex with Rudy "though it is against my will. But here is the thing. When he gets on me, I suddenly feel I am fat. I feel I am terrifically fat, so fat that Rudy is a tiny thing and hardly there at all" (6).

When the waitress tells these fantasies to Rita, neither woman "know[s] what to make of it" (6). The first takes place in the shower. She puts her hand on her "middle" and imagines not just an exceptionally fat child, but *what would happen* if she had such a "fatty." The child is ungendered, just fat. Her hand is on her skinny belly, but still from that belly she imagines producing a child without her debility: infinite thinness. Such an event would force *something* to happen in her life; in any case, the fantasy itself represents a shift away from the heterosexual narratives that circulate among the bodies she knows. In this sense, the transposition of the fat customer to a fat fantasy child reproduces the action of thinking about change, about emigrating to a semiotic field outside that in which she currently lives. Thus follows the second fantasy, in which Rudy becomes shockingly a "tiny thing" while the waitress herself becomes terrific and terrifying in her fatness.

If the first dream vision relinquishes the intelligibility of history and the body through the fat child's genderlessness, the second locates the waitress's emancipatory agency in a different fantasy, of control over space, context, size. When Rudy gets on and occupies her, she tries to begin to relax. But she relaxes into a fantasy in which *her* fatness so overwhelms the space of Rudy's person and the violation he enacts sexually that he becomes reduced to a "thing." It is tempting to read this thing as a penis — after all, Rudy is so rudely reduced at the moment he transfers his own agency to his private part, so private it is invisible. It is also possible to transfer her fantasy of fat childbirth to this moment, such that the tiny thing Rudy is can be read as a homunculus, a baby, or a fetus. This means either that she infantilizes him, or that sexual intercourse injects his entire body into hers, such that she becomes big with Rudy, which is why she cannot see him.

But what the waitress *says* is that he is "hardly there at all" (6). He is no longer there as an adult lover. He has been reduced, condensed, and displaced into a bare minimum facticity. Fat, she imagines, usurps the place of heterosexuality; it supervenes the place of embodied exchange not through abstraction but through superembodiment; it casts the shadow of its belly on the sexo-semiotic of sexual difference, and eradicates a man in the process.[10] It seems clear that the point of domestic entry to the narrator's own body has been her vagina, not her mouth, as in the case of the fat man. But after serving the fat man, she understands: power as pleasure comes from speaking for two. For the fat man, speaking for two involves becoming a supervalent site of autoerotic compulsion; for the heterosexual woman, speaking for two has meant speaking for the heterosexual couple that never quite achieves stability. But after the fat man, she sees another route to the power of superpersonality that speaking for two suggests: pregnancy. Her heterosexual fat will be less socially transgressive than the fat man's autoerotic corporeality, although as a pregnant woman she will certainly take up a kind of excessive space that similarly elicits commentary and interpretation. For the person who speaks for two has no privacy. The person who takes on the model of fat agency is entirely public and yet also represents a mystical or magical interiority. More surface, more depth, more dimensionality: the fat subject has explicitly and paradoxically given up control and become a stereotype of compulsive, helpless choosing, of selflessness and an excess of self. The difference between the fat man's fat and the heterosexual woman's fantasy pregnancy is coded in the morality of their excess. His is an excess of consumption. He wears and performs his excess in public, and he does not pay for his display by making himself available for others' erotic fantasies. Thus, his fat trespasses.

In contrast, if the waitress's fantasies of superpersonhood are merely wishes for change, her fantasy of taking over space with fatness serves as an easily containable compensation for the inevitable heterosexual saturation of her everyday life; if, on the other hand, the waitress is really pregnant, she has taken control over the possibilities of change by blurring the boundaries between her body and another's. Pregnancy, of course, expands her own corporeal horizon in a way her culture will support. But this seems not to be her motive for entering the state of becoming-pregnant. This seems to be located in the rapture, the feeling of change she secures, which is an erotic feeling for which she has no social support and of which she herself has little understanding outside the improvisations of fantasy. Speaking for two creates a space for an expanded definition of personhood, and although it takes a maternalist fantasy to do it, the waitress, for the first time, feels authorized to think expansively, to make her body magical. This magical feeling is opposite to what she experiences at work. It releases her from the compulsion to "relax" while she is being violated against her will; it opens up what Eve Sedgwick calls a "space of permission" for the kind of change that will authorize her feeling for it.[11] No longer constrained by the violations of sexuality and interpretation that characterize heterosexuality, the fat/ fetus axis ungenders the woman and releases her from identity and definition. As the waitress says to her inquisitive lover, "Rudy, he is fat . . . but that is not the whole story" (5).

Taken as one woman's impulsive solution to her conscription to heterosexual womanhood, "Fat" maps out how what looks like a cross-margin identification with another corporeally marked person can disrupt the authority of public norms and rules of erotic decorum. Another reading of the story might put a much more negative spin on it.[12] Griselda Pollack argues that "any figured body is a complex of traces of fantasies of several bodies, bodies constantly oscillating between lack and plenitude, threat and restoration. *The* body of this scenario is the mother's body, the repressed body, and the one that obsesses the phallocentric system."[13] From this vantage point, the waitress has just reinvented for herself typical conditions of feminine representation, in which the pregnant woman's body is made into a fetish, both her abundant overpresence and her lack of femininity serving as sources of fascination, desire, repulsion, and disavowal. But the aim here is not to determine whether the waitress's sentimentality about fat and her fetal imaginary constitute true or false consciousness. Rather, it is to use her story as an example of the ways distortions of scale that falsify or transfigure notions of natural form become common routes to imagining fate and pain, on the one hand, and change and freedom, on the other.[14] The narrator of this tale enacts a metadistortion of form, and in so doing inhabits a space of change and exchange that uses ordinary apertures of incorporation, the mouth and the vagina, to dissolve boundaries between public and private, capitalist and domestic, and all corporeally conscripted spaces of identity. To imagine freedom in the fantasy, not in the lived experience, of noncompulsory female fatness or pregnancy, and to imagine speaking for two is not simply to perform the ritual inversions of carnival but instead to seek in representation a space of change for which there is yet no reliable structural, let alone skeletal, support.

I mean this moving iconicity, this impossible flickering image, this structure of self-displacement into supercorporeal identity, to represent a utopian moment of subjective and corporeal excess. But the cost of this subjectification is an excessive focus on the isolate body as the totality of its own political condition. The narrator of "Fat" has great expectations. Although these are both personal and social, however, they are not construed as political in the text, because the conditions of identity and specificity have been so miniaturized and banalized in the world of this tale that the historical and knowledge contexts of the narrator's life and change of life have been left entirely implicit. Many processes collaborate to make structural conditions of existence seem like properties of the body and the person. One of these is that the circulating library of the stereotype sifts through subjectivity to become a measure of a person's uniqueness and individuality, an antidistinguishing mark that measures anyone's relation to the implicit world of normativity. The narrator of "Fat" has an instinct about how to short-circuit this process of becoming an object/subject, making herself feel physically strange and estranged so that she might form an uncharted subjectivity to respond to her now alien body. The creativity of this kind of vague agency usually goes unnoticed in discussions of pregnancy, fat, and femininity.

The other side of this screen can be viewed in the certainty with which fetality or babyhood signifies the thing of value in life that is an absolutely known and fixed quantity, the source of a natural narrative that ought to unfold from conception. The world in which pregnancy could be considered a local event of personal privacy no longer exists: "Fat" is fabulously archaic, in this sense, which is one reason it should be read. It reminds us of the incomplete saturation of the quotidian by the contexts of law and politics that have so challenged the meanings of reproduction in the contemporary United States. The politics of abortion, birth control, sex, and sexuality have threatened to corrode the aura of nature and future that pregnancy and motherhood once betokened. In the next section we will look at the way this upheaval of the personal domain mirrors and reverberates in the delicate condition of citizenship. If it used to be the case that only powerful people had public pregnancies in the political sense, now every pregnancy vibrates to the law as though it were truly the mother's voice.

It's Morning (Sickness) in America

The conditions of American citizenship are always changing. But these transformations of pregnancy and fetality have had extreme cultural effects. The emergence of fetal personhood as a legal and medical category, and as a site of cultural fantasy, has been a major stimulus for thinking anew about what citizenship means as an index of social membership and a context for social agency. These changes have happened in a number of domains, and have more to do with contestations over who will control the vast material resources of the U.S. than anything about sexual, moral, or affective practice. But the combined effects of these complex changes have created a crisis in citizenship of which pregnant women and their fetuses are bearing an undue burden.

How to explain the concentration of complex citizenship issues on the fate and status of a bare minimum unit of human material? Let us start at a beginning. By merging the American counterdiscourse of minority rights with the revitalized providential nationalist rhetoric of the Reaganite right, the pro-life movement has composed a magical and horrifying spectacle of amazing vulnerability: the unprotected person, the citizen without a country or a future, the fetus unjustly imprisoned in its mother's hostile gulag. This spectacle periodically and strategically distracts the collective gaze from the class war currently raging in the United States, substituting patriotic images of a generic familial good life well-intentioned people can make for images of a world organized around the economic contexts in which specific people live. This aspect of fundamentalist politics has fundamentally altered the aggregate meaning of nature, identity, and the body in the construction of American nationality. Its transformations are of a scale unmatched in American history since the enfranchisement of African Americans in 1868, which not only added a new group of "persons" to "the people" but had two other effects relevant to this investigation: it changed fundamentally the relative meanings and rules of federal and state citizenship, and it called into crisis the norms and principles of national embodiment.

Clearly, unlike the African American subject, the fetus has no autonomous body. And unlike the African American subject, the fetus has no voice and thus cannot partake of the kinds of agency recognized in the protocols of the political public sphere. The success of the concept of fetal personhood depends on establishing a mode of "representation" that merges the word's political and aesthetic senses, imputing a voice, a consciousness, and a self-identity to the fetus that can neither speak its name nor vote. This strategy of nondiegetic voicing has two goals: (1) to establish the autonomy of the fetal individual; and, paradoxically, (2) to show that the fetus is a contingent being, dependent on the capacity of Americans to hear *as citizens* its cries *as a citizen* for dignity of the body, its complaints at national injustice.

Most Anglo-American feminist work on the politics of fetal personhood has focused on its theft of the meaning of gender, maternity, and childbirth from women. Rosalind Petchesky, Paula Treichler, Faye Ginsburg, Emily Martin, Rayna Rapp, Zillah Eisenstein, Barbara Duden, Marilyn Strathern, and many others have performed critical analyses crucial to this one.[15] They have profoundly explicated the ways new technologies and new modes of representation such as fetal imaging have created a nationwide competition between the mother and the fetus that the fetus, framed as a helpless, choiceless victim, will always lose — at least without the installation of surrogate legal and technological systems to substitute for the mother's dangerous body and fallen will. And collectively they have established a powerful argument for redefining the conditions of gendered identity in America according to the difference that the capacity to reproduce makes in the woman's access to sociality, power, and value.

In addition to witnessing the politics of woman's discipline to the norms of proper motherhood, it is important to recount this moment as a case study in the process of nation formation and its reliance on manipulations of the identity form to occlude the centrality of reproduction to the processes by which the nation rejuvenates itself.[16] In this light, the pregnant woman is the main legitimate space in which the category *female* converts into a national category and changes the meaning of citizenship — citizenship not just as a juridical category but also as a horizon of social practice and aspiration.

One reason the revitalization of this category is so crucial now is that pro-life rhetoric has seen the relation between nature and nation as central to its sacred logics. Citizenship is the category in which these two formations are supposed to merge, but the arguments for their relation differ in different contexts. First, the narrative of natural development from gendered womanhood to pregnancy and motherhood has provided one of the few transformational lexicons of the body and identity we have. It has framed womanhood in a natural narrative movement of the body, starting at the moment a child is sexed female and moving to her inscription in public heterosexuality, her ascension to reproduction, and her commitment to performing the abstract values of instrumental empathy and service that have characterized norms of female fulfillment. Some antifeminist antiabortion activists view the modern woman as no longer trained in or committed to the rigors of natural femininity; pregnancy appears not only to threaten a rupture in a traditional notion of the continuity between feminine value and motherhood but to threaten the national future as well.

Anxieties around the relation between proper womanhood and proper motherhood have long been evident in middle-class-identified women's reform movements. Since the mid-nineteenth century, movements populated by these usually white women sought to reform the sexuality of the poorer and often racially marked or immigrant women who seemed not to make properly graceful transitions from feminine sexuality to nonsexual motherhood. Now the gendered class hierarchy is often reversed by pro-life women, as they seek to reform the sexually profligate sisters blinded by selfish unwomanly fantasies of economic privilege and/or sexual autonomy.[17] In any case, the normativity of pro-life society dictates that once pregnant the woman loses her feminine gender, becoming primarily a mother — the current phrase is "pregnant mother" — and therefore becomes *uninteresting* in herself. In protecting the fetus from the woman they divide the woman into a nongenital "female" part — the maternal womb, which really belongs to the fetus — and a potentially malevolent section, composed of a sexual body (un)governed by a woman's pseudosovereign consciousness.[18]

In so recasting the pregnant body as, at its best, a vehicle for the state's "compelling interest" in its citizens, the pro-life nation that currently exists sanctions the pregnant woman as American only insofar as she becomes impersonal and public, committed to submitting her agency to the "compelling interests" of any number of higher powers. She is juridically and morally compelled to exchange the privacy protections of gender for a kinder, gentler state.[19] Claudia Koonz has documented a similar conversion of gender to nationality in the conscription of German women to reproduce citizens for the Third Reich.[20] At this time in America, however, the reproducing woman is no longer cast as a potentially productive citizen, except insofar as she procreates: her capacity for other kinds of creative agency has become an obstacle to national reproduction.

This is the logic by which the pregnant woman sutures femininity, nature, and nation. The emergence of pregnancy into ordinary representation makes this suture vulnerable to unraveling, and as it threatens to do so, so many of the hard-won political transformations in notions of women's authority over reproduction have unraveled as well. But if one effect of the discourse on fetal personhood is a crisis in the capacity of a maternalized gender to organize a discursive field that links women's private activity to national history and the future, from the point of view of fetality, counterclaims for female authority over the fetus seem to block or distort the narrative of natural development. Thus, in pro-life discourse, the aim of national reproduction merges with the claim that fetuses, like all persons, ought to have a politically protected right to natural development. This version of the costructuration of nature and nation is behind the pro-life appropriation of tactics from feminist and other minority-American "identity" movements: asserting that the "silence" and "invisibility" of the fetal person will be redressed by its imputed speech and visibility; assuming the point of view of victimized citizenship by redefining radically the meaning, the history, and the dimensionality of the body; challenging and transforming stereotypes that define identity in the public sphere, emphasizing the claim to the pure protection of the identity form American national membership is supposed to provide.

The movement for fetal rights is thus also a development in the history of national sentimentality, where complex political conditions are reduced or refined into the discourses of dignity and of the authority of feeling. It embodies how strongly the subject position of the national victim has become a cultural dominant in America: in this moment of mass nationality and global politics, power appears always to be elsewhere, and political authenticity depends on the individual's humiliating exile from somebody else's norm. A nationwide estrangement from an imagined hegemonic center seems now to dignify every citizen's complaint.

As the ways norms of representing privilege in the political public sphere shift, such that people seek minority status in order to trump other forms of national demand; as the mass media produces further transformations of the scale of political experience in America; as pro-life and aligned forces incite the law to renaturalize national identity; and as everyone seems to experience nationality as a species of trauma, it seems necessary to track and to challenge what has happened to the citizen form (its constellation of agency, identity, and embodiment) in the national public sphere. My aim is to be able to understand bumper-sticker slogans like "Support Our Future Troops!" and "Abortion Is Destroying America's Future . . . One Life at a Time."

What kinds of anxiety and theory of personhood are expressed by such slogans? How can we make sense of recent alliances between imperialism and pro-life patriotism, or between antichoice, pronatalist, antidrug propagandas and pedagogy, which collectively have produced the anti-Madonna, the mother who poisons or aborts her child, as a new traumatized national icon?[21] This new stereotype not only circulates through policy debates over abortion and fetal drug syndromes, but also surfaces in "nonpolitical" public-service announcements (PSAs) about maternal health care. For instance, a television PSA by the Partnership for a Drug-Free America casts the fetus as a philanthropic object for its own mother, in a montage that isolates the images and equates the sizes of a fetus, a crack pipe, and a mother's face. These images run under a voice-over that asks the mother to choose between her "pleasures" (the pipe) and the fetus's health. The aim of these distortions of scale and these false equations of value is to demonstrate visually a crisis in maternal value in which two objects, the fetus (starring as "life") and the pipe (starring as "pleasure"), vie for the woman's agency. Yet the panicky, ostensibly therapeutic act of breaking up the maternal body into the face, the fetus, and the pipe fortifies the toxic maternal stereotype it dissects by making maternity, under these conditions, *impossible* to imagine. (In Chicago in 1990 and 1991, this gothic public-service montage ran daily during the maternal melodrama *As the World Turns*.)

To understand how the pregnant woman and the fetus have become so fetishized, both in their fracture and in the fantasy of their reunification, we must also think about how national norms of corporeality work, and about the nation-making function of the minority stereotype. This critical project would not be possible without the unsettling redescriptive efforts of the postcolonial and sex-radical intellectual activists who

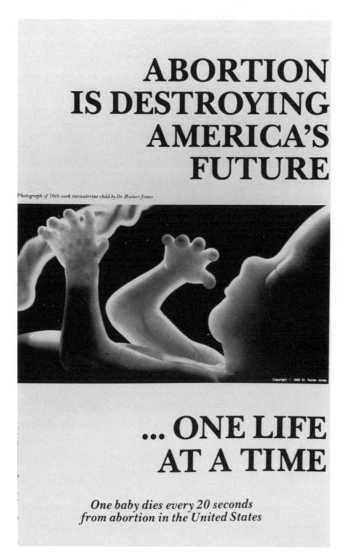

ABORTION
IS DESTROYING
AMERICA'S
FUTURE

Photograph of 16th week intrauterine child by Dr. Rainer Jonas

Copyright © 1982 Dr. Rainer Jonas

... ONE LIFE
AT A TIME

*One baby dies every 20 seconds
from abortion in the United States*

have countered the malignity of modern national body politics — for example, Gilles Deleuze and Félix Guattari, Gayatri Spivak, Eve Sedgwick, and Gayle Rubin.[22] Situated in very different national and international struggles for cultural and political transformation, this work details the tyrannizing strategies of a culture's caste-making gestures toward particular *kinds* of embodiment. Minority identity is often experienced as corporeal discomfort: in these texts the scandalous anus, the cancerous breast, the mouth that houses the speaking tongue, and a whole range of "perverted" sex acts serve as evidence of the places where cultures install normative truth and law on subjects' bodies at the expense of their dignity and status. But in this archive these intimate national and imperial wounds flag other possibilities as well: for example, that the story of the scarred-up subject can be made to interfere with the privatizing or shaming effects of domination by turning the bodily experience of structural conflict into a public affidavit of collective life, a museum of ordinary violence, a portable monument to the uncivil cruelty of even the most universalist ideology of democratic national abstraction.[23]

When the meaning of a person is reduced to a body part, the identity fragment figures as a sign of incomplete social personhood; its dialectical Other, the stereotype, masks this violence in false images of simple self-unity, as though the minoritized body were naturally and adequately described by the identity that names it violently. Homi Bhabha has argued that the stereotype is an essential mental ligament of modern national culture, as the common possession of aesthetic and discursive "national" objects provides an affective intimacy among citizens that no commonly memorized political genealogy or mass experience of democracy has yet successfully effected.[24] I have called the archive of these hieroglyphic images the "National Symbolic," and have suggested that the collective possession of these official texts—the flag, Uncle Sam, Mount Rushmore, the Pledge of Allegiance, perhaps now even JFK and Dr. Martin Luther King—creates a national "public" that constantly renounces political knowledge where it exceeds intimate mythic national codes.[25]

But the colonial spectacle or national stereotype serves more than to create national amnesia. Bhabha provides a "positive" explanation of the stereotype's ambivalent function in mass-cultural politics. To repeat and to elaborate on his argument: The colonial spectacle or the national stereotype is a hybrid form, a form of feeling, of alienation, and of sociality; the stereotype circulates between subjects who have power as a kind of cultural property they control; it circulates among minority subjects as a site of masochistic identification (the minority/colonial subject as cultural property recognizes itself in the objective circulation of its own form); it is additionally a site of social power, of apparent magical embodiment, and of collective authority. When the national hieroglyph is an object, its capacity to condense and displace cultural stress is made possible by its muteness as a thing. But when the national stereotype represents a "minority" person, the ambivalences of the culture that circulates the form are brought to the fore, for the national minority stereotype makes exceptional the very person whose marginality, whose individual experience of collective cultural discrimination or difference, is the motive for his/her circulation as an honorary icon in the first place.

This is how it happens, for example, that a homophobic culture loves its Liberace, and a racist culture its Eddie Murphy. In moments of intensified racism, homophobia, misogyny, and phobias about poverty, these "positive" images of national minority represent both the minimum and the maximum of what the dominating cultures will sanction for circulation, exchange, and consumption. As *iconic* minority subjects, these luminaries allow the hegemonic consuming public to feel that it has already achieved intimacy and equality with the marginal mass population; as minority exceptions, they represent heroic autonomy from their very "people"; as "impersonations" of minority identity, they embody the very ordinary conditions of subjective distortion that characterize stereotypic marginality.

In addition, we must see the hyperbolic politics of marginality in the context of mass political culture in America, as Michael Rogin has argued.[26] Since the Second World War, the American movie star has come to embody the fantasy form of iconic citizenship, of a large body moving through space unimpeded, as only a technologically protected person can do.[27] This explains why, as we will see in the following section, the culture of the star has become so central to fetal personhood. As the public terms of personal classification we denote when we speak of "identity" or "identity politics" shift and recombine, outrunning our political and aesthetic depictions of them, the citizen's body in its everyday size, time, and space becomes confusing: an embarrassment, a burden, a question.

Because it appears to be personhood in its natural completeness, prior to the fractures of history and identity, the fetus is supposed to be a solution, from the origin of human existence, to the corporeal, juridical, intimate violence that plagues America today. It has become an index of natural/national rights with respect to which adult citizens derive their legitimation. Thomas Laqueur has brilliantly shown how manipulations of scale have functioned to consolidate "sex" as an identity category, a hieroglyph of unbroken development; here, I want to suggest how shifts of scale function, in mass national culture, to constrict which kinds of national bodies can legitimately enter the body politic.[28] The material effects these political distortions have had can now be viewed concretely, in the patriotic, pro-life pages of *Life* magazine.

In 1965, the first photographic images of a wombed fetus were published in *Life* magazine. They were framed by *Life* as an American miracle in the realms of nature, technology, and domestic intimacy. These photos of origin, of natural development, and of "life" were repeated and renewed like wedding vows in *Life* in the summer of 1990. Human space and time have been entirely reconstructed through these "almost sacred" photographs; in addition, the fetus's revolutionary embodiment has accompanied and incited fundamental alterations in the place of visual media in American political culture. In this light, the chapter in the story of postmodern American citizenship fetal personhood occupies is also profoundly about how mass culture has spawned unpredictable events in mass nationality. The photography of *Life* magazine has coordinated the origins of human life with the snap of the shutter. This change in the time and space of human identity initiated an entirely new scopic regime, a whole new calendar, and finally, a whole new voice for the American citizen.

The "Fragmentation of the Aura":
Life *before Birth*

On April 30, 1965, *Life* magazine's cover story was titled "Drama of Life Before Birth," featuring on the cover a "Living 18-week-old fetus shown inside its amniotic sac."[29] This "unprecedented photographic feat" in color is unprecedented because the fetus was living at the time the "specially built super wide-angle lens and . . . tiny flash beam at the end of a surgical scope" (54) recorded its uterine existence; the rest of the pictures were taken of "surgically removed," miscarried, or aborted fetuses outside the womb and the maternal body. On *Life*'s cover, the fetus faces left and seems to look at the magazine's name, which confirms its own "life"; *Life*, the magazine, confirms life before birth, designating as life anything that can be photographed and captioned in its pages. John Berger points out that the sacred and documentary function of *Life* was an explicit part of its inaugural machinery:

> The first mass-media magazine was started in the United States in 1936. At least two things were prophetic about the launching of *Life*, the prophecies to be fully realized in the postwar television age.

The new picture magazine was financed not by its sales, but by the advertising it carried. A third of its images were devoted to publicity. The second prophecy lay in its [ambiguous] title. It may mean that the pictures inside are about life. Yet it seems to promise more: that these pictures *are* life. The first photograph in the first number played on this ambiguity. It showed a newborn baby. The caption underneath read: "Life begins . . ."[30]

This is to say that new regimes of textuality, of capital accumulation, of national discourse, of the family, and of human embodiment were unveiled as mutually reinforcing structures of value by *Life,* and more than simple pro-choice arguments are implied in such a conjunction of domains. In a magazine that conflates all documentation with nationality, celebrity, and intimacy, the baby circulates as the tabula rasa of consumer nationalism, as an object consumed and as a citizen recast. This formation consolidates the structure of agency in mass citizenship that, as Berger says, now dominates American politics.

We might not have predicted this specific change in 1965. The primacy of technology in the discourse of the magazine isolated instead two main features of change. The first is linking this technological event with the history of what Jonathan Crary has called "techniques of the observer," in which the camera at once comes to represent the scientific "norm of truthfulness" and becomes the index for an "objective" nonelite and disinterested perspective and semiotic field.[31] Walter Benjamin's "A Short History of Photography" calculated the opportunity for knowledge/ power this machine offers: "Photography . . . with its time lapses, enlargements," makes microknowledge of the body possible. "Through [its] methods one first learns of this optical unconscious, just as one learns of the drives of the unconscious through psychoanalysis. Concern with structure, cell forms, the improvement of medicine through these techniques: the camera is ultimately more closely related to these than to the moody landscape or the soulful portrait. At the same time, however, photography opens up in this material the physiognomic aspects of the world of images, which reside in the smallest details, clear and yet hidden enough to have found shelter in daydreams."[32] But, like the unconscious itself, the optical unconscious in mass culture operates according to a principle of trauma: "The camera will become smaller and smaller, more and more prepared to grasp fleeting, secret images whose shock will bring the mechanism of association in the viewer to a complete halt. At

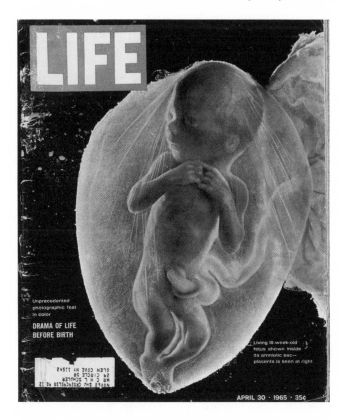

this point captions must begin to function, captions which understand the photography which turns all the relations of life into literature, and without which all photographic construction must remain bound in coincidences" (215). The capacity of *Life* to give new life to a fetus at eighteen weeks is rooted in the photographic control of scale, of magic, and of captioning the unprecedented but phantasmatically natural framed text it documents.

Benjamin argues that the process of abstracting the value of life into the representational norms of the photograph has fragmented the human aura, evacuating it of its unique value: first, by fixing the body's perfect organisms, gestures, and parts scientifically (thus substituting for the wholeness that had derived from God); second, by appropriating the magical aura of reproduction as a technological miracle whose spark has "burned through the person in the image with reality, finding the indiscernible place in the condition of that long past minute where the future is nesting, even today, so eloquently that we looking back can discover it" (202). Lisa Cartwright's work has shown that where the fetus is concerned, this procedure of making visible is precisely "anti-visual"; that is, more concerned with replacing subjective experiences of sight with "objective" ones.[33] The temporal transformation of the fetal photograph's aura, which memorializes its monumental and recent pasts, marks futurity by the very boundary it creates between the image and that horizon. These images, captioned by *Life* as "strangely complete in their clinical detail but at the same time strangely beautiful" (54), establish a "difference between technology and magic as a thoroughly historical variable," opening up the possibility that through the double movement of science and magic sacred and secular development might be secured, ad infinitum.

In the three decades between *Life*'s first and second installments of the fetal photographs, the meaning of this double movement between science and magic has changed, because of changes in political norms about personhood and political representation that these photographs themselves facilitated. Benjamin's notion that the photograph emits an aura of both the real person and also the person's death reminds us that the invasive installation of the camera in the womb ruptured a seemingly sacred or natural continuity between the mother and the fetus she carries. The mother remains involved with fetal nourishment, even under the new photographic regime. But prior to the new technology, the mother's expanded body had functioned both as the representation of the fetus's body and as its armor. The expansion of the fetus to human and even superhuman scale within the frame of the photograph shattered the aura of maternal protection, making the fetus miraculous in a new way, vulnerable in a new way, and human in an unprecedented way.

It necessitated a new mode of human description, one that might locate the "real" moment of viable life in *Life* when the sperm fertilizes the egg by isolating the exact moment of "the transition point where an embryo, a Greek word meaning to swell, starts being called technically a fetus, a Latin word meaning young one" (62). The transition from Greek to Latin seems to reproduce the providential political narrative of development we call the *translatio studii* and *imperii,* as if deep in the structure of medical language the westward movement of global power were hardwired into the body. (I will return to this global movement in the final section.) Additionally, as Daniels, Duden, Kaplan, Petchesky, Martin, and Stabile have shown, this transformation of representation and scale has pushed the mother into the fuzzy, unfocused part of the picture, throwing her body into a suspension of meaning and value with implications both intimate and national.[34] At the time of this first series of pictures, however, the antimaternalist implications of fetal photographic viability were unclear; nonetheless, the captions to these "revolutionary" images do clearly transfer the agency of the mother in fetal development to three other objects—the camera, the placenta (which, "[c]ontrary to popular belief, [produces] no direct connection whatever between the mother's circulation and the baby's" [71]), and the magazine, *Life* itself. In this way the unique emplacement of the photographed fetus becomes the *source* of its realness, the aura of death photography captures recycled into a captioning discourse on futurity, natural transformation, and inevitability, in *Life* / life.

The place of this magical technology in the increasingly privatized political public sphere of the U.S. present tense is made explicit in *Life*'s much more religious recelebration of what "life" means, in 1990.[35] Evidence can be found in the title's transformation, from "Drama of Life Before Birth" (1965) to "The First Pictures Ever of HOW LIFE BEGINS" (1990), which is supplemented inside by the biblical headline "The FIRST DAYS of Creation" (26). Evidence is also in the escalation of the magazine's rhetoric of fetal membership in *Life*'s national album of family photographs, and in the captioning rhetoric of the text, which has become newly infused with universalizing sacred language about MAN. The introduction to *Life*'s special section on life constructs the discursive field:

> Made visible here for the first time, the earliest moments of human development are no less mysterious than ever. A single fertilized cell will reproduce itself over and over again, and if all be well, it may blossom into a person. And maybe, like executive Dory Yochum, it will be the kind of person who can stretch expectations for double-X chromosomes in an XY corporate world. Then there are those who are blessed with all the right genetic stuff . . . but fail to thrive— while others are cursed with the worst of nature and nurture but unexpectedly flourish. Saint Augustine, wrestling with predestination and free will, was unable to resolve that dilemma without positing this: No matter the heavenly design, each human spirit can be touched by something he called grace—something that can transform even the destiny preordained by DNA. Such is the case of

young Carmelo, whose basic cellular coding is so flawed that each season brings a new and terrible blight. (25)

Most explicit about the possibilities of this technological transformation of personhood, publicity, and knowledge, though, is an interview with the photographer, Lennart Nilsson. Here the magazine raises the question of his power to be both God and the Supreme Court:

> His greatest subject, and his continuing lifetime project, is based on the way he sees a mother's womb — not as a social battleground but as a 'very interesting' world in which a magical process occurs. Oh, he will try to please the questioners, aid in their own, more narrow investigation. Out of sheer civility he will flip once more through his pictures in search of the key moment, but again and again, he cannot choose. There is always another moment, earlier or later in the process, that he loves just as much. . . . 'I cannot tell you. If I told you only ten days, or two days, or forty days, it would be wrong. It would. Look at the pictures. I am not the man who shall decide when human life started. I am a reporter, I am a photographer.' He smiles. 'Maybe the first moment of human life, it starts with a kiss.' (46)

In his bashful disinclination to engage in the political struggles that provide the main context of value for his work, Nilsson exposes some of the mechanisms by which the counterintuitive magic of social privatization happens. Most explicitly, photography's central role in the abortion debate is to provide that anyone can wield evidence of the human cost of aborting or not aborting: it seems to work by using the fetal image to mobilize a desire to protect the tissue whose violation by technology is at issue. We also witness the insertion of these pictures into the natural history of heterosexuality, which links the visual construction of fetal personhood to the pseudoinevitable trajectory of desire: "The two batches of chromosomes draw inexorably toward one another, like lovers across a crowded room. . . . Perhaps the beginning of life is as complicated and seamless a miracle as falling in love" (46). Lennart Nilsson cannot "choose," although he is the photographer; the fetus too cannot "choose," for the "choice" to reproduce, infinitely repeated in the fantasy of fetal agency developed in these captions, has taken place in the kiss, which must properly lead down the slippery slope to the fetus, to Nilsson's *A Child is Born* and *Behold Man* with their color

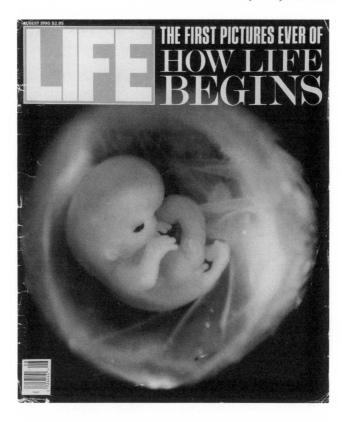

glossies of "life," and to *Life* magazine, with its aspiration to construct a mass-mediated national family of consumers. These visually conceivable changes in the meaning of fetuses, mothers, and "life" are propped on transformations in the represented body size of the fetus; they result in a revitalized fantasy of natural heterosexuality, in new definitions of knowledge, danger, and power; they evaporate the mother, who is now not "viable" outside the kissing couple of private citizens of the United States. In this regime of photographic evidence, the mother is not a "person" when she is pregnant: she is "public," and vulnerable to regulation like a veritable strip mall, or any kind of property. Her technical and political irrelevance to the child's reproduction in the new sacropolitical regime of "life" is a condition of political as well as visual semierasure, in which she can gain value only by submitting to the law and forfeiting the intense competition between American fetuses and their mothers.

THE MOVING FETUS

The Silent Scream and the Physician's Voice

An aura of covert communication hovers when the fetus is used as a public sign: it is something taboo or off-limits, as when a coat opens up to show the illicit — a row of hot watches? a naked body? In 1992 anti-abortion activists tried to deliver to the pro-choice Democratic-party candidate Bill Clinton an allegedly freshly aborted fetus, wrapped in tissue, tissue framed in a sheaf of tissues. According to a similar logic, Volvo has developed advertisements that star a fetal picture, which focus on the play between its authentic "presence" and its veiled or mediated existence, its residence away from the very scenes of anxiety and desire the ad means to prompt and provoke.[36] Featuring an x-ray of a car that frames a sonogram of a fetus protected by the Volvo (its phonemic proximity to and displacement of "vulva" speaks for itself), the printed text whispers to the conscience of the consumer: "Is Something Inside Telling You to Buy a Volvo?" The surprising displacement of the fetus from pulsating inadequate human flesh to "My Mother, the Car" depends on the sonogram photograph's ambivalent appearance: as a negative, a sound wave, an imminent presence; a vehicle for publicity, star quality; something unseeable that must be seen politically; something sanctified that, in a just world, would continue to be concealed by the maternal body that is its natural agent.

But in the context of contemporary intimacy politics, still photos of the floating fetus represent a breach between the fetus and its implied mother, and this crisis touches many domains: Petchesky writes, "a picture of a dead fetus is worth a thousand words. Chaste silhouettes of the fetal form, or voyeuristic-necrophilic photographs of its remains, litter the background of any abortion talk. These still images float like spirits through the courtrooms, where lawyers argue that fetuses can claim tort liability [and in the Supreme Court, where evidence of fetality is used to define what the law means by 'the state's compelling interest']; through the hospitals and clinics, where physicians welcome them as 'patients'; on billboards, in shopping center malls, in science fiction blockbusters . . . [acquiring] a symbolic import that condenses within it a series of losses — from sexual innocence to compliant women to American imperial might."[37]

The fetal photograph seems thus to have a specific use value: to serve as evidence of something, something invaluable, something paradoxically essential and historical, fragile and monumental, pulsating and frozen, sacred and scandalous too. In contrast, the cinema of living, moving fetuses reinflects the crisis of political and human value the fetus generally organizes. The moving fetus not only raises political questions about the relation between personhood and embodiment, but also forces consideration of agency and intention, and their relations to norms of representation and citizenship. *The Silent Scream* (1984), which was the first mass-distributed cinematic instance of fetal narrative realism, distinguishes itself not only for documenting abortion in what it calls "real time," the time of fetal uterine movement refracted through a sonogram, but for establishing "beyond a doubt" that fetuses are rational and self-reflective. At the start of film the narrator intones, "Now we can see for the first time abortion from the victim's vantage point. Ultrasound imaging has allowed us to see this, and so for the first time we are going to watch a child being torn apart, dismembered, disarticulated, crushed and destroyed, by the unfeeling steel instruments of the abortionist." This interpretation simply equates point of view with the bodily existence of the fetus; and having established that perspective is evidence of sentient subjectivity, the video projects intention onto all movements of the fetus in the maternal womb, regardless of the cause that generates physical effects. And so, in one nationally distributed antiabortion broadside, a picture of an active fetus is glossed this way: "She can make a tiny fist / get hiccups / suck her thumb / feel pain / yet she can be legally put to death by abortion at any time until the day she's born."

If fetuses become Cartesian subjects by virtue of being photographed in motion, many pregnant women testify ambivalently about the effects the new reproductive technologies have had on their sense of their own power in pregnancy. It is not just that the maternal body has been redefined as a disaster movie waiting to happen, or a technical "environment" that makes the fetus vulnerable to toxic invasions via the mother's mouth, veins, or vagina. It is also that the sonogram has come to attain higher truth value than many other knowledges of pregnancy, including the mother's feelings and experiences, and those of other women.[38] Of course, the deployment of new knowledge about fetality constantly incites the culture at large to unlearn a variety of things it used to think about the complex relation of maternity, science, the law, nationality,

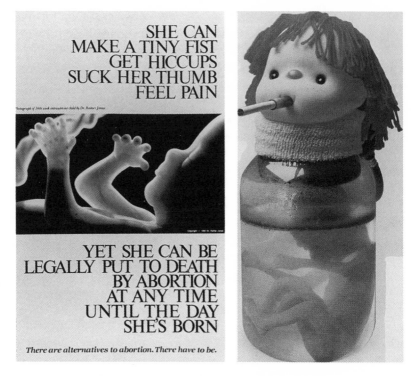

The name of this doll is "Smokey Sue Smokes for Two." (Right)

and citizenship. What is striking here, however, is the ways the conjuncture of medical and entertainment contexts for fetal circulation unsettle the already fragile condition of U.S. women's citizenship.

In my discussion of *Life* and "Fat," the nation has been a commercial sign, imminently or explicitly a scene of commodity exchange around the body, which was central to the production of national intimacy as a form of family feeling. The antiabortion documentaries *The Silent Scream, Eclipse of Reason,* and *Let Me Live* are more than visual video lyrics about the right of bodies to "life" in the abstract: they are sophisticated remediations of the national public sphere. They speak a patriotic language, yet they also construe the scenes and experiences of politics in ways that seek to undermine the juridical nation. This ambivalence toward the nation is fundamental to the ideology of the New Right—for example, it is evident in Ronald Reagan's 1984 *Abortion and the Conscience of the Nation,* written while he was a sitting president.[39] In this essay, Reagan characteristically positions himself as an outsider to the official nation of which he is president; citing the heroic precedents of Dred Scott and Abraham Lincoln (whose pictures here, as often, join Mother Teresa's as the iconic monuments of pro-life nationalism), Reagan demonstrates the crisis in his belief in the providentially sanctified nation by making historical America a contested term, in competition with other forms of authority. In Reagan's account, the abortion-saturated nation of the present tense is in an antagonistic relation to another, essentially real genealogy of American heroism, global culture, science, morality, experience, and, of course, to the abstraction "life" itself.

We can read the relation between fetality and nationality in each of these videos as an offspring of the image/caption relation Benjamin describes: in this kind of work, crucially, the main kind of caption is the voice-over.[40] This means that the videos enact their reconstruction of identity by coordinating different relations of displacement. First, their construction of visual knowledge relies heavily on a juxtaposition of totality (images of the whole fetus, the whole doctor, the whole family) and fragmentation (in montage sequences of broken-up fetal bodies, abortion clinics, women in mourning, doctors shrouded in antiseptic white, and "pictures of agony" related to other social ills like racism and homelessness that have already been legitimated as "American" problems in the political public sphere). Second, and in contrast to the internal dialectics of form, the voice-over both reconstructs authority by acting as a consoling guide to the new visually traumatized body and image archive and undermines the scene of any human authority by multiplying the kinds of voices silenced under the regime of *Roe v. Wade*. By relying on the pseudo-objectivity of science to stop the violence of interpretation, these texts seem to perform the objective truth of the fetus's self-evident right to (political) life in the United States.

As an aggregate, the pro-life videos claim to resituate all of human history and American law from the perspective of the fetal body. This horizon of meaning is not, from the beginning, considered fully in terms of citizenship, but overall an argument develops that disestablishes the credentials of American liberalism and American politics, especially where they value autonomy and social experience over "life" in the body. Yet, the kind of postmodern liberation theology this movement has developed envelops the mass-cultural icon as well, by appropriating the pseudointimacy of the relation between the star and the ordinary and generic individual.⁴¹ This relation between the value of the body itself and the fictive intimacy of individuals with media personalities produces new logics of meaning, value, and politics within hybrid generic forms: the videos fuse the anerotic sentimental structure of the infomercial and the docudrama with the pornotropic fantasies of the snuff film. The purpose here is to exhaust the banality of violence to the ordinary (read white, "American") body, to make violation once again a scandalous violence, and to reprivatize that body (within the patriarchally identified family); to recontain scandalous corporeality within mass culture and the minority populations of the nation; and to revitalize the national fantasy of abstract intimacy, but this time in a body that, visually available in its pure origin, receives protection from the juridical and immoral betrayals of national capitalism let loose by feminism and *Roe v. Wade.*

Let me briefly lay out the national contours in which the fetal image became not just captioned but spoken for, using these videos as examples of the analogy that has become common between the fetus, the woman, the nation. *The Silent Scream* is narrated by Dr. Bernard Nathanson, cofounder of the National Abortion Rights League (NARAL) and a self-described converted ex-abortionist. The video uses sonograms and implied fetal consciousness to democratize the expertise that will, he hopes, redefine American personhood. *Eclipse of Reason,* another Nathanson production, enlists the authority of television to place the fissure between the moral and the juridical nation in the context of both a global jeremiad and the authority of the Hollywood star system. You will note the Enlightenment citation in the title: knowledge brings light to the darkness of ignorance; only "reason" can save life; abortion is of a piece with irrationality, greed, passion, and other vices. Charlton Heston introduces *Eclipse of Reason,* lending his aura as Hollywood's Moses and as public representative of the National Rifle Association to broadcast true patriotic antinomian credentials. Finally, *Let Me Live* projects as a postpolitical, utopian horizon the political aims of the actually existing pro-life movement. It is a fetal national anthem, narrated and sung by Pat Boone and "thousands, maybe millions," of fetuses.⁴² The video's textual system returns the fetus visually to its disembodied state and then, as it grows, reinvents human time, space, value, and subjectivity by giving it a collective and an individual voice, or more particularly, a voice-over.

The Silent Scream premiered in 1984 in a media whirl of controversy around the authenticity of the "real-time" abortion it shows. These de-

bates were incited by the truth claims of the very first frames: opening
with a warning that explicit material will follow and with the credit line
"An American Portrait Film's Educational Production," the text then
moves to its first image, a sonogram. The triangular image of sonar
waves is surrounded by nothing, a plain orange matte, and a voice saying, "Now we can discern the chilling silent scream on the face of this
child, who is now facing imminent extinction." The "now" repeated in
this sentence refers to a number of coterminous temporalities: now, in
the viewing of this film; now, in the history of science; now, in the
history of the world; and now, in the magical time of textuality, where
the repetition of the destruction of the fetus is always "imminent," for
this fetus is all fetuses — from the point of view of its standing in the
sacred and the juridical law. The issues arising from the claim that a
videotaped sonogram is in "real time" are plain, but when *The Silent
Scream* finally enters its narrative, it is the history of science that establishes its transformation of expertise. Nathanson opens the conversation
autobiographically: "When I was a medical student in 1949, there was no
science called fetology. We were taught that there was something in the
uterus, but it really was an article of faith as to whether or not it was a human being and whether or not that human being had any unique qualities." Since the 1970s, the science of fetology exploded with methods
such as "ultrasound imaging, electronic fetal heart monitoring, hystero-
scopy, radio immunochemistry, and a host of other dazzling technologies which today constitute, in fact, the corpus of the science of fetology. . . . Those technologies, those apparatuses, that we use every day
have convinced us that the unborn child is indistinguishable in any way
from us." This is to say that "our" ordinary practice is already way ahead
of our conceptualization of it.

As he tells this story, Nathanson speaks technically about what ultrasound is. He then names the instruments that the abortionist uses on the
fetus. He uses plastic models of fetuses, larger than actual size, for purposes of demonstration, and then, switching from infomercial to docudrama format, crosscuts his representation of the abortion on the plastic
baby with the abortion viewed on real-time ultrasound wave images. In
his play-by-play narration of the abortion in real time, each movement of
the medical utensil, and each response of the fetus, is registered and
interpreted; the apparent movement taking place inside, from the abortion, as shown on the monitor, and the simulated abortion happening outside, on the plastic baby, bring the violence closer to "you," the

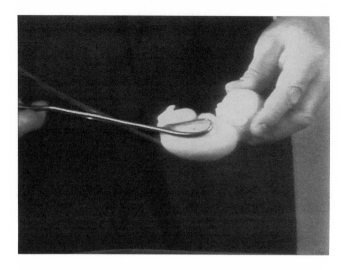

consumer, who is asked to choose between identification with the baby or with the medical personnel, with their power, money, and jargon. Nathanson comments, indeed, that medical personnel who have watched this representation, as we have, have undergone conversion experiences (they report these experiences on film in *Eclipse of Reason*) and have left behind the practice of abortion forever. This instance of technical and emotional pedagogy is followed by a series of arguments about the kind of context the United States provides for abortion. After giving the annual figures of American abortion, he associates, covertly, the U.S. government with the Mafia, which apparently now runs profitable abortion clinics much as it ran gin mills during Prohibition, in an analogous evil, underground industry promoted by a bad federal law.

This information segment is followed by one that repeats the structure of the voice intoning over the silently screaming sonogram. Over pictures of silent crying women, victimized by abortion, Nathanson begins the nationalist argument: that this film should be a part of the law's standard of informed consent, and that "I refuse to believe that Americans, who have put men on the moon, can't devise a better solution than the resort to violence." At "moon," the image text moves to a picture of a man on the moon, and then to a fetus, and at the moment the film ends, an image of Mount Rushmore flashes on the screen, as if to remind us that (1) in nature, all presidents were fetuses; (2) presidents are vulnerable like fetuses; (3) the monumentalizing memory of American political life should provide the kinds of guarantees of monumentality for each and every American, not just the ones whose futurity is secured by the privileges of the political public sphere.

The aim of *The Silent Scream* is to establish "documentation" that will transform the decision to abort from an effect of feeling or desire to the rational effect of true knowledge. Nathanson insists that this objective, graphic information would simply exterminate the capacity to advocate abortion: technical information about the sensations that both the fetus and the mother will experience during the procedure will have to substitute for the shaky vicissitudes of desire or mystification. Since the woman would see in it that the fetus consents to nothing, no woman, in Nathanson's view, would knowingly consent to abortion. The woman who aborts must then be blinded by liberal ideology, which has neither medical expertise nor the theoretical capacity to understand the pain of human embodiment. The fetus, in contrast, feels the unmediated truth, and its condition thus must be considered the truth of human existence. While Nathanson acknowledges that pro-choice advocates argue correctly that the self-understanding of a pregnant woman ought to figure prominently in decisions about abortion, and that without that right to exercise her capacity, she would earn the credentials of the victim so central to the vision of pro-life doctrine, he downplays the woman's pain as merely a social problem, minimal in the face of "life" itself.

In sum, two logics of fetal authenticity combine in the national counterpolitics of Nathanson's discourse. In one, the sensual basis of fetal experience stands in for a preideological condition: the fetus's pain equals the raised consciousness of the antiabortion advocate, for neither is mystified into the ideological distortion or bargaining that marks prochoice maternalism. In the second logic, contingencies of the social are sacrificed for ideality in the providential historical way. Speaking the patriotic discourse of American exceptionalism, Nathanson implicitly characterizes the fetus as an imperial American male who must return the fallen official state to the conditions of national election Americans have a fundamental responsibility to uphold.

If *The Silent Scream* uses the new *reproductive* technologies to reconstruct the identitarian logic of natural extension from fetus through science to national identity, *Eclipse of Reason* connects the new *information* technologies to a reconstructed global history to tell the story of abortion in America. This shift in focus from the conscience of the individual spectating consumer to the national mass-media public is coordinated with the much broader global consciousness of *Eclipse,* which sees the national crisis in terms of a moral, economic, and imperial world emergency. While the internal matter of the video repeats much of the same information and imaging that characterizes *The Silent Scream,* the narrative frame around *Eclipse of Reason* expresses the need for a political, mass-cultural consciousness to match the ethical and scientific claims made in the first instance. The frame, performed by Heston, is given here in its entirety:

> There are over 150,000 open-heart operations performed in this country every year. Did you know that? Probably you did, for there are good documentaries about it on television all the time. We all know something about single- and double-bypass surgeries and how many lives have been saved. That's good. But the kind of surgery most frequently done in America is abortion, and that's not meant to save lives. In this country, we perform and submit to one and one-half million abortions every year — that's ten times the number of open-heart surgeries. Now, the average abortion only takes five or six minutes, but they've never shown the complete operation on any television channel, any time. That's not good. That's a big part of what television is for, to explore public questions we care about. Abortion is surely that — the feelings generated, the passionate debates and the issues, safety, morality, long-term consequences. All these intrude on the public conscience much more strongly than any surgery ever has. Political candidates are not expected to take a stand on coronary bypass. The Supreme Court has yet to rule on the constitutionality of heart transplants. People don't take to the streets in thousands to demonstrate their opinions on artificial hearts. Yet, the press and television tell us a lot more about heart surgery than they ever have about abortion. I think the media have failed here badly in what they claim is their responsibility to inform the public who will make the final decisions on abortion. If you're looking at me on television now, then they've accepted that responsibility to inform.
>
> The film you're about to see is graphic. Some of you may find it too graphic: there's blood, and death — we all remember the horror of the film from the death camps in Europe, the grisly images of the broken victims of Hiroshima. I was in Ethiopia myself; you'll recall the gut-wrenching pictures of starving babies we sent back from

there. Well, the babies in this film are not starving. But with those other terrible images, they serve the right of the people to know, to know the victim. When he accepted the Nobel Prize, Elie Wiesel said, 'I swore never to be silent whenever and wherever human beings endure suffering and humiliation. We must always take sides. Neutrality helps the oppressor, never the victim. Silence encourages the tormentor, never the tormented.' No one has ever spoken more eloquently than that on behalf of the victim. Since 1973, abortion has claimed more than twenty million mute and innocent victims. This film speaks for them. The silence has to stop.

The broken body of the fetus hovers over this monologue like a ghost, but there is no fetal image here, just Heston. His masculine authority offers up the form of celebrity power as a sign of what all political agents must seize: since the media has failed to assume its obligation to inform us about the true state of the global / national body, each pro-life activist / consumer must in essence *become* Charlton Heston. What would this transformative identification mean? To refuse the false position of neutrality would require seeking out and broadcasting painful knowledge about immoral power all over the land. It would be to think African / Jew / fetus as the iconic sign of tyrannized citizenship in a nation dominated by a corrupted state. It would be to remember that an abortion culture is on the "subtle, slippery slide to Auschwitz," as C. Everett Koop elsewhere argues.[43] It would be to remember, therefore, important failures in America's political leadership that must be reversed by mass political action.

Heston's segment is straightway followed by an announcement: "During the next eight minutes this child will be destroyed before your eyes." But even if the violence we witness in the video pains us, this means to be Armageddon, the violence to end all violence. The terrible images we see are the price we have to pay for sustaining a terrible political culture that cannot visualize the human value of the fetus, a culture whose global, national, and local parameters are made cinematically graphic, via maps imprinted by statistics detailing the *facts* of abortion culture; through transnational images of *faces* in pain, such as those of the starving children from Ethiopia Heston mentions; and through moving and still fetuses, the hieroglyphs of contemporary inhuman practice. Heston wants his viewers to borrow his star aura, the aura of super-citizenship. To do this they must assume custody of the fetal body, must represent it corporeally, like an actor or a politician. Moreover, to represent the fetus politically is to caption it, put a gloss on its image. Speaking to it, around it, with it, and for it, the eloquent ventriloquism of pro-life politics brings the fetus to "life."

Eclipse of Reason itself is the usual encyclopedia of technical information: an aborted fetus in still and moving pictures; a real and a plastic demonstration; a sequence of national maps and statistics that join with both technical and commonsense definitions of personhood to reconstruct expertise; a wide variety of ignorant responses by people on the street and knowing responses by postabortion subjects experiencing trauma about the abortions they've had. These shameful scandals provide the evidence that justifies the intimacy politics the video promotes, which involves a knowledge revolution that will help to eclipse the eclipse of reason abortion culture betokens. In the video's final section, two montage sequences summarize the lesson. Nathanson introduces them to document "the unmistakable trademark of the irrational violence that has pervaded the twentieth century. There's no rightful place for violence in a world of reason. Those qualities which grace such a world of light and reason are kindness, compassion, patience, and love. This is the face of the world of violence." This speech is followed by a montage punctuated by music, with no voice-over: *(1) aborted baby-mound on table; (2) protester being bitten by police dog; (3) Hiroshima; (4) Khaddafi; (5) needle/drug/arm; (6) "terrorist" in stocking cap throwing bomb; (7) the sign of a destroyed abortion clinic — "George R. Tiller, M.D., Women's Health Care P.A."; (8) two hooded Klansmen; (9) bag lady; (10) Ethiopian starving child.* This trauma montage requires no voice-over, because the violences it represents are iconic: traumas made famous in the mediascape of everyday news and entertainment. The text holds out this chain of violence as a site of proliferation — there is no end in sight to its catalog of destruction. But because the pro-life movement wants to return to a body bounded by ordinary, unspectacular dignity, the video offers another montage: *(1) Mother Teresa holding a baby (over which it is announced, "This is the face of the world of love"); (2) man standing behind a wheelchair sharing laughter with a man in the chair; (3) two women hugging; (4) wedding picture; (5) mother and baby; (6) grandmother and young boy; (7) two women with two babies; (8) family portrait; (9) yawning baby and smiling mother; (10) little kids playing musical instruments.*

"What kind of a world do you want?" is the last line of the video, which means, "Which montage are you in?" These images are thus the new sentimental icons of national culture, images of virtuous pain and evil power. These are the choices offered up for the future of personhood in America. In the first, pain is political, regulated by nations, racism, imperialism, and global capitalism; it is public, it is a terrified and terrorized world of/in black and white. The pro-life field of pleasure is, in contrast, intimate, familial, corporeal, nonpenetrative, intergenerational, and historical only in the private sense, imbued with the sensuality of color. It promotes a relation among surfaces, and suggests a world where the only means necessary for survival is love and where all bodies have one "face." For if love is your capital, a world that exchanges value in its currency will beget no poverty, racism, or government. Pain proves victimization; victimization signals unjust power; the world of light will be achieved only when the body is safe for the future. This is what star power is, and here celluloid becomes, again, the place where the human body's essential substance and imaginary voice see their realization in fantasy.

You will notice that fetal and pregnant bodies have practically evaporated from my own discussion of these pro-life videos. What I have been trying to describe here, indeed, is the process by which the fetus was produced, invested with aura and scandal, and then made banal — as its minor existence in the montage of national icons in *Eclipse of Reason* demonstrates. Let me summarize. When the fetus was an article of fantasy or faith, as in "Fat," it was indescribable or multiply describable. It provided a structure of improvisation, which opened a space for change beyond what the female narrator knew how to desire, much less depict. Her voice-over is thus partial and intuitive in its construction of ways bodies might be imagined acting in excess of themselves, to unleash new species of identity. When the fetus became available to photography, making "life" miraculous in a new way, it came to occupy a new scale of existence, often taking up an entire frame like a portrait. In the process of becoming bigger, it pushed the externally visible bodies involved in reproducing it outside the family picture, making the mother and the father, I think, ancestors before their time.

As it came more into play as a political substance, the fetus's iconicity became a nostalgic horizon. The narrative of fetal violation by bad mothers and unjust nations was visually confirmed by images that shuttled between the still perfection of the fetal icon and the icon's horrifying violation — by the nation, by persons, by forced historicity. The solution these texts offer is to reimagine America as a place where, paradoxically, the body is safe, but only as a stereotype. This is a political fantasy of the end of history, in a realm of postpolitics, beyond everyday life, maternity, racism, law, regulation; it is represented as a possibility for us by the hyperspace of mass culture, whose very commitment to pleasure produces a clean, well-lighted decontextualized celebrity.

The celebrity's capacity to move through space unimpeded by obstacles in the mode of imperial being not only repossesses the constitutional ideal of abstract personhood, but does it in a body. Thus although this discourse remains maternalist and patriotic, it can only imagine the fetus, the mother, and the nation with one "face"; although it is a rhetoric suspicious of the bodily pleasure and sexuality mass culture promises, it still sees in this displacement of the juridical to the simulated national culture a route to constructing new fantasy norms, not only of pleasure but of citizenship.

Not a Pretty Picture: Fetal Celebrity
and National Culture

In short, your fetus is what you eat — and what you don't eat. As you can probably guess, a baby made up of candy bars and colas is quite different from a baby made up of whole grain breads and milk. . . . Not a pretty picture. . . . While you can eat what you choose to eat, a fetus has no choice. It eats what you've chosen, whether the selection serves its nutritional interests or not. It can't order in a bowl of shredded wheat to supplement your breakfast doughnut, or an extra serving of protein to augment that lunchtime hot dog. It can't leave the fries if it's surfeited with fat, or opt for a glass of milk instead of that cola when the craving is for calcium. — Arlene Eisenberg, Heidi E. Murkoff, Sandee E. Hathaway, *What to Eat When You're Expecting*[44]

The celebrity fetus is among us now, starring in political documentaries, Hollywood films, commodity advertisements, and home videos.[45] Like all celebrities, the identity its body coordinates exists fully in a public sphere of superpersonhood, where it radiates authenticity and elicits strong identification — in part by the miraculous auratic ways its own magnificent body can be represented and in part by its displacement from an authentic voice. For although the fetus may be a living thing, it is also, as a representation, always a special effect.[46] This is a condition of extreme vulnerability and also of immense power, and its effects and authority go way beyond their typical narrative articulation. In this sense, the fetus follows the celebrity logic of the diva, whose majesty derives from her bigness on the screen, her intimacy with pain and death, her capacity to survive by being a space of permission for the expression and bodily demonstration of excess sentiment. The difference is that the diva has a voice, and it matches her body for bigness. The new reproductive media have attempted to disavow this difference in ways that have radically reframed how political identity is represented in a national context. This has to do with the refraction of the commodity form in the construction of postmodern American subjectivity, identity, and identification. Here are two related, but not identical, examples.

Pat Boone's *Let Me Live* is an MTV-style music video that establishes the conditions of lyric subjectivity for the fetus. The conceit of the song is a dream, Boone's dream, of a chorus of fetal voices that sing to him in his sleep, in the mode of a children's choir. The fetal voices he hears appear to him as myriad stars, or as a thousand points of light; they converge on the camera lens like snowflakes on a car windshield. He remembers the dream as "indescribable," "so profound / so troubling / [he] woke up trembling in tears"; and when he wakes he knows that "thousands of unborn children were singing to me / from their mothers' wombs / and they're not just mindless bits of flesh / they're human beings."[47] What has happened to take him from the "indescribable" moment of feeling to a place of expertise? The genre of the fetal song that Boone's commentary frames is something called the fetal diary, and it is a major invention of the pro-life movement, although not historically unprecedented. In this diary, the fetus records its sensations from the moment of conception and establishes a prehistory to any public sign of its existence. The internal narrative of *Let Me Live* extends from one to three months, beginning before the moment the imperfect maternal body can register knowledge of itself and ending when the fetus realizes the mother knows it exists. The visuals are suffused with crosscutting between fetal images and slow-motion images of visibly generic, happy family life. It does this to establish that the fetus knows about, and participates in, family life long before the mother even knows the fetus exists. In the meantime the fetus speaks to Pat Boone. Presumably, it speaks to him because he has a personal relation to God, and perhaps because he himself is a "star," and stars respond to him. It is also because he is not a mother that he can experience what she cannot feel in her body. She is numb to her knowledge, while he trembles from the sensation of it.

It is hard to think of a better example of how powerfully the diva fetus

DIARY OF AN UNBORN CHILD

OCTOBER 5— Today my life began. My parents do not know it yet, I am as small as a seed of an apple, but it is I already. And I am to be a girl. I shall have blond hair and blue eyes. Just about everything is settled though, even the fact that I shall love flowers.

OCTOBER 19— Some say that I am not a real person yet, that only my mother exists. But I am a real person, just as a small crumb of bread is yet truly bread. My mother is. And I am.

OCTOBER 23— My mouth is just beginning to open now. Just think, in a year or so I shall be laughing and later talking. I know what my first word will be: MAMA.

OCTOBER 25— My heart began to beat today all by itself. From now on it shall gently beat for the rest of my life without ever stopping to rest! And after many years it will tire. It will stop, and then I shall die.

NOVEMBER 2— I am growing a bit every day. My arms and legs are beginning to take shape. But I have to wait a long time yet before those little legs will raise me to my mother's arms, before these little arms will be able to gather flowers and embrace my father.

NOVEMBER 12— Tiny fingers are beginning to form on my hands. Funny how small they are! I'll be able to stroke my mother's hair with them.

NOVEMBER 20— It wasn't until today that the doctor told mom that I am living here under her heart. Oh, how happy she must be! Are you happy, mom?

NOVEMBER 25— My mom and dad are probably thinking about a name for me. But they don't even know that I am a little girl. I want to be called Kathy. I am getting so big already.

DECEMBER 10— My hair is growing. It is smooth and bright and shiny. I wonder what kind of hair mom has.

DECEMBER 13— I am just about able to see. It is dark around me. When mom brings me into the world it will be full of sunshine and flowers. But what I want more than anything is to see my mom. How do you look, mom?

DECEMBER 24— I wonder if mom hears the whispering of my heart? Some children come into the world a little sick. But my heart is strong and healthy. It beats so evenly: tup-tup, tup-tup. You'll have a healthy little daughter, mom!

DECEMBER 28— Today my mother killed me.

annihilates what Nathanson calls the merely "social": class, race, gender, sexuality, nationality, global economy, and markets in reproductive technology and policy. All of the obstacles to constructing generic expectations for personhood itself are not merely marginalized or replaced here — as they are in the earlier examples — they are canceled out as material for knowledge and memory. The fetus is incompetent to think about power as contingent. It speaks only of God's creation.

But this kind of propaganda about power and ethics is not intrinsic to the cinematic attribution of voice to the fetal body. Amy Heckerling's *Look Who's Talking* films take up and exploit the problem in a sophisticated, and a sophistic, way, demonstrating what Paula Treichler has called "the national spirit of utter confusion" with respect to the meaning and the value of reproduction.[48] The films are caught in a cluster of contradictions organized around questions of survival. Linking the logics of feminist consciousness to pro-life arguments about person-hood, the mother and the fetus live parallel plots; staging problems of intimacy and technical competence at negotiating metropolitan culture, sexuality, and motherhood, the films demonstrate the contexts for their comedy as saturated by real, hard problems for women, but they also entertain consumers through a slapstick dialectic of feminine/maternal failure and mastery.

As for fetal representation itself, each film seems to come right out of Pat Boone and George Bush's image archive, while demonstrating as well genuine political distance from the semiotic field it uses. They both climax their opening scenes of copulation with similar scenes that take place visually in the tissues of the penis, vagina, and uterus. Adopting as well the mise-en-scène of music video, they represent conception in the form of a primal sexual violence, the rape of an egg by a sperm. The egg, which has a female voice, never wants to be penetrated by the sperm, who has been egged on to this deed by the enthusiasm of other hearty, vocal male-voiced sperm produced in the ejaculation, and by a Beach Boys soundtrack gloss. The sperm always want to penetrate the egg, and there always seems to be an egg ready to be penetrated: heterosex appears to tend naturally toward reproduction, whether or not the persons having it are having it for mere pleasure. The sequel is distinguished from the original by representing married, not passionate, sex, and by representing an actual diaphragm around the cervix that gets circumvented by an especially creative and articulate sperm. Each of these conceptions is an "accident." On penetration, the child is conceived immediately, in a burst of starry points of light. Soon thereafter, the embryos are talking that nondiegetic fetus talk, where ordinariness and celebrity meet, in the celluloid voices of Bruce Willis, Joan Rivers, and Roseanne.[49]

Yet the films do narrate as a symptomatic social problem the becoming-stereotypical of the modern woman — usually white, middle-class, and American. Anna Tsing argues that "[i]n inverting all that is proper, [modern] 'anti-mothers' join female monsters of the 1960s and 1970s — monsters such as the fat woman (the anti-beauty) and the female boss — in the ongoing production and negotiation of gender."[50] In *Look Who's Talking*, Kirstie Alley plays a high-powered accountant, covertly involved with George Segal, a client who runs a company named Chubby Charles.[51] Segal plays a middle-aged white man with a tight stomach who displays enormous pictures of hugely fat art deco women on the walls of his office while surrounded by women with eating disorders and pushing products that encourage identification with fat. He is, in other words, a hysteric addicted to a world of compulsive consumption but in disavowal of his own desire for it—which is why he falls for his accountant, whose job is to keep track of appetite and accumulation without indulging in it herself.

Segal says, nonetheless, that he cannot divorce his wife, because she is bulimic ("Every time I say the word 'divorce' she loses five pounds"). Shortly after this conversation, we cut to Alley's head in the toilet, discharging loud vomiting sounds. This tableau seems unsettling and pathological for a moment, an emblem of femininity's current association with stress, food hysteria, and therapy culture. But while Alley first seems to be imitating the lover's wife by vomiting, it turns out that this is morning sickness, and that Alley is pregnant. The fat that she will gain happily is proper heterosexual fat, and she is not doomed to mime the emaciated starvation of the desperate wife nor the autoerotic amplitude we witnessed as a social offense in "Fat."

Although Alley is out of control, has transgressive sex, overeats in public, makes scenes, hits men, and yells and screams, she always looks robust and beautiful. She drinks apple juice; she eats massive bars of Dove ice cream. There is a kind of glow to heterosexual fat, although it is accompanied by terror that it might remain postpartum, and turn into the other, immoral kind. John Travolta, who by chance helps deliver her child (and then follows the condition of the fetus by becoming its father), remarks with approval that after the birth Alley quickly recoups her "figure," her cultural capital. But unmarried and with no visible sign of her heterosexuality, which has been kept implicit by the love affair's illicitness, Alley remains abnormal. The film's code word for this condition is "lesbian," a term of disgrace she twice encounters. Because she is unintelligible at the very moment she should be most pregnantly iconic, she is caught in the discourse of sexual difference, capital exchange, class turmoil, sexual humiliation, and compulsory heterosexuality. This is the stuff of comedy. The films do not minimize its significance or typicality for a minute.[52] Alley's assertion of control over sexuality and reproduction disturbs the gender norms of her class: her decline in status licenses the love plot she enters with Travolta, a working-class cab driver who aspires to transcend ground transportation by becoming a pilot (the melodrama of his class ascension through marriage motivates *Look Who's Talking Too*).

In the last months of Alley's pregnancy, she walks into her cheating lover's office as a beautiful woman leaves it. Alley whines, "Albert, do you think that woman out there is pretty?" and announces, in contrast, "I look like a big fat Pilgrim." She says this because she is wearing a black dress with a white collar, the way an American Pilgrim might, and in saying this makes herself iconic, but also archaic, a body from the past. Her alterity to herself is a sign of what happens when an icon fails, becomes historical. Alley's self-description, on the other hand, designates a condition of coerced, alienated nationality and affiliates her with the stereotypes of African American women and other corporeal outsiders who have provided much matter for Hollywood comedy (although it must be noted that none of the fetus-driven comedies Hollywood cinema and television have generated feature African American, Hispanic, Asian, or strongly ethnicized women, who are still marked with class identities and therefore are not representable as abstractable citizen-subjects in the American popular cultural lexicon. These marked subjects have been available only, if at all, for maternal melodrama).[53]

Alley's portrait of herself as a Pilgrim amounts to a mere breath she takes before diving back into the search for a comfortable stereotype to inhabit, like a snail. But as mass nationality and mass culture meet on Alley's body to stage a contest between hegemonic icons and marginal stereotypes, and as we witness her screwball incompetence at both the small and important technicalities of the body in everyday life, the foreignness of the fat, pregnant, female American Pilgrim seems a good place to suspend this cinematic genealogy of the hybrid icon of fetal motherhood — its uncanny scale, its double interiority, its complex corporeality — not with an astrological image of the imperial fetus itself, or with an icon of sacred stellar maternity, but with a constellation of questions about gender, fetality, and nationality.

The pro-life image of the nation as parent with a compelling interest in its children / citizens has produced an image of the autonomous fetus — a cruel, inhuman image, both because of the vulnerability of its body and because of its violent expropriation from the maternal site. The structure of rescue this image forces any ethical subject to assume almost invariably, and with devastating effects, erases other images: of specific maternal bodies, of adult women in their contexts of domestic and public work, women who act in history and have value beyond their specific place in the sacred national temporality of reproduction. In this occluded archive of women's practical lives, the pilgrimage of women toward full U.S. citizenship travels a map nobody has seen. It is made of multiple, overlapping semitransparencies. There is the scenic route of natural extension, in which girls naturally reproduce, producing new generations of Americans; the civic, interstate route of national everyday life, in which a maternal ethic limits women to the realm of social power and denies the importance of a non-privacy-oriented politics for them, which impedes women's participation in a more materialist general discussion of what the collective good life might become. On yet another map, covered with incomplete roads and dotted lines, is the national space yet to be zoned, where women might experience their value as something other than and exorbitant to the infantile national public sphere, in which fetuses star as citizen celebrities and women appear as little more than stage mothers to the nation. It is this condition of pilgrimage — through public spheres, where identity forms are undergoing rapid and uneven transformations of scale and value — that makes the woman, despite all appearances, both a citizen manqué and an expert witness to the crisis in conceiving, not just of children, but of actually democratic political agency in contemporary America.

"Hi, Hon!": Or, How I Got My Evidence

I carry in my mind a picture of a child who was never born. A child I aborted. A picture that changes as the years go by. I imagine him growing tall, with dark hair and eyes. Again and again my mind returns to that ghost of a child, who would have been twelve this spring. If you think abortion is an easy choice, that you can just forget about it, it's not true, you can't.

Life. What a Beautiful Choice (a public-service-style announcement sponsored by the Arthur S. DeMoss Foundation)

When the woman in "Fat" experiences her customer's fat agency as a lesson in the power of bigness, the fetus she imagines producing is unreal to her, an object of a fantasy game in which playing with public norms of corporeal discipline and transgression provides an opportunity not for changing into *something* but for imagining or teasing change toward some barely conceived horizon. Fatness suggested the effacement of a violated personality by a surplus of body; it was less clear what, if anything, would happen once the new regime of embodied superpersonhood was achieved. When I first imagined this essay, I thought I would have to write something about my own relation to fat, thinking that my readers would wonder, Is she fat? Since the paper's first incarnation was as a talk, this anxiety faded: the audience had ocular evidence.

I have no anxiety about my reader's thinking that I am currently a fetus, but I find that I cannot allay questions that my encounters with fetality have raised, questions of evidence, of professional discourse, and of autobiography, and their relation to the political contexts in which, I have argued, intimacy has been transformed from a private relation to a structuring aspect and affect of citizenship in the contemporary U.S. public sphere. When I decided to write this essay, I thought it would be about the reinvention of American personhood from the point of view of fetal inner space. I suspected that the sound waves of the sonogram and the special effects of the photograph had secured a privileged perspective on changes taking place in the legal and aesthetic production of identity meanings in America. I expected to trace the escalating competition between the fetal "person" in the abstract, whose virtue and value appear morally uncontestable, and the women who claim priority over their bodies, since in the fundamentalist epoch of the 1980s and 1990s, women's very capacity to think, to choose, to act politically, and to desire nonreproductive sex makes their very claims of authority appear suspect, grotesque, self-indulgent, and immoral, like fat.

Under the pressure of isolating this problem in its condensed forms, I surveyed the cinema of the fetus for the ways it situates national and sexual fantasy in the same discursive field: for example, *2001: A Space Odyssey* (dir. Stanley Kubrick, 1968), and its comic inversion in Joe Dante/Steven Spielberg's *Innerspace* (1987); the works of David Cronenberg that dramatize reproductive technologies (*The Brood* [1979],

Videodrome [1983], *Dead Ringers* [1988]); the *Alien* series (dir. Ridley Scott, 1979; James Cameron, 1986; David Fincher, 1992); *Look Who's Talking* and *Look Who's Talking Too* (dir. Amy Heckerling, 1989 and 1990); and surrogacy or prosthetic family films like *Immediate Family* (dir. Jonathan Kaplan, 1989), *Angie* (dir. Martha Coolidge, 1994), *Junior* (dir. Ivan Reitman, 1994), and *Nine Months* (dir. Chris Columbus, 1995). Because the reproductive maternal body is considered broken or irrelevant—or, in Emily Martin's terms, *flexible,* a mobile sign[54]—in this moment of feminist backlash and imperial fetology, I also thought it necessary to read professional and lay pregnancy books; in particular, to compare the relation between professional discourses on fetal and maternal bodies and the kinds of communication addressed to the nonprofessionals, the mothers.[55] I was particularly interested in popular notions of fetal and maternal health, especially where the nutritional interests of the fetus seemed to clash with the anxiety new mothers regularly report about losing the "baby fat" gained during pregnancy.[56]

My university library had no books of this sort. So I called my sister, Valerie, who had just had a child. I asked her advice. After rattling off a bibliography, she offered to send me some of her favorite books, and a videotape of the sonogram her husband, Richard, had taken. The tape she sent me, titled *Zak Davis: From Sonogram to Two Years,* incorporated more than I had expected. Valerie enclosed a note with the videotape: "Richard thought you might like to see Zak grow up, so he included highlights from his first two years."

The contents of this tape moved and informed me in ways I could not have predicted. As I thought about bringing into representation the banalization of the fetus in America, the affective charge of the tape created static in my thinking: precisely what did the language of national public spheres, identity politics, fetal motherhood, commodity identification, and mass culture have to do with the tape my brother-in-law constructed and my sister circulated privately to me? How did this communication from personal life provide information about the distortions of scale that govern the struggle being waged, on behalf of the fetus, over the national future? This fight is being cast as a struggle over life-and-death ethics, sexual propriety, national privilege, and what counts as a claim to justice in the United States. But even this description forgets that the "body" over which this strife continues is (1) two bodies, sutured; (2) a corporeal complexity inhabited as a fact of ordinary experience; (3) a realm of activity and agency whose *untranslatability* into the discourses of nationality and identity remains a vitalizing and threatening political irritant. The contingency of this familial communication, the ease with which the videotape provided a local context for reading the fetus, the "softness" of the anecdotal evidence: these accidents of information must be read not only as incidents in my life but as a part of a communication network about fetality, family, and the technology of memory that enters the register of public discourse in ways oblique to the rest of this essay.[57]

To provide a different context for the previous discussion of the ways mass publicity and mass politics saturate reproductive meaning in contemporary America, I want to trace in the following pages three moments in the production of fetal publicity, all of which involve an encounter between the technology and the contingency of reproductive knowledge. We will see that publicity is not simply public or nondomestic. The affective charge in the abortion controversy, as with all identity struggles, partly arises from the improvisations people make during moments of upheaval in their personal lives, whether or not their lives seem to intersect with struggles for power and legitimacy in the hegemonic public sphere. Sometimes, the experience of reproduction seems to circumvent the constraints of public discourse, seems wholly irrelevant to politics; yet sometimes even intensively personal experiences of intimate life register a virtually political sense that everything fragile and precious can fall apart, especially when one's intimate identity appears to be up for revision in public terms that are radically, incommensurably Other. In the latter case, reproductive politics can appear as a ghost or a euphemism in the way pregnancy and reproduction are described: a part of what is taken for granted in the way a woman and her partner negotiate the big change that is coming.

"I LOVE LUCY, AND SHE LOVES ME": WHO?[58]

No sweeter example of the anxiety wrought by changes in technology and privacy can be found than in the moment when, in October 1953, entertainment television became a reproductive technology. Due to the efforts of Desi Arnaz to incorporate the pregnant body of his wife, Lucille Ball, into that of the character Lucy Ricardo, real-time pregnancy was fictively narrated for the first time on American television. The discursive shift the narrative of Lucy's pregnancy represents involved exposing marital sexuality to the "domestic" national market: Arnaz had to argue with the sponsor, Philip Morris, and the Catholic Church, that pregnancy and childbirth in the domestic space of the Ricardo family would enhance the show's public status as moral exemplum and might additionally increase consumer identification with the family, the show, and the products whose advertisements make narrative consumption on television seem "free."[59]

Linking pregnancy to romance, sexuality, and foreignness by announcing Lucy's condition in French, the episode of *I Love Lucy* titled "Lucy Is *Enceinte*" broke the taboo on real-time reproductive representation that American television had always honored, and plotted its breaking of the silence as a rupture of other relations as well. Ethel walks into Lucy's apartment: "Hi, honey! Where are you going so early?"[60] Lucy responds that she feels "dauncy," and explains that this is a word her grandmother used to describe feeling "bleah" without being sick. Ethel wonders if Lucy is "going to have a baby." Lucy, incredulous, says, "A baby?" Ethel: "Baby. That's the word *my* grandmother made up for tiny little people." When the pregnant and ecstatic Lucy returns from the doctor, she says, "Ethel, we're going to have a baby!" Ethel responds, "We are? . . . I never had a baby before! I mean, I've never been let in on it so soon." Ricky Ricardo closes the show singing the song "We're Having a Baby, My Baby and Me," thus confirming that he, and not Ethel, is the baby's other parent. (Even Ricky's lucidity about the familial lines of reproduction is unsettled by the news: On hearing it he announces to his nightclub audience, "I'm going to be a father! Let me introduce you to my mother!") But the early scenes depicting Ethel and Lucy's confusion about the status of their intimacy remind us how thoroughly new knowledge about reproduction requires ad-libbing about identity and sociality outside the position "mother." Who is *having* the baby? The people who are "let in" to the reproduction via the forms of intimacy the mother deploys.

I Love Lucy introduces its consumers to pregnancy by contrasting the conventional practices of feminine masquerade with the world of actual theatricality, which includes, on this show, Ricky's professional work as a singer-actor.[61] Lucy describes to Ethel how often, in their lives, she has imagined the scene in which she tells Ricky, "Ricky, darling, our dream has come true. You and I are going to be blessed with something that means more to us than anything in the whole world." As she tells this to Ethel she makes such passionate love to her own hand that the embarrassed Ethel leaves the room. And when Ricky finally learns the news, after Lucy has given up on telling him directly, he is actually in a tuxedo

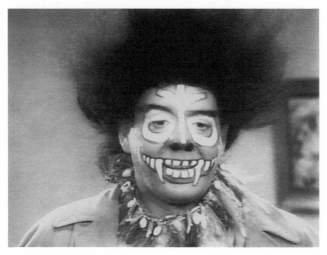

at the nightclub performing for an audience. When the baby is born, six episodes later, Ricky is also in the middle of a performance.

Ricky thinks he is singing "We're Having a Baby" to an unknowing husband/father-to-be, whose wife has sent a note to Ricky, asking him to deliver the message musically. Lucy is sitting in the audience. When Ricky sees the luster on Lucy's radiantly nodding face, he does the kind of theatrical double take one regularly sees in scenes of real-life surprise, realizing that the song he is singing about "our baby" is a song about himself. He brings Lucy up on stage and takes her in his arms, dances with her, and croons to her in her ear. They both weep while he is singing. The filmed audience becomes an absent fact and the TV viewer feels up close and personal. Because the announcement of pregnancy is so ritually invested with the promise of magical life transformation, because Lucy is actually the pregnant Lucille, and because, apparently, this fictional event mirrored the ten-year span of the actors' own failed attempts to get pregnant, the acted scene dissolves, the streaming tears of Lucy and Desi burning through the show's comic mediation of their marriage, merging the publicness and theatricality of pregnancy in ordinary life and the real struggles of intimate existence with the televisual "situation."

This surplus of failed performances reveals something of the wild improvisation pregnancy induces in the people whose world becomes officially unpredictable with its revelation: how do you tell, what do you tell, who do you tell, what are you telling, when you tell, even your closest friends, that you are pregnant? Even if you are sure that any baby you have might, as Ricky suggests, end up "at the White House," pregnancy reveals the motility of privacy and the chaos, not the certainty, of even the most authentic knowledge of authenticity that a baby is said to represent. The anarchy pregnancy incites in the most stable domestic world is further established in the birth episode, called "Lucy Goes to the Hospital," in which Ricky's national and sexual alterity to Lucy is figured in the costume he wears throughout the show: a barbarous mask and Afro wig for the "voodoo" number he performs in Spanish at the club. He frightens the hospital staff with it and they call the police onto the scene. But it is Ricky who finally faints from fright, when he sees the baby's newborn face.

INNERSPACE

When "star quality" refers to the relation between outer space and reproductive technologies, the aura of the natural that accompanies the fetus merges privacy and nationality in a way quite different than in the domestic scene of *I Love Lucy*. Zoe Sofia and Vivian Sobchack have expertly described the national/imperial politics of the final image of *2001: A Space Odyssey:* a huge, Lennart Nilssen-like fetus floating in space. This fetal image joins the movie camera and the special effect to the history of the telescope and the microscope's centrality to national fantasy: the authenticity putatively beyond family and nation that science secures for empire. They describe how the capacity to miniaturize made possible the lightness of the computer and the spaceship, enabling artificial knowledge to surpass self-knowledge, family identity, capital, politics, and earth itself; the fetus, in this regard, is the vehicle for merging technology with nature in its most primal incarnation. Sofia argues that the aura of nuclear annihilation becomes a part of an imperial/patriarchal erotics that focuses on the fetus as a sign that pure life will exist in the universe after nuclear death. Sobchack adds that "during this period, patriarchal and capitalist America was searching for a way to transform its moral guilt and its political, economic, and social failures at home and abroad into something more supportable. Toward the end of the seventies, popular imagery began transcoding American bourgeois culture's *lack of effectivity* into *child-like innocence,* and its *failed aggressivity* into a *transcendent victimization.*"[62]

Back on earth, nineteen years later, the same configuration of anxiety and aggressivity reappears in the film *Innerspace* (1987), a fetal screwball comedy, with its focus on the corporeal and imperial fantasies of the military-industrial complex. It has no interest in establishing providence and national holiness through fetal astral projection but rather locates the relation between fetality and banality within contemporary U.S. history and culture. In *Look Who's Talking,* the fetus is a featured player with more savvy wit and subjectivity than any adult: indeed, the film enacts the fetus's auratic decay as synonymous with the process of growing up. *Innerspace,* in contrast, describes, appropriately for its title, the banalization of private life, of the unspectacular everyday failed body, sexuality, and health of everyone who lives in Postmodernia, U.S.A. — Silicon Valley, California. In this context, the fetus represents the utopian Other — of everything imaginable. Untainted by the waste and violence of U.S. state capitalism, corporate bureaucracies, information culture, and consumer decadence, the miraculousness of the fetus is nonetheless available to Americans only by way of these very domains.

In addition, the forms of corporate power available to postmodern science fiction are here actively mapped onto disruptions of sexual norms. To map the heterosexual surface of the traditional screwball comedy onto sexual identifications after the 1960s requires redescribing, as well, the relation between gender, sexuality, and codes of humiliation in the Hollywood film. The fetal moment of *Innerspace* is the effect of many causes: Dennis Quaid, an alcoholic former ace Air Force officer, has been miniaturized and inserted into a syringe that will be shot into a rabbit (a rabbit test, whose archaic symbolic force as a medical test for pregnancy is not lost on the film); then, an attempt at international industrial espionage (the animus that drives the "plot") disrupts and botches the injection of Quaid into the rabbit; the scientist who escapes with the needle that contains Quaid gets shot from behind, staggers into a mall, where Martin Short, a grocery-store cashier, has just purchased cruise tickets; the scientist injects Dennis Quaid into Martin Short's derriere. The backside has been designated the body part of erotic choice by the end of the film's first segment, as a butt-naked Quaid is left howling on the streets of San Francisco after his journalist girlfriend, Meg Ryan, strips him of his towel, his sexual security, his self-esteem. This cathexis on, and injection into, the male derriere signifies this as an AIDS- and certainly a gay-conscious text, although not in a coherent way: the exchange of fluids and bodies in this sexual triangle plays a crucial role in vitalizing masculine heterosexuality in the narrative. Martin Short's femininity, established by his well-known Katharine Hepburn impersonation, is central to the star aura of the text; but Short, playing a nervous, sexually insipid hypochondriac, is actually masculinized and heterosexualized by carrying Quaid in his body. Inseminated with Quaid, he gets to be a spy, a policeman, a knight; he gets to act as a sexual relay between Quaid and Ryan.

In sum, *Innerspace* offers a kind of polymorphous sexual mobility as the heterosexuality of late capitalism. In the key scene of fetal imaging, Short romantically kisses Ryan and through his saliva transfers Quaid into her body. At first, Quaid, confused by the huge rush of fluid Short's arousal provokes in his body, floats in Ryan's body unaware, thinking he has remained in Short's. Suddenly, as his spaceship floats down, Quaid beholds a shocking thing: a fetus Ryan carries, a fetus Quaid and Ryan begot in the days when he was bigger than a sperm. The scene remasculinizes Quaid. He becomes a master of knowledge and its disciplinarian: on finally emerging from Short's body, his first question to Ryan is, "Why didn't you tell me?" Of course, she doesn't know that she's pregnant.

One lesson of *Innerspace* is that the cinematic fetus registers the emergence of cyborg masculinity, in contrast to the transformation of feminine power in the situation of the comedy in *I Love Lucy*. In addition, *Innerspace* shows that the cinematic meaning of "inner space" circulating around the fetus increasingly depends on conventions of communication outside a sacred/national discourse of "abstract" power. It takes up instead, as crisis, the secular problem of patriarchal sexual intersubjectivity in an age of miniaturization. (As one character in *Innerspace* says, "Space is a flop. Miniaturization, Jack: that's the ticket.") Miniaturization—or diminished expectations? The comedy of *Innerspace* is dark and bleeds into the male melodrama the public cinema of reproductive technology repeatedly stages: nightmares in which American white men can no longer assume a priori jurisdiction over space, nation, women, knowledge, scale, and size—in science, politics, and everyday life.

ZAK DAVIS: FROM SONOGRAM TO TWO YEARS

We can assume, by now, that explicit representations of the fetus in contemporary U.S. culture always refer to the semiotic fields of abortion, heterosexuality, gender properties, constitutional law, and national fantasy. But if the fetus must be revealed, must become photogenic, the historical information about power, authenticity, and futurity that its figure condenses must be linked to its utility as a sign of the ordinary as well. I have noted the new forms of affectivity that sonographic representation has generated for mothers. Their sensational knowledge of pregnancy superseded by the technical mastery of fetology, women report adapting to the prebirth personhood by giving the fetus interim names, framing its image, sharing it with friends and relatives. Hard evidence for this emerging transformation in the boundedness of domestic privacy is hard to come by, though the social energy generated by circulating sonograms and other new prenatal information is easy to come by anecdotally.[63] Ask anyone who has recently been pregnant. After seeing sonograms, my sister Valerie named one fetus "Buford" and another "Spud"; another friend called hers "Cletus the Fetus"; another named hers "Shrimp," another "Thumper," and so on. A standard comic hieroglyph for this phenomenon can also be found in an MTV-style video montage following the progress of Kirstie Alley's pregnancy in *Look Who's Talking*. Going through the motions of pregnancy sans husband, she gathers her women friends around her. Among sequences of their comic incompetence at decorating the baby's room and putting together baby furniture, the women cluster around Alley to coo at a series of sonogram images. The world-making force of the fetal image has also been used narratively as a charm to transform men from technical to affective fatherhood: in the film *Nine Months,* Hugh Grant succumbs to the lure of paternity on seeing the video of his potential son's sonogram (including the now conventional thrill at seeing a sonographic penis);

140

periodically, on the daytime soaps, men are roped into marriage by the aesthetic power that constitutes the agency of the imaged fetus.[64]

The nostalgic energy for a family that does not yet exist and has never existed enables the new reproductive technologies — which now include cinema and television — to exploit commodity identification for the purpose of promoting "family values," which are said to exist outside politics. The "family" is constituted by control over knowledge and representation, and has little to do with anyone's control over everyday practice or performance. In *Look Who's Talking,* the motivation for domesticity the cinema of the fetus represents might be a simple variation on the formula of the screwball comedy, in which the comedy of remarriage is modified into a comedy of marriage: the body of the sexually active, single, and pregnant woman represents the "family" already broken, a body whose wholeness resides only in the romantic fantasy lives of Alley and her friends. The creative child-care collaboration of Alley and John Travolta retrieves that fantasy into the reality of the film by the end, when Alley has a second baby and makes a nuclear, natural family from the scraps of intimacy it can collect.

Zak Davis: From Sonogram to Two Years is similarly a document of family-making, and like the other examples it could easily be characterized as a document tracing privileged assertions of intimate normativity. But I have tried to show that the aspiration to iconic normalcy denotes not the exception of identity formation in America but the conventional capital of mass national culture, the place where glamour and ordinariness meet in practical subjectivities. This videotape opens in the sonogram room, where my sister (Valerie), my mother (Joanne), the technician, and my brother-in-law (Richard) are commenting on the sonogram screen. Valerie and my mother are briefly visible in this scene; otherwise, the commentary is disembodied and the sonogram machine dominates the frame. Richard's voice carries a great deal of authority — he's a doctor, and he knows how to make home videos and to interpret the images Valerie generates. "Say 'Hi,' hon," Richard says to Valerie in the opening shot. "Hi, hon!" she says. Throughout, my sister makes jokes about her body (she shows the camera that her belly button has popped, she says "no crotch shots," she says she feels like a whale), but basically she is quiet and attentive; my pro-choice mother glosses the hard-to-read sonogram image ("He's a little person!"), hears an ambulance siren, makes a Nazi joke ("They're coming to get us!"), and conflates viewing with eating the fetus ("Isn't he delicious?"); Richard talks to the technician, alternating delight with shoptalk. In the next scene, the camera returns to the friendly salute, "Say 'Hi,' hon"/"Hi, hon!" Valerie shifts between explaining to the camera that she is in labor, and asking Richard the ordinary questions of domestic intimacy ("Do you think we should call the synagogue from the hospital?"). We see many segments of her descent or ascent into labor, each punctuated with "Say 'Hi,' hon"/"Hi, hon!" In the last, Valerie huddles in a fetal position, as if she is resting. She is connected to many monitors. She is green and shaking intensely in the dusky room. In response to Richard's request to say "'Hi,' hon," she lifts her hand at the camera and closes her eyes, exhausted.

The next sequences record the quite stunning baby right after the birth — getting weighed, being covered with a latex hat, crying. Richard talks empathetically to him from behind the camera, calls him "buddy"; then the grandparents join the parents and infant in the hospital room. The shots in the room are so beautifully, symmetrically arranged — one set of grandparents on each side of the bed, one set holding the baby, then the other — there seems nothing accidental or improvisational about this particular sequencing of family performance. Once he leaves the hospital, Zak's emergence into motor and psychic autonomy becomes visible: Zak is a lump with eyes dressed in clothes; Zak, propped on pillows, grabs helium balloons; Zak plays in the bathtub and watches himself in the mirror as his parents dry him. Richard and Valerie act as relaxed as laypeople being filmed can be, adapting the conventional oscillations of home-movie subjects between self-consciousness and obliviousness, involved as they are in the routines of everyday bodily maintenance in the nuclear household.

Then we arrive at Zak's first birthday. There is a special poignancy for me watching this first birthday, for I well remember Valerie's (she's five years younger than I am; we had just moved to a new house). On her first birthday, she was set in front of a huge chocolate-frosted cake; she delighted us all by smearing it all over her face and everything, in her first official assertion of agency and competence, or sentience. Either Zak has inherited this will to pleasure from his mother, or the home movies and pictures from Valerie's birthday have become so iconic in the rituals of our family memory that she arranged his scene as a repetition of her own. In any case, the scene of my memory is reproduced in the video, as from a painting.[65] At one point, Valerie sets Zak up with his presents. We watch him learning what a gift is, and learning how to prolong anticipation by

opening it slowly. As a one-year-old, he is barely competent to sit up, anticipate, and open presents all at once. Finally, he gets the wrapping off the huge present his grandparents have given him. This present seems not especially to move him (the way his Teenage Mutant Ninja Turtles delight him on his second birthday), but Valerie and Richard seem to watch with pleasure as Zak pulls from his first-birthday-present box — what else? — six videotapes.

When I watched this, I felt how totally appropriate it was that Zak received videotapes on his first birthday. He was constituted in Valerie's memory as a sonogram, in his own and mine as a sonogram on a videotape. He is fundamentally the star of his own video, his life. He identifies totally with the stars he watches on the VCR and takes on their identities in play. The ease with which video can be made, purchased, copied, and circulated brings the quotidian into our collective memory of him in such a way that the accident of the cartoon videos he received seemed also an accidental truth about him, and the future of his history. For even if the fetus as a person has become ordinary in popular discourse, the new technology also generates a sense of surprise, contingency, and accident that foregrounds the ways popular technologies alter the possibilities of enacting identity in personal, as well as political, domains of information and entertainment.

This is not simply an instance of evaluating the technology of middle-class familial theatricality in late capitalism: the video camera is a direct extension of the portable camera, whose mass production reconstructed childhood and domestic memory, as Bourdieu and Barthes have described, since the turn of the century.[66] In addition, the contrast between the formal superpersonality of Zak, Buford, Spud, Cletus the Fetus, and Shrimp, on the one hand, and the generic fetality of the unnamed "unborn" heralded by pro-life activists, on the other, is worth investigating, because the authority of the information that circulates around them and gives them identity reveals harshly the fault lines that separate forms of identity politics in America today, showing, as well, the limits of identity and expressivity as forms of optimism and resistance. As in the case of Alley's figure in *Look Who's Talking*, we witness a bubbling over of hegemonic icons and marginal stereotypes, in a way that marks its politics as epochal, historic, and in the present tense.

Benedict Anderson writes that the entombed "unknown soldier" must be personally anonymous in order to sanctify the nationality of life and death: the muteness of the soldier's historicity is the setting for the jewel of his nationality.[67] I read that the Roman Catholic Church plans to erect Tombs of the Unknown Fetus in Catholic cemeteries throughout America; the anonymity of the fetus becomes a necessary precondition to the form of politically useful empathy constructed by the pro-life movement.[68]

But it does not follow that naming or any kind of imaging secures historicity and human justice to the person. Nor does it follow that pro-choice citizens must produce a counterfetus of some sort to supplant the powerful and banal subject that has been installed in the archive of the National Symbolic, for this image would at best only be additive. There is no formal solution to the problem of citizenship the exposed fetus raises for fetuses, women, mothers, Americans. When the state regulates foreign-aid packages according to the birth-control policies of less industrialized nations while profiting from military-industrial labor exploitation in America and elsewhere, or when social-welfare policies can be justified only for the sake of "the children," we know that the political imagination's displacement away from adults to the horizon of "our children" or "the unborn" signifies a widespread incapacity to conceive, with the overabundance of information we already have, a positive sense of the present or the future of the adult American. Fetuses become the "problem" in the absence of a sustained critical national political culture. Meanwhile, the ongoing practices of a personal-information public generate new forms of sociality that displace the spheres of mass politics, with consumers bored and alienated from even the banalized sensational versions of their own lives they receive from docudrama, infomercials, and political news propaganda. "Hi, hon!" As I write this sentence, a letter to unnamed recipients (who might respond, "I'm Batman!"), the television news anchor reports that someone else's home video has become important news. She closes the story, noting, "This video is being sent to the Smithsonian."

4   Queer Nationality

(written with Elizabeth Freeman)

. . . now the skins felt powerful and human.
They became lords of sounds and lesser things.
They passed nations through their mouths.
They sat in judgement.
  — Zora Neale Hurston

We Are Everywhere. We Want Everything.
  — Queer Nation, Gay Pride parade, New York, 1991

I Pledge Allegiance to the F(l)ag

At the end of Sandra Bernhard's *Without* You *I'm Nothing*, the diva wraps
herself in an American flag. This act, which emblazons her interpretation
of Prince's "Little Red Corvette," culminates her performance of feminine drag, feminist camp. Staging not a cross-dressing that binarizes sex
but a masquerade that smudges the clarity of gender, Bernhard frames
"woman" within a constellation of sexual practices whose forms of publicity change by the decade, by subcultural origin, by genres of pleasure (music, fashion, political theater), and by conventions of collective
erotic fantasy. But having sexually overdressed for the bulk of the film,
Bernhard strips down to a flag and a sequined red, white, and blue
G-string and pasties, and thus exposes a national body, her body. This
national body does not address a mass or abstract audience of generic
Americans, nor does it campily evoke a "typical" American citizen's nostalgia for collective memory, ritual, and affect. Bernhard flags her body
to mark a fantasy of erotic identification with someone present, in the
intimate room: it is a national fantasy, displayed as a spectacle of desire,
and a fantasy apparently external to the official national frame, of com-
munion with a black woman whose appearance personifies authenticity.

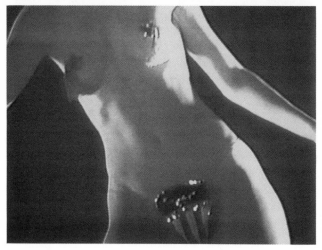

At the same time, also in 1990, Madonna responded to a civic crisis marked by voter apathy among youth by performing in a pro-voting commercial stripped down to a bikini and wrapped alluringly in an American flag. In this commercial, the blond bombshell is flanked by a black man and a white man, both of whom are dressed in the clone semiotic that flags a certain East Coast urban gay community style. These men sing "Get Out and Vote" in discordant comic harmony with Madonna, while they wave little flags and she flashes her body by undulating a big one.

In March 1991, the Sunday fashion section of the *Chicago Tribune* featured the Gulf War as a fashion event. Adding to the already widely publicized rush by citizens to own their very own gas masks and military fatigues, supplementing the fad for patriotic T-shirts and sweatshirts bearing American flags and mottoes like "These Colors Won't Run," this style section featured the new rage in feminine fashion: red, white, and blue. Mobilized by the patriotic furor generated by the war, women en masse were signifying through the color combination and not the icon, capitalizing on the capacity of the flag's traces to communicate personal politics without explicit polemic. The dissolution of the flag into flagness also protected the consumer from being charged with desecrating the flag, should it become stained with food or sweat, or singed with the dropped ashes of a cigarette.

In 1991 *RFD,* a magazine for rural gays with connections to the Radical Faeries, released a poster featuring a naked young white man with an erection on a pedestal, set against the background of an American flag. Two captions graced this portrait: "BRING OUR BOYS HOME AND WHOLE THIS SOLSTICE PEACE NOW!" and "What could be more American than young, hard man/boy flesh?"

A rhetorical question? Having witnessed this rush to consume the flag, to fuse it with the flesh, we conclude that at present the nation suffers from Americana nervosa, a compulsive self-gorging on ritual images. This grotesque fantasy structure was paraded in the 1988 presidential election by the Republican flap over whether citizens should be legally obliged to say the Pledge of Allegiance. It was further extended from mass public struggle into the Supreme Court by constitutional battles over whether the flag should be exposed to mortality's contagion in the form of its own ashes or dirt, and has recast national patriotism as a question, not of political identity, but of proper public expression, loyal self-censorship, and personal discipline. No longer is the struggle to secure national discursive propriety located mainly on the general terrain of "freedom of speech," state policies against certain sexual practices, and the regulation of privately consumed sexual images within the U.S. mail: the struggle is now also over proper public submission to national iconicity and over the nation's relation to gender, to sexuality, and to death.

If, in the wake of the election and the remilitarization of America, official patriotic discourse casts the American flag in an epidemic crisis and struggles to manage its public meaning through a sublime collective manufactured consent, the consumption of nationality in the nineties appears motivated not by a satisfaction that already exists but by a collective desire to reclaim the nation for pleasure, and specifically the pleasure of spectacular public self-entitlement. Queer Nation has taken up the project of coordinating a new nationality. Its relation to nationhood is multiple and ambiguous, however, taking as much from the insurgent nationalisms of oppressed peoples as from the revolutionary idealism of the United States. Since its inception in 1990, it has invented collective local rituals of resistance, mass cultural spectacles, an organization, and even a lexicon to achieve these ends. It aims to capitalize on the difficulty of locating the national "public," whose consent to self-expression founds modern national identity.[1]

Queer Nation's outspoken promotion of a national sexuality not only discloses that mainstream national identity touts a subliminal sexuality more official than a state flower or national bird, but also makes explicit how thoroughly the local experience of the body is framed by laws, policies, and social customs regulating sexuality. Queer Nation's tactics of invention appropriate for gay politics both grassroots and mass-mediated forms of countercultural resistance from left, feminist, and civil-rights movements of the sixties — the ones that insisted that the personal is political, engaging the complex relation between local and national practices. Also, in the nostalgic impulse of postmodernism, Queer Nation redeploys these tactics in a kind of guerrilla warfare that names all concrete and abstract spaces of social communication as places where "the people" live, and thus as "national" sites ripe for both transgression and legitimate visibility.[2] Its tactics are to cross borders, to occupy spaces, and to mime the privileges of normality — in short, to simulate "the national" with a camp inflection. This model of political identity imitates not so much the "one man, one vote" caucus polemic mentality of mainstream politics, but rather the individual and mass identities of consumers: Queer Nation, itself a collection of "local" affinity groups, has produced images, occupied public spaces of consumption, like bars and malls, and refunctioned the culture of the trademark.[3] Exploiting the structures of identification and the embodied and disembodied scenes of erotic contact, substitution, publicity, and exchange so central to the allure of nationalism and capitalism, Queer Nation operates precisely in the American mode.[4]

In this chapter we seek to understand the political logic of Queer Nationality and to trace the movement's spectacular intentions and effects. We will, in the next three sections, describe Queer Nation in its strongest tactical moments, as when it exploits the symbolic designs of mass and national culture in order to dismantle the standardizing apparatus that organizes all manner of sexual practice into "facts" of sexual *identity*,[5] as when it mobilizes a radically wide range of knowledge — modes of understanding from science to gossip — to reconstitute "information" about queerness, thus transforming the range of reference "queer" has by multiplying its specifications.[6] Whether or not Queer Nation survives as an organization past the present tense of our writing,[7] the movement provides us with these discursive political tactics not simply as fodder for history but also as a kind of incitement to reformulate the conditions under which further interventions into the juridical, policy, and popular practices of contemporary America must be thought and made.[8]

This demands an expanded politics of description. We might say "an expanded politics of *erotic* description," but crucial to a sexually radical movement for social change is the transgression of categorical distinctions between sexuality and politics, with their typically embedded divisions between public, private, and personal concerns. The multiplicity of social spaces, places where power and desire are enacted and transferred, need to be disaggregated and specified. The abstract, disembodied networks of electronic visual, aural, and textual communication, the nationalized systems of juridical activity and official public commentary, the state and local political realms that are not at all simply microcosmic of the national: all coexist with both the manifestly pleasuring or money-making embodiments of local, national, and global capitalism, and with the random or customary interactions of social life — this sentence could, and must, go on interminably. These spaces are hard to describe, because they are all unbounded, dialectically imagined, sometimes powerful, and sometimes irrelevant to the theory, practice, and transformation of sexual hegemony. Whatever they are, at the moment they are resolutely national. Queer Nation's nationalist-style camp counterpolitics incorporates this discursive and territorial problem, shifting between a utopian politics of identity, difference, dispersion, and specificity and a pluralist agenda, in the liberal sense, that imagines a "gorgeous mosaic" of difference without a model of conflict. Our final section, "With *You* Out We're Nothing, and Beyond," supports and extends Queer Nation's contestation of existing cultural spaces, but seeks to reopen the question of nationalism's value as an infidel model of transgression and resistance, for the very naturalizing stereotypes of official nationality can inflect even the most radical insurgent forms. In other words, this is an antiassimilationist narrative about an antiassimilationist movement. It must be emphasized, however, that disidentification with U.S. nationality is not, at this moment, even a theoretical option for queer citizens: as long as PWAS (People with AIDS) require state support, as long as the official nation invests its identity in the pseudoright to police nonnormative sexual representations and sexual practices, the lesbian, gay, feminist, and queer communities in the United States do not have the privilege to disregard national identity. We are compelled, then, to read America's lips. What can we do to force the officially constituted nation to speak a new political tongue?

Recently, official America has sought to manage an explicit relation between national power and the vulnerable body by advertising an unironic consecration of masculine military images and surgical incisions into the borders of other sovereign nations. Queer Nation, in dramatic contrast, produces images in response to the massive violence against racial, sexual, gendered, and impoverished populations within the U.S. borders, a violence emblematized by, but in no way limited to, the federal response to AIDS. A brief history of the movement will help explain the genesis of its polymorphous impulses. Founded at an ACT UP New York meeting in April of 1990, Queer Nation aimed to extend the kinds of democratic counterpolitics deployed on behalf of AIDS activism for the transformation of public sexual discourse in general. Crimp and Rolston's *AIDS Demo Graphics* is to date the fullest and most graphic record of ACT UP's intervention into local, state, and national systems of power and publicity.[9] This specification of mainstream sites of power was made necessary by federal stonewalling on the subject of AIDS treatment, support, and education among institutions in the political public sphere, where the bureaucratic norm is to disavow accountability to vulnerable populations. ACT UP recognizes the necessity to master the specific functions of political bureaucracies and to generate loud demands that these live up to their promise to all of "the people." Among other strategies, it exploits the coincidence between national and commercial spectacle by pirating advertising techniques: an alliance with the political artists called Gran Fury has produced a sophisticated poster campaign to transform the passive public space of New York into a zone of political pedagogy. Queer Nation takes from ACT UP this complex understanding of political space as fundamental to its insistence on making all public spheres truly safe for all of the persons who occupy them, not just in psychic loyalty but in everyday and embodied experience. To be safe in the national sense means not just safe from bashing, not just safe from discrimination, but safe *for* demonstration, in the mode of patriotic ritual, which always involves a deployment of affect, knowledge, spectacle, and, crucially, a kind of banality, ordinariness, popularity.

> Through its activism Queer Nation seeks to redefine the community—its rights, its visibility—and take it into what's been claimed as straight political and social space. "QUEERS READ THIS" asks to be read as the accompanying declaration of nationalism. It says: In this culture, being queer means you've been condemned to death; appreciate our power and our bond; realize that whenever one of us is hurt we all suffer; know that we have to fight for ourselves because no one else will. It says, this is why we are a *nation* of queers, and why you must feel yourself a part. Its language seems to borrow from other, equally "threatening" power movements—black nationalist, feminist separatist.[10]

The key to the paradoxes of Queer Nation is the way it *exploits* internal difference. That is, Queer Nation understands the propriety of queerness to be a function of the diverse spaces in which it aims to become explicit. It names multiple local and national publics; it does not look for a theoretical coherence to regulate in advance all of its tactics: all politics in the Queer Nation are imagined on the *street*. Finally, it always refuses closeting strategies of assimilation and goes for the broadest and most explicit assertion of presence. This loudness involves two main kinds of public address: internal, for the production of safe collective queer spaces, and external, in a cultural pedagogy emblematized by the post-Black Power slogan "We're Here. We're Queer. Get Used to It." If "I'm Black and I'm Proud" sutures the first-person performative to racial visibility, transforming the speaker from racial object to ascendant subject, Queer Nation's slogan stages the shift from silent absence into present speech, from nothingness to collectivity, from a politics of embodiment to one of space, whose power erupts from the ambiguity of "here." Where?

Inside: I Hate Straights, and
Other "Queeritual" Prayers

Nancy Fraser's recent essay on postmodernity and identity politics argues that countercultural groups engage in a dialectic with mainstream public culture, shifting between internal self-consolidation and reinvestment of the irrelatively essentialist "internal" identity into the normalizing discussions of the mass public sphere.[11] In this dialectic, the subaltern indeed becomes a speaking player in her own public identity, for the public is an intelligibly "dominant" space characterized by collective norms. Fraser's model does not work for Queer Nation, which neither recognizes a single internal or privatized interest nor certifies one mainstream whose disposition constitutes the terrain for counterpolitics. This distinguishing mark of Queer Nation — its capacity to include cultural resistance, opposition, and subcultural consolidation in a mix of tactics from identity politics and postmodern metropolitan information flows — will thus govern our inside narrative. We will shuttle between a dispersed variety of Queer National events, falsely bringing into narrative logic and collective intentionality what has been a deliberately unsystematized politics.

If there is one manifesto of this polyvocal movement, defining the lamination of a gay liberation politics and new gay power tactics, it is, famously, the "I Hate Straights" polemic distributed as a broadside at the Gay Pride parades in New York and Chicago in the summer of 1990. "I Hate Straights," printed (at least in Chicago) over the image of a raised clenched masculine fist, is a monologue, a slave narrative without decorum, a manifesto of rage and its politics. Gone, the assimilationist patience of some gay liberation identity politics; gone, the assertive rationality of the "homosexual" subject who seeks legitimacy by signifying, through "straight" protocols, that "civilization" has been sighted on the cultural margin.[12]

"I Hate Straights," instead, "proceeds in terms of the unavoidable usefulness of something that is very dangerous."[13] What is dangerous is rage, and the way it is deployed both to an "internal" audience of gay subjects and an "external" straight world. The broadside begins with personal statements: "I have friends. Some of them are straight. Year after year, I see my straight friends. I want to see them, to see how they are doing . . . [and] [y]ear after year I continue to realize that the facts of my life are irrelevant to them and that I am only half listened to." The speaker remains unheard because straights refuse to believe that gay subjects are in exile from privilege, from ownership of a point of view that American social institutions and popular cultural practices secure: "insiders claim that [gays] already are" included in the privileges of the straight world. But gay subjects are excluded from the privileges of procreation, of family, of the public fantasy that circulates through these institutions: indeed, it seems that only the public discipline of gayness keeps civilization from "melt[ing] back into the primeval ooze."

In the face of an exile caused by this arrogant heterosexual presumption of domestic space and privilege, the speaker lights into a list of proclamations headed by "I hate straights": "I" hates straights on behalf of the gay people who have to emotionally "take care" of the straights who feel guilty for their privilege; "I" hates straights for requiring the sublimation of gay rage as the price of their beneficent tolerance. "You'll catch more flies with honey," the speaker hears; "Now look who's generalizing," they say, as if the minoritized group itself had invented the "crude taxonomy" under which it labored.[14] In response, the flyer argues, "BASH BACK . . . LET YOURSELF BE ANGRY . . . THAT THERE IS NO PLACE IN THIS COUNTRY WHERE WE ARE SAFE."

The speaker's designation of "country" as the space of danger complexly marks the indices of social identity through which this invective circulates. "I" mentions two kinds of "we": gay and American subjects, all of whom have to "thank President Bush for planting a fucking tree" in public while thousands of PWAs die for lack of political visibility. The nation of the Bush and the tree here becomes a figure of "nature" that includes the malignant neglect of AIDS populations, including and especially (here) gay men. Straights ask the gay community to self-censor, because anger is not "productive." Meanwhile, the administrators of straight America commit omissions of policy to assert that healthy heterosexual identity (the straight and undiseased body) is a prerequisite to citizenship of the United States. The treatise goes on to suggest that the national failure to secure justice for all citizens is experienced locally, in public spaces where physical gay-bashing takes place, and in even more intimate sites like the body: "Go tell [straights] to go away until they have spent a month walking hand in hand in public with someone of the same sex. After they survive that, then you'll hear what they have to say about queer anger. Otherwise, tell them to shut up and listen."

The distribution of this document to a predominantly gay population at Gay Pride parades underscores a fundamental Queer Nation policy. *Visibility* is critical if a safe public existence is to be forged for American gays, for whom the contemporary nation has no positive political value. The cities where Queer Nation lives already contain local gay communities, locales that secure spaces of safe embodiment for capital and sexual expenditures. For Queer Nation, they also constitute sites within which political bases can be founded. This emphasis on safe spaces, secured for bodies by capital and everyday life practices also, finally, constitutes a refusal of the terms national discourse uses to frame the issue of sexuality: "Being queer is not about a right to privacy: it is about the freedom to be public. . . . It's not about the mainstream, profit-margins, patriotism, patriarchy or being assimilated. . . . Being queer is grass roots because we know that everyone of us, every body, every cunt, every heart and ass and dick is a world of pleasure waiting to be explored. Everyone of us is a world of infinite possibility." Localness, here transposed into the language of worldness, is dedicated to producing a new politics from the energy of a sentimentally and erotically excessive sexuality. The ambiguities of this sexual geography are fundamental to producing the new referent, a gay community whose erotics and politics are transubstantial. Meanwhile, in the hybrid Queer/American nation, orthodox forms of political agency linger, in modified form. For example, Queer Nation proclaims, "An army of lovers cannot lose!" But this military fantasy refers in its irony to a set of things: counterviolences in local places, sixties movements to make love, not war, and also the invigorated persecution of queer subjects in the U.S. military during the Reagan/Bush years.

Thus too the "queeritual" element in some Queer Nation productions exceeds American proprieties, replacing the secular pledge to the flag in broadsides headed "I praise life with my vulva" and "I praise God with my erection."[15] Although we might say that this queerituality is reactionary, reflecting a suprapolitical move to spiritual identity, we might also say that this is literally conservative, an attempt to save space for hope, prayer, and simple human relations—a Queer Nation "Now I lay me down to sleep." These pieties assert the luck the praying subjects feel to be sleeping with someone of their own sex, thus promoting "homosexuality" in the way Queer Nation wants to do, as a mode of ordinary identification and pleasure. But these prayers also parody the narrative convention of normative prayer to find a safe space for eluding official and conventional censorship of public sexuality: *Thing* magazine reports, indeed, that the broadside has come under criticism for seeming to promote promiscuity.[16] In our view, the prayers counter the erotophobia of gay and straight publics who want to speak of "lifestyles" and not sex. Finally, just as the genre of the circulating broadside reveals how gay and straight populations topographically overlap, so does this use of prayer itself avow the futility of drawing comprehensive affective boundaries between gay and straight subjects. Queer Nation's emphasis on public language and media, its exploitation of the tension between local embodiment and mass abstraction, forfeits the possibility of such tax-onomic clarity.

Outside: Politics in Your Face

On February 23, 1967, in a congressional hearing concerning the security clearance of gay men for service in the Defense Department, a psychiatrist named Dr. Charles Socarides testified that the homosexual "does not know the boundary of his own body. . . . He does not know where his body ends and space begins."[17] Precisely—the spiritual and other moments of internal consolidation which we have described allow the individual bodies of Queer Nationals to act as visibly queer flashcards, in an ongoing project of cultural pedagogy aimed at exposing the range and variety of bounded spaces upon which heterosexual supremacy depends. Moving out from the psychological and physical "safe spaces" it creates, Queer Nation broadcasts the straightness of public space, and hence its explicit or implicit danger to gays. The queer body—as an agent of publicity, as a unit of self-defense, and finally as a spectacle of ecstasy—becomes the locus where mainstream culture's discipline of gay citizens is written and where the pain caused by this discipline is transformed into rage and pleasure. Using alternating strategies of menace and merriment, agents of Queer Nation have come to see and conquer places that present the danger of *violence* to gays and lesbians, to reterritorialize them.

Twenty-three years after Dr. Socarides' mercifully brief moment of fame, New Yorkers began to display on their chests a graphic interpretation of his fear for the national defense. The T-shirt they wore portrays a silhouette of the United States, with the red tint of the East Coast and the blue tint of the West Coast fading and blending in the middle. Suddenly, the heartland of the country is a shocking new shade of queer: red, white, and blue make lavender. This, Queer Nation's first T-shirt, extends the project of an earlier graphic produced by Adam Rolston, which shows a placard that reads, "I Am Out, Therefore I Am." But Queer Nation's shirt locates the public space in which the individual Cartesian subject must be out, transforming that space in order to survive. Queer Nation's design maps a psychic and bodily territory which cannot be colonized—lavender territory—and expands it to include, potentially, the entire nation. This lamination of the country to the body conjoins individual and national liberation: just as Dr. Socarides dreaded, the boundaries between what constitutes individual and what constitutes national space are explicitly blurred. "National defense" and "heterosexual defense" become interdependent projects of boundary maintenance that Queer Nation graphically undermines, showing that these colors *will* run.

While the Queer Nation shirt exploits heterosexist fears of the "spread of a lifestyle" through dirty laundry by publicizing its wearer as both a gay native and a missionary serving the spread of homosexuality, not all of their tactics are this benign. The optimistic assertion that an army of lovers cannot lose masks the seriousness with which Queer Nation has responded to the need for a pseudomilitia on the order of the Guardian Angels. The Pink Panthers, initially conceived of at a Queer Nation meeting (they are now a separate organization), provided a searing response to the increased violence that has accompanied the general increase of gay visibility in America. The Panthers, a foot patrol which straddles the "safe spaces" described in the first section of this chapter and the "unsafe spaces" of public life in America, not only defend other queer bodies but aim to be a continual reminder of them. Dressed in black T-shirts with pink triangles enclosing a black paw print, they move unarmed in groups, linked by walkie-talkies and whistles. In choosing a uniform which explicitly marks them as targets, as successors of the Black Power movement, and as seriocomic detectives, the Panthers bring to-gether the abstract threat implicit in the map graphic described above, the embodied threat implicit in individual queers' crossing their sub-cultural boundaries, and the absurdity that founds this condition of sexual violence.

The Panthers' slogan is "Bash Back." It announces that the locus of gay oppression has shifted from the legal to the extralegal arena, and from national-juridical to ordinary everyday forms.[18] The menace of "Bash Back" reciprocates the menace of physical violence that keeps gays and lesbians invisible and/or physically restricted to their mythically safe neighborhoods. But rather than targeting specific gay bashers or lashing out at random heterosexuals, the Panthers train in self-defense tech-niques and travel unarmed: "Bash Back" simply intends to mobilize the threat gay bashers use so effectively — strength not in numbers but in the presence of a few bodies who represent the potential for widespread violence — against the bashers themselves. In this way, the slogan turns the bodies of the Pink Panthers into a psychic counterthreat, expanding their protective shield beyond the confines of their physical "beat." Perhaps the most assertive "bashing" that the uniformed bodies of the Pink Panthers deliver is mnemonic. Their spectacular presence counters heterosexual culture's will not to recognize its own intense need to reign in a sexually pure environment.

While the rage of "Bash Back" responds to embodied and overt violence, Queer Nation's "Queer Nights Out" redress the more diffuse and implicit violence of sexual conventionality by mimicking the hackneyed forms of straight social life. Queer Nights Out are moments of radical desegregation with roots in Civil Rights-era lunch counter sit-ins; whereas the sixties sit-ins addressed legal segregation, these queer sorties confront customary segregation. Invading straight bars, for example, they stage a production of sentimentality and pleasure that broadcasts the ordinariness of the queer body. The banality of twenty-five same-sex couples making out in a bar, the silliness of a group of fags playing spin the bottle, efface the distance crucial to the ordinary pleasures straight society takes in the gay world. Neither informational nor particularly spectacular, Queer Nights Out demonstrate two ominous truths to heterosexual culture: (1) gay sexual identity is no longer a reliable foil for straightness; (2) what looked like bounded gay subcultural activity has itself become restless and improvisatory, taking its pleasures in a theater near you.

Queer Nights Out have also appropriated the model of the surprise attack, which the police have traditionally used to show gays and lesbians that even the existence of their subcultural spaces is contingent upon the goodwill of straights. Demonstrating that the boundedness of heterosexual spaces is also contingent upon the (enforced) willingness of gays to remain invisible, queers are thus using exhibitionism to make public space psychically unsafe for unexamined heterosexuality. In one report from the field, two lesbians were sighted sending a straight woman an oyster, adding a sapphic appetizer to the menu of happy-hour delights. The straight woman was not amused.[19] Embarrassment was generated — the particular embarrassment liberals suffer when the sphere allotted to the tolerated exceeds the boundaries "we all agree upon." Maneuvers such as this reveal that straight mating techniques, supposed to be "Absolutely Het," are sexual lures available to any brand of pleasure: "Sorry, you looked like a dyke to me."[20] This political transgression of "personal space" can even be used to deflect the violence it provokes. Confronted by a defensive and hostile drunk, a Queer Nation gayboy addresses the room: "Yeah, I had him last night, and he was terrible."

In this place of erotic exchange, the army of lovers takes as its war strategies "some going-down and buttfucking and other forms of theatre."[21] The genitals become not just organs of erotic thanksgiving, but weapons of pleasure against their own oppression. These kinds of militantly erotic interventions take their most public form in the Queer Nation kiss-in, in which an official space such as a city plaza is transfused with the juices of unofficial enjoyment: embarrassment, pleasure, spectacle, longing, and accusation interarticulate to produce a public scandal that is, as the following section will reveal, Queer Nation's specialty.

Hyperspace: "Try Me On, I'm Very You"[22]

In its most postmodern moments, Queer Nation takes on a corporate strategy in order to exploit the psychic unboundedness of consumers who depend upon products to articulate, produce, and satisfy their desires. Queer Nation tactically uses the hyperspaces created by the corporeal trademark, the metropolitan parade, the shopping mall, print media, and, finally, advertising, to recognize and take advantage of the consumer's pleasure in vicarious identification. In this guise, the group commandeers permeable sites, apparently apolitical spaces through which the public circulates in a pleasurable consensual exchange of bodies, products, identities, and information. Yet it abandons the conciliatory mode of, for instance, Kirk and Madsen's plan to market "positive" (read "tolerable") gay images to straight culture.[23] Instead, it aims to produce a series of elaborate blue-light specials on the queer body. The Queer National corporate strategy — to reveal to the consumer desires he didn't know he had, to make his identification with the product "homosexuality" both an unsettling and a pleasurable experience — makes consumer pleasure central to the transformation of public culture, thus linking the utopian promises of the commodity with those of the nation.

One particular celebrity oscillates between local/embodied and corporate/abstract sexual identification: the bootleg "Queer Bart" T-shirt produced by Queer Nation in the summer of 1990. Queer Bart reconfigures Matt Groening's bratty white suburban "anykid," Bart Simpson, into the New York gay clone: he wears an earring, his own Queer Nation T-shirt, and a pink triangle button. The balloon coming out of his mouth reads, "Get used to it, dude!" Like all bodies, Queer Bart's body is a product that serves a number of functions. In the first place, he provides a countertext to the apparent harmlessness of the suburban American generic body: Queer Nation's Bart implicitly points a finger at another bootleg T-shirt on which Bart snarls, "Back off, faggot!" and at the heterosexuality that Regular Bart's generic identity assumes. In the second place, the original Bart's "cloneness," when inflected with an "exceptional" identity—Black Bart, Latino Bart, and so on—not only stages the ability of subcultures to fashion cultural insiderhood for their members but also reinscribes subcultural identity into mainstream style. The exuberant inflection of Bart Simpson as queer speaks to the pleasures of assuming an "official" normative identity, signified on the body, for those whom dominant culture consistently represents as exceptional.

Queer Nation's reinflection of Bart's body, which, precisely because it *is* a body, readily lends itself to any number of polymorphously perverse identities, graphically demonstrates that the commodity is a central means by which individuals tap into the collective experience of public desire. Queer Bart, himself a trademark, is a generic body stamped with Queer Nation's own trademarked aesthetic, which then allows the consumer to publicly identify him-/herself as a member of a trademarked "nation."[24] Thus, Bart embodies the nonspaces we will discuss in the following paragraphs. His own unboundedness as a "commodity identity" exploits the way that the fantasy of "being" something else merges with the stereotype to confer an endlessly shifting series of identities upon the consumer's body.[25]

The genealogy of the Queer Bart strategy extends from the Gay Pride parades of the 1970s, when, for the first time, gay bodies organized into a visible public ritual. In addition to offering gays and lesbians an opportunity to experience their private identities in an "official" spectacle, the parades also offered flamboyant and ordinary homosexuality as something the heterosexual spectator could encounter without having to go "underground"—to drag shows or gay bars—for voyeuristic pleasure or casual sex.[26] In the last twenty years, the representation of "gayness" in the Gay Pride parade has changed, for its marching population is no longer defined by sexual practice alone. Rather, the current politicization of gay issues has engendered broadly based alliances, such that progressive "straights" can pass as "queer" in their collective political struggles.[27] As a result, the Gay Pride parade no longer produces the ominous gust of an enormous closet door opening; its role in consolidating iden-

tity varies widely, depending on what kind of communication participants think the parade involves. While Gay Pride parades have not yet
achieved the status in mainstream culture of, for instance, St. Patrick's
Day parades (in which people "go Irish for a day" by dressing in green),
they have thus become pluralistic and inclusive, involving approval-
seeking, self-consolidating, and saturnalian and transgressive moments
of spectacle.[28] Although Queer Nation marches in traditional Gay Pride
parades, it has updated and complicated the strategy of the parade, recognizing that the planned, distanced, and ultimately contained nature of
the form offers only momentary displacement of heterosexual norms:
after all, one can choose not to go to a parade, or one can watch the scene
go by without becoming even an imaginary participant.

   In parades through urban American downtowns, Queer Nationals
often chant, "We're here, we're queer, we're not going shopping." But
shopping itself provides the form of a tactic when Queer Nation enters
another context: the Queer Shopping Network of New York and the
Suburban Homosexual Outreach Program (SHOP) of San Francisco
have taken the relatively bounded spectacle of the urban pride parade to
the ambient pleasures of the shopping mall. "Mall visibility actions" thus
conjoin the spectacular lure of the parade with Hare Krishna-style "conversion" and "proselytizing" techniques. Stepping into malls in hair-
gelled splendor, holding hands and handing out fliers, the queer auxili-
aries produce an "invasion" which conveys a different message: "We're
here, we're queer, *you're* going shopping."

   These miniature parades transgress an erotically, socially, and economically complex space. Whereas patrons of the straight bar at least understand the bar's function in terms of pleasure and desire, mall-goers invest
in the shopping mall's credentials as a "family" environment, an environment which "creates a nostalgic image of a clean, safe, legible town
center."[29] In dressing up and stepping out queer, the Network uses the
bodies of its members as billboards to create what Mary Ann Doane calls
"the desire to desire."[30] As Queer Shoppers stare back, kiss, pose, they
disrupt the antiseptic asexual surface of the malls, exposing them as
sites of any number of explicitly sexualized exchanges — cruising, people
watching, window-shopping, trying on outfits, purchasing commodities, and having anonymous sex.[31]

The inscription of metropolitan sexuality in a safe space for suburban-
style normative sexual repression is just one aspect of the Network's

critical pedagogy. In addition, mall actions exploit the utopian function
of the mall, which connects information about commodities with sensual expressivity and which predicts that new erotic identities can be
sutured to spectacular consuming bodies. The Queer Shopping Network understands the most banal of advertising strategies: sex sells. In
this case, though, sex sells not substitutions for bodily pleasures — a car, a
luxury scarf — but the capacity of the body itself to experience unofficial
pleasures. While the Network appears to be merely handing out another
commodity in the form of broadsides about homosexuality, its ironic
awareness of itself as being on display links gay spectacle with the window displays that also entreat the buyers. Both say "buy me," but the
Queer Shopping Network tempts consumers with a commodity that, if
they could recognize it, they already own: a sexually inflected and explicitly desiring body. Ultimately, the mall spectacle addresses the consumer's own "perverse" desire to experience a different body and offers
itself as the most stylish of the many attitudes on sale in the mall.

Queer Nation exploits the mall's coupling of things and bodies by
transgressively disclosing that this bounded, safe commercial space is
also an information system where sexual norms and cultural identities
are consolidated, thus linking it with Queer Nation's final frontier: the
media. As it enters the urban media cacophony, Queer Nation scatters
original propaganda in the form of graffiti, wheat-pasted posters, and
fliers into existing spaces of collective, anonymous discursive exchange.
While the mall circulates and exchanges bodies, print media circulate
and exchange information in the most disembodied of spaces. Queer
Nation capitalizes on the abstract/informational apparatus of the media
in a few ways, refunctioning its spaces for an ongoing "urban redecora-
tion project" on behalf of gay visibility.[32] First, it manipulates the power
of modern media to create and disseminate cultural norms and other
political propaganda: Queer Nation leeches, we might say, onto the
media's socializing function. Second, Queer Nation's abundant interventions into sexual publicity playfully invoke and resist the lure of
monumentality, frustrating the tendency of sexual subcultures to convert
images of radical sexuality into new standards of transgression.

In addition to manufacturing its own information, Queer Nation's
mass mediation takes on a more ironic "Madison Avenue" mode, "queering" advertisements so that they become vehicles of protest against and
arrogations of a media that renders queerness invisible, sanitary, or spectacularly fetishized. More ambiguous than the tradition of political de-

facement from which it descends — feminist spray-painting of billboards with phrases like "this offends women," for example[33] — Queer Nation's glossy pseudoadvertisements involve replication, exposure, and disruption of even the semiotic boundaries between gay and straight. The group's parodies and reconstructions of mainstream ads inflect products with a sexuality and promote homosexuality as a product: they lay bare the "queerness" of the commodities that straight culture makes and buys, either translating it from its hidden form in the original or revealing and ameliorating its calculated erasure. In short, the most overtly commercial of Queer Nation's campaigns, true to the American way, makes queer good by making goods queer.

One form this project takes is an "outing" of corporate economic interest in "market segments" with which corporations refuse to identify explicitly. The New York Gap series changes the final *p* in the logo of stylish ads featuring gay, bisexual, and suspiciously polymorphous celebrities to a *y*. For the "insider," these acts "out" the closeted gay and bisexual semicelebrities the Gap often uses as models. But the reconstructed billboards also address the company's policy of using gay style to sell clothes without acknowledging debts to gay street style: style itself is "outed," as are the straight urban consumers who learn that the clothes they wear signify "gay."

Whereas the Gap ads confront both the closetedness of a corporation and the semiotic incoherence of straight consumer culture, another series addresses the class implications of advertising's complicity in the national moral bankruptcy. A series of parody Lotto ads exposes the similarities and differences between the national betrayal of poor and of gay citizens. The "straight" versions of a series of advertisements for New York's Lotto depict generic citizens of various assimilated genders and ethnicities, who voice their fantasies about sudden wealth underneath the caption "All You Need is a Dollar Bill and a Dream." The ads conflate citizenship and purchase, suggesting that working-class or ethnic Americans can realize the American dream through spending money. One of Queer Nation's parody ads shows an "ordinary citizen" in one of the frank, casual head-and-shoulders poses that characterize the real ads. The caption reads, "I'd start my own cigarette company and call it Fags." The Queer Nation logo appears, along with the slogan "All You Need is a Three-Dollar Bill and a Dream." Again, the ads link citizenship with capitalist gain, but the ironized American dream cliché also establishes the group's resistance to a liberal "gay business" approach to social liberation, in whose view capitalist legitimation neutralizes social marginality. Queer Nation recognizes that the three-dollar bill remains non-negotiable tender. The transformed caption reveals that the lottery's fundamental promise does not hold true for the nation's gay citizens in terms of the freedom to pursue sexual pleasure, which costs more than any jackpot or bank account has ever amassed.

In posing as a countercorporation, a "business" with its own logo, corporate identity, and ubiquity, Queer Nation seizes and dismantles the privileges of corporate anonymity.[34] It steals the privilege that this anonymity protects, that of avoiding painful recrimination for its actions. As it peels the facade of corporate neutrality, Queer Nation reveals that businesses are people with political agendas, and that consumers are citizens to whom businesses are accountable for more than the quality of their specific products. Abstracting itself, Queer Nation embodies the corporation. The Lotto ad finally promises an alternative to the capitalist dream machine: its Queer Nation logo, juxtaposed against the "All You Need is a Three-Dollar Bill and a Dream" caption, appeals to the consumer to invest in its own "corporate" identity.

The Queer Nation logo itself, then, becomes a mock twin to existing national corporate logos. Just as red, white, and blue "Buy U.S.A." labels, yellow ribbons, and flag icons have, by commodifying patriotism, actually managed to strengthen it, so does the spread of Queer Nation's merchandise and advertising expand its own territory of promises.[35] Because Gap clothes and lottery fantasies confer identities as much as flag kitsch does, Queer Nation has the additional power to expose or transform the meaning of these and other commodities — not simply through the reappropriation that camp enacts on an individual level but through collective mimicry, replication, and invasion of the pseudoidentities generated by corporations, including the nation itself.

Queer Nation's infusion of consumer space with a queer sensibility and its recognition of the potential for exploiting spaces of psychic and physical permeability are fundamental to its radical reconstitution of citizenship. For in the end, an individual's understanding of himself as "American" and/or as "straight" involves parallel problems of consent and local control: both identities demand psychic and bodily discipline in exchange for the protection, security, and power these identities confer. If the official nation extracts public libidinal pleasure as the cost of political identity, queer citizenship confers the right to one's own specific pleasures. In the final analysis, America, understood not as a geographic but as a symbolic locus in which individuals experience their fundamental link to 250 million other individuals, is the most unbounded of the hyperspaces we have been describing. The official transformation of national identity into style — of flag into transvestite "flagness" — offers Queer Nation a seamless means of transforming "queerness" into a camp counternationality, which makes good on the promise that the citizen will finally be allowed to own, in addition to all the other vicarious bodies Queer Nation has for sale, his very own national body.

With You Out We're Nothing, and Beyond

We have territorialized Queer Nation and described the production of a queer counterpublic out of traditional national icons, the official and useful spaces of everyday life, the ritual places of typical public pleasure (parades, malls, bars, and bodies), and the collective identities consumers buy in the mode of mass culture. The effect of casting gay urban life and practices as ongoing and scandalously ordinary is simultaneously to consolidate a safe space for gay subjects and to dislocate utterly the normative sexual referent. If nationality as a form of fantasy and practice provides a legal and customary account of why American citizens in the abstract are secure *as heterosexuals,* Queer Nation exploits the disembodied structure of nationality by asserting that xenophobia would be precisely an inappropriate response for a straight community to have toward gay Americans. By asserting that straight and gay publics are coextensive with Americans at large, Queer Nation shows that the boundaries that might secure distinctions between sexual populations are local (like neighborhoods), normative (like taxonomies), and elastic (like latex). But these distinctions, in any event, must not be considered national, and in this sense Queer Nation's relay between everyday life and citizen's rights seems fitting.

Yet if Queer Nation tactically engages the postmodernity of information cultures, cutting across local and disembodied spaces of social identity and expressivity to reveal the communication that already exists between apparently bounded sexual and textual spaces, the campaign has not yet, in our view, left behind the fantasies of glamour and of homogeneity that characterize American nationalism itself. We might comment on the masculine apriority that dominates even queer spectacle; we might further comment on the relative weakness with which economic, racial, ethnic, and non-American cultures have been enfolded into queer counterpublicity.[36] In short, insofar as it assumes that "queer" is the only insurgent "foreign" identity its citizens have, Queer Nation remains bound to the genericizing logic of American citizenship and to the horizon of an official formalism — one that equates sexual object choice with individual self-identity. We concede the need to acknowledge the names people use for themselves, even when they originate in the service of juridical and medical discipline. Popular forms of spectacle and self-understanding are crucial for building mass cultural struggle. But it is not enough to "include" women, lesbians, racial minorities, and so on in an ongoing machine of mass counternationality. Achieving the utopian promise of a Queer Symbolic[37] will involve more than a story of a multicultural sewing circle sewing the scraps of a pink triangle onto the American flag, or turning that flag, with its fifty-times-five potential small pink triangles, into a new desecrated emblem; more than a spectacle of young, hard girl/woman flesh outing the pseudoabstraction of masculine political fantasy. Queer culture's consent to national normativity must itself be made more provisional.

We have argued that America has already become marked by a camp aesthetic in the nineties. Camp America enrages, embarrasses, and sometimes benignly amuses official national figures and gives pleasure to the gay, the African American, the feminist, and the left-identified communities who understand that to operate a travesty on the national travesty is to "dissolve" the frame that separates national fantasy from ordinary bodies. But the verb "dissolve" is a temporal fantasy, of course: tactical interventions, such as Dred Scott's flag doormat in Chicago's Art Institute or Kelly and Ronnie Cutrone's transformation of the flag into a sheet for polymorphous lovemaking in New York, have momentarily disintegrated national abstractness by turning bodies into national art and actually making censorship law look silly. These gestures were potentially dangerous and legally scandalous. But contained in museums/galleries, they depended on the usual protections of free high "artistic" expression to purchase the right to scandalize national iconography. At a time when existing laws against public and private sex are being newly enforced, the class distinction between sexual art and sex practices must be replaced by an insurgent renaming of sexuality *beyond* spectacle.

In other words, the exhibition of scandalous direct contact between oppositional stereotypes of iconic America and its internally constructed "Others" — say, of the "body" and the "nation" — solves as spectacle a problem of representation and power that is conceptually much harder

166

to solve. But the indeterminate "we" from which we are writing, comfortable on neither side of most taxonomies, seek to occupy a space of a more complexly dimensional sexuality and political identity than these simple sutures suggest. This is, as Monique Wittig contends, not simply a question of "dedramatiz[ing] these categories of language. . . . We must produce a political transformation of the key concepts, that is of the concepts which are strategic for us."[38] As a gesture toward mapping this unsanctioned terrain, let us return to the problem of Sandra Bernhard: her pasty body wrapped in the flag, her extremely (c)little "red corvette," and her desire to seduce cathartically an African American woman through a lesbian erotics that manipulates sentimentality, national parody, and aesthetic distance. This final seductive moment, when Bernhard utters "Without me/you I'm nothing," is framed by the "you" in the film's opening monologue. There, Bernhard wishes the impossible — that "you," the disembodied, autoerotic spectator, would traverse the space of aesthetic and celluloid distance to kiss her right "here," on a facial place where she points her finger; no such contact with the audience happens in the frame of the film. In the end, after the masquerade, the racial, regional, ethnic, and class drag, and during the American striptease, the film stages a response that goes beyond the star's original request: the generic black-woman-in-the-audience about whom the film has periodically fantasized in nonnarrative, naturalistic segments writes on the café table with a lipstick, "FUCK SANDRA BERNHARD." This syntactically complex statement — a request, a demand, and an expletive — situates the black woman as an object of desire, as an author of feminine discourse, and as an image of the film's hopelessly absent audience. Her proximity to Bernhard's final lesbian/nationalist striptease thus suggests neither a purely sentimental "essentialist" lesbian spectacle, nor a postmodern consumer feminine autoerotics, nor a phallocentrically inspired lust for lesbian "experience," but all of these, and more.

In this encounter, Bernhard tries to merge national camp with lesbian spectacle.[39] She produces scandalous erotic pleasure by undulating between the impossibility of laminating the flag onto her body and the equal impossibility of ever shedding the flag altogether: as she peels off her flag cape, she reveals three more in the form of a red, white, and blue sequined G-string and patriotic pasties, leaving us no reason to think that this exponential multiplication of flags would ever reach its limits. This undulation of the body and the flag, which eroticizes the latter as it nationalizes the former, is coterminous with the tease and the denial of the cross-race, homoerotic address to her consumer — the black-woman-in-the-audience. That is to say, the political liberation the flag promises and the sexual liberation its slipping off suggests makes a spectacle of the ambiguity with which these subjects live American sexuality.

Bernhard's refusal to resolve her feminine and sexual identities into a lesbian love narrative also illustrates how the eroticization of female spectacle in American public culture frustrates the political efficacy of transgressive representations for straight and lesbian women. The film imagines a kind of liberal pluralistic space for Bernhard's cross-margin, cross-fashion fantasy of women, but shows how lesbophobic that fantasy can be, insofar as it requires aesthetic distance — the straightness of the generic white woman-identified woman — as a condition of national, racial, *and* sexual filiation. Her desire for acceptance from the black-woman-in-the-audience perpetuates the historic burden to represent embodiment, desire, and the dignity of suffering that black women in cinema have borne on behalf of white women, who are too frightened to strip themselves of the privileges of white heterospectacle. Thus in addition, the rejection Bernhard receives from the black-woman-in-the-audience demonstrates the inability of cinematic public spectacle to make good on its teasing promise to dignify feminine desire in any of its forms. Bernhard's inability to bridge the negativity of anyone's desire focuses the lens on female spectacle itself, staging it as a scene of negativity, complete with producer, consumer, audience resistance, and the representation of multiple and ambiguous identifications.

The failed attempt to represent and to achieve a lesbian/national spectacle foregrounds the oxymoronic quality of these two models of identification. In the remainder of this essay we mean to explain how this failure to conflate sexual and political spectacle can provide material to transfigure queer as well as American nationality — not to commandeer the national franchise for our particular huddled masses but instead to unsettle the conventions that name identity, frame expressivity, and provide the taxonomic means by which populations and practices are defined, regulated, protected, and censored by national law and custom. Lesbian/national spectacle emerges here as the measure of a transitory space, a challenge to revise radically the boundaries of the normative public sphere and its historical modes of intelligibility, among which are male homosociality, a very narrowly defined set of public "political" interests, and garbled relations between politics and affect.[40] We understand that to define sexual expressivity as public political speech, and to resist censorship by expanding the range of erotic description, is simultaneously to exercise a fundamental privilege of American citizenship and to risk forsaking the refuge of camp. But these are risks that queers/Americans cannot afford to pass on. Indeed, the question of whether female/lesbian sexuality can come into any productive contact with the political public sphere is a founding problem of lesbian political writing of the last fifteen years, and this problem is a problem for us all, by which we refer to "us" queers and "us" Americans.

Female subjects are always citizens in masquerade: the more sexual they appear, the less abstractable they are in a liberal corporeal schema. Lesbian theory's solution to this dilemma has been to construct *imaginable* communities, which is to say that America's strategies for self-promotion have not worked for lesbians, who have historically and aesthetically often embraced the "space-off" in expatriate expression of their alienation from America.[41] The female body has reemerged in the safe spaces of lesbian political theory outside the political public sphere, in tribal structures that emphasize embodied ritual and intimate spectacle as a solution to the indignities women, and especially lesbians, have had to endure. The blinking question mark beside the word "nation" in Jill Johnston's separatist *Lesbian Nation;* the erotogenic metamorphoses of the body, sex, and knowledge on the island of Monique Wittig's *The Lesbian Body;* and even the personal gender performances central to Judith Butler's sexual self-fashioning in *Gender Trouble* all reveal an evacuation of liberal nationality as we know it.[42] But for what public?

Separatist withdrawal into safe territories free from the male gaze secures the possibility of nonpornotropic embodiment in everyday life and aesthetic performance by emphasizing intimacy, subjectivity, and the literally local frame.[43] We do not mean to diminish the benefits of separatist expatriation: in its great historical variety, separatist withdrawal has expressed a condition of political contestation lesbians and gays already experience in America and has used the erotics of community to create the foundation of a different franchise. However, by changing the locus of spectacle — transporting it over state lines, as it were — lesbian theory has neglected to engage the political problem of feminine spectacle in mass society. Even Butler's metropolitan polymorphous solution to the politics of spectacle limits the power of transgression to what symbolic substitution on the individual body can do to transform custom and law. And as Queer Nation has shown us, no insistence on "the local" can secure national intimacy and national justice, where spectacle is intimacy's vehicle, and the vehicle for control. If the spectacle of the body's rendezvous with the flag has seemed to yoke unlike things together, the distance between persons and collective identities must also be read not only as a place to be filled up by fantasy, but as a negative space, a space where suddenly the various logics of identity that circulate through American culture come into contradiction and not simple analogy.

Along this axis, the negativity of national life for nonwhite and/or non-male queers has reemerged in a more radical diacritic: the queer fan-zine.[44] We move away from the word "lesbian" and toward these de-scriptions of negative identity because it is this space—the space of nonidentification with the national fantasy of the white male citizen—that is both the symptom of even "queered" Enlightenment nationality and the material for its refunctioning. As a rule, underground fanzines make explicit their refusal of a property relation to information and art, repudiating the class politics of mainstream gay for-profit journals like the *Advocate* and *Outweek,* and shunning the mock Madison Avenue production values of Queer Nation, Gran Fury, and ACT UP.[45] The Toronto fanzine *BIMBOX* writes that the magazine is free because "the truth is, you have already paid for *BIMBOX.* We have all paid for it—dearly. We have paid for it in blood and we have paid for it in tears. Unrelenting pain is our credit limit, and we are cursed with intermi-nable overdraft protection."[46] Xerox collage, desktop publishing, and other photo-techniques have combined in a medium of comic and politi-cal communication, whose geographically isolated examples have con-verged into the infocultural version of the tribe: a network.[47] Thus, the contest over the territory of the Queer Symbolic has resulted in what Bitch Nation, a manifesto in *BIMBOX,* calls a civil war.

The fanzines' only shared identity is in their *counterproductivity*—a multifold mission they share with other sexual radicalisms to counter American national and Queer National culture's ways of thinking about political tactics and sexual intelligibility.[48] In the first place, the zines show that "obscenity" itself is political speech, speech that deserves con-stitutional protection. Transforming "the American flag into something pleasant," Sondra Golvin and Robin Podolsky's "Allegiance/Ecstasy" turns "i pledge allegiance" into an opportunity to add "my cunt help-lessly going molten," "her clit swelling to meet my tongue," "my fist knocking gently at her cunt" to the national loyalty oath.[49] Additionally, the zines have widened the semantic field of sexual description, moving sexual identity itself beyond known practical and fantastic horizons — as when *BIMBOX* imagines "fags, dykes, and USO's (*Unidentified Sexual Objects*)." But they are also magazines in the military sense, storehouses for the explosives that will shatter the categories and the time-honored political strategies through which queers have protected themselves. Queer counterspectacle might well be read as a means for aggressively achieving dignity in the straight world; in the zine context, however, these spectacles are also icons that require smashing. The suspicion of existing tactics and taxonomies runs deep: "Dykes against granola lesbians. Fags against sensitive gay men. And bitches against everyone else."[50]

Along with joining queer culture's ongoing politics of dirty words, then, some zines engage in what would seem to be a more perverse activity: the aggressive naming and negation of their own audience. If citizenship in the Queer Nation is voluntary and consensual, democratic and universalist in the way of many modern nationalisms, the application for citizenship in the Bitch Nation, for example, repudiates the promise of community in common readership, the privileges of a common language, and the safety of counteridentity. "And — don't even bother trying to assimilate any aspect of Bitch Nation in a futile attempt to make your paltry careers or lame causes appear more glamorous or exciting. We won't hesitate to prosecute — and the Bitch Nation court is now in session!!"[51] As Bitch Nation endangers the reader who merely quotes, abstracts, and appropriates zine culture, many zines engage in a consumer politics of sexual enunciation, forcing the reader to see where she is situated, or to resituate herself politically — and culturally. Thus, when the cover of *Thing* magazine proclaims that "She Knows Who She Is," it mobilizes the common gay use of the feminine pronoun in the ventriloquized voice of the "woman's magazine" to categorize "insiders" by attitude rather than by gender or sexual identity, disarming many different kinds of essentialism through arch indirect address.

This move to materialize the spectator as *different* from the spectacle with which she identifies has powerful political force for women, whose collective and individual self-representations are always available for embarrassment, and most particularly for lesbians, whose sexual iconography has been overdetermined by the straight porn industry. By reversing the direction of the embarrassment from the spectacle toward the spectator, the zines rotate the meaning of *consent*. In severing sexual identity from sexual expressivity, the spectacle talks dirty to *you*, as it were, and you no longer have the privilege to consume in silence, or in tacit uncon-

sciousness of or unaccountability for your own fantasies. As *Negativa,* a Chicago lesbian fanzine, puts it, "What you looking at bitch?"

Linked complexly to the enigma of consensual sex is that of consensual nationality, which similarly involves theories of self-identity, of intention, and of the urge to shed the personal body for the tease of safe mutual or collective unboundedness. American national and Queer National spectacle depend upon the citizen's capacity to merge his/her private, fractured body with a collectively identified whole one. Uncle

Sam points his finger and says he wants *you* to donate your whole body literally and figuratively to the nation, and Queer Nation uses the allure of commercial and collective embodied spectacle to beckon *you* toward a different sort of citizenship. But the fanzines' postnational spectacle disrupts this moment of convergence: just as *you,* the desiring citizen, enter the sphere of what appears to be mutual consent, an invisible finger points back at you. It unveils your desire to see the spectacle of homoculture without being seen; it embarrasses you by making explicit your desire to "enter" and your need for "permission" to identify; and it insists that you declare your body and your goods and that you pay whatever political and erotic duty seems necessary.

Thus, like Queer Nation, the zines channel submission and bitterness into anger and parody. Queer Nation and allied groups struggle to reoccupy the space of national legitimation, to make the national world safe for just systems of resource distribution and communication, full expression of difference and rage and sexuality. Parody and camp thus become the measure of proximity to the national promise, as well as the distance from access to its fulfillment. Gestures of anger, parody, and camp in the zine network, by contrast, represent a disinvestment in authenticity discourse that moves beyond the intelligibility of gender, of sexual object choice, and of national identity by cultivating a passionate investment in developing the negative for pleasure and politics. In their drive to embody *you,* the citizen / spectator / reader / lover, by negating your disembodiment, the zines represent the horizon of postpatriarchal and postnational fantasy.

Even in their most parodic manifestations, gestures of sexual and national intelligibility — both oppressive and emancipatory — are part of a process of making norms. The zines acknowledge the necessity, and also the reality, of stereotypical self-identity and at the same time try to do violence to normative forms that circulate in America. In staging the process by which stereotypes become hybrid forms, their clarifying function as sites of identity and oppression exhausted, the zines do more than deconstructively put the icon "under erasure."[52] The negated stereotype remains available: mass politics requires a genuinely populist currency. But the stereotype is expensive. The fanzines' gestures in countering national political sovereignty, then, lead us in another direction. They suggest a space of politics in which to be "out" in public would not be to consent parodically to the forms of the political public sphere but rather to be *out beyond* the censoring imaginary of the state and the information culture that consolidates the rule of its names. We support Queer Nation and ACT UP's commitment to occupy as many hegemonic spaces as possible in their countering moves. What we seek to describe, in addition, is the value in converting the space of negativity that distinguishes queer American identity into a discursive field so powerful that the United States will have to develop a new breed of lexical specialists to crack the code of collective life in a hot war of words about sex and America, about which the nation already finds itself so miserably — and yet so spectacularly — archaic.

5   The Face of America and the State
of Emergency

When can I go
into the supermarket
and buy what I
need with my good looks?
  — Allen Ginsberg, "America"

The Political Is the Personal

"The tradition of the oppressed teaches us that the 'state of emergency' in which we live is not the exception but the rule. We must attain to a conception of history that is in keeping with this insight. Then we shall clearly realize that it is our task to bring about a real state of emergency."[1] When Walter Benjamin urges his cohort of critical intellectuals to foment a state of political counteremergency, he responds not only to the outrage of fascism in general, but to a particularly brutal mode of what we might call *hygienic governmentality:* this involves a ruling bloc's dramatic attempt to maintain its hegemony by asserting that an abject population threatens the common good and must be rigorously governed and monitored by all sectors of society.[2] Especially horrifying to Benjamin are the ways the ruling bloc solicits mass support for such "governing": by using abjected populations as exemplary of all obstacles to national life; by wielding images and narratives of a threatened "good life" that a putative "we" have known; by promising relief from the struggles of the present through a felicitous image of a national future; and by claiming that, because the stability of the core image is the foundation of the narratives that characterize an intimate and secure national society, the nation must at all costs protect this image of a way of life, even against the happiness of some of its own citizens.

In the contemporary United States it is almost always the people at the bottom of the virtue/value scale—the adult poor, the nonwhite, the unmarried, the nonheterosexual, and the nonreproductive—who are said to be creating the crisis that is mobilizing the mainstream public sphere to fight the good fight on behalf of normal national culture, while those in power are left relatively immune. For example, while the public is incited to be scandalized by so-called welfare queens, the refusal of many employers to recompense their workers with a living wage and decent workplace conditions engenders no scandal at all. Indeed, the exploitation of workers is encouraged and supported, while it is poor people who are vilified for their ill-gotten gains. The manufactured emergency on behalf of "core national values" advanced by people like William Bennett, magazines like the *National Review,* and organizations like FAIR (Federation for American Immigration Reform) masks a class war played out in ugly images and ridiculous stereotypes of racial and sexual identities and antinormative cultures.[3] As Stephanie Coontz has argued, this core U.S. culture has never actually existed, except as an ideal or a dogma.[4] But the cultural politics of this image of the normal has concrete effects, both on ordinary identity and the national life the state apparatus claims to be representing.

In this chapter I am going to tell another story about the transformation of the normative citizenship paradigm from a public form into the abstracted time and space of intimate privacy. I will start with a reading of the film *Forrest Gump* (dir. Robert Zemeckis, 1994) and other scenes of mass politics and end with the video of Michael Jackson's song "Black or White" (dir. John Landis, 1991). In between, and comprising the crux of this chapter, I will be engaging another fictitious citizen: the new "Face of America" who, gracing the covers of *Time, Mirabella,* and the *National Review,* has been cast as an imaginary solution to the problems of immigration, multiculturalism, sexuality, gender, and (trans)national identity that haunt the U.S. present tense.

This imaginary citizen or "woman" was invented in 1993 by *Time* magazine. She is a nameless, computer-generated heterosexual immigrant, and the figure of a future core national population. In previous chapters, I have described the constriction of modal citizenship into smaller and more powerless vehicles of human agency: fetuses and children. Joining this gallery of incipient citizens, the computer-generated female immigrant of our *Time* cannot act or speak on behalf of the citizenship she represents; she is more human than living Americans, yet less invested with qualities of personhood. With no capacity for agency, her value is also in her irrelevance to the concerns about achievement, intelligence, subjectivity, desire, demand, and courage that have recently sullied the image of the enfranchised American woman. Her pure isolation from lived history also responds to widespread debate about the value of working-class and proletarian immigrants to the American economy and American society. In the following pages I will show how sectors of the mainstream public sphere link whatever positive value immigration has to the current obsessive desire for a revitalized national heterosexuality and a white, normal national culture.

Thus this is a story about official storytelling and the production of mass political experience.[5] It is also an opportunity to ask what it means that, since "'68," the sphere of discipline and definition for proper citizenship in the United States has become progressively more private, more sexual and familial, and more concerned with personal morality. How and why have other relations of power and sociality — those, for example, traversing local, national, and global economic institutions — become less central to adjudicating ethical citizenship in the United States?[6] How and why have so many pundits of the bourgeois public sphere (which includes the popular media, the official discourses and practices of policy making, and the law) come to see commitments to economic, racial, gender, and sexual justice as embarrassing and sentimental holdovers from another time? And how might the privatization of citizenship help devalue political identification itself for U.S. citizens?

To begin to answer these questions, it might help first to see a bigger picture of the ways the spaces of national culture have recently changed, at least in the idealized self-descriptions of contemporary U.S. official culture. Conservative attempts to restrict citizenship have so successfully transformed scenes of privacy into the main public spheres of nationality that, for example, there is nothing extraordinary about a public figure's characterization of sexual and reproductive "immorality" as a species of "un-American" activity that requires drastic hygienic regulation. This general shift has at least three important implications for the attempt to understand the cultural politics of citizenship in the official U.S. present tense.

First, the transgressive logic of the feminist maxim "The personal is the political," which aimed radically to make the affects and acts of intimacy in everyday life the index of national/sexual politics and ethics, has now been reversed and redeployed on behalf of a staged crisis in the legitimacy of the most traditional, apolitical, sentimental patriarchal family values. Today, the primary guiding maxim might be "The political is the personal." Reversing the direction of the dictum's critique has resulted in an antipolitical nationalist politics of sexuality whose concern is no longer what sex reveals about unethical power but what "abnormal" sex/reproduction/intimacy forms reveal about threats to the nation proper/the proper nation. As registered in the anti-gay-citizenship film *The Gay Agenda* (1993), the pro-gay response *One Nation Under God* (dir. Teodoro Maniaci and Francine M. Rzeznik, 1994), and many pro-life pamphlets, the religious right calls the struggle to delegitimate gayness and return sexual identity to tacitness, privacy, and conjugal heterosexuality "the Second Civil War."[7] This general shift also informs the increasing personalization of politics, where "character" issues have come to dominate spaces of critique that might otherwise be occupied with ideological struggles about public life, and where the appearance of squeaky cleanness (read: independently wealthy conjugal heterosexuality) is marketed as an index of personal virtue (as in the recent cases of Michael Huffington in California and Mitt Romney in Massachusetts).

But personalizing citizenship as a scene of private acts involves more than designating and legislating sexual and familial practices as the main sites of civic ethics. Relevant here as well is an increasing tendency to designate political duty in terms of individual acts of consumption and accumulation. Two major economic platforms in the last twenty years bear this out: (1) the increasing emphasis on boycotts to enforce conservative sexual morality in the mass media (often on behalf of "our youth"); and (2) the staggering contention, by Presidents Reagan, Bush, and Clinton and their cohort, that receiving federal welfare funds so morally corrupts individuals that they are responsible for the quotidian violence and decay of the inner city, and indeed more generally for the decline of the nation as a whole. This assertion refuses to account for many things racial, gendered, and economic, including the dramatic drop in employment opportunities and wages in the metropolitan industrial sector over the last twenty years, and the social devastation that has taken place precisely in those defunded areas; its logic of displacement onto the consumer reveals how the personal morality citizenship card being played by ruling blocs is central to the ideology of unimpaired entrepreneurial activity that was sanctified as free-market patriotism during and after the Reagan regime.[8]

The second effect of citizenship's privatization has to do with the relation of mass media to national culture. If individual practice in and around the family is one nodal point of postmodern national identity, another intimate sphere of public citizenship has been created as sentimental nationality's technological mirror and complement: the mass-mediated national public sphere. As I will elaborate shortly, embodied activism performed in civic spaces has become designated as a demonized, deranged, unclean (a)social mob activity.[9] In contrast, every article about the Internet shows us that accessing and mastering national/ global mass-media forms has become widely construed as the *other* most evolved or developed scene for the practice of being American.[10] While at other moments in U.S. history the mediations of mass culture have been seen as dangers to securing an ethical national life, the collective experiences of national mass culture now constitute a form of intimacy, like the family, whose national value is measured in its subjugation of embodied forms of public life.

Finally, I have described a dialectic between a privatized "normal" nation of heterosexual, reproductive family values and the public sphere of collective intimacy through which official mass nationality stays familiar, and suggested that these two domains now saturate what counts as mass community in the contemporary United States. The compression of national life into these apparatuses of intimacy also advances the conservative desire to delegitimate the embodied public itself, both abstractly and in its concrete spatial forms. Michael Rogin has called this kind of wholesale deportation of certain embodied publics from national identity "American political demonology." This involves "the inflation, stigmatization, and dehumanization of political foes" by populist, centrist, and right-wing politicians and thinkers.[11] We see it happening in the right-wing and neoliberal loathing of a cluster of seemingly disparate national scenes: public urban spaces and populations; sexualities and affective existences that do not follow the privacy logic of the patriarchal family form; collectivities of the poor, whether of inner-city gangs or workers at the bottom of the class structure; the most exploited (im)migrants; nonpaternal family forms; and racially marked subjects who do not seem to aspire to or identify with the privacy/property norms of the ostensibly core national culture. The "American way of life" against which these deviancies are measured is, needless to say, a fantasy norm, but this fantasy generates images of collective decay monstrous and powerful enough to shift voting patterns and justify the terms of cruel legislation and juridical decree.

Persons categorized as degenerate typically enter the national register through stereotype, scandal, or unusually horrible death: otherwise their lives are not timely, not news of what counts as the national present. That is, they are part of the present but are unassimilable to the national in its pure form. The disfiguring marks of disqualified U.S. citizenship are inscribed within the present tense by tactics ranging from the manufacture of scandal to strategies of throwaway representation, like jokes; and when collective contestation does happen, it becomes cast as a scene of silly and/or dangerous subrationality, superficiality, or hysteria.[12] But my aim in this essay is not solely to explicate the ways public lives uncontained by the family form and mass mediation have become bad objects in the political public sphere. It is also to seek out and explore the moments of world-building optimism within the normalizing discourse of national privacy, to better understand what kinds of life are being supported by the privatization of U.S. citizenship, and what kinds of good are being imagined in the ejection of entire populations from the national present and future.

On Being Normal, Average, Common, Ordinary, Standard, Typical, and Usual in Contemporary America[13]

One of the most popular vehicles celebrating citizenship's extraction from public life is the film *Forrest Gump,* which uses spectacles of the nation in crisis to express a nostalgic desire for official national culture, and which retells the story of recent U.S. history as a story about the fragility of normal national personhood. Like the *Contract with America,* which expresses the wish of the now mythic "angry white male" voter who feels that his destiny has been stolen from him by a coalition of feminists, people of color, and social radicals, *Forrest Gump* narrates the recent history of the United States using an image archive from contemporary rage at the radical movements of the 1960s and the culture of desire that borrowed their energy to challenge previously protected forms of American pro-family patriarchal pleasure and authority. To perform this act of rage as though it were a show of love, the film situates a politically illiterate citizen in the place of civic virtue, and reinvents through him a revitalized, reproductive, private, and prepolitical national heterosexuality. It is telling, here, that Forrest Gump is named after Nathan Bedford Forrest, founder of the Ku Klux Klan, and that an early film clip of the Klan with Tom Hanks in Klan drag cites *The Birth of a Nation* as *Forrest Gump*'s earliest cinematic progenitor. What does it

suggest that these nostalgic, familial references to nationally sanctioned racial violence are translated through someone incapable of knowing what they mean?[14]

Forrest Gump follows the youth and middle age of an infantile citizen, a man who retains his innocence because he is five points shy of normal intelligence. We know he is such a statistical person because the principal of his school says so: to explain Forrest's horizon of life opportunity, the principal holds up a sign with statistics on it, which are clustered into the categories Above, Normal, and Below. Forrest has an IQ of seventy-five, which would force him to attend what Mrs. Gump bitingly calls a "special" school: eighty is normal, and would give the child access to the standard pedagogical resources of the state. Forrest's mother refuses to submit to the rule of numbers, since she believes that people must make their own destinies. Therefore she lubricates Forrest's way into normal culture by having sex with the principal of his school, her body in trade for five points of IQ and the privileged protections of normality.

Therein begins a simple story about gender, heterosexuality, and nationality that nonetheless articulates complicated ideas about how U.S. citizens inhabit national history. First, *Forrest Gump* seeks to eradicate women from public life and nonreproductive sex from the ideal nation. As Mrs. Gump demonstrates, a virtuous woman does her business at home and organizes her life around caretaking, leaving the domestic sphere only to honor her child. Even more insidious than this 1950s-style gender fantasy is the way the film sifts through the detritus of national history since the protest movements of the 1960s and their challenge to what constitutes a national public. The narrative replays the history of post-1968 America as a split between the evil of intention, which is defined as a female trait, and the virtue of shallowness, which is generally a male trait (except if the man has lusted after women, in which case his passions are figured both as violent to women and tainted by the cupidity/rapacity of feminine desire). Forrest Gump's "girl," Jenny Curran, inherits Mrs. Gump's horizon of historical possibility, organizing with her libidinous body a narrative of the corrupted national public sphere. Like Mrs. Gump, Jenny is there to have sex and to be sexually exploited, humiliated, and physically endangered in every intimate encounter she has with a man. Between 1971 and 1982 Jenny goes through each form of public, sensual degradation available in the *Time*-mediated version of American culture: the sexual and political revolution of the '60s, the drugs and disco culture of the '70s, and then, finally, the AIDS pandemic of the '80s. (Although the disease goes unnamed, Jenny seems to die of a special strain of AIDS that makes you more beautiful as your immune system collapses.) To add insult to history, the film seems to locate the bad seed of the '60s in the sexual abuse of Jenny by her alcoholic father. It is as though, for the family to be redeemed as a site of quasi-apolitical nation formation, the pervasiveness of abuse has to be projected out onto the metropolitan public. Jenny's private trauma comes to stand not for the toxicity of familial privacy or patriarchal control of children, but for a *public* ill whose remedy seems bizarrely to require a return to the family, albeit a kinder, gentler, more antiseptic one. Before Jenny dies she is redeemed from her place as an abject sexual and historical subject via an act of reproductive sex with Forrest. The family is then fully redeemed by Forrest's single fatherhood of his eponymous son: symbolically eradicated from the nasty public world, women and friends are ultimately separated from the family form as well, absent the way public history is, except as animating memory.

In his random way, Forrest enters the national narrative too. But he encounters history without becoming historical, which in this film means becoming dead, gravely wounded, or degenerate. Because he is mentally incapable of making plans or thinking conceptually, he follows rules and orders literally. Someone says, "Run, Forrest," he runs; someone says shrimp, he shrimps. This is why he can become an "All-American" football hero and why, in the Army, Gump is considered a genius. This is why he can survive Vietnam while others around him fall and falter; why he endures when a hurricane obliterates every other shrimp boat in the South (which produces "Bubba Gump," a financial empire made from shrimp and clothing tie-ins with the company logo); and why, when his friend Lt. Dan gambles on some "fruit" company called Apple, Gump is financially fixed for life. He takes risks but experiences nothing of their riskiness: a Vietnam with no Vietnamese, capitalism with no workers, and profit at a distance both from production and exploitation.[15] While Jenny deliberately seeks out the deteriorating political and aesthetic public culture of modern America, Gump notices nothing and excels at everything he decides to do. He is too stupid to be racist, sexist, and exploitative; this is his genius and it is meant to be his virtue.

In addition to enjoying the patriarchal capitalist entitlements of American life as a man of football, war, and industry, and in addition to inventing the treasured and complexly linked national banalities "Have a Nice Day" and "Shit Happens," Gump makes three pilgrimages to the White House, where he meets Presidents Kennedy, Johnson, and Nixon. Each time he shakes a president's hand the president automatically inquires as to his well-being, a question that conventionally seeks a generic citizen's response, such as "Fine, Mr. President." But to Kennedy, Gump says, "I gotta pee." With Johnson, Gump pulls down his pants to show the war wound on his "buttocks." With Nixon, he discusses his discomfort in Washington: Nixon transfers him to his favorite place, the Watergate Hotel, where Gump sees flashlights in the Democratic National Committee headquarters and calls Frank Wells. Forrest notices that Nixon soon resigns, but this event is as random to him as the white feather that floats in the film's framing shots. "For no particular reason," he keeps saying, these nice presidents are shot, assaulted, or disgraced, along with George Wallace, John Lennon, Bobby Kennedy, Gerald Ford, and Ronald Reagan. No mention of Martin Luther King, Medgar Evers, or Malcolm X is made in *Forrest Gump*.

Gump narrates the story of his unearned and therefore virtuous celebrity to a series of people who sit on a park bench next to him in Savannah, Georgia. They all assume he's stupid, partly because he repeats his mother's line "Stupid is as stupid does" so often it begins to make sense. But then the fact that this movie makes any sense at all is a tribute to two technologies of the gullible central to contemporary American life. The first is the digital technology that makes it possible to insert Tom Hanks /

Forrest Gump into nationally momentous newsreel footage from the past three decades. Using the technologies called "morphing" and blue-screen photography, which enable computers to make impossible situations and imaginary bodies look realistic on film, *Forrest Gump* stages five national "historical" events.[16] In these moments the nation, often represented through the president's body, meets "the people," embodied by Gump, who has made a pilgrimage to Washington. Gump's clear anomalousness to the national norm, signaled in the explicit artificiality of Hanks' presence in the newsreel images, makes his successful infantile citizenship seem absurd, miraculous, or lucky; on the other hand, the narrative of his virtue makes him seem the ideal type of American. The technology's self-celebration in the film borrows the aura of Gump's virtuous incapacity to self-celebrate: the film seeks to make its audience *want* to rewrite recent U.S. history into a world that might have sustained a Forrest Gump. To effect the audience's desire for his exemption from the traumas of history, the writers and director broadly ironize and parody an already wildly oversimple version of what constituted the 1960s and beyond. But the intensity of the visual and aural maneuvers the film makes suggests a utopian desire for one political revolution (the Reaganite one) to have already happened in the 1960s, and another (the counterculture's) never to have begun at all.

The second technology of the gullible, then, available in the film's revisionary historicism, is the right-wing cultural agenda of the Reagan revolution, whose effects are everywhere present. The ex-president is literally represented for a minute, in one of the film's many scenes of national trauma. But Reagan's centrality to the historical imaginary of *Forrest Gump* is signaled as powerfully by the *People* magazine his first interlocutor reads. This has Nancy Reagan on the cover, standing in both for her presidential husband and for the grotesqueness of feminine ambition. Although it has the historical and technological opportunity, the film never shows Gump meeting, or even noticing, this president. Why should it? He *is* Reagan—Reagan, that is, as he sold himself, a person incapable of duplicity, who operates according to a natural regime of justice and common sense in a national world that has little place for these virtues.[17]

With its claim to be without a political or sexual unconscious, and with its implied argument that to have an unconscious is to be an incompetent or dangerous American, *Forrest Gump* is a symptomatic product of the conservative national culture machine, with its desire to establish a simple, privacy-based model of normal America. This machine involves creating a sense of a traditional but also an urgently contemporary mass consent to an image/narrative archive of what a core national culture should look like: through an antipolitical politics that claims to be protecting what it is promoting—a notion of citizenship preached in languages of moral, not political, accountability—the national culture industry seeks to stipulate that only certain kinds of people, practices, and property that are, at core, "American," deserve juridical and social legitimation. The modal normal American in this view sees her/his identity as something sustained in private, personal, intimate relations; in contrast, only the abjected, degraded, *lower* citizens of the United States will see themselves as sustained by public, coalitional, non-kin affiliations.

Forrest Gump produces this political hierarchy too. For all its lightness and irony, there is something being wished for when the film has Forrest "unconsciously" ridicule the Black Panthers and the left-wing cultural and political imaginary, which is reduced to achieving the revolutionary liberation of the word "fuck" from the zone of "adult" language into public political discourse.[18] For all its idealization of Jenny Curran, the film is never more vicious about the desire to be and to have a public than when she leaves her terrible home to experiment in nonfamilial contexts. I have suggested that the crisis of the contemporary nation is registered in terms of threats to the imagined norm of privatized citizenship: *Gump* defines "normal" through the star's untraumatized survival of a traumatic national history, which effectively rewrites the traumas of mass unrest of the last few decades not as responses to systemic malaise, exploitation, or injustice, but as purely personal to the dead, the violent, and the violated.

Explicating this ejection of a nonconjugal and non-mass-mediated public life from the official/dominant present tense in the United States involves coordinating many different plateaus of privilege and experience. It also involves taking up Benjamin's challenge: to the state of emergency the official nation is now constantly staging about the ex-privilege of its elite representatives there must be a response, involving the creation of a state of counteremergency. To do this will at least be to tell the story of a symbolic genocide within the United States, a mass social death that takes place not just through the removal of entire populations from the future of national political life and resources but also through cruel methods of representation in the mainstream public sphere and in the law. This is to say that the United States that the law recognizes is generated in representations of public opinion and custom; to take seriously the ordinary representations of the official public sphere is to enter a war of maneuver, an uncivil war that is currently raging everywhere around us.

Making Up Nations (1): Postmodern Mobocracy and Contemporary Protest

As anyone can see on the television news, a terrible state of political emergency exists on the streets of the contemporary United States. There, ordinary conflicts among different publics about what the good life should entail are recast as menaces to national society, and images of political life "on the street" become evidence that a violent change threatens an idealized version of the national. Despite occasional attempts to caption images of public dissent respectfully, the typical modern TV news report represents the right and left through their most disorderly performances of resistance, to indicate that collective opposition is based not on principle, but on passions that are dangerous and destabilizing for the commonweal. Whether their acts are cast as naive, ridiculous, insipid, and shallow, or merely serious and unpragmatic, protesters are made to represent the frayed and fraying edges of national society.[19] Yet in news footage of police activity during feminist, abortion, antiwar, civil-rights, and Yippie demonstrations, we see that violent disorder is in fact rather more likely to come from the actions of police.[20] Michael Warner has argued that media sensationalism around collective public citizenship acts is partly driven by a desire to increase ratings and to whet the consuming public's appetite for mass disaster.[21] More important than that, though, is the chilling effect such framing has on conceptions of political activism. Nonetheless politicians and the dominant press tend to ascribe the disorder to the resisters and, more insidiously, to the world they want to bring into being.

The double humiliation of protest in the mainstream media, making it both silly and dangerous, subtracts personhood from activists, making their very gestures of citizenship seem proof that their claims are illegitimate. This is especially germane to the portrayal of pro-life and gay collective actions. In contrast, political suffering is still palatable when expressed as a trauma or injury to a particular person. This narrowing in the means for making a legitimate claim on public sympathy has had a significant effect in a certain strain of U.S. legal theory, where some are arguing that words and images can produce harms to a person as substantial as those made by physical acts of violence, such that violent and cruel talk should be actionable the way physical assault is.[22] But more than this, talk shows and other forms of gossip media have helped make scenes of personal witnessing the only political testimony that counts. It is not just that everybody loves a good sob story. Trauma makes good storytelling and, as journalistic common sense constantly reminds us, it puts a "face" on an otherwise abstract issue.[23] Moreover, the sheer scale of the systematically brutal hierarchies that structure national capitalist culture can be overwhelming, leading to a kind of emotional and analytic paralysis in a public that cannot imagine a world without poverty or violence: here too, the facialization of U.S. injustice makes it manageable and enables further deferral of considerations that might force structural transformations of public life. In the meantime, while the embodied activities of anonymous citizens have taken on the odor of the abject, the personal complaint form now bears a huge burden for vocalizing and embodying injustice in the United States.

Yet there *is* a kind of public and collective protest that the media honors. Take, for example, press reports of the thirtieth anniversary of Martin Luther King's March on Washington, and contrast them to reports on the gay and lesbian march on Washington on April 25, 1993. In 1963, the approach of King's march created panic and threats of racist counterviolence. But in retrospect, this event has been sanitized into a beautifully choreographed mass rationality, an auteurist production of the eloquent, rhetorically masterful, and then martyred King. These solemn reports wax nostalgic for the days when protest was reasonable, and protesters were mainly men speaking decorously with their bodies, while asking for reasonable things like the ordinary necessities of life.[24]

This media legitimation of orderly national protest has a long history. The 1933 film *Gabriel Over the White House* (dir. Gregory La Cava), for example, details with particular clarity the limited kind of citizenship activity a privacy-based mass democracy can bear, especially in times of economic crisis. Like other films of the depression,[25] *Gabriel* explores the seeming fraudulence of the claim that democracy can exist in a capitalist society, by focusing on the "forgotten men" who had fought World War I for a United States that could not support them afterward. To the "forgotten man" the depression broke a contract national capitalism had made with national patriotism, and the possibility of a legitimate *patriotic* class war among men was palpable everywhere in the United States.

In response to this decline in national/masculine prestige, the culture industry produced narratives that performed ways of sending rage into remission. I quote *Gabriel* at length to demonstrate Americans' long-standing ambivalence toward democracy's embodiment in collective struggle; but also to set up these images of collective dignity and sacrifice as the nostalgic horizon that official culture "remembers" in its scramble to codify the proprieties of mass national culture in the present tense.

Speaking on the radio during the depression is "John Bronson," leader of an army of unemployed men who are marching on their way to Washington from New York to find out whether the federal nation feels accountable to their suffering. As Bronson speaks, the film shows the president having a treasure hunt in the Oval Office with his nephew and then eating the marshmallow treasures he has hidden. They are not attending to the disembodied and dignified voice coming from the radio: this difficult task is left to the viewers, who hear it while their eyes are distracted by the president's play.

> People of America. This is John Bronson speaking, not for himself, but for over a million men who are out of work, who cannot earn money to buy food because those responsible for providing work have failed in their obligations. We ask no more than that which every citizen of the United States should be assured: the right to live, the right to put food in the mouths of our wives and children. Our underlying purpose is not revolutionary. We are not influenced by militant leaders. None of us are reds. We merely want work, and we believe this great United States of America under proper leadership can provide work for everybody. I have appealed to the president for an interview and the president says he will not deal with us because we are dangerous anarchists. We are not. We are citizens of America with full confidence in the American democracy, if it is properly administered. The people of America are hopelessly [speech drowned out by conversation between an African American valet and the president about what coat the president will wear] prosperous and happy. I ask your president now if he has ever read the Constitution of the United States as it was laid out by those great men that day in Philadelphia long ago, a document which guarantees the American people the rights of life, liberty, property, and the pursuit of happiness. All we ask are to be given those rights. This country is sound. The right man in the White House can bring us out of despair into prosperity again. We ask him at least to try.

Almost instantly after this speech Bronson is murdered, and enters the pantheon of antinational patriotic martyrs (the "army of the unemployed" sings the almost eponymous "John Brown's Body" as it marches from city to city); but there is no violence by the workers. Indeed, becoming by executive order an official reserve army for American capital, they trade rage for wages the government pays them (the president eventually sets up utopian boot camps for the working poor, in support of the men's prestige in the family). As in the case of King's March on Washington, this suggests that the only way Americans can claim both rights and mass sympathy is to demonstrate, not panic, anger, demand, and desire, but ethical serenity, hyperpatriotism, and proper deference. Political emotions like anxiety, rage, and aggression turn out to be feelings only privileged people are justified in having. America's breach of its contract with its subordinated peoples becomes in this model of mass politics an opportunity for elites to feel sorry for themselves, and sympathy for the well-behaved oppressed: but the cruelty of sympathy, the costs it extracts in fixing abject suffering as the only condition of social membership, is measured in the vast expanse between the scene of feeling and the effects that policies exert.

This distortion of the origins and aims of disorder is not just due to the confusion of the moment, nor merely to the traditionally grotesque representation of public bodies made by political elites and editorial cartoonists. As a force in framing the contemporary conditions of national power, the misattribution of public disorder is a strategy to delegitimate antiprivacy citizenship politics, especially where it seeks to unsettle the domains of white patriarchal nationalism. The mainstream press's representation of the serious carnival of women's liberation and antiwar activity of the early 1970s is not, after all, so far from the representation of sexual politics in mainstream places like *Newsweek* and *The Gay Agenda,* which features graphic descriptions of sexual display in Gay Pride parades and marches on Washington to equate negatively the spectacular modalities of the parade with the utopian national imaginary of queers.[26] Accusations that political activists on parade are animals unable to assimilate to the rational norms of civic life are crucial weapons in the denationalization of these populations. There is no appreciation for the desire for continuity between everyday life and political activism expressed in these serious carnivals. Take Marlon Riggs's *Tongues Untied* (1989), where the specific beauty and self-pleasure of protesters in parades is a form of sexual *and* political happiness, a part of the erotics of public personhood that queer politics imagines as central to the world of

unhumiliated sexuality (at least for gay men) it means to bring forth in America: "Black men loving Black men is the Revolutionary Act."

Finally, John Grisham's *The Pelican Brief* (1992), and the film of it (dir. Alan J. Pakula, 1993), summarize strikingly how the fear of mobocracy both constitutes and threatens to efface the popular spaces and animate bodies of adult citizens in the contemporary nation. The film opens outside the Supreme Court in the middle of a demonstration. This, the first of four major street/mob scenes in the film, means to measure a crisis of national power brought on, or so it seems, by the people who insist on being represented by it. The opening shot of the protesters quotes the iconic images from the 1968 Democratic Convention in Chicago: wild-haired youths and police in helmets struggling to move, to hit, to fall, and to remain standing; loud, incoherent, angry voices.

The camera pulls back to reveal a disorderly mob, in which some faces are obscured by the sheer number of people and the placards that are being brandished. What is the protest about? I catalog the signs and slogans: "abortion is murder"; uncaptioned pictures of aborted fetuses; "handgun control"; "no justice no peace"; "save our cities"; "AIDS cure now"; "Silence=Death"; "Come out come out wherever you are"; "gun control now"; "fur is death"; "pass gun control"; "execution is no solution"; "Death to Rosenberg" (this uncannily anticommunist sign actually refers to a liberal judge who is shortly thereafter assassinated for political reasons that are not at all linked to this cluster of protests). From this mélange of complaints we can conclude that in the contemporary United States collective social life is constituted within a sublime expanse of nationally sanctioned violent death, a condition that the animated mob breaks down to its discrete evidences and testifies to by shouting out.

At the end of the film, the camera rests happily on the smiling face of Julia Roberts, who is watching Denzel Washington on television reporting that "she's just too good to be true." By this time we have entirely lost the trace of the opening protest. It turns out that there is nothing important about the scene, it is entirely gratuitous to the narrative. The activist judge is killed because he threatens the property privilege of a fat capitalist. This capitalist, Victor Mattiece, has contributed millions to the campaign of the film's vacuous Reagan-style president; in contrast, we never see the criminal in the flesh, only a newspaper photo of him. In short, citizens acting en masse seem to be protesting *the wrong things,* and to have irrelevant views about what kinds of corruption constrain their free citizenship.

Yet the logic of the book/film is more complex. We see that when the state imagines popular resistance, its paranoia invents mass political entities like the "underground army," an underdefined institution of faceless and random radicals.[27] But when the state itself is reimagined here as a corrupt cabal of businessmen, lawyers, and politicians, the corruption is *personal* and does not rub off onto the institution, which apparently still works well when "good men" are in it. Likewise, Julia Roberts plays Darby Shaw, a sexy law student who writes the "Pelican Brief" not from a political motive, but out of love for her lover/law professor (whose mentor was Justice Rosenberg); Denzel Washington plays Gray Grantham, disinterested reporter for the *Washington Post,* out to get a story. Together they manage to create a non-subaltern-identified asexual, apolitical wedge of objective knowledge about the corrupt state. And in the end it is Roberts, with her guileless youth, her detached sexuality, her absolute privacy, her enormous smile, and her mass-mediated star aura, who becomes the horizon of the law's possibility and of a sanitized national fantasy, the new face of a remasculinized America where the boundaries are drawn in all the right places, and the personal is as vacuous as the political.[28]

Making Up Nations (2): "A Melding of Cultures"[29]

In contrast to the zone of privacy where stars, white people, and citizens who don't make waves with their bodies can imagine they reside, the immigrant to the United States has no privacy, no power to incorporate automatically the linguistic and cultural practices of normal national culture that make life easier for those who can pass as members of the core society. This is the case whether or not the immigrant has "papers": indeed, the emphasis placed on *cultural* citizenship by books like *The De-Valuing of America, Alien Nation,* and *In Defense of Elitism* confirms that acquiring the formal trappings of legitimate residence in the country is never sufficient to guarantee the diminution of xenophobic.[30]

These books argue that, where immigrants are concerned, the only viable model for nation-building is a process of "Americanization." I have suggested that, even for birthright citizens, the process of identifying with an "American way of life" increasingly involves moral pressure to identify with a small cluster of privatized normal identities. But what kinds of special pressure does this process involve for immigrants? What kinds of self-erasure, self-transformation, and assimilation are being imagined by those who worry that even the successful "naturalization" of immigrants will equal the denaturalization of the U.S. nation? What does the project of making this incipient citizen "American" tell us about the ways national identity is being imagined and managed in the political public sphere?

When a periodical makes a "special issue" out of a controversy, the controversy itself becomes a commodity whose value is in the intensity of identification and anxiety the journal can organize around it, and this is what is happening to immigration as a subject in the U.S. mainstream. Captioning *Time*'s first "special issue" on immigration, *Immigrants: The Changing Face of America* (8 July 1985), is a passage that describes what kinds of boundaries get crossed and problems get raised when the immigrant enters the United States:

> Special Issue: Immigrants. They come from everywhere, for all kinds of reasons, and they are rapidly and permanently changing the face of America. They are altering the nation's racial makeup, its cities, its tastes, its entire perception of itself and its way of life.[31]

The emphasis on time and space in this framing passage — "they" come from everywhere, "they" incite rapid change — suggests that there is something "special" about the contemporary immigrant to the United States that ought to create intensified anxieties about social change, even despite the widely held axiom that the United States is fundamentally "a nation of immigrants." The something that the force and velocity of

immigrant cultural practices is radically changing is people's everyday lives in the nation, but that "something" is underspecified. We see in particular a change in the default reference of the category "race," and concurrently the city and its dominant "tastes." These unsettlements, in turn, have forced alterations in what had ostensibly been a stable national self-concept, based on common affinities and ways of life.

Of course, every crisis of immigration in U.S. history has involved the claim that something essentially American is being threatened by alien cultural practices. In the 1985 *Time* magazine variant on this national anxiety, however, immigrants to the United States are made stereotypical in newly ambivalent ways. *Time* first represents their challenge to the "us" and the "our" of its readership — everywhere implicitly native-born, white, male salaried citizens — through a cover that shows a classic huddled mass made up mostly of Latinos and Asians of all ages, with lined or worried faces. Their faces are in various stages of profile facing the reader's right, as though the "changing" face of America that the title declares is made visible in the dynamism of their rotation. In the present tense of a new national life, they are looking off toward the edge of the page at something unidentified: their future, America's future, the scene of their prospects contained in the magazine whose pages are about to be opened. The diverted gaze of the immigrants frees the reader from identification with them: the readers too, from their side of the border, are positioned to open the magazine and see their future prophesied and plotted.

I overread this cover story in part to set up a frame for thinking about the 1993 special issue of *Time* on immigration and national life, but also to look at how national publics are characterized and made in an age of mass mediation. *Time* presents its immigrants in segmented populations, which are defined in relation to the totality "Americans": "Hispanics," "Asians," and "Blacks" each get their own article. But *Time*'s task is not merely to document changes: to name a racial or ethnic population is to name for the public a difficult problem it faces. Specifically, the magazine responds to particular issues created by the 1965 Immigration and Nationality Act, which dissolved official preference given to European migration to the United States.[32] While some section headings confirm that immigrants like "Asians" as a class and talented individuals like the Cuban poet Heberto Padilla contribute superbly to the core U.S. national culture, alien cultures are named mainly because they seem to pose threats. For "Blacks" (said to be "left behind" by the wave of new races), and the rest of the United States, "Hispanics" are the new "problem" population, so disturbing they get their own section and dominate several others, including "Business," "Policy," "The Border," "Religion," "Video," and "Behavior."

Yet the explicit rhetoric of the special issue is nothing if not optimistic: overall, the essays have a tinny and intense enthusiasm about immigration's effect on national life, and it is the ambivalent tone of voice they use to support optimism about the process of assimilation that is of interest here. An immigrant is defined by *Time* as a national alien who comes to America consciously willing to be exploited in exchange for an abstraction: "opportunity."[33] But in lived terms opportunity is not abstract. If the immigrant's value is in her/his willingness to be economically exploited for freedom, *Time* also argues that the intense labor of mass assimilation into cultural literacy itself will further enrich the already existing indigenous "national culture."[34]

> The American schoolroom has traditionally provided a hopeful glimpse of the nation's future, and some people still imagine it to be a Rockwellian scene of mostly pink-cheeked children spelling out the adventures of Dick and Jane. But come for a moment to the playground of the Franklin elementary school in Oakland, where black

girls like to chant their jump-rope numbers in Chinese. "See you mañana," one student shouts with a Vietnamese accent. "Ciao!" cries another, who has never been anywhere near Italy. And let it be noted that the boy who won the National Spelling Bee in Washington last month was Balu Natarajan, 13, who was born in India, now lives in a suburb of Chicago, and speaks Tamil at home. "Milieu" was the word with which he defeated 167 other competitors. Let it also be noted that Hung Vu and Jean Nguyen in May became the first Vietnamese-born Americans to graduate from West Point.[35]

Like their parents, these child immigrants are imagined as a heterogeneous population that lives mainly outside and on the streets of America. They compose a population whose tastes in food and art and whose creative knowledges ("Spanglish" is featured elsewhere)[36] are easily assimilable to the urges for commodity variation and self-improvement that already saturate the existing indigenous mass national "milieu." There are also *three* essays on elite immigrants who have freely brought "wealth," "brain power," and "culture" to enrich the land of opportunity that is the United States. Children and the elite: these good immigrants are good, in *Time*'s view, because they are the gift that keeps giving, willing to assimilate and to contribute difference and variation to American culture.

Meanwhile, in separate articles on immigrant women and children, we see that worthy migration is determined not only by intercultural influence and economic activity, but also by its utility as symbolic evidence for the ongoing power of American democratic ideals. That is, immigration discourse is a central technology for the reproduction of patriotic nationalism: not just because the immigrant is seen as without a nation or resources and thus as deserving of pity or contempt, but because the immigrant is defined as *someone who desires America*.[37] Immigrant women especially are valued for having the courage to grasp freedom. But what is freedom for women? *Time* defines it not as liberation from oppressive states and economic systems, but as release from patriarchal family constraints, such that the free choice of love object is the pure image of freedom itself. Indeed, an explicit analogy is drawn between the intimacy form of consensual marriage and the value of American national culture:

> Women migrate for the same reasons that men do: to survive, because money has become worthless at home, to find schooling and

jobs. But they also have reasons of their own. Single women may leave to escape the domination of their old-fashioned families, who want them to stay in the house and accept an arranged marriage. . . . [For] home, like parentage, must be legitimized through love; otherwise, it is only a fact of geography or biology. Most immigrants to America found their love of their old homes betrayed. Whether Ireland starved them, or Nazi Germany persecuted them, or Viet Nam drove them into the sea, they did not really abandon their countries; their countries abandoned them. In America, they found the possibility of a new love, the chance to nurture new selves. . . . [Americanization] occurs when the immigrant learns his ultimate lesson: above all countries, America, if loved, returns love.[38]

I will return to the utopian rhetoric of national love anon. Although *Time* admits that there are other reasons people come to the United States — for example, as part of the increasingly global proletarian workforce[39] — its optimism about immigration is most powerfully linked not to the economic and cultural *effects* of immigration on the United States or its current and incipient citizens, but to the symbolic implications immigration has on national vanity: it is proof that the United States is a country worthy of being loved. This is, after all, the only imaginable context in which the United States can be coded as antipatriarchal. Come to America and not only can you choose a lover and a specially personalized modern form of quotidian exploitation at work, but because you can and do choose them, they must be prima facie evidence that freedom and democracy exist in the United States.

Meanwhile, for all its optimism about immigrant-American nation formation, *The Changing Face of America* clearly emerges from a panic in national culture, and one motive for this issue is to substitute a new panic about change for an old one. Explicitly the issue responds to the kinds of nativist economic and cultural anxiety that helped shape the Immigration Reform and Control Act of 1986 and, more recently, California's Proposition 187. Three specific and self-contradictory worries predominate: the fear that immigrants, legal and illegal, absorb more resources than they produce, thus diverting the assets of national culture from legal citizens; the fear that immigrants, legal and illegal, are better capitalists than natal citizens, and thus extract more wealth and political prerogative than they by birthright should; and the fear that cities, once centers of cultural and economic capital, are becoming unlivable, as spatial boundaries between communities of the very poor, workers, and affluent residents have developed in a way that threatens the security of rich people and the authority of "the family."

The essay that most fully expresses this cluster of fears is the title essay, "The Changing Face of America," which provides a remarkable caption to the cover image. But what is striking about this essay, which equates "face" with place of national origin ("That guy is Indian, next to him is a Greek, next to him is a Thai," says one neighborhood tour guide),[40] is not the American xenophobia-style apprehension it expresses, acknowledges, and tries to manage. This panic of mistrust in the viability of a non-European-dominated "America" almost goes without saying in any contemporary mainstream discussion of the immigrant effect: it is expressed in the chain of almost equivalent signs "immigrant," "alien," "minority," "illegal"; it is expressed in the ordinary phrase "wave of immigrants," which never quite explicitly details the specter of erosion and drowning it contains, a specter that has long haunted American concerns about the solidity of national economic and cultural property.

Instead, what distinguishes this special issue on immigration is the way it characterizes birthright American citizenship, and particularly how it codes the relationship between the animated corporeality of immigrant desire and the enervation of the native or assimilated American. The essay about America's changing face is illustrated by photographs of immigrants who have just landed within the hour at New York's Kennedy Airport. The photographs are not meant to tell stories about the immigrants' histories. Rather, *Time* claims that the captured image of the face in the picture records an immigrant's true feeling at the threshold, the feeling of anticipation that history is about to begin again, in the context of the new nation: "The moment of arrival stirs feelings of hope, anxiety, curiosity, pride. These emotions and many others show in the faces on the following pages."[41] (These phrases caption a picture of a sleeping baby.) The immigrant portraits are like fetal sonograms or baby pictures. The specific bodies matter little. Their importance is in the ways they express how completely generic immigrant hopes and dreams might unfold from particular bodies, and they tell a secret story about a specific migrant's odds for survival — by which *Time* means successful Americanization.

The photographs of new immigrants are also made in an archaic style, often taking on the design of formal family daguerreotype portraits. Given *Time*'s explicit commitment, in this issue, to refurbishing Ellis

Island, it is not surprising that these threshold images make the immigrants American ancestors before the process of living historically as an American has happened. What are the aims of this framing modality? First, to borrow the legitimating aura of American immigrants from past generations, with whom even Euro-Americans can still identify. Second, to signal without saying it that the "wave" is no mob, but actually a series of families, bringing their portable privacy to a land where privacy is protected. Third, the structure of generationality provides a strong model of natural change, evolutionary reproduction being the most unrevolutionary structure of collective transformation imaginable, even while worries about burgeoning new-ethnic populations (of color) seem to threaten the future of (white) modern nationality. Fourth, as Roland Barthes argues, the portrait photograph is a figure of displacement and a performance of loss or death[42]; and as the immigrant has long been said to undergo a death and rebirth of identity in crossing the threshold to America, so too the picture might be said to record the "changing" over of the face as the subjects change the register of their existence.

Yet if death (of identities, identifications, national cultures) is everywhere in this issue of *Time,* and if these processes are linked complexly to the production of America, it is not simply the kind of death one associates with the iconic symbolics of national rebirth; nor its opposite, in the privileged classes' typical construction of ghetto violence and its specters as the end of America as "we" know it; nor in the standard depiction of an undervalued and exploited underclass with a false image of the *class's* undervaluation of "life" — although the special issue periodically cues up this cruel translation in essays on the unlivable city. Mainly, *The Changing Face of America* deploys images of national death to say something extraordinary about the logics by which the American desire for property and privacy makes citizenship itself a death-driven machine.

The essay on America's changing face captions its photographs with a story about what happens to the immigrant's sensuous body in the process of becoming American.

> America is a country that endlessly reinvents itself, working the alchemy that turns "them" into "us." That is the American secret: motion, new combinations, absorption. The process is wasteful, dangerous, messy, sometimes tragic. It is also inspiring.

"The story, in its ideal, is one of earthly redemption," the magazine proclaims.[43] But the process of alchemy turns out to be virtually vampiric.

It was America, really, that got the prize: the enormous energy unleashed by the immigrant dislocations. Being utterly at risk, moving into a new and dangerous land, makes the immigrant alert and quick to learn. It livens reflexes, pumps adrenaline. . . . The immigrant who travels in both time and geographical space achieves a neat existential alertness. The dimensions of time and space collaborate. America, a place, becomes a time: the future. . . . In this special issue, *Time* describes the newest Americans and addresses the myriad ways in which they are carrying on an honored tradition: contributing their bloodlines, their spirit and their energy to preserve the nation's vitality and uniqueness.[44]

The immigrant is full of vitality, and he/she provides an energy of desire and labor that perpetually turns America into itself. What then of the native citizen? Throughout the text the problem of immigration turns into the problem of abject America: we discover that to be an American citizen is to be anesthetized, complacent, unimaginative. "There is nothing deadened or smug about immigrants," the editors write. In contrast, U.S. citizenship is a form of annulment, for the attainment of safety and freedom from the anxiety for survival national capitalism promises turns out, again and again, to make old and new citizens enervated, passive in the expectation that at some point their constitutionally promised "happiness" will be delivered to them. This passivity is central to America's economic and cultural decline, implies *Time;* the metaphysics of "success" leads to the evacuation of ambition in the present tense, and threatens the national future.[45]

Thus along with the problem of cultural transformation that immigration presents to the anxious native public is a threatening, half-obscured question of national identification and identity: in 1985 *Time* proclaims the *new* immigrant as the only true American, while casting birthright and naturalized citizens as subject to enervation, decay, and dissolution. The very promise that lures persons to identify with their native or assumed U.S. national identity, the promise of freedom unearned and privacy enjoyed, is cast as an unmitigated economic disaster.

This is, perhaps, why *The Changing Face of America* emphasizes the difference between the economic and the ideal United States: if masses of immigrants are necessary to provide the proletarian and creative cultural energy for the nation's well-being, the essential nation itself must be untouched by the changing face of America, must be a theoretical nation where success is measured by civic abstractions and moral obligations.

"Love" of "home" turns out to be *Time*'s foundation for democratic American morality; American morality turns out to be the reality effect of national culture. If America is constituted metaphysically, as an ethical space of faith or belief, then intimacy with the principles of American democratic culture—property, privacy, and individuality—is the only ground for the true practice of nationhood. There are no immigrants or citizens there, in that zone of abstraction: it is a dead space, dead to the fluctuations of change. All the rest is just history.

Making Up Nations (3):
Another New *Face of America*

When in 1993 *Time* revised its earlier construction of the immigrant effect, the magazine felt compelled to do so not only because of the conflictual economic and cultural conditions of the present, but also because a new future was being assessed: it had just become common knowledge that "sometime during the second half of the 21st century the descendants of white Europeans, the arbiters of the core national culture for most of its existence, are likely to slip into minority status . . . '[w]ithout fully realizing it,' writes Martha Farnsworth Riche, director of policy studies at Washington's Population Reference Bureau."[46] The directionality of the earlier special issue on immigrants has reversed: whereas in the 1980s, the issue was immigration and the politics of assimilation (to Americanness), in the 1990s the issue seems to be the necessary adaptation all white Americans must make to the new multicultural citizenship norm, even the ones who don't live in New York, El Paso, and Los Angeles.

This special issue is thus a cultural memento mori for the white American statistical majority, but it is also a call to a mass action. What kind of mass action? At the moment of its statistical decline, it becomes necessary to reinvent the image archive of the nation in a way that turns the loss of white cultural prestige into a gain for white cultural prestige. To perform this process of transfiguration, the cover of this issue is both more and less than a death mask; it is a new commercial stereotype advertising the future of national culture: "Take a good look at this woman. She was created by a computer from a mix of several races. What you see is a remarkable preview of The New Face of America."

The changes this special issue rings on the citizen-energy crisis of the earlier issue is indicated in the facelift the newer version gives to the

SPECIAL ISSUE

Take a good look at this woman. She was created by a computer from a mix of several races. What you see is a remarkable preview of ...

THE NEW FACE OF AMERICA
How Immigrants Are Shaping the World's
First Multicultural Society

faciality of the earlier immigrant cover. Two particular domains of assimilation that have framed immigrant representation in the past are importantly altered here: in the threat and allure of the immigrant's body, and its relation to the ways assimilation is imagined, whether through generational change or the relation of labor and education to citizenship. What will count as full citizenship in the future which is also the now of the new? Whereas the earlier cover depicts multiple living ethnic-faced persons apparently involved with imagining their own future lives in America, the second cover foregrounds a single, beautiful woman looking directly out of the page, at the reader, who is, in turn, invited to "Take a good look." The earlier faces were lined — texts of history written on the body; the new face of America reveals only the labor of a faint smile on a generically youthful face. The earlier faces are clearly artificial, standing in for a "wave" of face types that Americans, in their national anxiety, have difficulty seeing as human; the second image looks like a photograph of an actually existing human being who could come from anywhere, but she is actually a Frankenstein monster composed from other "ethnic" human images, through a process of morphing. The new face of America involves a melding of different faces with the sutures erased and the proportions made perfect; she is a national fantasy from the present representing a posthistorical — that is, postwhite — future.

The "new face of America," then, has been manifestly individuated and gendered, specified and symbolized, in the eight years between *Time*'s special issues. Moreover, the contexts for the immigrant image have also changed in the interval. In the first issue immigrants are public, collective, constructed by the activity of changing nations and subjectivities on the way to becoming American; in the second, the background to the new girl in the polis is merely a phenotypic index, a subject effect. Behind her is a field of other immigrant faces, barely visible: the matrix of blurry faces, barely intelligible dots, is the dominant image of mass immigrant life in this *Time,* which is dedicated to disaggregating, categorizing, and managing the circulation and value of the contemporary immigrant population. The dots declare the immigrant a weak or faded sign, real only as an abstract racial type rather than as persons distinguished by movement through concrete and abstract spaces of any sort. As they recede behind the face of the future that is also called the "new face of America" in a kind of whirl of temporalizing, the immigrant dots are also already being forgotten.

The new American face also has a body. In the first issue the changing faces sit atop clothed bodies, because these persons are figured as social agents, capable of making history; in the second issue, the bodies are still and naked, hidden demurely behind the screen of the text, but available for erotic fantasy and consumption. This again raises images of the national fetal person, but differently than in its first incarnation. In 1985, the immigrants photographed in situ of their transition into the status "foreign national" were fetal-style because they were officially or wishfully caught as persons prior to their incorporation within the American national story: that is, the potential of their unfolding history was indistinguishable from their new identities as potential U.S. citizens. In 1993, the new face of America has the corporeality of a fetus, a body without history, an abstraction that mimes the abstraction of the American promise that retains power *because* it is unlived.

In short, the cover situates American posthistory in prelapsarian time. Appropriately, where the first issue describes the "possibility of finding a new love" in the national context as a matter of collectively inhabiting lawful national spaces or "homes," the latter text proclaims, early on, a kind of carnal "love" for the computer-generated cover girl's new face of America.[47]

But what of love's role in the technology of assimilation and nation building? What is the labor of love, if not to lose sight of the labor of the immigrant in the blinding bright light of patriotic gratitude for the possibility that there will be, if "we" do not slip unawares into multiracial society, an intelligible national future after all? In the previous special issue, the female immigrant fleeing an archaic patriarchal family represented the limits of what immigration could do to alter America. To repeat, the narrative image of the woman in flight from intimate authoritarian structures translates into a figure of and desire for America, not the abject lived-in United States where suffering takes place and survival is decided locally, but abstract America, which foundationally authorizes an elastic language of love and happiness that incorporates and makes claim on any aspiring citizen's intimate desire, as long as the citizen is, in a deep way, "legal." Likewise, in 1993, an image of a sexualized cyborg gendered female explicitly bears the burden of mature and natural national love, which involves representing and effacing the transition the privileged classes of the United States must make to a new logic of national identity and narrative.

But love amounts to even more than this when it comes to revitalizing the national narrative. Desiring to read the immigrant like the fetus and the child, whose histories, if the world is "moral," are supposed to unfold from a genetic / ethical kernel or rhizome, *Time* in 1993 installs the future citizen, not in a family that has come from somewhere else, but in a couple form begotten by a desire to reproduce in private; that is to say, in a postpolitical domain of privacy authorized by national culture and law. It further illustrates this future through a series of photographic images, which are organized into a seven-by-seven square according to visible ethnicities now procreating in the United States. The principles by which an American ethnic type is determined are very incoherent: "Middle Eastern," "Italian," "African," "Vietnamese," "Anglo-Saxon," "Chinese," "Hispanic." These images are organized on the page following the model of those squares children use to learn the multiplication tables. Within these "reproduction squares" the images are morphed onto each other so that their future American "progeny" might be viewed in what is almost always its newly lightened form.[48] The nationalist heterosexuality signified by this racial chain is suffused with nostalgia for the feeling of a stable and dominant collective identity. In the now of the American future *Time* sets forth, the loving heart is a closed-off border open only to what intimacy and intercourse produce, and even American strangers cannot enter the intimate national future, except by violence.[49]

Love of the new face embodies three feelings less hopeful than the

204

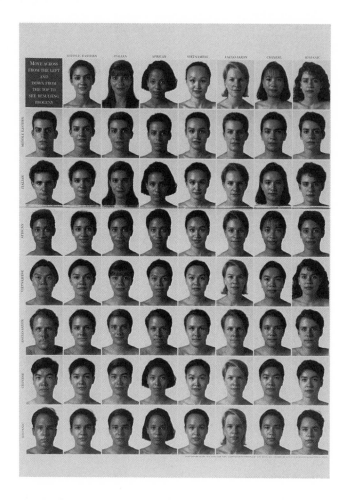

ones I've been following so far: disappointment in and disavowal of the cultural and economic violence of the present tense; a counterinsurgent rage at what has been called "the new cultural politics of difference"; and an ambition for the nation's future.[50] Let me briefly address each of these. First, *Time* reinvents the "new" but not yet achieved or experienced American future in the context of a more conventional engagement with issues of immigrant practice, never hesitating to trot out the same old categories (illegals, immigrant high culture, transformed metropolitan life, and so on) and the same old defensive bromides (Tocqueville and the *Federalist* papers are the real core of national identity that no immigrant culture can disturb). The ambition of the ex-privileged is to be able to narrate from the present a national scene of activity, accumulation, and reproduction that never becomes unintelligible, unmanageable: the wish of the dream cover is that American racial categories will have to be reinvented as tending toward whiteness or lightness, and whiteness will be reinvented as an ethnic minority (as in the story "III Cheers for the WASPS," which asserts that "Americanization has historically meant WASPification. It is the gift that keeps on giving"; moreover, it is the essence of America's "national character," which is in danger of "slipping into chronic malfunction").[51]

Time, admitting the bad science of its imaging technologies, nonetheless makes a claim that crossbreeding, in the reproductive sense, will do the work of "melding" or "melting" that diverts energy from subcultural identification to what will be the newly embodied national scene. "For all the talk of cultural separatism," it argues, "the races that make the U.S. are now crossbreeding at unprecedented rates" such that "the huddled masses have already given way to the muddled masses."[52] "Marriage is the main assimilator," says Karen Stephenson, an anthropologist at UCLA. "If you really want to effect change, it's through marriage and child rearing." Finally, "Those who intermarry have perhaps the strongest sense of what it will take to return America to an unhyphenated whole."[53] This ambition about what "the ultimate cultural immersion of interethnic marriage" will do for the nation is an ambition about the natural narrative of the national future.[54] The promise of this collective narrative depends on a eugenic program, enacted in the collective performance of private, intimate acts, acts of sex and everyday child-rearing. The American future has nothing to do with vital national world-making activities, or public life: just technologies of reproduction that are, like all eugenic programs, destructive in their aim.

Of course you wouldn't hear the violence of this desire in the tone of the special issue, which demonstrates an overarching optimism about the culturally enriching effects of all kinds of reproduction: the intimate private kind, and its opposite, from within the mass-mediated public sphere. You will remember that the special issue begins with the morpher's fantasy of cybersex with the fair lady's face he creates; it ends where "The Global Village Finally Arrives." *Time*'s excitement about globality is very specific: if the new national world of America will be embodied in private, the new global world will be public and abstract.

It would be easy, seeing all this, to say that the world is moving toward the *Raza Cósmica* (Cosmic Race), predicted by the Mexican thinker José Vasconcelos in the '20s — a glorious blend of mongrels and mestizos. It may be more relevant to suppose that more and more of the world may come to resemble Hong Kong, a stateless special economic zone full of expats and exiles linked by the lingua franca of English and the global marketplace.[55]

In other words, the melding of races sexually is not a property of the new world order, which *Time* describes as "a wide-open frontier of polyglot terms and post-national trends." This global scene is economic and linguistic, it has no narrative of identity, it is the base of capitalist and cultural expansion that supports the contraction of the intranational narrative into a space covered over by a humanoid face.

It remains to be asked why this national image of immigration without actual immigrants is marketed now, in the 1990s, and in a way that elides the optimism and anxiety about immigrant assimilation of the previous decade. To partly answer this, one must look at the essay by William A. Henry III "The Politics of Separation," which summarizes much in his subsequent book *In Defense of Elitism*.[56] This essay blames multiculturalism, political correctness, and identity politics for the national fantasy *Time* promotes in this issue: "one must be pro-feminist, pro-gay rights, pro-minority studies, mistrustful of tradition, scornful of Dead White European Males, and deeply skeptical toward the very idea of a 'masterpiece,' " says Henry.[57]

Henry equates the discord of identity politics and its pressures on the terms of cultural literacy and citizenship competence with something like an antiassimilationist stance that might be taken by immigrants. Indeed, he bemoans the ways the dominant narratives that marked competency at citizenship themselves have become "alien," thanks to the allegedly dominant fanatical multiculture that reduces the complexity of culture and power to authoritarian countercultural simplicities. As a result, "Patriotism and national pride are at stake," for "in effect, the movements demand that mainstream white Americans aged 35 and over clean out their personal psychic attics of nearly everything they were taught — and still fervently believe — about what made their country great."[58]

Henry's passionately committed essay is not merely cranky. It is also a symptomatic moment in the struggle that motivates the "new face of

America" to be born. This is a culture war over whose race will be the national one for the policy-driven near future, and according to what terms. For example, if whites must be racialized in the new national order, racial identity must be turned into a national family value. If race is to be turned into a national family value, then the nonfamilial populations, the ones, say, where fathers are more loosely identified with the health of the family form, or affective collectivities not organized around the family, must be removed from the national archive, which is here organized around a future race of cyborgs, or mixed-race but still white-enough children. It is in this sense that the defensive racialization of national culture in this issue is genocidal. It sacrifices the centrality of African American history to American culture by predicting its demise; it sacrifices attention to the concrete lives of exploited immigrant and native people of color by fantasizing the future as what will happen when white people intermarry, thus linking racial mixing to the continued, but masked, hegemony of whiteness; it tacitly justifies the continued ejection of gays and lesbians and women from full citizenship, and deploys national heterosexuality to suppress the complex racial and class relations of exploitation and violence that have taken on the status of mere clichés — that is, accepted truths or facts of life too entrenched to imagine surpassing — by the panicked readership of *Time*. After all, the entire project of this issue is to teach citizens at the core culture to remain optimistic about the U.S. future, and this requires the "new face" the nation is already becoming not to have a memory.

This epidemic of quasi-amnesia was sponsored by the Chrysler Corporation, a company sure to benefit from the translation of the immigrant into an image of an immigrant's future racially mixed granddaughter from a nice family in a white American suburb. And it should not be surprising that the "new face of America" generated even more new faces: on the cover of the *National Review,* which shows a young African American child running away from a graffiti mustache he has drawn on the "new face" of *Time*'s cover, accompanied by a story that blasts *Time*'s refusal to engage directly in the class and race war it is romancing away;[59] on the cover of *Mirabella,* in which a picture of a morphed woman and a computer chip makes explicit the desire to love and aspire only to faces that have never existed, unlike one's pitiful own; and in at least two marketing magazines,[60] which were directly inspired by *Time*'s "new face" to think of new ethnic markets in cosmetics, so that "ethnic" women might learn how simultaneously to draw on and erase the lines on their faces

that distinguish them as having lived historically in a way that threatens their chances of making it in the new future present of America.

Making Up Nations (4): Face Value and Race

In *Time* we have learned that the experience of the national future will be beautiful, will be administered by families, will involve intimate collective patriotic feelings, and will take place in the domestic private, or in foreign publics, places like Hong Kong or, say, CNN, the contemporary American postnation. In reinventing the national icon, embodied but only as an abstraction, *Time* delinks its optimism about national culture from the negativity of contemporary public politics: in the abstract here and now of *Time*'s America, the rhetorics of victimhood and minority that identity politics and multiculturalism have deployed are given over to the previously unmarked or privileged sectors of the national population; in the abstract here and now of this America, people at the bottom are considered American only insofar as they identify with and desire the status of the unmarked.

In this light we can better see more motives for official America's embrace of heterosexuality for national culture. For one thing, *Time*'s fantasy logic of a tacitly white or white-ish national genetic system integrated by private acts of consensual sex that lead to reproduction provides a way of naturalizing its separation of especially African American history and culture from the national future, and thus implicitly supports disinvestment in many contexts of African American life in the present tense. In making the main established taxonomy of race in the United States an archaic formation with respect to the future it is projecting as already here or "new," the issue of *Time* makes core national subjectivity itself racial along the lines of scientific racism through images of what it calls "psychic genes" that mime the genes that splice during reproduction to produce new likenesses.

Second, heterosocial marriage is a model of assimilation like e pluribus unum, where sexual and individual "difference" is obscured through an ideology/ethics of consensual "melding" that involves channeling one's world-making desires and energy into a family institution through which the future of one's personhood is supposed to unfold effortlessly. So too the new face of America, having been bred through virtual sex acts, projects an image of American individuals crossbreeding a new citizenship form that will ensure the political future of the core national culture. In sum, the nationalist ideology of marriage and the couple is now a central vehicle for the privatization of citizenship: first, via moralized issues around privacy, sex, and reproduction that serve as alibis for white racism and patriarchal power; but also in the discourse of a United States that is not an effect of states, institutions, ideologies, and memories, but an effect of the private citizen's acts. The expulsion of embodied public spheres from the national future/present involves a process I have been describing as an orchestrated politics of nostalgia and sentimentality marketed by the official national culture industry, a politics that perfumes its cruelty in its claim to loathe the culture war it is waging, blaming social divisions in the United States on the peoples against whom the war is being conducted.

In itself, there is nothing cruel in using racial morphing to make up fantasy images of a new national identity, especially insofar as the purpose might be to counter the national/global traffic in stereotypes of nationality, race, sexuality, and gender. Indeed, this is what morphing was invented to do, to represent the unintelligibility of the visible body, and thus to subvert the formulaic visual economy of identity forms, which are almost always monuments to the negativity of national power. Yet the morphing technology *Time* uses to make its racial, sexual, economic, and national imaginary appear to be a visible reality is haunted by the process of amnesia / utopia that must accompany the seamlessness of these corporeal transformations. Nowhere is this haunting more manifest than in Michael Jackson's video for the song "Black or White." I say "haunting" because the ghosted forms of the bodies left behind by this mode of racial and sexual futurism are instructively and insistently visible in Jackson's fantasy. The visual scene of the video is at first located in public, collective, and historically saturated spaces of dance and ends with Jackson's utter solitude. In this translation of space, the video seems to repeat the pattern of privatization I have been describing, which supports disinvesting in cultural, collective forms of personhood while promoting an image of the legitimate, authentic individual situated in the spaces of intimate privacy. Yet the video also disinvests in privatized citizenship, by representing in complicated and powerful ways the world of national, racial, sexual, and class injustice the politics of privacy ejects from the dominant national narrative.

The video is split into two. First, the song "Black or White," during which Jackson shuttles among a frenetic montage of national images. Neither the song's lyrics nor its music refers to nationality: this mise-en-scène is invented for the visual text, which has its own narrative that meets up with, or morphs into, the song's love story in the section's final minutes. The story of the lyric is the story about love that modern sentimentality has long told: traditions of violence between people like us that might keep us apart do exist, but it doesn't matter, I can still love you; all the cruel forces of history could seek to hurt me for being with you and I would still love you. Absent the video, the pop lyric enters just enough into both the racial conflicts of contemporary U.S. life and the self-esteem pedagogies of much pop music to tell the absent lover that as far as Jackson's concerned, "It doesn't matter if you're black or white": history is "history," and conceivably anyone who wants to can be his "baby" or his "brother."

But the visual story reorganizes the song's emphasis on love's transcendence of the violence of racism, locating itself in the stereotypes and forms of intelligibility that characterize *national* cultures, as though the nation form were racism's opposite and the solution to the problem of "black or white," a racial taxonomy which the visuals reveal as ridiculously oversimple by virtue of the multicultural casting of the national scenes. Each national image Jackson encounters gets its own pseudo-authentic set, and each population is represented by the stereotyped version of itself that saturates the American popular-cultural imaginary.

National types from Africa, from India, from Russia, from the Native American Southwest, and from the U.S. inner city dance national dances in open, public spaces, and as Jackson migrates transglobally through these scenes, he dances improvisations on the dances of the other national cultures.

But then every context for a national dance becomes subverted by shots of the video's production apparatus. There is, apparently, nothing authentic about the dances themselves: they are valued *because* they are invented traditions and joyous expressions of a desire for national form, especially for the artificiality of form. Michael Jackson himself wears no stereotyped national costume, although in wearing black pants and white shirts he starkly represents what doesn't "matter" in the song. His decision to sing the chorus "It don't matter if you're black or white" while standing on an artificial image of the Statue of Liberty, however, suggests that his absence of a stereotyped national body *is* his performance of being American. In addition, the U.S. inner-city scene is populated by the unmarked adult's symbolic Other, a group of infantile citizens, and at a certain point, a black baby and a white baby in diapers sit atop the globe playing peacefully with a toy that contains and minimizes the hard history the song is telling. Indeed, as though it were advertising *Time*'s desire to eradicate multicultural citizenship politics, the video has the child actor Macaulay Culkin lip-synching, to the voice of an adult, male African American rapper, the lines "It's a turf war / on a global scale / I'd rather hear both sides of the tale / it's not about races, just places, faces."

The final segment of the video's first half takes literally the lyric's assertion "I'm not going to spend my life being a color," by performing through computer-morphing technology what the lover would like to perform with his will: the end of racial and gender boundaries. The video moves through the space marked by a series of differently sexed and multiply raced faces. Their bodies are naked, stripped of the national costume. Absent any "cultural" boundaries, the faces happily turn into each other while singing the words "It's black, it's white, yeah, yeah, yeah." Despite the politically saturated differences of race and gender in their faces, all of them have shining eyes, great hair, and beautiful teeth.

But countering the frenetic glossing of the stereotype with a lyric about a star's refusal to live his intimate life and his public life within the American-style color scheme, Jackson choreographs another segment, which created such a scandal that Jackson cut it from the video directly after its television premiere on November 14, 1991. It is now available in its complete state in video stores. The uncut video, from Jackson's *Dangerous: The Short Films,* opens with a tabloid-style montage of the sensation the second part of the video created. The scandal was provoked mainly by Jackson's masturbatory self-groping and destruction of property in this scene, which people took to imply an advocacy of these kinds of acts. Jackson issued a public apology which said that he had meant no harm, and that he had not intended to promote either violence or masturbation.

In the suppressed segment, Jackson is alone in a city. There are no other persons there but himself—although it is not clear he *is* himself, for he enters the screen morphed into the body of a black panther—I mean the *Panthera pardus* kind. He enters the inner-city scene as the panther, and his body emerges silently out of its body. Although this is part of the "Black or White" video, in this segment there is neither music nor song. There is no language either, but a series of screams, accompanied by dance. There is no happiness or optimism, but rage and destruction of property, property that displays the signs of white American racism by which Jackson, as a citizen, is always surrounded and endangered.

In the past, when Jackson has entered an imitation inner city—notably in the videos for "Beat It," "Thriller," and "The Way You Make Me Feel"—the inner city has been a place where a crumbling environment, a black public sphere, and heterosexual tension are entirely intertwined. The environment of "The Way You Make Me Feel" in particular predicts "Black or White" with its desolate and graffiti-laden surroundings. But the crisis "The Way You Make Me Feel" expresses is sexual. (In its first two lines someone says to Jackson, "You don't know about women. You don't have that kind of knowledge.") But in the suppressed segment of "Black or White" no one can question Jackson's sexual competence— he's a successful masturbator. Instead, the crisis here is racial.

On the walls and on the glass of the inner city he lives in we see the graffiti slogans "Nigger go home," "No More Wet Backs," "KKK Rules," a swastika. Like the protest signs in *The Pelican Brief,* these epithets emanate from diverse sites and address different problems in American life. But if in *The Pelican Brief* slogans and rallies issue from the spaces of subordination, in "Black or White" the fighting words are uttered from the extremes of a contested racial/national privilege greedy for more domination. Screaming and dancing, Jackson breaks the windows that broadcast these messages. Amidst a cascade of sparks bursting in air from the sign of the "Royal Arms Hotel" that collapses from the sheer force of Jackson's rage, he howls a counter-national anthem beyond language and music. At one point he throws a trash can through a big generic storefront window. As when Mookie throws the trash can through the window of Sal's Famous Pizzeria to begin a riot in Spike Lee's *Do the Right Thing* (1989), Jackson's extraordinary violence performs the limit of what his or anyone's eloquence can do to change the routine violence of the core national culture. His act, isolated and symbolic, is almost as much a blow against a politically dissociated cultural studies.

One might say more about the films this segment quotes — *Singin' in the Rain*,[61] *Do the Right Thing*, and *Risky Business*.[62] But I want to focus on the dominant political intertext: the black panther, the animal that is Jackson's technological origin and end. By this single sign he signals the amnesiac optimism or the absolute falseness of the utopian performative "It don't matter if you're black or white."

Most importantly, the eloquent dance Jackson dances in the second segment, which refuses syntactic language in a hailstorm of howling, performs the violence of the traffic in U.S. stereotypes, in order to show that *having an identity in the culture of the stereotype makes a citizen public, makes the citizen definitionally on the streets, not privileged by any privacy protections, constantly in danger,* and thus, here, for a minute, Dangerous. In other words, life on the streets in this video reminds us that the fantasy of a private, protected national space is a fantasy only a nonstigmatized person, a privileged person, can realistically imagine living. This is the kind of person who can freely use the waste and stereotype-laden languages of national culture, like jokes, graffiti, and gossip, and who can, without thinking, keep coaxing the stereotype's reference away from the cartoon it should mean, back to the real it does mean, thereby making unsafe the contexts in which the stereotyped peoples live. As the last shot of the video proclaims in large type, "Prejudice is Ignorance."

"Black or White" seems to argue that the stigmatized person cannot use realism to imagine a world that will sustain her/him, for the materials of that world are saturated with a history of ordinary violence, violence so prosaic it would be possible to wield without knowing it, violence that feels like a fact of life. To break the frame of ordinariness, the stigmatized person seems to have two aesthetic choices: spare, howling, formalist minimalism, as in the second part of the video; or lush fantasy diva activity, as in the broad oversimple wishfulness and technologically supported impossibility of the first part.[63]

And yet the processing of U.S. racism in this video goes on. In 1995, Jackson released a greatest-hits album of sorts, titled *History*. With it he released a greatest-hits video collection, which claims that it includes "Black or White." However, *History* dramatically changes the story this video tells. While the rereleased version follows *Dangerous* in returning

the black panther segment to its rightful place next to "Black or White," it also sanitizes this segment, but in ways that should not, by now, surprise.

In the expurgated version of the black panther portion, all the masturbatory images of Jackson remain. But all the racist graffiti has been cleansed from the scene: no KKK, no "nigger," no swastika, no "wet back" anywhere. The clip of Jackson captioned by "Prejudice is Ignorance" is also edited out. The destruction of racism by fantasy solutions, refused by the video's first edition, is now completed in the video called *History*, and it requires the self-destruction of Jackson's own text, which has had to further bury its memories through a kind of horrifying mnemoplasty. These memories seem to have been digitally lifted, following the same logic that had Forrest Gump digitally edited into spaces he could not have historically experienced. That is, Jackson continues to revise history, and particularly the history of national racism, by revising what its images tell you about what it takes him to survive in America.

In the reedited version, Jackson's destruction of property and his howling appear to be solely the expression of his physical and sexual power, frustration, and self-consolation. This shift from racial to sexual corporeality might be explained by the immediate context in which *History* was marketed: accused of sexually abusing children after so long identifying himself with advancing their happiness in the hard world, Jackson attempts to use *History* to make himself appear safe, and in several ways. He includes a brochure with the record that contains images of his abuse as a child, assertions of spiritual and not sexual feelings for children, and testimonials to his rectitude by mainstream American celebrities like Steven Spielberg and Elizabeth Taylor. He also draws attention to his very public heterosexual marriage to Lisa Marie Presley, and in the iconography of the *History* cover art he casts himself as a heroic monument — to children and to "history." Thus in the reedited version of "Black or White" Jackson attempts to assert conflicting views of himself: his safety to children, his self-contained sexuality, and his virile adult heterosexuality. To do this the signs of history, nationality, transnationality, racism, and the urban black public sphere are sacrificed from the black panther segment of "Black or White," remaining only in their smudged traces in the song's happy lyric. His struggle for citizenship becomes fully sexual, and Jackson now appears animated by a desire for an infinitely expanding zone of privacy.

Imagine what kind of scandal the latter part of "Black or White" would have created were there dozens or hundreds of angry black men screaming, destroying, dancing, groping. Before the revision, both segments expressed a wish for a public, a collective culture, perhaps a movement culture (of the Black Panther kind), one that supports a world that no longer polices the way one inhabits race, gender, or the isolations of ordinary privatized sexuality. Absent collective struggle, Jackson's own very public and painful relation to sexual anomaly, to racial ambivalence, to animals, and to bodily transformation is everywhere visible. Watching any version of "Black or White," it is impossible not to think of the compulsive self-morphing Jackson's own body has undergone to try to erase his vulnerability to the nationally supported violence of race, gender, class, and sexuality — at least from his face. We can see the ravages of this violence in their incomplete effacement.

When *Time* magazine deploys the immigrant morph it is not to provide any kind of lens through which the most banal forms of national violence can be viewed and reexperienced painfully. Its essay on the morph takes us back to where we began, in the universe of *Forrest Gump:* the special issue is introduced by the headline "Rebirth of a Nation." Can it be an accident that the new face of America is captioned with a citation of D. W. Griffith's racist nationality? (An answer: Sure, racist citation can be unconscious or unintentional — that is what makes the simple pun and other cruel and popular forms of dominant cultural privilege so hard to contest.) When the magazine next participates in the logic of the morph, in the summer of 1994, it is to darken the face of O. J. Simpson, accused of killing his wife and a friend of hers. *Time* was saying many things in translating Simpson into darker hues: not only had the celebrity allegedly killed two people, but he had seemed to do it while passing as someone who had transcended his "origin," a word used broadly in the Simpson literature to denote poverty while screaming "race." Even now, passing is a crime against white people's desire to dominate race through fantasy scenes and fixed definitions. Simpson had seemed successfully to morph himself, but his arrest and the revelations of battery and drug use that quickly followed peeled away the new face to reveal a "darker" kid from the ghetto who was unassimilable to the "lighter" game face he used in his crossover career.[64]

When a human morphs himself without a computer, through ambition or plastic surgery or assimilation to a putatively normal lifestyle or, say, through interracial marriage to a more racially and class-privileged person, that identification and that passing makes him more likely to be a member of the core national culture, according to the logic of normalization I have been describing. But when his passing up the hierarchy of value fails and falls into a narrative about the real trauma in which visible order is actually a screen over terrible misrule, he unsettles the visual discipline of the American identity form that makes white people feel comfortable, and thus fouls the space of abstract personhood, ostensibly the American ethical space. In Simpson, racial and class morphing come to look like an abuse of the national privilege to be abstract, tacit, entitled, normal: or this is the view of *Time,* whose "optimistic" desire for the new face of America to create a posthistorical future in which all acts take place in a private space of loving citizen discipline attempts and fails to screen out an ongoing race and class struggle of unbeautiful proportions; a sex war of outrageous exhibition; a global conflict about the ethics of labor and ideologies of freedom; and a political public sphere where adult citizens identify powerfully with living in the complex, jagged edges of a terrible and terribly national present tense.

Coda: A Scar across the Face of America

"There is a terrible scar across the face of America the beautiful," said Pat Buchanan in 1992, as he ran for president of the United States.[65] The scarred face to which Buchanan refers seems unrelated to the hypothetical forms — fetal, normal, cyborg — in which so much fantasy of a revived American way of life is now being invested. It is nothing like the face of America that *Time*'s computer produced, a prosthetic image of a hopeful national future. It is nothing like the body of *Forrest Gump,* which transcends national trauma to produce beautiful children. And it is nothing like Michael Jackson's computer-generated (re)vision of a national body liberated from racial and sexual humiliation, strangeness, violence, and history. It is more like *Time*'s representation of the darkened face of O. J. Simpson, which is the current model moral image of what a damaged and veiled social subjectivity looks like, a once-beautiful thing whose degeneracy registers on the surface as a distortion, an eruption, a gash, or a scar, with a brutal and unforgettable historicity that the body registers externally and eternally. Buchanan never represents what the face of America looked like before it was scarred; it was just beautiful, a luminous abstract image of the righteous body politic. It is as though the scar itself makes the face concrete, human, fallen, and representable. In any case, he argues, the once-iconic face of American beauty has been scarred, and "terribly" — by "1.5 million abortions per year."

To Buchanan and many antiabortion rhetoricians, the devastating violence of 1.5 million abortions per year by women in the United States destroys the natural beauty of America, a space which has nothing to do with anything remotely ecological. Instead, the beauty to which the presidential candidate alludes is an abstraction for a natural way of life that is also a specific version of American national culture. These days, identification with this natural, national way of life is cast as part of a holy nation-building project by much of the secular and religious right — in considerable pro-life material, and also in the three volumes of the Republican and Christian *Contract with America*.[66] In the image archives of these reactionary movements, the aborting or improperly sexual person is not only self-destructive, but destructive of nature, culture, and spirit as well. Nor does she figure as a citizen of the nation Buchanan imagines. In his rhetoric, the fetus is the unmarked, perfect face of America, and its abortion is a visible self-mutilation. This horrible image supports an allegory of wasted life, a wasted way of life, and a culture of degenerate citizenship in a declining nation.

As we have seen, one embodiment strategy of both the religious and the secular right, which has been adopted more fuzzily by the dominant media, is to produce a revitalized image of a future United States from the genetic material of what was dominant, and then to build a new national public sphere around this past/future image of the good life in the United States. The prepolitical child and other infantile and incipient citizens have become so important to public-sphere politics partly because the image of futurity they convey helps fend off more complex and troubling issues of equity and violence in the present. The recent book *Alien Nation* demonstrates this process, when the author, Peter Brimelow, explains his desire to bring into being a white, postimmigrant America: "My son, Alexander, is a white male with blue eyes and blond hair. He has never discriminated against anyone in his little life. . . . But public policy now discriminates against him" in favor of the " 'protected classes' that are now politically favored, such as Hispanics," a population he sees lamentably expanding, pushing his innocent son to the margins from his rightful place in the center.[67] Yet while inciting racialist and nationalist panic in the present through images of white pain in the future, national sentimentalists like Brimelow claim that their politics are superior to politics as usual. Driven by ethical and spiritual commitments to natural justice, common sense, and a good, long, intimate generic family life, they promote a mode of being they think is at once sacred, ahistorical, and national.

One response to this politics among progressive writers has been to represent the "voices" of or put "faces" on American citizens who do not live and/or aspire to membership in the institutions and life narratives described by the American dream, so that those with prerogative in the formerly unmarked populations, those white, financially fixed, or heterosexually identified people, for example, might recognize that people unlike them are humans worth full citizenship after all. Books in the important tradition of Studs Terkel's *Working,* Faye Ginsburg's *Contested Lives,* or Marilyn Davis's *Mexican Voices/American Dreams* might indeed teach the persons who read them to break with their own xenophobia, misogyny, racism, sex bigotry, or aversion to the relatively and absolutely poor. Likewise, every time someone who has suffered makes the pilgrimage to Washington to testify before Congress about the hard effects of the law, it is surely possible that someone else might see it and imagine millions of people so testifying in a way that changes the kinds of nationally sanctioned prejudice and harm they are willing to support. But the nation has witnessed Anita Hill, and many others, testifying without making an irrevocable difference that counts. One person, one image, one face can only symbolize (but never meet) the need for the radical transformation of national culture, whose sanitary self-conception these days seems to require a constant cleansing of the nonnormal populations — immigrant, gay, sexually nonconjugal, poor, Hispanic, African American — from the fantasy scene of private, protected, and sanctified "American" life.

The changes that would make such testimony central to an undefensive democratic culture in the United States can only be effected in collective and public ways — not simply by changing your individual feelings about something to which you used to be averse. To effect such a transformation requires sustained, long-term, collaborative, multiply mediated agitation against the narrow, privatized version of the American way of life everywhere: in the political public sphere, in the courts, in the middlebrow media, at work, in the labor of living every day, in all the avant-gardes, subcultures, and normal spaces we can imagine. This means not killing off the family or intimacy, but inventing new scenes of sociality that take the pressure off the family form to organize history for everything from individuals to national cultures. Only by taking the risk to make demands that will render people vulnerable (first, to changing their minds) will it be possible to make the culture here called "national" adequate to any of the things and all of the people for which it ought to stand, in this current state of emergency.

6   The Queen of America Goes to Washington

City: Notes on Diva Citizenship

On Diva Citizenship

What would it mean to write a genealogy of sex in America in which
unjust sexual power was attributed not to an individual, nor to patriarchy, but to the nation itself? Such an account would expose the
circuits of erotic and political dominance that have permeated collective
life in the United States: it would register how intensively *sexual* white
Americans' relations have been to African American people, as well as to
other people of color, and it would demonstrate the perverse play of
attraction and aversion in the political life of the polis; it would show
how vital the existence of official sexual underclasses has been to national
symbolic and political coherence, linking experiences of violated sexual
privacy to the doctrine of abstract national personhood; it would radically transform what is considered *national* about the history of the
"public" and the "private" in the United States; finally, it would establish
an archive for a different history, one that claimed the most intimate stories of subordinated people as information about *everyone's* citizenship.

To inaugurate the long view of citizenship's sexual history, I begin
with three cases: Harriet Jacobs's slave narrative *Incidents in the Life of a
Slave Girl* (1861), Frances E. W. Harper's postslavery novel *Iola Leroy*
(1892), and the Senate testimony of Anita Hill (1991). These cases, life
stories of African American women transcribed across the span of a
century, speak volumes about subaltern survival in a nation where coerced sexualization is both banal and a terrorizing strategy of control in
the interstices of democracy.[1]

But how can Hill's contemporary example, neither a text nor a narrative of slavery, be spoken of in the same breath with Jacobs's and

Harper's work? Narrating such a genealogy as even a broken lineage of citizenship threatens to flatten out the complex intersecting histories they register, of race, sex, class, gender, and national identity in the U.S. public sphere from the Civil War to Civil Rights.[2] Hill, an Ivy League-educated, African American attorney who worked a string of high-status corporate, federal, and academic jobs, must live in a different universe, and a different nation, from the African American women who preceded her, as well as most of her contemporaries. Yet despite these differences, there have been devastating and telling continuities in the material limits to dignity and citizenship the women here found. The cases of Jacobs, Hill, and the fictional Iola Leroy harmonize in ways that not only unsettle easy periodization but offer an opportunity both to rethink and to remake radically the lexicons, contexts, and publics central to the story of being American.

How can U.S. "minorities" abide, just one more day, the ease with which their bodies — their social labor and their sexuality — are exploited, violated, and saturated by normalizing law, capitalist prerogative, and official national culture? Mass violence by subordinate citizens must seem an ongoing possibility to anyone who knows U.S. history, anyone who has seen occasional moments of violence flash up only to be snuffed out in a mist of hegemonic hand-wringing, supression, neglect, and amnesia.[3] What are the *technologies of patience* that enable subaltern people to seem to consent to, or take responsibility for, their painful contexts? What are national subjects taught that causes them to channel the energy of collective distress into the work of deferring a demanding response to it?[4]

Moments of optimism for the transformation of U.S. political and social culture abound in the stories of subordinated peoples. The spectacle of Anita Hill testifying before the Senate and the American people manifested to me the importance of grasping the unlikely rhetoric of these moments. A member of a stigmatized population testifies reluctantly to a hostile public the muted and anxious history of her imperiled citizenship. Her witnessing turns into a scene of teaching and an act of heroic pedagogy, in which the subordinated person feels compelled to recognize the privileged ones, to believe in their capacity to learn and to change; to trust their desire to not be inhuman; and trust their innocence of the degree to which their obliviousness has supported a system of political subjugation. These moments are acts of strange intimacy between subaltern peoples and those who have benefited by their subordination. These acts of risky dramatic persuasion are based on a belief that the privileged persons of national culture will respond to the sublimity of reason.

I call these moments acts of Diva Citizenship. Diva Citizenship does not change the world. It is a moment of emergence that marks unrealized potentials for subaltern political activity. Diva Citizenship occurs when a person stages a dramatic coup in a public sphere in which she does not have privilege. Flashing up and startling the public, she puts the dominant story into suspended animation; as though recording an estranging voice-over to a film we have all already seen, she renarrates the dominant history as one that the abjected people have once lived sotto voce, but no more; and she challenges her audience to identify with the enormity of the suffering she has narrated and the courage she has had to produce, calling on people to change the social and institutional practices of citizenship to which they currently consent.[5]

Diva Citizenship has a genealogy that is only now beginning to be written; the fate of its time- and space-saturating gesture has been mostly to pass and to dissolve into nostalgia, followed by sentences like "Remember that moment, just a second ago, when X made everything so politically intense that it looked like sustained change for good would happen?" The centrality of publicity to Diva Citizenship cannot be underestimated, for it tends to emerge in moments of such extraordinary political paralysis that acts of language can feel like explosives that shake the ground of collective existence. Yet in remaking the scene of public life into a spectacle of subjectivity, it can lead to a confusion of willful and memorable rhetorical performance with sustained social change itself.[6]

In the primary texts to follow, the diva-auratic moments are variously pessimistic and optimistic about the kinds of social transformation speaking in public might make. They also measure how big the national public is, traversing a variety of media forms and public spheres — from the Old Testament to CNN. They resonate with images from some current work in cultural studies, texts by Donna Haraway, bell hooks, Wayne Koestenbaum, and others.[7] For Haraway, the fantasy political project is to cultivate "cyborg citizenship." This postmodern marriage of bodies and technologies into hybridized identities and counterhegemonic coalitions takes all forms of personhood to be public, and vanquishes the "private identity/public world" distinction to the dustbin of modernist history. Hooks derives a similar politics of the "third world diva girl" from the everyday forms of assertive and contesting speech she absorbed among "Southern black folk." These forms of diva speech violate norms of class decorum between and among white, Third World, and African American feminists who try to limit the ways other women can legitimately take, hold, use, respect, or demonize public authority: hooks argues that the transgression of a gentility that pretends social relations are personal and private rather than public, political, and class-based must be central to any liberation politics. For Koestenbaum, the diva emerges in a public "ordinariness touched by sublimity." He argues that the diva form has already been crucial to the emergence of a "collective gay subcultural imagination," performing the public grandiosity of survival and the bitter banality of negotiating everyday life in a way that creates a transgressive and threatening counterculture. "Where there is fever," he writes, "the need for police arises." Crossing police barricades and the civilizing standards of public life, Diva Citizenship takes on as a national project the need to redefine the scale, the volume, and the erotics of "what you can do for your country."

One diva-tinged strategy of the women in our particular archive has been its royalist strain.[8] In *Iola Leroy,* Harper locates the promise of Diva Citizenship in the biblical story of Queen Esther. Iola Leroy is a mulatta, daughter of Marie, a Creole slave, and Marie's white owner, Eugene Leroy, who had fallen in love with his slave and illegally married her. Prior to the marriage, the owner/lover sent his wife-to-be from his plantation to a finishing school. *Iola Leroy* narrates the day of Marie's graduation. Marie makes an abolitionist speech, executing a performance of refracting ironies, for she is a Creole slave woman speaking to a free white audience on the day she graduates from the "finishing" school that will enable her to pass as a white wife. "Like Esther pleading for the lives of her people in the Oriental courts of a despotic king, she stood before the audience, pleading for those whose lips were sealed, but whose condition appealed to the mercy and justice of the Nation."[9] The analogies between Marie and Esther are myriad. Forced to pass as a Persian in the court of Ahasuerus, the king and her husband, Esther speaks as a Jew to save her people from genocide. She mobilizes the contradictions of her identity to unsettle the representational and political machinery of a dominant culture; she makes it desire her. It is thus not only in the gesture of special pleading that Marie absorbs Esther, but in the analogy between the passing mulatta and the assimilated Jew. Esther's capacity to pass not only made her erotic masquerade the default activity of her everyday embodiment, but gave her sexual access to power — which she used, not in a prevaricating way, but under the pressure of a diasporic ethics. Purim, Queen Esther's holiday, is offered as a day of masquerade, revelry, and rage at tyranny — although as a story additionally about a wronged queen (Vashti) and a holocaust, its status as an origin tale of domestic and imperial violence cannot be glossed over.[10] But Queen Esther stands in Harper's text as a monument to Diva Citizenship: a foreign national separated at birth from the privileges of nationality, and also a slave to masterly fantasies of sexual hierarchy and sensational excess who learned to countertheatricalize her identity, and to wield it against injustice.

Harriet Jacobs's contribution to this monarchial fantasy politics deploys a queen too, but not as a figure of tactical self-distortion, instrumental sexual intimacy, and rhetorical optimism. Instead, the diva queen of this text stands like a colossus, a rhetorical figure of superior physical power who remediates and remakes the relations between politics and the body in America. The context for the queen's emergence is a chapter of *Incidents in the Life of a Slave Girl* titled "What Slaves Are Taught to Think of the North." Jacobs represents the "state of civilization in the late nineteenth century of the United States" by showing a variety of indirect and noncoherent ways the nation came into deliberate contact with slaves — through scandalous and petty torture. In turn, Jacobs shows how the slaves misrecognize, in potentially and sometimes strategically radical ways, what constitutes the nation. She describes at great rageful length the double strategy of subordination masters use: sexual brutality to male and female slaves, and lies, what she calls "the pains" masters take, which construct false scenarios about "the hard kind of freedom" that awaits freed or escaped slaves in the North. Jacobs writes that some male slaves, thoroughly demoralized by the impossibility of imagining political freedom, become actively complicit in the scene of sexual savagery, actually sneaking "out of the way to give their masters free access to their wives and daughters,"[11] because sexuality is the only exchange value the slaves pseudopossess. Disgusted by the soul-killing effects of unjust rhetorical and sexual power, Jacobs seizes the master's tools of misrecognition and affective distortion and turns them back, not on the master, but on the nation:

> One woman begged me to get a newspaper and read it over. She said her husband told her that the black people had sent word to the queen of 'Merica that they were all slaves; that she didn't believe it,

and went to Washington city to see the president about it. They
quarrelled; she drew her sword upon him, and swore that he should
help her to make them all free.

That poor, ignorant woman thought that America was governed
by a Queen, to whom the President was subordinate. I wish the
President was subordinate to Queen Justice. (45)

Let us suppose it were true that the queen of America came down to
Washington and put the knife to the president's throat. Her strategy
would be to refute his privilege, and that of citizens like him, to be above
the sensational constraints of citizenship. The queen of America educates
him about his own body's boundaries with a cold tip of steel, and he
emancipates the slaves. But Jacobs, never one to give the nation credit for
even potentially recognizing its excesses, closes this anecdote not advocating violence on this individual president but subversively transfer-
ring the horizon of national identity to its illiterate citizens. She does this
in order to counter what Haraway has called "the informatics of domination."[12] Using the misrecognitions of everyday life as the base of her
national archive, Jacobs shows how national consciousness truly cuts a
path through gossip, deliberate lies of the masters, the political illiteracy
of "the people," the national press, the president of the United States
who lives in Washington, the queen of America who is dislocated from
any specific capital, and the queen of Justice who rules, perhaps in a
parallel universe to that of the other queen, and who has no national
boundaries. In so creating this genealogy, this flowchart of power whose
boundaries expand with every sentence written about America, Jacobs
dislocates the nation from its intelligible official forms. She opens up a
space in which the national politics of corporeal identity becomes displayed on a monarchial body, and thus interferes with the fantasy norms
of democratic abstraction; in so doing, she creates an American history
so riddled with the misrecognitions of mass nationality that it is unthinkable in its typical form, as a narrative about sovereign subjects and their
rational political representation. For no American president could be
subordinate to any queen — of America or of Justice. Bracketing that
horizon of possibility, it becomes imperative to witness the scandalous
promise of Jacobs's version of Diva Citizenship, which is to exploit a
fantasy of cutting across the space that doesn't exist, where abstract and
corporeal citizenship come into their contradictory contact not on the
exploited and minoritized body but on *the body of the nation*.

In contrast, Anita Hill says that she did not intend to be a Diva Citizen. Her story highlights the ongoing historical importance of testifying, showing that at any minute a text, a gesture, an event can be saturated with the political potential for representing unpredictable change. As we will see, at the time of her emergence into the public imagination, she saw herself as not "political," but "ordinary," the opposite of a queen.[13] Her own testimony was not launched as a divine counter to the sexual world of white heteroracial erotics, but as a complaint made in the rational tones of an insulted professional colleague. Indeed, in Hill's testimony, two genealogies of exploitation converge. In both domains of experience, this kind of violation has been a widespread social practice protected by law. One is the sexual history of African American women in white heterosexual culture, to which I have referred. The other is revealed in the discourse of sexual harassment. Invented as a technical legal category when middle-class white women started experiencing the everyday violations of sexual dignity in the workplace that working-class women have long endured, sexual harassment has provided a way to link the ordinariness of female sexualization to other hard-won protections against worker exploitation and personal injury.[14] It has also contributed to vital theoretical and policy reconsiderations of what constitutes consent and privacy in public: according to sexual harassment law, there is no space of work that is private and personal, not even under the aegis of national-democratic protections. Hill's testimony generated a widespread optimism that, finally, men would "get it"; that is, would understand that the workplace is a public space in which women's sexual and economic vulnerabilities are constantly being irritated by both deliberate cruelty and the unthinking casualness of privilege. Despite her failure to convince the Senate about Thomas and his alleged proclivities, Hill's testimony turned into an act of national pedagogy that still generates commentary, controversy, and political struggle: an act of Diva Citizenship.

Jacobs, Harper, and Hill are not identical, but the tactics of their pedagogy and the conditions of their constraint in America link them unequivocally. They risked rhetorical and political failure under what they perceived to be the pressure or the necessity of history, to behave as native informants to an imperial power; that is, they mimed the privileges of citizenship in the context of particular national emergencies. These national emergencies are, in chronological order, slavery, Reconstruction, and the dismantling of the civil-rights project of which the nomination of Clarence Thomas to the Supreme Court was both symptom, symbol, and instrument. These emergencies were experienced first as personal, intimate, and private. Hill, Harper, and Jacobs responded to these emergencies, these experiences of national sexuality, by producing what might be read as a counterpornography of citizenship. For the next two sections I will characterize this critical genre through readings of the nineteenth-century texts, and then shift historical perspective to Anita Hill. In the closing section, I will talk about the poverty of a mass politics that must build its coalitions via grandiose public dramatic performances of injured subjectivity. A sexually toxic American culture and a national fantasy of corporeal dignity will characterize this story throughout.

A Meditation on National Fantasy, in Which Women Make No Difference

The hierarchies of American citizenship can be tracked according to the distribution and coding of sensations. Two distinct moments in the nineteenth-century texts crystallize the conditions and fantasies of power that motivate its modes of affective domination, and so represent the negative space of political existence for American women in the last century. It may not appear that the sexual and affective encounters I will describe are indeed national, for they take place intimately between persons, in what look like private domains. But the women's enslavement within the sensational regime of a privileged heterosexuality leads, by many different paths, to their transposition of these acts into the context of nationality. Even if sexual relations directly forced on these women mark individuals as corrupted by power, the women's narratives refuse to affirm the private horizon of personal entitlement as the cause of their suffering. America becomes explicitly, in this context, accountable for the sexual exploitation it authorizes in the guise of the white male citizen's domestic and erotic privilege.

Incidents in the Life of a Slave Girl registers many moments of intense corporeal stress, but one particular transitional gesture measures precisely on Harriet Jacobs's body the politics of her situation: hers is a hybrid experience of intimacy and alienation of a kind fundamental to African American women's experience of national sexuality under slavery. A mulatta, she was thought by some whites to be beautiful, a condition (as she says) that doubles the afflictions of race. She writes that the smallest female slave child will learn that "If God has bestowed beauty upon her, it will prove her greatest curse. That which commands admiration in the white woman only hastens the degradation of the female slave" (28). Racial logic gave America a fantasy image of its own personal underclass, with European-style beauty in the slave population justifying by nature a specific kind of exploitation by whites, who could mask their corporeal domination of all slaves in fantasies of masculine sexual entrapment by the slave women's availability and allure. For dark-skinned, "black," women, this form of exploitation involved rape and forced reproduction. These conditions applied to mulatta women too, but the lightness of these women also provided material for white men's parodic and perverse fantasies of masking domination as love and conjugal decorum.[15] Theatrically, they set up a parallel universe of sexual and racial domestic bliss and heterosexual entitlement: this involved dressing up the beautiful mulatta and playing white-lady-of-the-house with her, building a little house that parodied the big one, giving her the kinds of things that white married ladies received, only in this instance without the protections of law. Jacobs herself was constantly threatened with this fancy life, if only she would consent to it.

This relation of privilege, which brought together sexual fantasy and the law, disguised enslavement as a kind of courtship, and as caricature was entirely a production of the intentions and whims of the master. Harriet Jacobs was involved in an especially intricate and perverse game of mulatta sexual guerrilla theater. One of her moves in this game was to become sexually involved with a white man other than her owner, Dr. Flint. (This man's *nom de théâtre* is "Mr. Sands," but his real name was Samuel Tredwell Sawyer and he was a U.S. congressman, a status to which I will return in the next section.) Jacobs reports that Mr. Sands seemed especially sympathetic to her plight and that of their two children, and when he is introduced in the narrative's first half, he seems to represent the promise of a humane relation between the sexes in the South — despite the fractures of race, and in contrast to the sexual and rhetorical repertoire of violences with which Dr. Flint tortures Jacobs and her family. But the bulk of *Incidents* finds Jacobs in constant psychic torture about Sands himself. Her anxiety about whether he will remember her when she is gone, and remember his promises to free their children, makes her risk life and limb several times to seek him out:

> There was one person there, who ought to have had some sympathy
> with [my] anxiety . . . but the links of such relations as he had

formed with me, are easily broken and cast away as rubbish. Yet how protectingly and persuasively he once talked to the poor, helpless, slave girl! And how entirely I trusted him! But now suspicions darkened my mind. (142)

No longer believing that Sands is a man of his word, Jacobs at length decides to escape — not at first from the South, but from Dr. Flint, following an intricately twisted path through the swamps, the hollow kitchen floors, and the other covert spaces of safety semisecured by the slave community.[16] This spatial improvisation for survival culminates in a move to her grandmother's attic, where she spends seven years of so-called freedom, the price of which would be lifelong nervous and muscular disruptions of her body.

On the last day of her transition from enslavement, which is also the end of her freedom of movement, Jacobs walks the public streets of her hometown (Edenton, North Carolina) in disguise, one that required perverse elaborations of the already twisted "epidermal schema" of slavery.[17] In her traveling clothes she does not assume white "lady's" apparel, but hides her body in men's "sailor's clothes" and mimes the anonymity of a tourist, someone who is passing through; in this last appearance in her native town she appears in blackface, her skin darkened with charcoal. A juridically black woman whose experience of slavery as a mulatta parodies the sexual and domestic inscription of whiteness moves away from slavery by recrossing the bar of race and assuming the corporeal shroud of masculinity. This engagement with the visible body fashions her as absolutely invisible on the street. Moving toward escape, she passes "several people whom [she] knew," but they do not recognize her. Then "the father of my children came so near that I brushed against his arm; but he had no idea who it was" (113).

When Mr. Sands does not recognize Jacobs, though he sees her and touches her body, it becomes prophetically clear how specific his interest in her was. He desired a mulatta, a woman who signifies as white but provides white men a different access to sexuality. Dressed as a man, she is invisible to him. With a black face, she is invisible to him, no longer an incitement to his desire. Touching him she thinks about other kinds of intimacy they have had — she calls him the father of their children — but in a certain sense her body registers what is numb to his because he is privileged. He has the right to forget and to not feel, while sensation and its memory are all she owns. This is the feeling of what we might call the slave's two bodies: sensual and public on the one hand; vulnerable, invisible, forgettable on the other. It is not surprising in this context that until Jean Fagin Yellin performed her research, the scholarly wisdom was that Harriet Jacobs could not have produced such a credible narrative. Her articulate representation of her sensational experience seemed itself evidence for the fraudulence of her claims to authorship.[18]

If Jacobs experiences as a fact of life the political meaninglessness of her own sensations, Harper represents the process whereby Iola is disenfranchised of her sensations. In the following passage Iola discovers that she is a slave, politically meaningful but, like Jacobs, sensually irrelevant. Harper meticulously narrates Iola's sustained resistance to the theft of her senses by the corporeal fantasies of the slave system.[19] This resistance is a privilege Iola possesses because of the peculiar logic of racial identity in America, which draws legal lines that disregard the data of subjectivity when determining the identity of "race." Iola is a mulatta raised in isolated ignorance of her mother's racial history. As previously described, her mother, Marie, was a Creole slave of Eugene Leroy's, manumitted and educated by him before their marriage. Against Marie's wishes, the father insists that the children grow up in ignorance of their racial complexity, the "cross" in their blood. He does this to preserve their self-esteem, which is founded on racial unselfconsciousness and a sense of innate freedom. When the father dies, an unscrupulous cousin tampers with Marie's manumission papers and convinces a judge to negate them. He then sends a lawyer to trick Iola into returning South and thus to slavery. Her transition between lexicons, laws, privileges, and races takes place, appropriately, as a transition from dreaming to waking. She rides on the train with the lawyer who will transport her "home" to the slave system, but she is as yet unknowing, dreaming of her previous domestic felicity.

> In her dreams she was at home, encircled in the warm clasp of her father's arms, feeling her mother's kisses lingering on her lips, and hearing the joyous greetings of the servants and Mammy Liza's glad welcome as she folded her to her heart. From this dream of bliss she was awakened by a burning kiss pressed on her lips, and a strong arm encircling her. Gazing around and taking in the whole situation, she sprang from her seat, her eyes flashing with rage and scorn, her face flushed to the roots of her hair, her voice shaken with excitement, and every nerve trembling with angry emotion. (103)

When, like the prince in a debauched *Sleeping Beauty,* the lawyer kisses Iola, he awakens her and all of her senses to a new embodiment. At first Iola dreams of life in the white family, with its regulated sexualities and the pleasure of its physical routine. Feeling her father's arms, kissing her mother, hearing the servants, snuggling with mammy: these are the idealized domestic sensations of white feminine plantation privilege, which provides a sensual system that is safe and seems natural. This is why Iola does not understand the lawyer's violation of her body. Since he already sees her as public property, authorized by a national slave system, he feels free to act without her prior knowledge, while she still feels protected by white sexual gentility. Thus the irony of her flashing-eyed, pulsating response: to Iola this is the response of legitimate self-protectiveness, but to the lawyer the passion of her resistance actually increases her value on the slave market. Her seduction and submission to the master's sexuality would reflect the victory of his economic power, which is a given. Her sensations make no sense to the slave system; therefore, they are no longer credible. Her relation to them makes no difference. This is the most powerful index of powerlessness under the law of the nation.

Slavery, Citizenship, and Utopia: Some Questions about America

I have described the political space where nothing follows from the experience of private sensation as a founding condition of slave subjectivity, a supernumerary nervous system here inscribed specifically and sexually on the bodies and minds of slave women. We see, in the narratives of Jacobs and Iola Leroy, that the process of interpellating this affective regime was ongoing, and that no rhetoric could protect them from what seemed most perverse about it: the permission it seemed to give slave owners to create sexual fantasies, narratives, masquerades of domesticity within which they could pretend *not* to dominate women, or to mediate their domination with displays of expenditure and chivalry.

But if this blurring of the lines between domination and play, between rhetorical and physical contact, and between political and sexual license always worked to reinforce the entitled relation to sensation and power the master culture enjoyed, both *Incidents* and *Iola Leroy* tactically blur another line — between personal and national tyranny. In the last section, I described the incommensurate experiences of intimacy under slavery.

Here I want to focus on how these intimate encounters with power structure Jacobs's and Harper's handling of the abstract problem of *nationality* as it is experienced — not as an idea, but as a force in social life, in experiences that mark the everyday. For Jacobs, writing before Emancipation, the nation as a category of experience is an archive of painful anecdotes, bitter feelings, and precise measurements of civic failure. She derives no strength from thinking about the possibilities of imagined community: hers is an anti-utopian discourse of amelioration. In contrast, Harper writes after the war and enfranchisement. These conditions for a postdiasporic national fantasy provide the structure for her reimagination of social value and civic decorum in a radically reconstructed America. The felt need to transform painful sexual encounters into a politics of nationality drove both of these women to revise radically the lexicon and the narratives by which the nation appears as a horizon of both dread and fantasy.

Jacobs's *Incidents* was written for and distributed by white abolitionists, whose purpose was to demonstrate not just how scandalous slavery was, but how central sexuality was in regulating the life of the slave. Yet the reign of the master was not secured simply through the corporeal logics of patriarchy and racism. Jacobs shows a variety of other ways her body was erotically dominated in slavery — control over movement and sexuality, over time and space, over information and capital, and over the details of personal history that govern familial identity — and links these scandals to a powerful critique of America, of the promises for democracy and personal mastery it offers to and withholds from the powerless.

Jacobs's particular point of entry to nationality was reproductive. The slave mother was the "country" into which the slave child was born, a realm unto herself whose foundational rules constituted a parody of the birthright properties of national citizenship. Jacobs repeatedly recites the phrase "follow the condition of the mother," framed in quotation marks, to demonstrate her only positive representation in the law, a representation that has no entitlement, a parodically American mantra as fundamental as a phrase about following she had no right to use, "life, liberty, and the pursuit of happiness."

But the technicalities of freedom would not be enough to satisfy Jacobs that America had the potential to fulfill its stated mission to be a Christian country. To gain free, unencumbered motherhood would be to experience the inversion of the sexual slavery she has undergone as a condition of her noncitizenship: at the end of the text, her freedom legally secured, she considers herself still unfree in the absence of a secure domestic space for her children.[20] But if Jacobs's relation to citizenship in the abstract is bitter and despairing, her most painful nationally authorized contact was intimate, a relation of frustrating ironic proximity.

I have characterized her sexual and reproductive relation with Mr. Sands, the U.S. congressman Samuel Tredwell Sawyer. A truly sentimental fiction would no doubt reveal something generous about Congressman Sawyer, about a distinguished political career that might have included, somehow, traces of the influence Jacobs had on Sawyer's consciousness, revealed in a commitment to securing legal consensus on the humanity of slaves; and it would be simply trivial to note that issues of the *Congressional Globe* from 1838 reveal him in another universe of political consciousness, entirely undistinguished (he seems concerned with laws regulating dueling). More important, *Incidents* establishes that his rise to national office directly correlated with his increasing disregard for his promises to emancipate their children and her brother, both of whom he had bought from Flint in isolated acts of real empathy for Jacobs. Like many liberal tyrants, Sawyer so believes that his relative personal integrity and good intentions place him above moral culpability that he has no need to act morally within the law. Indeed, the law is the bar to empathy. When Harriet's brother, William, escapes from him, Sawyer says petulantly, "I trusted him as if he were my own brother, and treated him as kindly . . . but he wanted to be a free man. . . . I intended to give him his freedom in five years. He might have trusted me. He has shown himself ungrateful; but I shall not go for him, or send for him. I feel confident that he will soon return to me" (135–36).

Later, Jacobs hears a quite different account from her brother, but what's crucial here is that the congressman whose sexual pleasure and sense of self-worth have been secured by the institution of slavery is corrupted by his proximity to national power. Yet Jacobs speaks the language of power, while Sawyer speaks the language of personal ethics; she looks to political solutions, while his privilege under the law makes its specific constraints irrelevant to him. Under these conditions Jacobs concludes three things about the politics of national sexuality. One is borne out by the performative history of her own book: "If the secret memoirs of many members of Congress should be published, curious details [about the sexual immorality of official men] would be unfolded" (142). The second she discovers as she returns from a trip to England where she has found political, sexual, racial, and spiritual peace and regeneration: "We had a tedious winter passage, and from the distance spectres seemed to rise up on the shores of the United States. It is a sad feeling to be afraid of one's native country" (186). Third, and finally, having established America as a negative space, a massive space of darkness, ghosts, shame, and barbarism, Jacobs sees no possibility that political solutions will ameliorate the memory and the ongoing pain of African American existence — as long as law marks a border between abstract and practical ethics. By the end of *Incidents* national discourse itself has become a mode of memorial rhetoric, an archive of dead promises.

I have identified two kinds of experience of the national for Jacobs: the actual pain of its practical betrayals through the many conscriptions of her body that I am associating with national sexuality, and a psychic rage at America for not even trying to live up to the conditions of citizenship it promises in law and in spirit. After Emancipation, in 1892, when Frances Harper is writing *Iola Leroy,* speaking at suffrage conferences, at the National Congress of Negro Women, and at the Columbian Exposition, she imagines that citizenship might provide a model of identity that ameliorates the experience of corporeal mortification that has sustained American racisms and misogyny.[21] Harper argues that "more than the changing of institutions we need the development of a national conscience, and the upbuilding of national character," but she imagines this project of reconstruction more subtly and more radically than this kind of nationalistic rhetoric might suggest.[22] She refuses the lure of believing that the discourse of disembodied democratic citizenship applies to black Americans: she says, "You white women speak here of rights. I speak of wrongs. I, as a colored woman, have had in this country an education which has made me feel as if I were in the situation of Ishmael, my hand against every man, and every man's hand against me."[23] But Jacobs's solution to the enigma of social life under racism and misogyny, to make familial relations the index of social justice, was not the only solution to this violent touching of hands. In contrast to Jacobs's narrative, Harper's *Iola Leroy* seizes the scene of citizenship from white America and rebuilds it, in the classic sense, imagining a liberal public sphere located within the black community.[24] More than a critical irritant to the white "people," the text subverts the racially dominant national polity by rendering it irrelevant to the fulfillment of its own national imaginary. Harper's civic and Christian black American nationality depends not only on eliding the horizon of white pseudodemocracy; she imagines that African American nationalism will provide a model of dignity and justice that white American citizens will be obliged to follow.

A double movement of negation and theorization transforms the condition of citizenship, as the novel imagines it. Harper's critical tactic banishes white Americans from the utopian political imaginary activity of this text. The initial loss of white status is performed, however, not as an effect of African American rage, but rather as an act of white political rationality. A general in the Northern army, encountering the tragedy of Iola's specific history and the detritus of the war, disvows his own identification as an American. He thinks, "Could it be possible that this young and beautiful girl had been a chattel, with no power to protect herself from the highest insults that lawless brutality could inflict upon innocent and defenseless womanhood? Could he ever again glory in his American citizenship, when any white man, no matter how coarse, cruel, or brutal, could buy or sell her for the basest purposes? Was it not true that the cause of a hapless people had become entangled with the lightnings of heaven, and dragged down retribution upon the land?" (39). This repudiation envelops national, racial, and gendered self-disenfranchisement, and clears the way for a postpatriarchal, postracist, Christian commonwealth. Its ethical aura hovers over the novel's postwar narrative as well: Iola's experience of racism and misogyny in the metropolitan and commercial spaces of the North induces more pronouncements by whites about the unworthiness of white people to lead America in official and everyday life, since it is white national culture that has transformed the country from a space of enlightenment to a place of what she calls shadows and foreshadowing.

Such political self-impeachments by whites make it possible for Harper to reinvent a truly African American–centered *American* citizenship. In this sense race in *Iola Leroy* is not solely a negative disciplinary category of national culture but becomes an archive of speech and life activities recast as a political arsenal. The originary form for African American insurgent community-building derives from the subversive vernacular practices of slave life — from, as the first chapter title suggests, "The Mystery of Market Speech and Prayer Meetings." The narrative opens in the marketplace, where the slaves are shown to use an allegorical language to communicate and to gossip illegally about the progress of freedom during the Civil War. Just as the white masters travel, "talking politics in . . . State and National capitals" (7), slaves converse about the freshness of butter, eggs, and fish, but these ordinary words turn out to contain covert communication from the battlefield (7–8). In addition to exploiting the commercial space, the slave community performs its political identity at prayer meetings, where more illegal communication about the war and everyday life under slavery also transpires in allegory and secrecy.

The internal communications and interpretations of the community became public and instrumental in a different way after the war, when the place where the community met to pray to God and for freedom is transformed into a site where families dispersed by slavery might recombine. "They had come to break bread with each other, relate their experiences, and tell of their hopes of heaven. In that meeting were remnants of broken families — mothers who had been separated from their children before the war, husbands who had not met their wives for years" (179). These stories demonstrating kinship locate it not, however, in memories of shared lives or blood genealogies but rather in common memories of the violence of familial separation and dispersal. Under the conditions of legal impersonality which had governed slave personhood, the repetition of personal narratives of loss is the only currency of personhood the slaves can exchange. The collective tactic here after slavery is to circulate self-descriptions in the hope that they will be repeated as gossip and heard by relatives, who will then come to the next convention and recite their own autobiographies in the hope that the rumor was true, that their stories had echoes in someone else's life.

The collective storytelling about the diasporic forces of slavery is reinvented after the migration north, in salons where what Harper calls *conversazione* takes place. Habermas and Landes have described the central role of the salon in building a public sphere.[25] Its function was to make the public sphere performatively democratic, more permeable by women and the ethnic and class subjects who had been left out of aristocratic privilege and who learn there to construct a personal and collective identity through the oral sharing of a diversity of written ideas. Harper explains at great length how conventions and *conversazione* transformed what counted as "personal" testimony in the black community: the chapter "Friends in Council," for example, details papers and contentious conversations about them entitled "Negro Emigration," "Patriotism," "Education of Mothers," "Moral Progress of the Race," and a poem written by Harper herself entitled "Rallying Cry." All of these speeches and the conversations about them focus on uplifting the race and rethinking history, and the conditions of uplifting require imagining a just America, an America where neither race nor sexuality exists as a mode of domination. As Iola's friend Miss Delaney says, "I want my pupils to do all in their power to make this country worthy of their deepest devotion and loftiest patriotism" (251). Finally, after these face-to-face communities of African Americans seeking to transform their enslaved identities into powerful cultural and political coalitions are established, a literary tradition becomes possible: Iola herself is asked to serve the race by writing the novel of her life that is this novel. Harper, in the afterword to the novel, imagines a new African American literature, "glowing with the fervor of the tropics and enriched by the luxuriance of the Orient." This revisionary aesthetic will, in her view, fulfill the African American "quota of good citizenship" and thus "add to the solution of our unsolved American problem" (282). In sum, the transmission of personal narrative, inscribed into the interiority of a community, becomes a vehicle for social transformation in *Iola Leroy,* recombining into a multicultural, though not multiracial, public sphere of collective knowledge. In reconstructing through mass-circulated literature the meaning of collective personhood, and in so insisting on a "quota system" of good citizenship based not on racial assimilation but on a national ethics, the African American community Harper imagines solves the problem of America for itself.

The Strange Case of Clarence and Anita

When you are born into a national symbolic order that explicitly marks your person as illegitimate, far beyond the horizon of proper citizenship, and when your body also becomes a site of privileged fantasy property and of sexual contact that the law explicitly proscribes but privately entitles, you inhabit the mulatta's genealogy, a genealogy of national experience. The national body is ambiguous because its norms of privilege require a universalizing logic of disembodiment, while its local, corporeal practices are simultaneously informed by that legal privilege and — when considered personal, if not private — are protected by the law's general proximity. The African American women of this narrative understood that only a perversely "un-American" but nationally addressed text written from the history of a national subculture could shock white citizens into knowing how compromised citizenship has been as a category of experience and fantasy, not least for the chastised American classes.

This question of sexual harassment is thus not just a "woman's" question. A charged repertoire of private domination and erotic theatricality was licensed by American law and custom to encounter the African

American women of whom I have written here, and many others, whose locations in hierarchies of racism, homophobia, and misogyny will require precisely and passionately written counterhistories. In twentieth-century America, anyone coded as "low," embodied, or subculturally "specific" continues to experience, with banal regularity, the corporeal sensation of nationality as a sensation over which she/he has no control. This, in the broadest sense, is sexual harassment. These texts break the sanitizing silences of sexual privacy in order to create national publics trained to think, and thus to think differently, about the corporeal conditions of citizenship. One of these conditions was the evacuation of erotic or sexual or even sensational life itself as a possible ground of personal dignity for African American women in America. As the rational, anti-passional logic of *Incidents* and *Iola Leroy* shows, the desire to become national seems to call for a *release* from sensuality—this is the cost, indeed the promise, of citizenship.

It is this phantasmatic body that the Anita Hill/Clarence Thomas hearings brought to us in the delusional week before the vote. It was alluded to in the corporeality of Thomas himself: in his alleged exploitation of personal collegiality in federal workspaces; in the racist fantasies that he evoked to account for his victimization by Hill and on the Hill; in the aura of the minority stereotype that black authority represents as a "token" on the Supreme Court. The national body is signified in Hill's own body as well, which displayed all of the decorums of bourgeois national polity while transgressing the veil between official and private behavior that grounds the erotic power of the state. Finally, the body of the nation was configured in the images of senators sitting in judgment and in the experts they brought in to testify to the law and to issues of "character" and "appearance."[26]

What I want to focus on is a displaced mediation of the national embodiment Hill and Thomas produced, in a television sitcom about the activities of a white- and female-owned southern business: the episode of *Designing Women* entitled "The Strange Case of Clarence and Anita" that aired shortly after the Senate vote. In many ways, this episode reproduces the legitimacy of masculine speech over feminine embodiment in the political public sphere, most notably by contrasting news clips of powerful men who are speaking to clips that represent Hill only in tableau moments of demure silence before the Senate Judiciary Committee. Thus the show's stifling of Hill reproduces a version of the imperial fantasy Gayatri Spivak describes, one in which white women "heroically" save brown women from brown *and* white men.[27] But while Hill herself demonstrated respect for national decorums and conservative ideologies of authority, her *case* substantially disrupted norms of embodiment of the national space and, indeed, revealed and produced disturbances in what counts as the national space itself.

In this episode, the characters share private opinions about Thomas and Hill, along with painful personal memories of sexual harassment; but under the pressure of historical circumstance, the ordinary space of intimacy they share comes into contact with a media frenzy: T-shirts they buy at the mall that say "He did it" or "She Lied" turn their bodies into billboards, which they flash angrily at each other; opinion polls that register the microfluctuations of "public sentiment" generate conversation about linguistic bias and motivate assertions of their own superiority to the numerically represented "people"; CNN, reinstated as the source of national identity, transforms the undifferentiated stream of opinions from all over the country into national data as "official" as that emanating from Washington itself; the television set focuses the collective gaze, such that domestic and public spheres become merged, as do news and entertainment (the character Julia Sugarbaker, for example, suggests that Thomas belongs not on the Supreme Court, but in the National Repertory Theater; their friend Bernice calls Senator Alan Simpson "Bart Simpson" and confuses Hill with Anita Bryant); and in the climactic moment, a local television reporter tapes an interview with Suzanne Sugarbaker, a Thomas supporter, and Mary Jo Shively, a self-described "feminist," right in their living room. What's striking about the condensation of these media forms and forms of embodied political intimacy is how close so many different and overlapping American publics become — and in the context not of a soap opera, but of a situation comedy that refuses, this time, to contain the "situation" within the frame of its half hour. Judge Thomas and Professor Hill turn into "Clarence" and "Anita" in this situation, like TV neighbors having a domestic row, and the diverse, incorrect, passionate, and cynical opinions that flow from viewers in the room take on the status of personal and political gossip. This is not just gossip about judges or licentious senators but about the intimate details of national identity.

At one point Mary Jo explodes in rage at Senator John Danforth's claim, shown on CNN, that Anita Hill suffered from a delusional disease, "erotomania," which made her project her own desire for power onto Thomas himself, misinterpreting his professional patronage as sexual desire. Hearing Danforth's pleasure in this pop-psych diagnosis rouses Mary Jo to call his office in Washington. But she is frustrated in this desire, because the line is busy. I myself wanted to call Washington during Hill's testimony or to testify in any way to my own banal/expert knowledge of the nonconsensual erotics of power we code as "harassment." The desire for contact sometimes took the phantasmatic form of a private letter to a senator, or one to a newspaper, sometimes a phone encounter, sometimes a fantasy that a reporter from the national news or *Nightline* would accost me randomly on the street and that my impromptu eloquence would instantly transport me to the televisual realm of a Robert Bork, where my voice and body would be loud, personal, national, and valorized.

In my view this ache to be an American diva was not about persuasion. It derived from a desire to enter a senator's body and to dominate it through an orifice he was incapable of fully closing, an ear or an eye. This intimate fantasy communication aimed to provoke sensations in him for which he was unprepared, those in that perverse space between empathy and pornography that Karen Sànchez-Eppler has isolated as constitutive of white Americans' interest in slaves, slave narratives, and other testimonials of the oppressed.[28] And in appealing to a senator's authority over the terms in which I experience my (theoretically impossible) sexualized national being, I imagined making him so full and so sick with knowledge of what he has never experienced officially that he would lose, perhaps gratefully, his sensual innocence about, not the power of his own sexuality, but the sexuality of his own power, and . . .

This is where my fantasy of swearing out a female complaint would falter, stop knowing itself and what it wanted. The desire to go public, to exploit the dispersed media of national life, became my way of approximating the power of official nationality to dominate bodies — a motive which, in a relation of overidentification, I and many others had mapped onto Hill. The final narrative image of *Designing Women* also takes up this desire to sustain Hill's Diva Citizenship into the practices of everyday life, merging a radical embodied feminist politics with the aura of the star system. Annie Potts, who plays Mary Jo Shively, wears Bette Davis drag. Dixie Carter, who plays Julia Sugarbaker, masquerades as Joan Crawford. Having come directly from a dress rehearsal of a local theatrical adaptation of *What Ever Happened to Baby Jane?* they sit on the couch, exhausted. They are not exhausted from the rehearsal, but from the rage they have expended on what they call this "day of [national] infamy."

Meanwhile, their friends slow-dance the night away, like kids at a slumber party. Bette asks Joan to dance with her. They get up and look at each other. "Who should lead?" asks Bette Davis. "Well, Bette," says Joan Crawford, "considering who we are, I think we both should." And who are they? As Joan says to Bette in an earlier moment, "two of the toughest talking big-shouldered broads ever to live in this country."

The fantasy of addressing the nation directly, of violating the citizen's proper silence about the sensations of citizenship, is a fantasy that many Americans live.[29] The bodily distortions and sensual intimacy of national media degrade and swell representations of political agency so extremely that diva manipulations of publicity might always bleed into a space of surprise where anything can happen, including political experiments in reimagining agency and critical practice that burn through citizenship's anesthesia. Yet these queenly gestures and impulses toward freedom, with their fabulous and parodistic irrelevance to anything remotely transgressive, remind us that the horizon of critical national possibility lies neither in a technological solution — orchestrating mass culture and mass nationality through the intimate forms of celebrity — nor in the pseudoimmediacy of "electronic town halls" or cyberculture, as currently offered everywhere as a solution to the impersonality of power in the United States. These media forms, like the diva form itself, reproduce the utter privacy that constitutes the conservative imaginary of citizenship in contemporary national life: privacy, a sacred zone where democracy's intimate failures are constantly performed, played out, and minimized, made so miniaturized and banal as to seem "obviously" not of the public interest. But what *is* the public interest in a nation where optimism about collective life can only seem to be sustained by sanitized images of intimacy?

On the Limits of Personal Testimony and the Pedagogy of Failed Teaching

For many readers of Harriet Jacobs, the political uncanniness of Anita Hill has been a somber and illuminating experience. To summarize, these cases intersect at several points: at the experience of being sexually violated by powerful men in their places of work; at the experience of feeling shame and physical pain from living with humiliation; at the use of "going public" to refuse their reduction to sexual meaning, even after the "fact" of such reduction; and at being African American women whose most organized community of support treated gender as the sign and structure of all subordinations to rank in America, such that other considerations—of race, class, and political ideology—became both muted and insubordinate.[30] In these cases, and in their public reception, claims for justice against racism and claims for justice against both patriarchal and heterosexual privileges were made to compete with each other: this competition among harmed collectivities remains one of the major spectator sports of the American public sphere. It says volumes about the continued and linked virulence of racism, misogyny, heterosexism, economic privilege, and politics in the United States.

In addition to what we might call these strangely nonanachronistic structural echoes and political continuities, the cases of Hill and Jacobs expose unsettled and unsettling relations of sexuality and U.S. citizenship—two complexly related sites of subjectivity, sensation, affect, law, and agency. I close with long excerpts from Harper's novel, Jacobs's narrative, and Hill's testimony. Although interpretive norms of production, consumption, and style differ among these texts, each author went public in the most national medium available to her. For this and other reasons, the rhetorical gestures that rhyme among these passages provide material for linking the politics of sex and the public sphere in America to the history of nationality itself, now read as a domain of sensation and sensationalism, and of a yet unrealized potential for fashioning "the poetry of the future" from the domains where citizens register citizenship, along with other feelings.[31]

> [Iola Leroy] 'I was sold from State to State as an article of merchandise. I had outrages heaped on me which might well crimson the cheek of honest womanhood with shame, but I never fell into the clutches of an owner for whom I did not feel the utmost loathing and intensest horror.' . . .
> [Dr. Gresham] 'But, Iola, you must not blame all for what a few have done.'
> [Iola] 'A few have done? Did not the whole nation consent to our abasement?' (Frances E. W. Harper, *Iola Leroy,* 115–16)

I have not written my experiences in order to attract attention to myself; on the contrary, it would have been more pleasant to me to have been silent about my own history. Neither do I care to excite sympathy for my own sufferings. But I do earnestly desire to arouse the women of the North to a realizing sense of the condition of two millions of women at the South, still in bondage, suffering what I suffered, and most of them far worse. . . . [My] bill of sale is on record, and future generations will learn from it that women were articles of traffic in New York, late in the nineteenth century of the Christian religion. It may hereafter prove a useful document to antiquaries, who are seeking to measure the progress of civilization in the United States. (Harriet A. Jacobs, *Incidents in the Life of a Slave Girl*, 1)

It is only after a great deal of agonizing consideration that I am able to talk of these unpleasant matters to anyone but my closest friends. . . . As I've said before, these last few days have been very trying and very hard for me and it hasn't just been the last few days this week.

It has actually been over a month now that I have been under the strain of this issue. Telling the world is the most difficult experience of my life, but it is very close to having to live through the experience that occasioned this meeting. . . . The only personal benefit that I have received from this experience is that I have had an opportunity to serve my country. I was raised to do what is right and can now explain to my students first hand that despite the high costs that may be involved, it is worth having the truth emerge. (Anita Hill, *New York Times* 12 October 1991, sec. 1: 1; 15 October 1991, sec. 1: 1)

When Hill, Jacobs, and Harper's Iola Leroy speak in public about the national scandal of their private shame, they bring incommensurate fields of identity into explosive conjunction. Speaking as private subjects about sexual activities that transpired within the politically charged spaces of everyday life, their testimony remains itself personal, specifically about them, their sensations and subjectivity. We hear about "my experiences," "my own suffering," "unpleasant matters"; we hear of desires to return to silence, and of longings to be relieved of the drive to consign this material to public life, which requires the speaker to reexperience on her body what her rhetoric describes. But as their speech turns "incidents" of sexuality into opportunities for reconstructing what counts as national data—that is, since each of these sexual autobiographies aims to attain the status of a *finding*, an official expert narrative about national protocols—the authors must make themselves representative and must make the specific sensational details of their violation exemplary of collective life. It is always the autobiographer's task to negotiate her specificity into a spectacular interiority worthy of public notice. But the minority subject who circulates in a majoritarian public sphere occupies a specific contradiction: insofar as she is exemplary, she has distinguished herself from the collective stereotype; and at the same time, she is also read as a kind of foreign national, an exotic representative of her alien "people" who reports to the dominant culture about collective life in the crevices of national existence. This warp in the circulation of identity is central to the public history of African American women, for whom coerced sexualization has been a constitutive relay between national experience and particular bodies.

Hence the specifically juridical inflection of "personal testimony." This hybrid form demarcates a collectively experienced set of strains and contradictions in the meaning of sexual knowledge in America: sexual knowledge derives from private experiences on the body and yet operates as a register for systemic relations of power; sexual knowledge stands for a kind of political counterintelligence, a challenge to the norms of credibility, rationality, and expertise that generally organize political culture; and yet, as an archive of injury and of private sensation, sexual knowledge can have the paradoxical effect of *delegitimating* the very experts who can represent it as a form of experience. These three women produced vital public testimony about the conditions of sexuality and citizenship in America. Their representations of how nationality became embodied and intimate to them involve fantasies of what America is, where it is, and how it reaches individuals. This requires them to develop a national pedagogy of failed teaching. Emerging from the pseudoprivate spaces where many kinds of power are condensed into personal relations, they detail how they were forced to deploy persuasion to fight for sexual dignity, and how they lost that fight. They take their individual losses as exemplary of larger ones, in particular the failure of the law and the nation to protect the sexual dignity of women from the hybrid body of white, patriarchal official and sexual privilege. They insist on representing the continuous shifting of perspectives that constitute the incommensurate experience of power where national and sexual affect meet. They resist, in sum, further submission to a national sexuality that blurs the line between the disembodied entitlements of liberal citizenship and the places where bodies experience the sensation of being dominated. For all these verbs of resistance, the women represent their deployment of publicity as an act made under duress, an act thus representing and performing unfreedom in America. And in manifesting their previous failures to secure sexual jurisdiction over their bodies, they challenge Americans to take up politically what the strongest divas were unable, individually, to achieve.

How Can We Keep Our Children Safe?

LIFE

NEGLECT

SEXUAL ABUSE   VIOLENCE

ABDUCTION   DRUGS

TELEVISION   VULGARITY

ACCIDENTS   ALIENATION

JULY 1995 $2.95

Newsweek

BAILING OUT MEXICO

WHAT COLOR IS BLACK?

Science, Politics and Racial Identity

DIVERSITY IS

EAUTIFUL

A RADICAL NEW FORM OF PLASTIC SURGERY
GAINS POPULARITY AMONG "PRO-LIFE" MEN

★ ELECTION '95 ★

Tribune photo by James Ma[r]

Campaign manager Jim Stahel (from left) joins newly elected Naperville Mayor George Pradel; his son, George Pradel; and campaign committee member Dwight Hollonbeck for a champagne toast in a victory celebration whirlpool bath Wednesday.

Notes

Introduction: The Intimate Public Sphere

1   In 1996, both the Republican and Democratic presidential nominating conventions
     were organized around the patriotic image of a nation made of and for children. The
     image of the citizen-child took its authority and intensity not from the moralizing
     hostility of Republican "family values" rhetoric that marked the previous election,
     but from the optimistic liberalism about privatization issued by Hillary Rodham
     Clinton. Clinton's book *It Takes a Village* argues in chapters such as "Children Are
     Citizens Too" that the most powerful motive for an expanded context of social justice
     in the United States is the world adults will bring into being for their children. In
     1996, the Republicans argued that it takes a "family," not a "village," to raise a child;
     the Democrats responded by claiming that raising nontraumatized citizens requires
     the beneficent service of a much more broadly defined population of trusted guard-
     ians that includes families, communities, teachers, childcare workers, police, social
     service agencies, and so on. Despite their differences, each of these positions locates
     the nation's virtue and value in its intimate zones, in personal acts of pedagogy and
     sustenance. For more serious and complicated engagements with these issues on a
     local, national, and global scale, see Stephens, *Children and the Politics of Culture.*
2   Much has been written about the psychological, sociological, and economic conse-
     quences for U.S. "white males" who see subaltern-rights movements as having put in
     place unjust obstacles to their achievement and social value. (According to one arti-
     cle, in the seven months after the November 1994 elections, fourteen hundred news
     columns used the phrase "angry white men" to describe the bloc of voters who voted
     the Republicans into office [*Detroit News* 30 May 1995: A9].) My guess is that the
     population identified this way is actually much more diverse in membership. Many
     people of color and women identify with the world of desire for accumulation and
     self-extension attributed, here, to "white men." In addition, the *USA Today* article
     that initiated this postelection conclusion actually specified the "AWM" as a male,
     working-class, high-school graduate: as usual in analyses of national politics, class
     motives are subordinated to the corporealized identity form.
         For commentaries that employ the concept of the angry white male citizen, see E. J.
     Dionne, "A Fashionable Stereotype That Explains Very Little," *International Herald*

Tribune 4 May 1995; Dumm, *united states;* Ehrenreich, *The Snarling Citizen;* Faludi, *Backlash;* Richard Goldstein, "Save the Males," *Village Voice* 7 March 1995: 21–29; J. Hoberman, "Victim Victorious," *Village Voice* 7 March 1995: 31–33; Jeffords, *Hard Bodies;* Pfeil, *White Guys;* Pollitt, *Reasonable Creatures,* 31–41, 115–23; Paul Rockwell, "These Angry White Men Say Yes to the Concept," *San Francisco Herald Examiner* 19 June 1995: A15; James Toedtmann, "Poll Warns of Angry Women Voters," *Newsday* 6 October 1995: A64.

3 On this point, see Cindy Patton's brilliant analysis, "Refiguring Social Space."

4 As chapter 1, "The Theory of Infantile Citizenship," suggests, cartoons have a long and hallowed place in the production of critical discourse in the U.S. public sphere. But political cartoons have used the body to represent, *in extremis,* the distorting tendencies of power and identity that political culture engenders. (For more on this, see chapter 3, "America, 'Fat,' the Fetus.") At this moment, I am arguing, extreme images of personhood count as modal citizenship in the identity politics contexts of the United States, which seems to be ravaged by a farce-style moral and civil war between icons and hyphenated stereotypes. As Congresswoman Patricia Schroeder (Democrat of Colorado) opines about the realpolitik context in which she operates, "Many progressives think you have to have big reports with lots of analysis and details. And I'm saying we need to have the equivalent of verbal cartoons to show what these people [the currently vigorous Christian/conservative right-wing alliance in the U.S. Congress] are doing. When I called Reagan the 'Teflon President,' people got it. What good is a 900 page report if the people never read it?" *Ms:* 6, no. 8 (March/April 1996): 24.

5 Habermas, *The Structural Transformation of the Public Sphere,* 27–37, 43–51, 151–75, and 231–50.

6 My argument that the Reaganite right has attempted to privatize citizenship by reframing it as an intimate form of social membership might seem to suggest that the dominant nation now uncannily repeats the conservative politico-familial mood of the U.S. postwar period. There are some important confluences too, especially in the continuing and paradoxical public-sphere worry that commodity culture both fulfills people and has potentially immoral effects on individuals, family life, and the nation generally. But contemporary work on sex, gender, race, and citizenship generally argues that while the early cold war era placed the white, middle-class family at the core of postwar national consumer and political culture, the family sphere was not considered the moral, ethical, and political *horizon* of national or political interest. There are many reasons for this dissimilarity. One has to do with the particular ways familialism played in the externalization of the communist/totalitarian threat to the United States during the cold war. This process produced the normative "American" family as a site of symbolic/ideological vulnerability that both symbolized the danger the nation faced and emphasized the difference between families and the tutelary state, which had a knowledge/power apparatus that could, if strong enough, protect ordinary citizens. Furthermore, challenges to state racism during this period of the welfare state's expansion put pressure on *public* institutions in the United States to catch up to citizen desire for more equivalence between democratic ideals and national/capitalist practices. In contrast, as the cold war waned and both the state and the industrial sector contracted, the intimacy wars have escalated, producing citizens

whose proper horizon of national interest is said to be the family and its radiating zones of practice. See Corber, *In the Name of National Security;* Rogin, *Ronald Reagan, the Movie;* Dolan, *Allegories of America: Narratives, Metaphysics, Politics;* Myerowitz, *Not June Cleaver;* May, *Homeward Bound;* Omi and Winant, *Racial Formation in the United States.* For a prophetically longer view of the emergence of intimacy as the index of normativity in the United States, see Sennett, *The Fall of Public Man.*

7 For an aligned project of understanding the ambiguous impulses at play in the contemporary United States, involving identity, nationality, commodity identification, and public-sphere intimacy forms, see Gilroy, " 'After the Love Has Gone.' "

8 Tocqueville, *Democracy in America;* see also Rogin, *Ronald Reagan, the Movie.*

9 I take the logic of the nervous system as an image of the social machinery of politics and subjectivity from Taussig, *The Nervous System.*

10 On the popular contexts of right-wing culture in the everyday of the nation see Diamond, *Roads to Dominion;* and Grossberg, *We Gotta Get Out of This Place.*

11 President Bush used the phrase (penned by speechwriter Peggy Noonan) "a thousand points of light" to describe the new, defederalized, post-welfare-state nation both in his speech accepting the presidential nomination and in his inaugural speech five months later. See the *New York Times* 19 August 1988: A14, and 21 January 1989: A10.

12 See Gillespie and Schellhass, *Contract with America;* Moore, *Restoring the Dream;* Christian Coalition, *Contract with the American Family.*

13 Much has been written about the ways media conglomerates are advancing the U.S. public sphere's atrophy. See especially the special issue of *The Nation* titled "The National Entertainment State," vol. 262, no. 22: 3 June 1996. For earlier and fuller analyses of the material, as opposed to psychic, subordination of the citizen to private "public" media interests in a complicated collusion with the security sector of the federal government, see Schiller, *Information and the Crisis Economy* and *Culture, Inc;* and Mowlana, Gerbner, and Schiller, *Triumph of the Image: The Media's War in the Persian Gulf — A Global Perspective.*

14 One recent exception to this general conservative tendency to use a highly moralized intimacy rhetoric as a distraction from the discussion of citizenship's material contexts is the populism of Patrick Buchanan, a perennial national presidential candidate and pundit who simultaneously wields morality rhetoric and taps into workers' rage at the amoral abandon with which corporate downsizing has been taking place. But the protectionist policy Buchanan offers as the solution to the problem of globalization is all tied up with a nationalist intimacy rhetoric that demonizes foreignness and nonnormative difference in general, promoting a linkage among all sorts of phobias — xenophobia and homophobia in particular.

15 In particular the influential work of Chantal Mouffe, from which I have learned much, presumes the inefficacy of class rhetorics for the progressive revitalization of citizenship discourse. Mouffe chooses an antiessentialist form of identity politics, which focuses on the contingencies of identity, and its potential for alliance building, in her reconstruction of citizenship. However, the unassimilability of class discourse to identity politics could just as easily be the *model* for what a conjunctural alliance politics might look like: Mouffe's exclusion of the economic (and class experience) from the realm of cultural politics seems a critical flaw in her imagination of new

social movements. See Mouffe, "Preface, Democratic Politics Today" and "Democratic Citizenship and the Political Community," in *Dimensions of Radical Democracy*, 1–14, 225–39.

16 For example, the nonprofit organization Focus on the Family, headed by the radio and print journalist and minister, Dr. James C. Dobson, lobbies for family values in everyday life and the national public sphere with sacred verve and rational clarity. See his magazines *Focus on the Family* and *Citizen*, the latter of which gives encouragement, explanation, argument, and tactical maps for being effective in the political public sphere. See also note 12.

17 For texts that imagine a mutual transformation of subaltern and capitalist culture see, for example, *The Black Public Sphere*, ed. The Black Public Sphere Collective (Chicago: University of Chicago Press, 1995), especially Austin, "'A Nation of Thieves': Consumption, Commerce, and the Black Public Sphere," 229–52; D'Emilio, "Capitalism and Gay Identity"; Griggers, "Lesbian Bodies in the Age of (Post)mechanical Reproduction"; Sedgwick, *Epistemology of the Closet*. See also chapter 4 of this book, "Queer Nationality." Queer theory in particular has generally occupied the scene of tactical subversion rather than anticapitalist radicalism: for critical analyses of this tendency, see Hennessey, "Queer Visibility in Commodity Culture"; Lauren Berlant and Michael Warner, "Sex in Public" (*GLQ*, forthcoming). For a critique of the capitalist optimism of cultural studies in general, see Berland, "Angels Dancing."

18 This includes most liberal and materialist social theory, and would require an interminable note.

19 To break down analytic distinctions between political, economic, and cultural domains of experience and analysis has long been a project of a certain strain of Marxist cultural theory. In my own development, the promise and challenge of *Social Text* 1 (winter 1979) remains vital. See especially Jameson, "Reification and Utopia in Mass Culture"; and John Brenkman, "Mass Media: From Collective Experience to the Culture of Privatization," 94–109. See also Jameson, "Five Theses on Actually Existing Marxism."

20 For an analytic that engages the ways the dominant media of the contemporary U.S. public sphere produce national knowledge via a series of discrete, unrelated events (thus frustrating the formation of a critical culture) see Hansen, foreword, in *Public Sphere and Experience*. Taken as a whole, Negt and Kluge's work on fantasy, experience, and political life is central to the thinking in this book. See especially chapter 1, "The Public Sphere as the Organization of Collective Experience," 1–53.

21 Again, this note would be interminable. One might begin with Habermas, "On the Concept of Public Opinion," in *The Structural Transformation of the Public Sphere*, 236–50; Herman and Chomsky, *Manufacturing Consent;* Heath, "Representing Television"; and Schwoch, White, and Reilly, *Media Knowledge*.

22 Since its inception as a kind of radical thought around abolition in the U.S. mid-nineteenth century, national sentimentality has been a project of privileged white citizens dedicated to reframing citizenship. In the nineteenth century this involved replacing citizenship's original status as a property- or identity-based condition of political legitimacy with a notion of citizenship as a private and personal formation based on subjective relations of identification and similarity. In the nineteenth century, national sentimentality was a terribly flawed vehicle for inducing a more racially

and economically equitable mass national democracy: in the late twentieth century, the reverse is the case. See Samuels, *The Culture of Sentiment.* See also Mohanty, "Cartographies of Struggle."

23 For theoretical accounts of banality, violence, and national life, see Baudrillard, *In the Shadow of the Silent Majorities* and "From the System to the Destiny of Objects"; Mbembe, "Prosaics of Servitude and Authoritarian Civilities"; Mbembe and Roit- man, "Figures of the Subject in Times of Crisis"; Morris, "Banality in Cultural Studies."

24 I often encounter people who think that "real" theory is philosophy while queer theory involves moralizing identity performances dressed up as thinking. This posi- tion strikes me as anti-intellectual and, need I say it, sexually anxious. In 1986 I heard a talk by Julia Lesage that argued for using citation not only to mark the range of a text's knowledge but also as a device for building alliances. The intellectual frames for this book come predominantly from queer and Marxist critical theory: rather than producing a huge bibliography of that theory here in an omnibus footnote, I have chosen to spread the news in the text and notes of the chapters to follow.

25 At the time of this writing a backlash against cultural studies is emerging in the humanities and humanistic social sciences. Some important concerns are expressed in this resistance: about the risks of cultural or historical anachronism and comparison; about the status of scholarship that seems at times motivated by an unselfconscious presentism and/or a smug moralism that is legitimated as "politics"; about the ana- lytic status of critical writing that uses autobiography or other forms of generic syncretism; and about nonrigorous engagements with a mass culture that is all too available for reading. Many progressive scholars join traditional ones in this debate, agreeing that politicized work on culture should still follow certain established no- tions of evidence, argument, archival work, tone of voice, and theoretical and histor- ical rigor.

But it is certainly hasty and may be in bad faith to identify cultural studies generally as anecdotal, posturing, and easy to do. It is merely defensive to assume that its sites of challenge and its critical experimentality inherently produce work that is lacking in consequential knowledge and serious concepts. Those of us who work with theory have all seen people use the strategy of generalizing about the value of a threatening kind of thinking by distorting and amplifying weak sentences or underdeveloped concepts in particular cases: for example, one colleague uses the phrase "another essay about Madonna's nipples" to inveigh against cultural studies. But this kind of cheap shot, and the more subtle ones, must be countered, and for a number of reasons. The backlash against cultural studies is frequently a euphemism for discomfort with work on contemporary culture around race, sexuality, class, and gender. It is sometimes a way of talking about the fear of losing what little standing intellectual work has gained through its studied irrelevance (and superiority) to capitalist culture. It ex- presses a fear of popular culture and popularized criticism. At the same time it can express a kind of antielitism made in defense of narrow notions of what proper intellectual objects and intellectual postures should be. On the left it frequently ex- presses a fear that critical metatheory will lose its standing as the ground of politics and *real* thinking. I am not saying that work in cultural studies is always what I wish it were: but as the attacks on it cloak so many kinds of worthy and unworthy aggression and anxiety it behooves us to try to say what they are and to fight the unworthy ones in their real terms. It goes without saying that this list of counterinsurgent motives can and should be augmented.

26 For an aligned view about the place of irony and archival creativity in critical studies of nationality, see John Caughie, "Playing at Being American."

27 See, for example, Appadurai, *Modernity at Large;* Dominelli, *Women Across Continents;* Ginsburg and Rapp, *Conceiving the New World Order;* Grewal and Kaplan, *Scattered Hegemonies;* Kaplan and Pease, *Cultures of U.S. Imperialism;* Rouse, "Thinking through Transnationalism"; Schneider and Brian Wallis, *Global Television;* Shohut and Stam, *Unthinking Eurocentrism;* Spivak, "The Politics of Translation," and "Acting Bits / Identity Talk." See also chapter 5 of this book.

28 Habermas laments the exhaustion of the utopia of labor and privatization of society both in contemporary European and U.S. public spheres in "The New Obscurity: The Crisis of the Welfare State and the Exhaustion of Utopian Energies," in Habermas, *The New Conservatism,* 48–70.

29 On radical recontextualization as critical method and a condition of historical possibility see Spivak, *Outside in the Teaching Machine* and Bhabha, "The Commitment to Theory."

30 Jacobs, *Incidents in the Life of a Slave Girl,* 45.

31 Warner, introduction, *Fear of a Queer Planet.*

32 The literature on "identity" is, again, very large: some examples from it include Foucault, *The History of Sexuality,* v. 1–3; Butler, *Gender Trouble;* Katz, *The Invention of Heterosexuality;* Danielsen and Engle, *After Identity,* especially essays by Halley ("The Politics of the Closet") and Coombe ("The Properties of Culture and the Politics of Possessing Identity"); Rouse, "Questions of Identity"; and Spivak, *Outside in the Teaching Machine.* For an essay that opens new comparative ways of thinking about identity as property in the self, see Petchesky, "The Body as Property."

33 The bibliography on the historical relation between U.S. citizenship and corporealized quasi nationality or subnationality is substantial. I summarize it in *The Anatomy of National Fantasy,* 11–17, 222–23. For an important politico-philosophical engagement with the means by which a culture of democratic rights hypocritically produces a turbulent politics of race, gender, and ethnicity, see Balibar, *Masses, Classes, Ideas.*

34 Elshtain argues strenuously against the current U.S. drive to consign "shameful" identities to the private or to use shame to draw the boundary between full and incompetent citizenship, a desire she sees as making democracy impossible. See *Democracy on Trial,* especially chapter 2, "The Politics of Displacement," 37–63.

1 The Theory of Infantile Citizenship

Much thanks to Ben Anderson, Michael Warner, and the great audience at the Society for Cinema Studies for their critical engagement with this paper / project.

1 Caughie, "Playing at Being American." This chapter and this book are indebted to Benedict Anderson's pathbreaking work on the technologies of "emotional legitimacy" that sustain nation-states as the utopian form of political life. See *Imagined Communities.*

2 Lorde, *Zami,* 68–71.

3 Marian Anderson, an African American opera star, gave a concert at the Lincoln Memorial in 1939 because the racist Daughters of the American Revolution denied her request to sing *inside* Constitution Hall.

4 An excellent argument for thinking about national/capitalist space can be found in Berland, "Angels Dancing."

5 Lorde, *Zami,* 71.

6 In addition to Audre Lorde's *Zami* and the episode of *The Simpsons* titled "Mr. Lisa Goes to Washington," the archive for these observations about infantile citizenship in the national-pilgrimage plot includes *The Birth of a Nation* (dir. D. W. Griffith, 1915); *Washington Merry-Go-Round* (dir. James Cruze, 1932); *Gabriel Over the White House* (dir. Gregory La Cava, 1933); *The Littlest Rebel* (dir. David Butler, 1935); *Mr. Smith Goes to Washington* (dir. Frank Capra, 1939); *Adventure in Washington* (dir. Alfred E. Green, 1941); *Heavenly Days* (dir. Howard Estabrook, 1944); *Born Yesterday* (dir. George Cukor, 1950; remake dir. Luis Mandoki, 1993); *The Day the Earth Stood Still* (dir. Robert Wise, 1951); *The Manchurian Candidate* (dir. John Frankenheimer, 1962); *Coming Home* (dir. Hal Ashby, 1978); *Being There* (dir. Hal Ashby, 1979); *In Country* (dir. Norman Jewison, 1989); *The Distinguished Gentleman* (dir. Jonathan Lynn, 1992); *Dave* (dir. Ivan Reitman, 1993); *The Pelican Brief* (dir. Alan J. Pakula, 1993); *Forrest Gump* (dir. Robert Zemeckis, 1994). The film *Born on the Fourth of July* (dir. Oliver Stone, 1989) is an honorary member of this archive. I also thank Howard Horwitz for alerting me to the "Weenie Tots" episode of *Married with Children.*

7 Tocqueville, *Democracy in America,* vol. 1, 250–59, 336–37.

8 Negt and Kluge, "Selections from *The Proletariat Public Sphere.* "

9 Žižek, *The Sublime Object of Ideology,* 87–129.

10 Heath, "Representing Television," 278–79.

11 For the main arguments for the pervasiveness of televisual amnesia or information fatigue, see Doane, "Information, Crisis, Catastrophe." See also Feuer, "The Concept of Live Television."

12 The ongoing pedagogic/civic activity of television is more widely appreciated on the right, and the moral domination of the medium by conservatives has been central to the right-wing cultural agenda of the Reagan/Bush era. What counts as "public" access, "public" television, has undergone massive restrictive redefinition under the pressure of a certain pseudorepresentative form of "public" opinion, whose virtue is established by reference to a supposedly nonideological or non-interest-group-based politics of transcendence that must be understood as fundamentalist in its imagina- tion of a nation of pure, opinionated minds. For overviews and thoughtful reconsid- erations on the left, see Lipsitz, *Time Passages;* Rasula, "Nietzsche in the Nursery"; Schwoch, White, and Reilly, *Media Knowledge.*

13 Morse, "An Ontology of Everyday Distraction."

14 See Benedict Anderson, *Imagined Communities,* 37–46.

15 On the nationalist media contexts around the production and reception of *Mr. Smith Goes to Washington,* see Eric Smoodin's fine " 'Compulsory Viewing for Every Citizen.' "

16 Christensen, *Reel Pictures,* 45–48.

17 Another extensive and historically rich analysis of *Mr. Smith* focuses on its nationalist

media contexts in and outside the plot. See Wolfe, *"Mr. Smith Goes to Washington,"* 330–31.

18 The final function of the infantile citizen is to promote an image of what the normal citizen must do and be to occupy the nation properly. No more brazen example of the technology of normative patriotism can be found than in the film *Heavenly Days* (dir. Howard Estabrook, 1944), which sets out to define what a good national man is: the answer, repeated incessantly throughout the film, is "an average man." Fibber McGee, like all Americans, thinks that he is above average, and that his normative national identity secures that status for him. The film disabuses him of his self-esteem by linking the plot of his pilgrimage to Washington (to help with a state project of rebuilding postwar national morale) to a plot that features the real-life person of Dr. George Gallup. Molly McGee inspires Gallup to do a national poll to discover what kind of person the average U.S. man really is. Fibber wins the award from Gallup. First, Fibber is insulted and throws it out; but quickly he realizes what a resource his averageness is, and then stages a parade down Main Street to educate other citizens into proper (average, semiprivate) citizenship.

19 Spillers, "Mama's Baby, Papa's Maybe," 66.

20 On the class, gender, and sexual politics of the grotesque in contemporary America, see Kipnis, *"Reading Hustler."*

21 Lipsitz, *Time Passages,* 70–71.

22 In *The Anatomy of National Fantasy* I use the concept of the National Symbolic to describe the archive of official objects and narratives whose possession is foundational for producing citizens who identify themselves with other citizens and the nation form itself.

23 On the centrality of the Lincoln Memorial to organizing national identification and memory, see Sandage, "The Lincoln Memorial, the Civil Rights Movement, and the Politics of Memory, 1939–1963." For a more global view of nationalist monumentality that includes a discussion of Lincoln's memorial, see Benedict Anderson, "Replica, Aura, and Late Nationalist Imaginings."

24 The bibliography on national allegory is big and complex. For current arguments about its positive and negative effects, see Ahmad, *In Theory;* Jameson, *The Geopolitical Aesthetic.*

2 *Live Sex Acts (Parental Advisory: Explicit Material)*

Thanks to Roger Rouse, Kim Scheppele, Michael Warner, Jody Greene, and the great audiences at the University of Michigan, Rutgers, Harvard, and Brown for much-needed conversation and challenge.

1 Andrea Dworkin, quoted in de Grazia, *Girls Lean Back Everywhere,* 581.

2 Michael Kammen describes the particularly intensified manipulations of national nostalgia and amnesia during the gestation and rise of the Reaganite right in *Mystic Chords of Memory,* 618–88.

3 Michael Taussig names this saturation of politics by the nation "state fetishism." This is a condition in which the state uses a sublime and magical official story of national identity to mask the nation's heterogeneity. See *"Maleficium:* State Fetishism," in his *The Nervous System,* 111–40, 223.

4   The original texts meant to be reviewed were Assiter, *Pornography, Feminism, and the Individual;* Chester and Dickey, *Feminism and Censorship;* Dworkin, *Pornography;* Gubar and Hoff-Wilson, *For Adult Users Only;* Hawkins and Zimring, *Pornography in a Free Society;* Itzin, *Pornography.* I have also read more widely in the literature pro and con, and assume the entire oeuvre of Catharine MacKinnon in this essay as well.

    Of those listed above, the British feminist texts (Assiter, Itzin, Chester and Dickey) share with the work of MacKinnon and Dworkin a sense that issues of sexual difference cannot be solved by U.S.-style liberal thinking about ontological selfhood, but must address the ways the state and the nation frame the conditions of sex, sexual identity, and gender value. Of the U.S. texts that do not take a clear pornography-is-patriarchy position, the most useful is *For Adult Users Only,* which rehearses and I think extends the feminist debate over the causes, effects, and possibilities pornography poses for American women.

    But the discussion over sexuality and public life is stunted by the referential dullness or hyperelasticity of the category "pornography," along with the unstated heteronormative assumptions (about what "good" sexuality is, about the relation of the natural and the normal, about what "bad" representations do) that almost always accompany these discussions. A scrupulous specificity is necessary for any discussion of politically rezoning the place where national culture meets intimacy forms like sex. This is why this chapter seeks to place this discussion of national sexuality in a context of thinking the sexual politics of citizenship in the contemporary United States.

5   *New York Times* 25 May 1993: A8.

6   I take this way of thinking about the processes of making an institution appear hegemonic from Chandra Mohanty, who takes it from Dorothy Smith. See Mohanty, "Cartographies of Struggle," 15–16; Dorothy E. Smith, *The Everyday World as Problematic,* 108.

7   Frohnmayer, *Leaving Town Alive,* 3, 337, and passim.

8   Ibid., 314, 202.

9   Ibid., 324.

10 Ibid., 326.

11 Wodiczko's "Homeless Vehicle" has generated a number of consequential essays, the most important of which for thinking subjectivity, capitalism, and citizenship is Neil Smith, "Contours of a Spatialized Politics."

12 Frohnmayer, *Leaving Town Alive,* 291, 324–25.

13 The "Helms amendment" was offered to the U.S. Senate on October 7, 1989. It reads: "None of the funds authorized to be appropriated pursuant to this Act may be used to promote, discriminate, or produce materials that are obscene or that depict or describe, in a patently offensive way, sexual or excretory activities or organs, including but not limited to obscene depictions of sadomasochism, homo-eroticism, the sexual exploitation of children, or individuals engaged in sexual intercourse." See *Congressional Record,* 1st sess., 1989, 135, no. 134: S12967.

14 Frohnmayer, *Leaving Town Alive,* 69.

15 De Grazia, *Girls Lean Back Everywhere,* 637.

16 Frohnmayer, *Leaving Town Alive,* 326, 328–29.

17 De Grazia, *Girls Lean Back Everywhere,* 4–5.

18 Ibid., 436–37. See also de Grazia, *Censorship Landmarks.*

19 Dworkin and MacKinnon, *Pornography and Civil Rights,* 48.
20 *Jacobellis v. Ohio,* 378 U.S. 184–204 (1964); see also de Grazia, *Girls Lean Back Everywhere,* 423–33.
21 Vance, "The Pleasures of Looking."
22 See Robin West, "Pornography as a Legal Text," in Gubar and Hoff-Wilson, *For Adult Users Only,* 108–30.
23 Attorney General's Commission on Pornography, *Final Report,* vol. 1, July 1986, 839.
24 Ibid.
25 Ibid., 839–40.
26 Dworkin and MacKinnon, *Pornography and Civil Rights,* 43, 45–46.
27 Bersani, "Is the Rectum a Grave?"
28 Dworkin and MacKinnon, *Pornography and Civil Rights,* 46.
29 Attorney General's Commission on Pornography, *Final Report,* vol. 1, 849.
30 Gore, *Raising PG Kids in an X-Rated Society.*
31 Ibid., 17.
32 Ibid., 18.
33 Ibid., 41.
34 Ibid., 28.
35 Ibid., 39.
36 Ibid., 42.
37 Ibid., 43–48.
38 Ibid., 11.
39 For all its greater liberalism and greater belief in the wisdom of a welfare state, Hillary Rodham Clinton's *It Takes a Village* fully joins Gore's *Raising PG Kids* in characterizing the ideal United States as a parental public sphere.
40 Gore, *Raising PG Kids in an X-Rated Society,* 167.
41 *Griswold v. Connecticut,* 381 U.S. 479 (1965), 479–531.
42 *Roe v. Wade,* 410 U.S. 159 (1973), 113–78.
43 Eley, "Nations, Publics, and Political Cultures."
44 Warner, "The Mass Public and the Mass Subject," 399–400.

3 *America, "Fat," the Fetus*

For rigorous and challenging responses, I thank Geoff Eley and CSST at the University of Michigan (1993); the working group in contemporary culture at Rutgers University (1994); the study group in feminism and visual culture at the University of Chicago (1994); seminars at Johns Hopkins and Miami of Ohio. Also, thanks to Bill Brown, Tom Mitchell, Tom Stillinger, Mary Poovey, Jody Greene.

1 Leff and Simmons, *The Dame in the Kimono,* 86, 88, 285.
2 See also Susan Bordo, "Are Mothers Persons? Reproductive Rights and the Politics of Subjectivity," in Bordo, *Unbearable Weight,* 71–97.
3 Berlant, "National Brands/National Body." See also Warner, "The Mass Public and the Mass Subject."
4 For excellent work on the class and gender politics of the grotesque in contemporary America, see Kipnis, "Reading *Hustler.* "
5 See, for example, the devastating evidence spread throughout Amott and Matthaei,

Race, Gender, and Work; Angela Davis, "Racism, Birth Control, and Reproductive Rights"; Nsiah-Jefferson, "Reproductive Laws, Women of Color, and Low-Income Women." For an amazing history of the different paths toward citizenship different genders have traveled in the U.S. welfare state (which shows, for example, how early-twentieth-century entitlements for men escaped the feminizing rhetoric of "dependency" by consolidating loyal voting blocs for particular political parties), see Skocpol, *Protecting Soldiers and Mothers.* For a deconstruction of the class aspects of fetal personhood, see Patricia J. Williams, "Law and Everyday Life."

6   Benjamin, "A Short History of Photography." For further consideration of the optical unconscious, see Hansen, *Babel and Babylon,* 110–11.

7   Carver, "Fat," 6. Subsequent references to this text will be noted parenthetically.

8   Jameson, "Postmodernism and Utopia," 30.

9   For a brilliant performance of the relation between the stresses and pleasures of fat's exorbitant corporeality and queer sexualities, see Moon and Sedgwick, "Divinity."

10   "Sexo-semiotic" was coined by Zoe Sofia, "Exterminating Fetuses," 48.

11   See Eve Kosofsky Sedgwick, "Axiomatic," in Sedgwick, *Epistemology of the Closet,* 1–63.

12   See, for example, Kaufmann, "Yuppie Postmodernism."

13   Pollock, "Missing Women," 219.

14   See Bordo, *Unbearable Weight;* Parker, *Literary Fat Ladies;* Stallybrass and White, *The Politics and Poetics of Transgression;* Stewart, *On Longing.*

15   The feminist bibliography on reproduction is considerable. Central to any investigation would be Patricia Smith, *Feminist Jurisprudence,* 299–383; Ginsburg and Tsing, *Uncertain Terms;* Jacobus, Fox Keller, and Shuttleworth, *Body/Politics;* and the two-volume special issue of *Camera Obscura* edited by Paula A. Treichler and Lisa Cartwright, *Imaging Technologies, Inscribing Science.* Many essays from these anthologies will reappear in these notes. See also Daniels, *At Women's Expense;* Duden, *Disembodying Women;* Eisenstein, *The Female Body and the Law;* Ginsburg, *Contested Lives;* Martin, "Body Narratives, Body Boundaries" and *The Woman in the Body;* Rayna Rapp, "Constructing Amniocentesis"; Gordon, *Woman's Body, Woman's Right;* Luker, *Abortion and the Politics of Motherhood;* Petchesky, *Abortion and Women's Choice;* Spallone, *Beyond Conception;* Strathern, *Reproducing the Future.*

16   For a more state- and public-sphere-conscious set of analyses of reproduction and citizenship, see Franklin, Lury, and Stacey, *Off-Centre.* See also Gilliam, "Women's Equality and National Liberation"; Heng and Devan, "State Fatherhood"; Davies, *Third World, Second Sex,* vols. 1 and 2. For a sensible comparative view that outlines a "middle way" for thinking citizenship and privacy rights, see Glendon, *Abortion and Divorce in Western Law.*

17   See Ginsburg, *Contested Lives;* and Luker, *Abortion and the Politics of Motherhood,* 192–216.

18   For a strong explication of the relation between the segmented female body and the new reproductive misogyny, see Spallone, *Beyond Conception.*

19   Spillers, "Mama's Baby, Papa's Maybe."

20   Koonz, *Mothers in the Fatherland.*

21   For discussions of the politics and cultural contexts of monstrous antilife motherhood, see Daniels, *At Women's Expense,* 57–131; Hartouni, "Fetal Exposures"; and

"Containing Women"; Tribe, *Abortion*, 127; Tsing, "Monster Stories," 282–99; Treichler, "Feminism, Medicine, and the Meaning of Childbirth," 113–38; Petchesky, *Abortion and Women's Choice*. For a pro-life argument against the culture of monstrous maternity, see Daughters of St. Paul, *Pro-Life Catechism: Abortion, Genetics, Euthanasia, Suicide, Child-Abuse* (Boston: St. Paul, 1984).

22 Deleuze and Guattari, "What Is a Minor Literature?"; Rubin, "Thinking Sex"; Spivak, "Draupadi" and "Breast-Giver," and "Woman in Difference"; Sedgwick, *Epistemology of the Closet* and "A Poem Is Being Written."

23 See also Kipnis, " 'The Phantom Twitchings of an Amputated Limb.' "

24 Bhabha, "The Other Question."

25 Berlant, *The Anatomy of National Fantasy*.

26 Rogin, *Ronald Reagan, the Movie*.

27 See, for example, the documentary *Hollywood Goes to War* (American Movie Channel, 1993).

28 Laqueur, *Making Sex*.

29 A. Rosenfeld and L. Nilsson, "Drama of Life Before Birth," *Life* 58 (30 April 1965), especially 62–69. Subsequent references to this issue will be noted parenthetically in the text.

30 Berger, *About Looking*, 49–50.

31 Crary, *Techniques of the Observer*.

32 Benjamin, "A Short History of Photography," 203.

33 Lisa Cartwright's *Screening the Body* provides indispensable archival and conceptual knowledge about the politics of the body in the procedural contexts of modern medicine and cinema.

34 Daniels, *At Women's Expense*, especially 9–29; Kaplan, *Motherhood and Representation*, 203–4; Petchesky, "Fetal Images"; Martin, "Body Narratives, Body Boundaries"; Duden, *Disembodying Women*; Stabile, *Feminism and the Technological Fix*, 68–98.

35 Lennart Nilsson, "The First Days of Creation," *Life* 13 (August 1990): 26–37. Subsequent references to this issue will be noted parenthetically in the text.

36 See Taylor, "The Public Fetus and the Family Car."

37 Petchesky, "Fetal Images," 263, 268.

38 See Rapp, "Feminism, Medicine, and the Meaning of Childbirth"; Stanworth, "Birth Pangs."

39 Reagan, *Abortion and the Conscience of the Nation*.

40 This discussion of the politics of the voice-over in pro-life representations of fetal personhood was anticipated in Barbara Johnson's analysis of abortion and the rhetorics of personhood, "Apostrophe, Animation, and Abortion." See also the pro-life poem "O Nameless and / Voiceless Child, / We will be / your name; / We will be your voice," in the *Chicago Tribune* 19 June 1991, sec. 1: 10–11.

41 See Denise Mann's argument that television produces the "auratic decay" of the Hollywood star, who transforms the signifying conventions of intimacy and domesticity the television situation comedy circulates by enfolding cinematic power into its everyday life simulacra and narratives. Mann argues that star aura miniaturized on television encouraged fantasy relationships between fans and stars, thereby distributing aura to the everyday life anxieties of the housewife represented in, consuming, and constructed in identification with the "situation" of the comedy. "Auratic decay"

might very well be another version of the "banalization" I've been describing. See Mann, "The Spectacularization of Everyday Life."

42   In the history of antiabortion cinema, there is precedent for the association of stars and heaven with the representation of the unborn. The 1916 pro–birth control, antiabortion film *Where Are My Children?* features allegorical scenes representing aborted fetuses as heavenly babies. For the social history of this cinematic genre, see Kuhn, *Cinema, Censorship, and Sexuality*, 28–48, 105–13.

43   C. Everett Koop, "The Slide to Auschwitz," in Reagan, *Abortion and the Conscience of the Nation*, 68.

44   Eisenberg, Murkoff, and Hathaway, *What to Eat When You're Expecting*, 41.

45   Adding to the work on the cultures of fetal visualization cited in notes 15 and 34, Janelle Sue Taylor has recently written on fetal visualization, the commodity form, and the hybridity of the fetus's traumatized/sacred body that I have gathered under the rubric "banalization." See Taylor, "The Public Fetus and the Family Car."

46   For an extended discussion of the imperial sexual politics of the special (fetal) effect, see Sofia, "Exterminating Fetuses," 47–59.

47   Here is what the fetus sings in the video *Let Me Live:*

> I'm one month old, I'm very small
> I feel me growing every day, in this warm dark place
> My heart is the biggest part of me, and it's beating
> I'm so glad to be alive, I'm very glad to be alive.

> Chorus:
> Let me live, let me walk into the sunshine
> Let me live, feel my mother's arms around me,
> Feel my father's love surround me,
> Be a part of God's creation, let me live.

> I'm six weeks old now, and I've grown so much
> Look at me, I'm a half-inch long already
> I have a little brain, and a big heart
> And eyes. I can't see yet, but I will, just give me time.

> Chorus:

> Fingers and toes my own now, my own lips
> And I'm two months old today.
> And my heart is beating fast.
> And I feel another heart, big and strong, somewhere, all around me. Is that my mother?

> Chorus:

> I'm three months old now, and my arms and legs have real bones.
> I'm growing, and kicking too, can you feel it?
> I can turn my head, I can squint and frown and make a fist.
> See, I can curl my toes! And I think my mother knows I'm here. I'm alive! I'm alive!

> Chorus, last line repeats

48 Paula A. Treichler, "Feminism, Medicine, and the Meaning of Childbirth," 115.

49 Willis's casting as a fetal presence in these films repeats the role he played in late episodes of *Moonlighting:* while Maddy (Cybill Shepherd) worries about the paternity of the baby she carries, he actually *plays* the fetus, solving the narrative problem of identity long before it is solved for the mother. See Joyrich, "Tube Tied."

50 Anna Lowenhaupt Tsing, "Monster Stories," 282.

51 In my discussion of the cinema of the fetus I use the actors' "star names" to describe what their characters do in the films, to focus on the structures of commodity identification in Hollywood cinema and their effects on the comic circulation of what had been politically contested signs.

52 For readings of Alley's typicality as a failed maternal icon, see Faludi, *Backlash;* E. Ann Kaplan, *Motherhood and Representation,* 205–9.

53 On gender, comedy, and carnivalesque inversion see Horton, *Comedy/Cinema/Theory,* especially Fischer, "Sometimes I Feel Like a Motherless Child." This excellent anthology says absolutely nothing about race comedy or race, genre, and the (re)production of marginality in Hollywood: starting places for that kind of discussion are Alexander, "Fatal Beauties"; Lipsitz, *Time Passages;* Neale and Krutnik, *Popular Film and Television Comedy.*

54 Martin, *Flexible Bodies.*

55 For more on doctor/patient contestations over expertise, see Martin, *The Woman in the Body;* Oakley, *The Captured Womb;* and Rapp, "Constructing Amniocentesis."

56 The baby-fat bibliography is itself quite big. Concerns on behalf of the child that the mother regulate her eating, of course, predate the political moment of fetal personhood. The following texts, which vary widely in the forms of expertise they offer, all register anxiety over the competition between mother and fetus as anxiety about the claims of health versus the moral, aesthetic, cultural, and psychological "need" for women to not be fat once they are not pregnant. American Academy of Pediatrics; American College of Obstetricians and Gynecologists, *Guidelines for Perinatal Care* (Evanston, IL, 1983), 166; Behan, *Eat Well, Lose Weight While Breastfeeding;* Brewer with Brewer, *What Every Pregnant Woman Should Know;* Dilfer, *"Your" Baby, "Your" Body;* Eisenberg, Murkoff, and Hathaway, *What to Eat When You're Expecting;* DeLyser, Fonda, and Schapiro, *Jane Fonda's Workout Book for Pregnancy, Birth, and Recovery;* Gates and Meckel, *Newborn Beauty;* Montagu and Montagu, *Life before Birth,* 32–46; O'Brien, *Birth and Our Bodies;* Verrilli and Mueser, *While Waiting,* 99; Phyllis S. Williams, *Nourishing Your Unborn Child.*

57 For an analogous point of entry into the study of mass culture and nation formation, see Morris, "Banality in Cultural Studies."

58 This phrase opens the chorus to the theme song of *I Love Lucy.* See McClay, *"I Love Lucy,"* xxii, 116, 270.

59 "Lucy Is *Enceinte*" is episode 50 of *I Love Lucy:* its narrative is told in McClay, *"I Love Lucy,"* 70–71, 158–61.

60 Because the characters on television are made more "real" to the audience through the commodity-structured repetition of their names, I use their character names here, in contrast to my earlier determination to focus on the star aura of the film actor in the ideological system of the film text.

61 Mellencamp, "Situation Comedy, Feminism, and Freud"; Spigel, *Make Room for TV.*

62 Sobchack, "Child/Alien/Father," 14–15. See also Sofia, "Exterminating Fetuses."

63 See the works by Ginsburg, Martin, and Rapp cited in note 15 above.

64 See, for example, *As the World Turns* (February 1996) and *The Young and the Restless* (March 1992).

65 After writing this, I called Valerie and asked her about the birthday scene on Zak's video, and she acknowledged that those images and repeated narratives of her childhood did indeed influence her construction of her son's birthday. My mother called shortly after to say that, contrary to both of our recollections, the memorialized event was Valerie's six-month birthday and that only one picture of it, taken by a neighbor, ever existed.

66 Barthes, *Camera Lucida;* Bourdieu et al., *Photography.*

67 Benedict Anderson, *Imagined Communities,* 17.

68 Katha Pollitt writes about the refusal of knowledge she finds in interviewing pro-life demonstrators in "The Mind of an Anti-Abortionist," *Nation* 24 January 1987: 1, 82–84.

4 Queer Nationality

We thank our collaboratrixes: Claudia L. Johnson, Tricia Loughran, Deborah N. Schwartz, Tom Stillinger, AK Summers, Michael Warner, the Gay and Lesbian Studies Workshop at the University of Chicago, and the Cultural Forms/Public Spheres study group at the Center of Psychosocial Research.

1 There is as yet no anthology or full history documenting Queer Nation, and its redefinitions in the print media are ongoing. For some contemporary accounts of Queer Nation, see the following articles: Bérubé and Escoffier, "Queer/Nation"; Chee, "A Queer Nationalism"; Esther Kaplan, "A Queer Manifesto," in Guy Trebay's article "In Your Face," 36; Kay Longcope, "Boston Gay Groups Vow New Militancy Against Hate Crimes," *Boston Globe* 2 August 1990: 25, 31; Maria Mag Maggenti, "Women as Queer Nationals," *Outlook: National Lesbian and Gay Quarterly* 11 (winter 1991): 20–23; Deborah Schwartz, "'Queers Bash Back,'" *Gay Community News* 24 June 1990: 14–15; Shilts, "The Queering of America"; Trebay, "In Your Face."

2 Bérubé and Escoffier, "Queer/Nation," 13–14.

3 These affinity groups include ASLUT (Artists Slaving under Tyranny); DORIS SQUASH (Defending Our Rights in the Streets, Super Queers United against Savage Heterosexuals); GHOST (Grand Homosexual Organization to Stop Televangelists); HI MOM (Homosexual Ideological Mobilization against the Military); LABIA (Lesbians and Bisexuals in Action); QUEER PLANET, an environmental group; QUEER STATE, which deals with state governments; QUEST (Queers Undertaking Exquisite and Symbolic Transformation); SHOP (Suburban Homosexual Outreach Program); UNITED COLORS, which focuses on experiences of queers of color. For the extended list, see Bérubé and Escoffier, "Queer/Nation," 15.

4 Our construction of the manifold publics, polities, and symbolic cultures that traverse American life emanates from a number of sources: Benedict Anderson, *Imagined Communities;* Berlant, *The Anatomy of National Fantasy;* Echols, *Daring to Be Bad;* Freeman, "Pitmarks on the History of the Country"; Mosse, *Nationalism and Sexuality;* Nicholson, *Feminism/Postmodernism;* Young, "Polity and Group Difference" and *Throwing Like a Girl.*

5   For the political need to postminoritize cultural experience through the manipulation of representational codes, see Lloyd, "Genet's Genealogy."

6   Three essays that argue for the need to retaxonomize sexual identity have inspired this essay: Newton and Walton, "The Misunderstanding"; Rubin, "Thinking Sex"; and Sedgwick, *Epistemology of the Closet,* 1–63.

7   This death knell was sounded as early as June 1991, in Toronto, according to *Xtra!* Toronto. "Quotelines," *Outlines* 5, no. 1 (June 1991): 7.

8   See Ross, *No Respect,* 135–70.

9   Douglas Crimp and Adam Rolston, AIDS *Demo Graphics* (Seattle: Bay Press, 1990).

10   Esther Kaplan, "A Queer Manifesto," in Trebay, "In Your Face," 36; Kaplan's emphasis.

11   Fraser, "Rethinking the Public Sphere."

12   Identity is linked to territorialization, both geographical and ideological: we mean to offer an account of a subcultural *topology,* a description of how modern space requires negotiating a complex relation between situated identities and mobilized *identifications.* The shifting terrain in the meaning of the phrase "gay community" symptomatized in Queer Nation's practices has been splendidly explicated by Richard Herrell, "The Symbolic Strategies of Chicago's Gay and Lesbian Pride Day Parade."

13   Spivak, "In a Word," 129.

14   See Sedgwick, *Epistemology of the Closet,* 1–63.

15   We cite the texts in their entirety. "I Praise Life": "I praise life with my vulva. I thank the gods for all the women who have kissed my lips. I praise life." "I Praise God": "I praise God with my erection. I thank God for all the men I've slept with. I praise God." They were created in 1990 by Joe Lindsay of Queer Nation Denver.

16   Ford, "Sacred Sex."

17   D'Emilio, *Sexual Politics, Sexual Communities,* 216.

18   D'Emilio, "Capitalism and Gay Identity," 110–13.

19   Trebay, "In Your Face," 36.

20   The "Absolutly Het" series, parodies of the ads for Absolut vodka, were produced by the anonymous group OUTPOST.

21   Trebay, "In Your Face," 39.

22   From Dee-Lite's song "Try Me On, I'm Very You," on the album *World Clique.* Elektra Entertainment, 1990.

23   Kirk and Madsen, *After the Ball.* Kirk and Madsen advise the gay community to present nonthreatening images of homosexuality to straight culture, a "marketing campaign" designed to win mainstream approval for the bourgeois homosexual at the cost of eliminating drag queens, butch lesbians, transsexuals, and so on from visibility.

24   For a discussion of the relationship between the trademark, commodity identification, and the colonized American body, see Berlant, "National Brands/National Body."

25   A powerful and extensive exploration of the role of this "stereotyped fantasy body" in the black gay voguing subculture is provided by Jennie Livingston's documentary *Paris Is Burning.* See also Berlant, "National Brands/National Body."

26   On the history of the Gay Pride parade, see D'Emilio, *Sexual Politics, Sexual Communities.*

27   See Ross, *No Respect.*

28 See Herrell, "The Symbolic Strategies." Herrell discusses how Chicago politicians annually assume at the parade pseudo-Irish last names such as "Mayor Richard O'Daley." The stigma attached to various cultural groups might well be discerned by such a litmus test: the unthinkable prospect of "Mayor Richard Gayley" suggests that there is, as yet, no such thing as "honorary" symbolic homosexuality.

29 See Friedberg, "Les Flâneurs du Mal(1)." Whereas Friedberg analyzes the mall as a theater, an illusory and ultimately nonparticipatory realm, we would argue that "mall erotics" extend beyond the consumer/commodity exchange she describes to include visual consumption of other people as products.

30 Doane, *The Desire to Desire*.

31 A letter in *Raunch* reveals that Southglenn Mall in Denver, Colorado, where guess-which-one-of-us hung out every Saturday for her entire adolescence, also used to contain one of the best arrays of glory holes in the country. Imagine my delight. McDonald, *Raunch*.

32 We first heard this phrase at Queer Nation Chicago, spring 1991.

33 See Jill Posener's photo-essay on the British and Australian feminist billboard spray-painting movement, in *Louder Than Words*.

34 Paradoxically, actual corporations have in turn exploited Queer Nation/Gran Fury's recognizable style to produce mock-gay ads such as the Kikit billboard which portrays two "lesbians" — actually an androgynous heterosexual couple — kissing.

35 The *New York Times* devoted a full section to paid advertisements supporting the Persian Gulf invasion and to commercial ads linking patriotism with purchase. Included were an ad for a Steuben glass flag paperweight, a Bloomingdale's spread saluting fathers' "devotion to family and country alike," and — in the most sinister pun of our times (apart from, perhaps, "Saddamize Hussein") — a Saks Fifth Avenue ad captioned "A woman's place is in the home of the brave and the land of the free" (*New York Times* 9 June 1991).

36 Fernandez, "Undocumented Aliens in the Queer Nation."

37 Our reference to a "Queer Symbolic" follows Berlant's analysis of the official "National Symbolic," which coordinates political affect in American life and extends the notion of a political counterlexicon to the current practices of Queer Nation. The National Symbolic is defined as "the order of discursive practices whose reign within the national space . . . transforms individuals into subjects of a collectively held history. Its traditional icons, its metaphors, its heroes, its rituals, and its narratives provide an alphabet for a collective consciousness or national subjectivity; through the National Symbolic, the historical nation aspires to achieve the inevitability of the status of natural law, a birthright. This pseudo-generic condition not only affects profoundly the citizen's subjective experience of her/his political rights, but also of civil life, private life, the life of the body itself" (Berlant, *The Anatomy of National Fantasy*, 20).

38 Wittig, "The Straight Mind."

39 We have been orally instructed on the genealogy of camp counterpolitics and its intersection with radical sexuality by Richard Herrell and Pam Robertson. For textual support, see Newton, *Mother Camp;* Ross, *No Respect;* and Robertson, "Guilty Pleasures."

40 For an aligned project, see Tucker, "Gender, Fucking, and Utopia."

41 See de Lauretis, *Technologies of Gender;* and Harris, "The More Profound Nationality of Their Lesbianism."

42 Judith Butler, *Gender Trouble: Feminism and the Subversion of Identity* (New York: Routledge, 1990); Jill Johnston, *Lesbian Nation: the Feminist Solution* (New York: Simon & Schuster, 1973); Monique Wittig, *The Lesbian Body,* trans. David Le Vay (Boston: Beacon Press, 1986).

43 Spillers, "Mama's Baby/Papa's Maybe."

44 Citational proprieties in the "University of Chicago style" are both inappropriate and virtually impossible with regard to the zines. Here is a selected list of those we consulted to make these generic observations: *BIMBOX* 2 (summer 1990); *Don't Tell Jane and Frankie* (n.d.); *Dumb Bitch Deserves to Die* 2 (winter 1989); *The Gentlewomen of California* 6 (n.d.); *Holy Titclamps* 6 (fall 1990); *Homoture* 2 (n.d.); *Manhattan Review of Unnatural Acts* (n.d.); *Negativa* 1–3 (March–May 1991); *No World Order* (1990); *Screambox* 1 and 2 (November 1990; May 1991); *Sister/My Comrade* (winter 1991); *Taste of Latex* 4 (winter 1990–91); *Thing* 4 (spring 1991).

45 See Crimp and Rolston, *AIDS Demo Graphics.*

46 *BIMBOX* 2.

47 In May 1991, the Randolph Street Gallery of Chicago hosted the first international queer fanzine conference, called "SPEW: the Homographic Convergence."

48 Rubin, "Thinking Sex"; and Duggan, "Sex Panics."

49 Golvin and Podolsky, "Allegiance/Ecstasy."

50 *Don't Tell Jane and Frankie,* no page number.

51 We understand the risk we take in citing Bitch Nation against its stated will: we look forward to our punishment at the hands of editrix G. B. Jones, who "takes her girls like Tylenol — 2 at a time" (see *Don't Tell Jane and Frankie*).

52 On the national stereotype and hybrid identities, see Bhabha, "The Other Question."

5 The Face of America and the State of Emergency

Much thanks to Arjun Appadurai, Carol Breckenridge, Cary Nelson, and Candace Vogler for goading me on to do this competently; and to Roger Rouse for his archival help, vast knowledge, intensive debate, and heroic labor of reading.

1   Benjamin, "Theses on the Philosophy of History," 257.

2   See Foucault, "Governmentality," especially 100–104. Foucault argues that modern states substitute a relatively decentered economic model of population control for the familial model of the sovereign, pre-Enlightenment state, and at the same time become obsessed with maintaining intimacy and continuity with its governed populations, an obsession that results in a fetishism of the kinds of knowledge and feeling that support the security of the state. Thus the intimate identity form of national fantasy accompanies the increasing segmentation and dispersal of state force, violence, and capital.

3   The literature on the "culture wars" is extensive. Inspiration for the conservative war to make a core national culture continues to be derived from Allan Bloom's *The Closing of the American Mind;* its current figurehead is former Secretary of Education, Chairman of the National Endowment for the Humanities, and director of the Office of National Drug Control Policy William J. Bennett. See *The De-Valuing of America*

and *Our Children and Our Country,* particularly the chapters "The Family as Teacher," 61–68, and "Public Education and Moral Education," 69–76; and the section "In Defense of the West," 191–218. Some samples of the anti-core-culture side of the struggle (mainly over the content of educational curricula and youth-culture entertainment) are Richard Bolton, *Culture Wars;* Gates, *Loose Canons;* Graff, *Beyond the Culture Wars;* and Jacoby, *Dogmatic Wisdom.*

4 Coontz, *The Way We Never Were.* See especially the chapters "A Man's Home Is His Castle: The Family and Outside Intervention," 122–48, and "Strong Families, the Foundation of a Virtuous Society: The Family and Civic Responsibility," 93–121.

5 This essay takes up the spirit of Ian Hacking's "Making Up People," with its arguments about the mutual and dialectical constructedness of categories of identity and kinds of subjectivity. See also Jameson, "Imaginary and Symbolic in Lacan."

6 The literature on race, gender, migration, state formation, and transnational capital is extensive: for a start, see Amott and Matthaei, *Race, Gender, and Work;* Dominelli, *Women across Continents;* Gilroy, *There Ain't No Black in the Union Jack;* Sassen, *The Mobility of Capital and Labor.*

7 Newt Gingrich has recently claimed that Republicans who oppose gays are "not representative of the future," and that the GOP is open to homosexuals "in broad agreement with our effort to renew American civilization." This concession to queer American nationality is amazing. However, in the context of the radical-right revitalization of the family as the nest for the future of national identity, it is clear that Gingrich has assimilated homosexuality to the project of reprivatizing sexual property in the person. See Gannett News Service wire report, "Gingrich: GOP Must Include Gays," 23 November 1994.

8 A most succinct analysis of the violent state- and capital-prompted disinvestment in the city and the national poor can be found in Mike Davis, "Who Killed LA? A Political Autopsy," *New Left Review* 197 (January/February 1993): 3–28, and "Who Killed Los Angeles? Part Two: The Verdict is Given," *New Left Review* 199 (May/June 1993): 29–54. In addition, see Robert Gooding-Williams's important anthology *Reading Rodney King/Reading Urban Uprising,* especially Ruth Wilson Gilmore, "Terror Austerity Race Gender Excess Theater," 23–37; Cedric J. Robinson, "Race, Capitalism and the Antidemocracy," 73–81; Rhonda M. Williams, "Accumulation as Evisceration: Urban Rebellion and the New Growth Dynamics," 82–96; Michael Omi and Howard Winant, "The Los Angeles 'Race Riot' and Contemporary U.S. Politics," 97–116; Melvin L. Oliver, James H. Johnson Jr., and Walter C. Farrell Jr., "Anatomy of a Rebellion: A Political-Economic Analysis"; *CovertAction Information Bulletin,* "An Interview with Mike Davis," 142–56; Thomas L. Dumm, "The New Enclosures: Racism in the Normalized Community," 157–77; and Elaine H. Kim, "Home Is Where the *Han* Is: A Korean-American Perspective on the Los Angeles Upheavals," 215–35.

9 Concepts of the protesting mass as a "mob" have even taken on Mafia tones since the Supreme Court, at Clinton's behest, allowed RICO antimob statutes to be used against nonviolent pro-life protesters. See *National Organization for Women Inc., et al. v. Joseph Scheidler, et al.,* 114 S.Ct. 798. For discussions of the Court's decision to link organized protest to racketeering, see the *Connecticut Law Tribune,* 12 June 1995, and the *Chicago Daily Law Bulletin,* 7 February 1995 and 25 July 1995.

10   See Hansen, foreword, *The Public Sphere and Experience.*

11   Rogin, *Ronald Reagan, the Movie*, xiii; see also chapters 1, 2, and 9.

12   An only apparent counterexample to the claim that public popular political activity has become a demonized and dominant form of containment for radical politics might be found in the *Washington Post* critique of the *New York Times* coverage of the 1994 Gay, Lesbian, and Bi-Sexual March on Washington, which, according to the *Post*, went out of its way to clean up the parade and edit out its powerfully sexual performances. But, as often, the inversion into the opposite reinforces the law: queer complexity must be suppressed. See Howard Kurtz, "Don't Read All About It! What We Didn't Say About the Gay March — and Why," *Washington Post* 9 May 1993, sec. C: 1.

13   This list of synonyms for "normal" is brought to you by the thesaurus of WordPerfect 5.1.

14   The ghost of U.S. racism that haunts the citizenship narrative of the film of *Forrest Gump* can also be traced to another text from which the film seems to have drawn some inspiration: Langston Hughes's "Simple" stories, written for the *Chicago Defender* between 1943 and 1966. Jesse B. Semple, or "Simple," as Hughes nicknamed him, is a "race man" who speaks a kind of street wisdom about the racial, sexual, class, and national politics of contemporary life in the United States. (Semple's wisdom is "simple" only in its vernacular informality. It has a critical and self-critical political edge — his is a pseudoinfantile citizenship.) Two speeches from the film, not found in the novel, suggest in particular that *Forrest Gump* borrows but whitewashes Semple's mode of commentary. First, Forrest Gump's opening speech, made to an African American nurse while sitting on a park bench, is about shoes: "Mama always said there's an awful lot you can tell about a person by their shoes — where they're goin', where they been. I've worn lots of shoes. I'll bet if I think about it real hard I can remember my first pair of shoes." In *The Best of Simple* (until recently the only widely available edited collection of Hughes's columns), the opening narrative is titled "Feet Live Their Own Life." Semple opens: "If you want to know about my life . . . don't look at my face, don't look at my hands. Look at my feet and see if you can tell how long I been standing on them. . . . Can't you tell by the shoes I wear — not pointed, not rockingchair, not French-toed, not nothing but big, long, broad, and flat — that I been standing on these feet a long time and carrying some heavy burdens? . . . Everything I do is connected up with my past life" (1). Second, in the film of *Forrest Gump*, Gump's African American friend Bubba Blue makes a long speech about all the things you can do with shrimp: "Anyway, like I was saying, shrimp is the fruit of the sea. You can barbecue it, boil it, broil it, bake it, sauté it. They's on shrimp kabobs, shrimp creole, shrimp gumbo, pan fry, deep fry, stir fry. Then there's pineapple shrimp, lemon shrimp, coconut shrimp, pepper shrimp, shrimp soup, shrimp slaw, shrimp salad, shrimp and potatoes, shrimp burger, shrimp sandwich." In *The Best of Simple*, Semple utters an uncannily similar passage about greens: responding to the narrator's comment that "Greens *are* good," Semple says, "Don't talk! . . . All boiled down with a side of pork, delicious! Greens make my mouth water. I have eaten so many in my life until I could write a book on greenology — and I would still like to eat many more. . . . Mustard greens, collard greens, turnip greens, dandelions, dock. Beet-tops, lamb's tongue, pepper grass, sheepcress, also poke. Good old mixed

greens! Spinach or chard, refined greens! Any kind of fresh greens" (121). The difference between these two "simple" citizens cannot be emphasized enough: Jesse B. Semple has common sense, wit, sensuousness, and intelligence; the filmic Forrest Gump has none of these, though he can pronounce the words. Jesse B. Semple's wisdom produced an antiracist best-selling series for Hughes; *Forrest Gump* involves a pro-white-normal-culture infantile citizenship series for Winston Groom and Robert Zemeckis, consumed by millions of U.S. citizens. See also Hughes, *The Return of Simple.*

15   In a long, commercially sold preview for the film *Forrest Gump,* titled *Through the Eyes of Forrest Gump,* director Robert Zemeckis and actor Tom Hanks clearly state their desire to write the history of the recent United States in a post-prepolitical vein of cultural memory (the screenplay was actually written by Eric Roth). Zemeckis says that "Forrest is a metaphor in the movie for a lot of what is constant and decent and good about America," and quite self-consciously goes on to show the film emerging from a revulsion at what he sees as the culture of negativity that begins to mark the political public sphere in the sixties. Take what happens to Vietnam in *Forrest Gump,* for example. From the pilgrimage-to-Washington material we know that the director could have placed Hanks / Gump in newsreel footage from Vietnam. But in *Through the Eyes of Forrest Gump* Hanks says, "We wanted to capture the reality without playing the same images that we've seen over and over again. And what we don't want to do is make that be yet another editorial comment on how bad a place it was or why. It just was." Significantly, *Through the Eyes of Forrest Gump* shows an alternative take to Gump's speech at the antiwar march on Washington the film represents. In the unreleased version of the scene, Gump says, "There's only one thing I can tell you about the war in Vietnam. In Vietnam your best good friend can get shot. That's all I have to say about that." This speech verbalizes the event from the novel: upset from thinking about his dead friend Bubba Blue, Forrest "heaves" his Medal of Honor at the crowd "as hard as he can" (Groom, *Forrest Gump,* 113). In contrast, in the released film, Gump's speech against the war is silenced by a "pig" who sabotages his microphone: the one moment when Forrest's "virtue" might come into critical contact with the nation is deliberately expurgated by Zemeckis.

16   For precise insider explanation of the technologies of corporeal transformation in the film *Forrest Gump,* see Pourroy, "Making Gump Happen." Thanks much to Julian Bleeker for sending this to me.

17   See the chapter "*Ronald Reagan,* the Movie," in Rogin, *Ronald Reagan, the Movie,* 1– 43. For another scene of infantile national politics that is a clear precedent both for Reagan and for *Forrest Gump,* see *Being There.* The novel is by Jerzy Kosinski; the film was directed by Hal Ashby (1979).

18   While generally the novel *Forrest Gump* is not nearly as reactionary as the film, it does predict the film's dismay at public political life. The novel represents the March against the War in Vietnam as "the most frightenin thing I have seen since we was back at the rice paddy where Bubba was kilt" (Groom, *Forrest Gump,* 78), and also describes a mass political movement for which Forrest is the inspiration, called the "I Got To Pee" movement (236).

19   Many examples of ridiculed protest representations against the left and the right abound at the present moment. Episodes from more liberal shows like *Roseanne, The*

Simpsons, and *Murphy Brown,* for example, mock right-wing protests as the acts of yahoos. Cinematic instances tend to be more conservative and confused. A film less ambitious than *The Pelican Brief* and *Forrest Gump* reveals the sheer ordinariness of protest's debasement: *PCU* (dir. Hart Bochner, 1994), for example, looks at the plague of "cause-ism" on contemporary college campuses, and after much sarcastic and hyperbolic cataloging of political activism by African Americans, gays and lesbians, vegetarians, eco-radicals, and so on, the campus comes together in the end under the rubric "Americans," chanting "We won't protest! We won't protest!" The film *S.F.W.* (dir. Jefery Levy, 1995) plays on three kinds of debased antinormative social movement activity: A "terrorist" group, "Split Image," whose politics is never defined, takes over a convenience store and, in exchange for not killing its youthful hostages, puts them on national television for thirty-six days, where the nation learns to heroize them. Next, a political movement sweeps the mass-mediated country, inspired by the courage of the captives, especially the surviving ones, the working-class Cliff Babb (Stephen Dorff) and the upper-crust Wendy Pfister (Reese Witherspoon). The movement's slogan is "S.F.W.," for "So Fucking What!" Babb is at first alienated by the shallowness of this movement, but as his face and fame spread across television and the covers of many national magazines, he comes to identify with his message, which is that "there is no message." Finally, Babb and Pfister are shot by a disgruntled leftist, "Babs" Wyler, whose slogan is "Everything Matters!" and who is very politically correct in the liberal way. The movie ends with Wyler becoming the national youth heroine of the moment; at the same "moment," the two stars agree to get married, and the movie ends. For yet a different set of contradictions, see the demonstration that introduces us to the fictional Columbus College in John Singleton's *Higher Learning* (1995). Starting with a shot of a crowd chanting "Fight! Fight! Fight!" and pointing their fists in the air, the film obscures whether this is a sports event or a political rally. The person who leads the rally, standing in front of a large American flag that provides the backdrop for the extremely political events to follow, then asks the cheering crowd two questions: "How many people came here to change the world?" and "How many people came here to learn to make a lot of money?" The last shot of the film is the silent stark caption "Unlearn."

20   Archive: the 1970 ABC documentary on "women's liberation" (from the series *Now*); the 1993 25th Anniversary Special commemorating 1968 (Fox, 1993); footage from CNN throughout the 1980s; footage from Chicago television news broadcasts during the 1990s. For an impressive, if overoptimistic, general history of recent protest in the United States and police brutality during it, see Terry H. Anderson, *The Movement and the Sixties.*

21   Warner, "The Mass Public and the Mass Subject."

22   Matsuda et al., *Words That Wound.*

23   In the contemporary U.S. public sphere, the rhetoric of the "face" flourishes in discourses of social justice: currently issues of welfare, AIDS, wife abuse, crime, racism, violence, war, and sexuality invoke this logic. Its function is a classically sentimental one, an attempt to solicit mass sympathy for or commitment to difficult social changes via a logic of personal identification. Some examples, culled from many: On welfare, Jennifer Wolff (text) and Kristine Larsen (photo-essay), "The Real Faces of Welfare," *Glamour* September 1995: 250–53; Rachel Wildavsky and Daniel R. Levine,

"True Faces of Welfare," *Reader's Digest* March 1995: 49–60. On AIDS, Bettijane Levine, "The Changing Face of AIDS," *Los Angeles Times* 16 June 1995, sec. E: 1; Lisa Frazier, "The Face of AIDS Is Changing," *New Orleans Times-Picayune* 8 March 1995, sec. B: 1; Douglas Crimp, "Portraits of People with AIDS"; and Stuart Marshall's video "Bright Eyes" (1984). On wife beating, Rheta Grimsley Johnson, "Nicole Has Given Wife Abuse a Face," *Atlanta Constitution* 15 May 1995, sec. C: 1. On race, Peter Watrous, "The Loss of a Star [Selena] Who Put a Face on a People's Hopes," *New York Times* 4 April 1995, sec. C: 15; and Gilbert Price, "Conservatism: A New Face," *Call and Post* sec. A: 4. On war, Catharine Reeve, "The Face of War," *Chicago Tribune* 7 May 1995, sec. 6: 3. On the death penalty, Linnet Myers, "Girl Puts Human Face on Death Penalty Debate," *Chicago Tribune* 5 February 1995, sec. 1: 3. See also Mills, *Arguing Immigration.*

Yet, as Gilles Deleuze and Félix Guattari argue, "Faces are not basically individual; they define zones of frequency or probability, delimit a field that neutralizes in advance any expressions of connections amenable to the appropriate significations." The face, in their view, is not evidence of the human, but a machine for producing tests for humanness at its limits. Likewise, this trend in the public sphere to put "faces" on social problems has the paradoxical effect of making the faces generic and not individual: thus the facializing gesture that promotes identification across the spaces of alterity is, in effect, an equivocal challenge to shift the political and cultural boundaries of what will count politically as human. Deleuze and Guattari, "Year Zero."

24   See, for example, *Chicago Sun-Times* 28 August 1993: 3, and 29 August 1993: 3; *Cleveland Plain Dealer* 29 August 1993: sec. A: 1; *Los Angeles Times* 29 August 1993, sec. A: 1; *New York Times* 29 August 1993, sec. 1: 18; *Washington Post,* 29 August 1993: 1.

25   *Gabriel Over the White House* comes from an anonymous novel of 1925, which reads American society as currently in a depression-style crisis mainly for the unemployed "forgotten men" who fought for the United States during World War I but reaped little prosperity from that sacrifice. The film of it takes bizarre twists. The president, an appetite-driven, politics-as-usual politician for the elite, drives too fast and dies in a car crash. But God, via the angel Gabriel, brings him back to life as an "ethical" person, in order to complete a short mission: the eradication of organized crime from the United States. To do this, he not only initiates a populist war on poverty by fiat but proclaims martial law, suspending the Constitution and all civil rights. For an excellent narration of the complex (fascist/democratic) political contexts of the book and the film's production, see McConnell, "The Genesis and Ideology of *Gabriel Over the White House.*"

26   See Berlant, "'68: Or, the Revolution of Little Queers."

27   Grisham, *The Pelican Brief,* 47, 55.

28   For the concept and the recent history of remasculinization, see Jeffords, *The Remasculinization of America.*

29   *Time* 8 July 1985: 24, 36.

30   Bennett, *The De-Valuing of America;* Brimelow, *Alien Nation;* Henry, *In Defense of Elitism.*

31   *Time* 8 July 1985: 1.

32   Ibid., 26.

33   Ibid., 3, 57.

34 Ibid., 33 ff.

35 Ibid., 29.

36 Ibid., 81.

37 Ibid., 82–83.

38 Ibid., 82, 100–101.

39 Ibid., 82.

40 Ibid., 26.

41 Ibid.

42 Barthes, *Camera Lucida*.

43 *Time* 8 July 1985: 24.

44 Ibid., 25.

45 There continues to be a vociferous debate on the right as to whether the benefit the United States might receive from immigrant "blood" is not less than the cost their practices and histories pose to the maintenance of normal national culture. See, for example, Peter Brimelow's *Alien Nation;* the issue of the *National Review* titled "Demystifying Multiculturalism" (21 February 1994); and William F. Buckley and John O'Sullivan, "Why Kemp and Bennett Are Wrong on Immigration," *National Review* 21 November 1994: 36–45, 76, 78; and Mills, *Arguing Immigration.*

46 *Time* 142, no. 21 (fall 1993): 5.

47 *Time* 8 July 1985: 100; *Time* 142, no. 21 (fall 1993): 3. Morphing as a model for humanity in general was apparently on *Time*'s "mind": the cover story of the previous issue (8 November 1993) asks dramatically, "Cloning Humans. The first laboratory duplication of a human embryo raises the question: Where do we draw the line?" "The New Face of America" answers this question by performing an erasure of the traces of social desire and aversion that such hierarchical line drawing embodies. Thanks to Carol Breckenridge for alerting me to this continuity.

48 *Time* 142, no. 21 (fall 1993): 66–67.

49 *Time*'s impulse to taxonomize and therefore to make firmer borders around racial types in the United States prior to their "melding" was evident in many places in the early 1990s. Another parallel example of the graphic unconscious is in the *Newsweek* cover story responding carefully to Richard Herrnstein and Charles Murray's reinvigoration of scientific racism in *The Bell Curve*, titled "What Color is Black?" and illustrated by a four-by-five square of differently shaded African American faces. As though randomly related, the three faces on the upper-right-hand corner are partly obscured by a yellow slash that reads, "Bailing Out Mexico." *Newsweek* 13 February 1995.

50 West, "The New Cultural Politics of Difference."

51 *Time* 142, no. 21 (fall 1993): 79.

52 Ibid., 64–65.

53 Ibid., 65.

54 Ibid., 9.

55 Ibid., 87. Henry, *In Defense of Elitism*. See also Henry's much less extreme prophecy of xenophobia to come, in the brief *Time* cover story "America's Changing Colors," 9 April 1990: 28–31.

57 Henry, *In Defense of Elitism*, 74.

58 Ibid., 75.

59 *National Review* 21 February 1994.

60 See *Cosmetics and Toiletries* 109, no. 2: 75; *Ethnic Marketing* 18 January 1993: 11.

61 On *Singin' in the Rain* and "Black or White," see Clover, "Dancin' in the Rain."

62 "Black or White" cites *Risky Business* (dir. Paul Brickman, 1983) in its frame narrative, which is also a part of the recorded song. In this scene, Macaulay Culkin gyrates and plays air guitar in his bedroom, like Tom Cruise in *Risky Business*, to libidinously pulsating rock and roll. Berated by his father (George Wendt) for playing the music too loud, Culkin retaliates with an electric guitar blast so loud that his father explodes, still in his armchair, out of his house and to the other side of the world (Africa). The phrase Culkin uses as he blasts his father is "Eat this." Culkin's body is thus deployed here to link white, male pubescent rock-and-roll excess to masturbation, awakening masculine heterosexuality, Oedipal rage, generational identity, commodity attachment, and a desire to inhabit the publics in which he *feels* himself at his happiest.

63 These two aesthetic horizons of possibility for a nationally minor literature are predicted by Deleuze and Guattari, "What Is a Minor Literature?"

64 A few weeks later (18 July 1994), *Time* no doubt unconsciously returned to the theme of racial/class passing in its cover story on "attention deficit disorder": it is illustrated by a caricature that looks uncannily like O.J.'s distorted icon, now the poster face both for distorted subjectivity and white despair over the alterity of darker faces.

65 Associated Press release, "Buchanan Courts Michigan Baptists," *Chicago Sun-Times* 16 March 1992: 14.

66 Gillespie and Schellhass, *Contract with America*; Moore, *Restoring the Dream*; *Contract with the American Family*.

67 Brimelow, *Alien Nation*, 11, 274.

6 The Queen of America Goes to Washington City:
Notes on Diva Citizenship

Special thanks to Gordon Hutner, Carla Kaplan, Miriam Hansen, audiences at Rutgers, the University of North Carolina, Chicago State, and MLA for their insightful and impassioned critical responses.

1 The strategy/tactics distinction is taken from Certeau, *The Practice of Everyday Life*.

2 On "intersectionality" and the traffic in national and subcultural identities in the United States, see Matsuda, *Words That Wound*.

3 For reading the dialectical image in contexts created through critical theorizing and historicizing, see Taussig, *Shamanism, Colonialism, and the Wild Man*, 366–92; and Jameson, "Reification and Utopia in Mass Culture."

4 Roberto Ungar comments on politics and psychoanalysis "in the rich countries of the contemporary Western world": "where politics are a narrow exercise in bargaining and drift, where the possibility that society might be deeply transformed through collective action is made to look like a revolutionary reverie, where permanent cultural revolution coexists with permanent political deadlock, and where the privileged devote themselves to the expensive, selfish, and impotent cultivation of subjectivity" (*Passion*, 298). This scenario of subjectification surely cuts across class divisions, although the forms of withdrawal from the political vary enormously according to the possession of cultural and economic capital.

5 "Abjection" is currently an important keyword for describing marginalized political

subjectivity in Western political contexts. Two important interlocutors for my thinking about this process are Butler, *Bodies That Matter;* and *The Abject, America,* a special
issue of *Lusitania* 1, no. 4 (n.d.). Abjection is generally thought to be the symbolic
and institutionally supported aura of pollution and prohibition associated with a
devalued population or type of social person. *The Abject, America* uses the work of
Georges Bataille and Slavoj Žižek to read the way the intensified, incoherent hegemonic processes of states reflect themselves in the overcoherent representations
of order that seem to organize dominant institutions and normative subjectivities;
Butler derives from Žižek and Julia Kristeva a notion of abjection that specifically
locates sexually Othered identities.

    My thinking about abjection differs from these in a few ways, which have to do
with tracking the political specificity of abjection's double process: as a kind of social
identity and as a kind of effect some people have on others. Kristeva actually talks
about abjection as a structure of *desubjectification* — in which "ordinary" subjects lose a
sense of their rationality or legitimacy as subjects in everyday and national life in
response to negatively invested social phenomena. She calls these abjected people
"dejects": faced with a substance or phenomenon that unsettles the constitutive rules
of order in their horizon of life expectation, dejects become shaken, aversive, incompetent to *subjectivity.* They feel a traumatic loss — of themselves.

    As I have argued throughout the book, in the contemporary United States abjec-
tion is a social descriptor that is assumed by people at many different junctures of
privilege / powerlessness, across the hierarchies that organize national culture and
national politics. Backlash politics is a politics of hegemonic abjection: but dominant
feelings of abjection would not be imaginable in the typical theoretical use of this
term. Meanwhile, insofar as citizens who consider themselves "normal" experience
abjection in proximity to socially marginal people and populations, marginal subjects
are indeed abject. But this is evident only in their effect on others who have some
definitional power in mass society. In addition, it would be hasty to assume that
subjects who create abjecting effects are abject to themselves, have abject *identities:*
people are not identical with the most negative versions of themselves that circulate in
the (national) public sphere. This suggests the need for greater critical skepticism
about the hierarchical clarity of a center / margin taxonomy in U.S. culture, and more
flexibility and rigorous description in the construction of political subjectivity, for
understanding the strange career of normative powerlessness and social abjection at
the present time. See also Kristeva, *Powers of Horror,* 1–31.

6   This worry, that changes in forms of subjectivity, norms of identification, and performances of rhetoric will seem merely to equal changes in the material conditions of
social life, distinguishes much Marxist / materialist social theory. See, for example,
Hennessy, *Materialist Feminism and the Politics of Discourse;* Lazarus, "Doubting the
New World Order."

7   Haraway, "A Manifesto for Cyborgs," 162; hooks, "Third World Diva Girls"; Wayne
Koestenbaum, "The Codes of Diva Conflict," chapter 3 of Koestenbaum, *The Queen's
Throat.* See also Kipnis, "Reading *Hustler*"; Miriam Hansen, "The Return of Baby-
lon: Rudolph Valentino and Female Spectatorship (1921–1926)," part 3 of Hansen,
Babel and Babylon; Ross, *No Respect;* Tyler, "Boys Will Be Girls"; Patricia J. Williams,
"A Rare Case Study of Muleheadedness and Men."

8   Weller, "The Royal Slave and the Prestige of Origins."

9   Harper, *Iola Leroy*, 75. Subsequent references will be noted parenthetically in the text.

10 I focus here on the analogy Harper seems to make between Esther's complicated ethnic masquerade and Marie's racial one, and the conditions for political speech that ensued. The Book of Esther as a whole tells a far more complex story. On the one hand, it might have provided Harper, and us, with a less patriarchalized model of feminine power: Queen Vashti, whose refusal to display her royal beauty to a banquet of drunken courtiers provoked Elizabeth Cady Stanton's *The Woman's Bible* to name her "the first woman recorded whose self-respect and courage enabled her to act contrary to the will of her husband . . . [in] the first exhibition of individual sovereignty of woman on record . . . true to the Divine aspirations of her nature" (86–88). On the other hand, the Book of Esther is a story about holocausts, a Jewish one averted, and a Macedonian one revengefully executed by the Jews themselves.

11 Jacobs, *Incidents in the Life of a Slave Girl*, 44. Subsequent references will be noted parenthetically in the text.

12 Haraway, "A Manifesto for Cyborgs," 161.

13 Anita Hill, on *60 Minutes*.

14 For the myriad transformations in legal theory and practical juridical norms regulating what counts as "injury" and "harm" to women see Fineman and Thomadsen, *At the Boundaries of Law;* and Bartlett and Kennedy, *Feminist Legal Theory.*

15 There is a large outstanding bibliography on this subject. It includes Carby, *Reconstructing Womanhood;* Foreman, "The Spoken and the Silenced in *Incidents in the Life of a Slave Girl* and *Our Nig,* " Gaines, "White Privilege and Looking Relations"; Spillers, "Notes on an Alternative Model — Neither/Nor" and "Mama's Baby, Papa's Maybe."

16 See Valerie Smith, " 'Loopholes of Retreat.' "

17 Fanon, *The Wretched of the Earth.*

18 See Yellin, *"Written by Herself."*

19 I adapt this notion of "theft" from Harryette Mullen's work on orality and writing in *Incidents in the Life of a Slave Girl.* See "Runaway Tongue."

20 On the counternational politics of gender and kinship in *Incidents,* see Spillers, "Mama's Baby, Papa's Maybe."

21 To place *Iola Leroy* in the context of Harper's complex political activities, see Carby, *Reconstructing Womanhood,* 63–94. Carby's chapter on Harper emphasizes the race/gender axis of her concerns, and provides crucial support to my thinking about nationality. See also Frances Smith Foster's introduction to *A Brighter Coming Day.*

22 Harper, "Duty to Dependent Races."

23 Foster, *A Brighter Coming Day,* 218.

24 The argument that nationality can overcome the fractures of race operates throughout Harper's speeches and poems as well. Perhaps the most condensed and eloquent of these was delivered at the Columbian Exposition. See "Woman's Political Future," in Sewall, *The World's Congress of Representative Women,* 433–38.

25 Habermas, *The Structural Transformation of the Public Sphere,* 31–43; Landes, *Women and the Public Sphere in the Age of the French Revolution,* 21–31.

26 See especially Wahneema Lubiano, "Black Ladies, Welfare Queens, and State Minstrels: Ideological War by Narrative Means," in Morrison, *Race-ing Justice, Engendering Power,* 323–63.

27 The original sentence, describing the mentality of "imperialist subject-production," is "White men are saving brown women from brown men." Spivak, "Can the Subaltern Speak?" 296.

28 Sànchez-Eppler, "Bodily Bonds."

29 The fantasy of diminishing the scale of America to make the nation a place one might encounter has a long history in American letters. See Berlant, *The Anatomy of National Fantasy;* Berland, "Angels Dancing"; and Caughie, "Playing at Being American."

30 The most incisive overview of the feminist, as opposed to class- and race-based, interpretations of the Hill/Thomas events is by Nancy Fraser, in "Sex, Lies, and the Public Sphere." Fraser sees this event as a symptom of transformations of and contestations over definitions of public and private, publicity and privacy. See also Rosemary L. Bray, "Taking Sides Against Ourselves," *New York Times Magazine* 17 November 1991: 56–97. Two volumes have recently emerged that perform repeatedly the adjustments between gender, race, class, and ideological identity categories I am describing here, with much emphasis on the "problem" of articulating "gender" not only with "race" but also with the political movements that make these categories contested and unstable ones in the political public sphere. *The Black Scholar* has assembled Chrisman and Allen, *Court of Appeal,* the following essays from which are directly germane: Calvin Hernton, "Breaking Silences," 86–91; June Jordan, "Can I Get a Witness?" 120–24; Barbara Smith, "Ain't Gonna Let Nobody Turn Me Around," 185–89; Rebecca Walker, "Becoming the Third Wave," 211–14. In Toni Morrison's edited volume *Race-ing Justice, En-gendering Power,* see especially Kimberlè Crenshaw, "Whose Story Is It Anyway? Feminist and Antiracist Appropriations of Anita Hill," 402–40; Christine Stansell, "White Feminists and Black Realities: The Politics of Authenticity," 251–68; Cornel West, "Black Leadership and the Pitfalls of Racial Reasoning," 390–401.

31 The word "experience" is important in the texts I am addressing and the one I am writing here, and requires some explication. The category "experience" is not meant to refer to self-evident autobiographical data over which the experiencing person has control: the experience of being dominated, for example, is subjective, and therefore incompatible descriptions of it might engender legitimate contestation. I take experience here more fundamentally to be something produced in the moment when an activity becomes framed as an event, such that the subject enters the empire of quotation marks, anecdote, self-reflection, memory. More than a category of authenticity, "experience" in this context refers to something someone "has," in aggregate moments of self-estrangement. Jacobs, Harper, and Hill are aware of the unreliability of experience as data both in their own perceptions and in their drives to produce convincing evidence to buttress their arguments for social change or informed consciousness. For a strong summary of the current historicist argument over the evidentiary use of experience, see Scott, "The Evidence of Experience"; and, more critically, Zavarzadeh and Morton, "Theory Pedagogy Politics: The Crisis of 'The Subject' in the Humanities," in their collection *Theory/Pedagogy/Politics,* 1–32; and Chris Weedon, "Post-Structuralist Feminist Practice," in the same volume, 47–63. The phrase "the poetry of the future" comes, famously, from Karl Marx, *The 18th Brumaire of Napoleon Bonaparte.*

Bibliography

Ahmad, Aijaz. *In Theory*. New York: Verso, 1992.

Alexander, Karen. "Fatal Beauties: Black Women in Hollywood." *Stardom: Industry of Desire*. Ed. Christine Gledhill. New York: Routledge, 1991. 45–54.

Amott, Teresa L., and Julie A. Matthaei. *Race, Gender, and Work: A Multicultural History of Women in the United States*. Boston: South End, 1991.

Anderson, Benedict. *Imagined Communities: Reflections on the Origin and Spread of Nationalism*. London: Verso, 1983.

——. "Replica, Aura, and Late Nationalist Imaginings." *Qui Parle 7*, no. 1 (fall/winter 1993): 1–21.

Anderson, Terry H. *The Movement and the Sixties: Protest in America from Greensboro to Wounded Knee*. New York: Oxford UP, 1995.

Appadurai, Arjun. *Modernity at Large: Cultural Dimensions of Globalization*. Minneapolis: U of Minnesota P, 1996.

Assiter, Allison. *Pornography, Feminism, and the Individual*. London: Pluto, 1989.

Austin, Regina. "'A Nation of Thieves': Consumption, Commerce, and the Black Public Sphere." *The Black Public Sphere*. Ed. the Black Public Sphere Collective. Chicago: U of Chicago P, 1995. 229–52.

Balibar, Etienne. *Masses, Classes, Ideas: Studies on Politics and Philosophy after Marx*. New York: Routledge, 1994.

Barthes, Roland. *Camera Lucida: Reflections on Photography*. Trans. Richard Howard. New York: Hill, 1981.

Bartlett, Katharine T., and Rosanne Kennedy. *Feminist Legal Theory: Readings in Law and Gender*. Boulder: Westview, 1991.

Baudrillard, Jean. "From the System to the Destiny of Objects." *The Ecstasy of Communication*. Trans. Bernard and Caroline Schutze. Ed. Slyvère Lotringer. New York: Semiotexte, 1987. 77–96.

——. *In the Shadow of the Silent Majorities . . . Or the End of the Social and Other Essays*. Trans. Paul Foss, Paul Patton, and John Johnston. New York: Semiotexte, 1983.

Behan, Eileen. *Eat Well, Lose Weight While Breastfeeding: The Complete Nutrition Book for Nursing Mothers Including a Healthy Guide to the Weight Loss Your Doctor Promised*. New York: Villard, 1992.

Benjamin, Walter. "A Short History of Photography." *Classic Essays on Photography*. Ed. Alan Trachtenberg. 1931. New Haven: Leete's Island, 1980. 202–3.

——. "Theses on the Philosophy of History." *Illuminations.* Trans. Harry Zohn. New York: Schocken, 1969. 253–64.

Bennett, William J. *The De-Valuing of America: the Fight for Our Culture and Our Children.* New York: Simon and Schuster, 1992.

——. *Our Children and Our Country: Improving America's Schools and Affirming the Common Culture.* New York: Simon and Schuster, 1988.

Berger, John. *About Looking.* New York: Pantheon, 1980.

Berland, Jody. "Angels Dancing: Cultural Technologies and the Production of Space." *Cultural Studies.* Ed. Lawrence Grossberg, Cary Nelson, and Paula Treichler. New York: Routledge, 1992. 39–55.

Berlant, Lauren. *The Anatomy of National Fantasy: Hawthorne, Utopia, and Everyday Life.* Chicago: U of Chicago P, 1991.

——. "National Brands/National Body: *Imitation of Life.*" *The Phantom Public Sphere.* Ed. Bruce Robbins. Minneapolis: U of Minnesota P, 1993. 173–208.

——. " '68: Or, the Revolution of Little Queers." *Feminism beside Itself.* Ed. Diane Elam and Robyn Wiegman. New York: Routledge, 1995. 296–311.

Bersani, Leo. "Is the Rectum a Grave?" *October* 43 (winter 1987). 197–222.

Bérubé, Allan, and Jeffrey Escoffier. "Queer/Nation." *Outlook: National Lesbian and Gay Quarterly* 11 (winter 1991): 13–15.

Bhabha, Homi K. *The Location of Culture.* New York: Routledge, 1994.

——. "The Commitment to Theory," in Homi K. Bhabha, *The Location of Culture.* New York: Routledge, 1994. 19–39.

——. "The Other Question: Stereotype, Discrimination, and the Discourse of Colonialism," in Homi K. Bhabha, *The Location of Culture.* New York: Routledge, 1994. 66–84.

Bloom, Allan. *The Closing of the American Mind.* New York: Simon, 1987.

Bolton, Richard, ed. *Culture Wars: Documents from the Recent Controversies in the Arts.* New York: New, 1992.

Bordo, Susan. *Unbearable Weight: Feminism, Western Culture, and the Body.* Berkeley: U of California P, 1993.

Bourdieu, Pierre, with Luc Boltanski, Robert Castel, Jean-Claude Chamboredon, and Dominique Schnapper. *Photography: A Middle-brow Art.* Trans. Shaun Whiteside. Stanford: Stanford UP, 1990.

Brewer, Gail Sforza, with Tom Brewer, M.D. *What Every Pregnant Woman Should Know: The Truth about Diets and Drugs in Pregnancy.* New York: Penguin, 1977.

Brimelow, Peter. *Alien Nation: Common Sense about America's Immigration Disaster.* New York: Random, 1995.

Butler, Judith. *Bodies That Matter.* New York: Routledge, 1994.

——. *Gender Trouble: Feminism and the Subversion of Identity.* New York: Routledge, 1990.

Carby, Hazel. *Reconstructing Womanhood: The Emergence of the Afro-American Woman Novelist.* New York: Oxford UP, 1987.

Cartwright, Lisa. *Screening the Body: Tracing Medicine's Visual Culture.* Minneapolis: U of Minnesota P, 1995.

Carver, Raymond. "Fat." *Will You Please Be Quiet, Please?: The Stories of Raymond Carver.* New York: McGraw, 1976. 1–6.

Caughie, John. "Playing at Being American." *Logics of Television: Essays in Cultural Criticism.* Ed. Patricia Mellencamp. Bloomington: Indiana UP, 1990. 44–58.

Certeau, Michel de. *The Practice of Everyday Life.* Trans. Stephen Randall. Berkeley: U of California P, 1984.

Chee, Alexander. "A Queer Nationalism." *Outlook: National Lesbian and Gay Quarterly* 11 (winter 1991): 15–19.

Chester, Gail, and Julienne Dickey. *Feminism and Censorship: The Current Debate.* Dorset: Prism, 1988.

Chrisman, Robert, and Robert L. Allen, eds. *Court of Appeal: The Black Community Speaks Out on the Racial and Sexual Politics of Clarence Thomas vs. Anita Hill.* New York: Ballantine, 1992.

Christensen, Terry. *Reel Pictures: American Political Movies from "Birth of a Nation" to "Platoon."* New York: Blackwell, 1987. 45–48.

Christian Coalition. *Contract with the American Family: A Bold Plan by the Christian Coalition to Strengthen the Family and Restore Common-Sense Values.* Nashville: Moorings, 1995.

Clinton, Hillary Rodham. *It Takes a Village: And Other Lessons Children Teach Us.* New York: Simon, 1996.

Coombe, Rosemary J. "The Properties of Culture and the Politics of Possessing Identity: Native Claims in the Cultural Appropriation Controversy." *After Identity.* Ed. Dan Danielsen and Karen Engle. New York: Routledge, 1995. 251–70.

Coontz, Stephanie. *The Way We Never Were: American Families and the Nostalgia Trap.* New York: Basic, 1992.

Corber, Robert J. *In the Name of National Security: Hitchcock, Homophobia, and the Political Construction of Gender in Postwar America.* Durham: Duke UP, 1993.

Crary, Jonathan. *Techniques of the Observer: On Vision and Modernity in the Nineteenth Century.* Cambridge: MIT P, 1990.

Crimp, Douglas. "Portraits of People with AIDS." *Cultural Studies.* Ed. Lawrence Grossberg, Cary Nelson, and Paula A. Treichler. New York: Routledge, 1992. 117–31.

Crimp, Douglas, and Adam Rolston. *AIDS Demo Graphics.* Seattle: Bay, 1990.

Daniels, Cynthia R. *At Women's Expense: State Power and the Politics of Fetal Rights.* Cambridge: Harvard UP, 1993.

Danielsen, Dan, and Karen Engle. *After Identity: A Reader in Law and Culture.* New York: Routledge, 1995.

Davies, Miranda. *Third World, Second Sex: Women's Struggles and National Liberation.* Vols. 1 and 2. London: Zed, 1983.

Davis, Angela. "Racism, Birth Control, and Reproductive Rights." *From Abortion to Reproductive Freedom: Transforming a Movement.* Ed. Marlene Gerber Fried. Boston: South End, 1990. 15–26.

Davis, Marilyn P. *Mexican Voices/American Dreams: An Oral History of Mexican Immigration to the United States.* New York: Holt, 1990.

Davis, Mike. "Who Killed LA? A Political Autopsy." *New Left Review* 197 (January/February 1993): 3–28.

———. "Who Killed Los Angeles? Part Two: The Verdict is Given." *New Left Review* 199 (May/June 1993): 29–54.

De Grazia, Edward. *Censorship Landmarks.* New York: Bowker, 1969.

———. *Girls Lean Back Everywhere: The Law of Obscenity and the Assault on Genius.* New York: Random, 1992.

De Lauretis, Teresa. *Technologies of Gender: Essays on Theory, Film, and Fiction.* Bloomington: Indiana UP, 1987.

Deleuze, Gilles, and Félix Guattari. "What Is a Minor Literature?" *Out There: Marginalization and Contemporary Cultures.* Ed. Russell Ferguson et al. Cambridge: MIT P, 1990. 59–69.

———. *A Thousand Plateaus: Capitalism and Schizophrenia.* Trans. and foreword by Brian Massumi. Minneapolis: U of Minnesota P, 1987.

DeLyser, Femmy, Jane Fonda, and Steve Schapiro. *Jane Fonda's Workout Book for Pregnancy, Birth, and Recovery.* New York: Simon, 1982.

D'Emilio, John. "Capitalism and Gay Identity." *Powers of Desire: The Politics of Sexuality.* Ed. Ann Snitow, Christine Stansell, and Sharon Thompson. New York: Monthly Review, 1983. 100–113.

———. *Sexual Politics, Sexual Communities: The Making of a Homosexual Minority in the United States, 1940–1970.* Chicago: U of Chicago P, 1983.

Diamond, Sara. *Roads to Dominion: Right-Wing Movements and Political Power in the United States.* New York: Guilford, 1995.

Dilfer, Carol Stahlmann. *"Your" Baby, "Your" Body: Fitness During Pregnancy.* New York: Crown, 1977.

Doane, Mary Ann. *The Desire to Desire: The Woman's Film of the 1940's.* Bloomington: Indiana UP, 1987.

———. "Information, Crisis, Catastrophe." *Logics of Television: Essays on Cultural Criticism.* Ed. Patricia Mellencamp. Bloomington: Indiana UP, 1990.

Dolan, Frederick M. *Allegories of America: Narratives, Metaphysics, Politics.* Ithaca: Cornell UP, 1994.

Dominelli, Lena. *Women Across Continents: Feminist Comparative Social Policy.* New York: Harvester, 1991.

Duden, Barbara. *Disembodying Women: Perspectives on Pregnancy and the Unborn.* Cambridge: Harvard UP, 1993.

Duggan, Lisa. "Sex Panics." *Democracy: A Project by Group Material.* Ed. Brian Wallis. Seattle: Bay, 1990. 209–12.

Dumm, Thomas L. *united states.* Ithaca: Cornell UP, 1994.

Dworkin, Andrea. *Pornography: Men Possessing Women.* New York: Dutton, 1989.

Dworkin, Andrea, and Catharine A. MacKinnon. *Pornography and Civil Rights: A New Day for Women's Equality.* Minneapolis: Organizing against Pornography, 1988.

Echols, Alice. *Daring to Be Bad: Radical Feminism in America, 1967–1975.* Minneapolis: U of Minnesota P, 1989.

Ehrenreich, Barbara. *Fear of Falling: The Inner Life of the Middle Class.* New York: Harper, 1989.

———. *The Snarling Citizen.* New York: Farrar, 1995.

Eisenberg, Arlene, Heidi E. Murkoff, and Sandee E. Hathaway. *What to Eat When You're Expecting.* New York: Workman, 1986.

Eisenstein, Zillah R. *The Female Body and the Law.* Berkeley: U of California P, 1988.

Eley, Geoffrey H. "Nations, Publics, and Political Cultures: Placing Habermas in the Nineteenth Century." *Habermas and the Public Sphere.* Ed. Craig Calhoun. Cambridge: MIT P, 1992. 289–339.

Elshtain, Jean Bethke. *Democracy on Trial.* New York: Basic, 1995.

Faludi, Susan. *Backlash: The Undeclared War against American Women.* New York: Crown, 1991.

Fernandez, Charles. "Undocumented Aliens in the Queer Nation." *Out/Look* 12 (spring 1991): 20–23.

Feuer, Jane. "The Concept of Live Television: Ontology as Ideology." *Regarding Television: Critical Approaches—An Anthology.* Ed. E. Ann Kaplan. University Publications of America, AFI, 1983. 12–22.

Fineman, Martha Albertson, and Nancy Sweet Thomadsen, eds. *At the Boundaries of Law: Feminism and Legal Theory.* New York: Routledge, 1991.

Fischer, Lucy. "Sometimes I Feel Like a Motherless Child: Comedy and Matricide." *Comedy/Cinema/Theory.* Ed. Andrew S. Horton. Berkeley: U of California P. 60–78.

Ford, Robert. "Sacred Sex: Art Erects Controversy." *Thing* 4 (spring 1991): 4.

Foreman, Gabrielle. "The Spoken and the Silenced in *Incidents in the Life of a Slave Girl and Our Nig.*" *Callaloo* 13, no. 2 (spring 1990): 313–24.

Foster, Frances Smith. *A Brighter Coming Day: A Frances Ellen Watkins Harper Reader.* By Frances Ellen Watkins Harper. New York: Feminist, 1990. 3–40.

Foucault, Michel. "Governmentality." *The Foucault Effect: Studies in Governmentality.* Ed. Graham Burchell, Colin Gordon, and Peter Miller. Chicago: U of Chicago P, 1991. 87–104.

———. *The History of Sexuality.* Vols. 1–3. Trans. Robert Hurley. New York: Pantheon, 1978, 1985, 1986.

Franklin, Sarah, Celia Lury, and Jackie Stacey. *Off-Centre: Feminism and Cultural Studies.* London: HarperCollins Academic, 1991.

Fraser, Nancy. "Rethinking the Public Sphere: A Contribution to the Critique of Actually Existing Democracy." *Social Text* 25/26 (1990): 56–80.

———. "Sex, Lies, and the Public Sphere: Some Reflections on the Confirmation of Clarence Thomas." *Critical Inquiry* 18 (spring 1992): 595–612.

Freeman, Elizabeth. "Pitmarks on the History of the Country: The Epidemic of Nationalism in Hawthorne's 'Lady Eleanore's Mantle.'" Unpublished ms., U of Chicago, 1990.

Friedberg, Anne. "Les Flâneurs du Mal(1): Cinema and the Postmodern Condition." *PMLA* 106, no. 3 (May 1991): 419–31.

Frohnmayer, John. *Leaving Town Alive: Confessions of an Arts Warrior.* Boston: Houghton, 1993.

Gaines, Jane. "White Privilege and Looking Relations: Race and Gender in Feminist Film Theory." *Screen* 18 (autumn 1988): 12–27.

Gates, Henry Louis Jr. *Loose Canons: Notes on the Culture Wars.* New York: Oxford UP, 1992.

Gates, Wende Devlin, and Gail McFarland Meckel. *Newborn Beauty: A Complete Beauty, Health, and Energy Guide to the Nine Months of Pregnancy and the Nine Months After.* New York: Viking, 1980.

Gillespie, Ed, and Bob Schellhass, eds. *Contract with America: The Bold Plan by Rep. Newt Gingrich, Rep. Dick Armey, and the House Republicans to Change the Nation.* New York: Times, 1994.

Gilliam, Angela. "Women's Equality and National Liberation." *Third World Women and the Politics of Feminism.* Ed. Chandra Talpade Mohanty, Ann Russo, and Lourdes Torres. Bloomington: Indiana UP, 1991. 215–36.

Gilroy, Paul. "'After the Love Has Gone': Bio-Politics and Etho-Poetics in the Black Public

Sphere." *The Black Public Sphere*. Ed. the Black Public Sphere Collective. Chicago: U of Chicago P, 1995. 53–80.

——. *There Ain't No Black in the Union Jack*. London: Hutchinson, 1987.

Ginsburg, Faye D. *Contested Lives: The Abortion Debate in an American Community*. Berkeley: U of California P, 1989.

Ginsburg, Faye D., and Rayna Rapp, eds. *Conceiving the New World Order: The Global Politics of Reproduction*. Berkeley: U of California P, 1995.

Ginsburg, Faye D., and Anna Lowenhaupt Tsing, eds. *Uncertain Terms: Negotiating Gender in American Culture*. Boston: Beacon, 1990.

Glendon, Mary Ann. *Abortion and Divorce in Western Law: American Failures, European Challenges*. Cambridge: Harvard UP, 1987.

Golvin, Sondra, and Robin Podolsky. "Allegiance/Ecstasy." *Screambox* 1 (November 1990): 20–21.

Gooding-Williams, Robert. *Reading Rodney King/Reading Urban Uprising*. New York: Routledge, 1993.

Gordon, Linda. *Woman's Body, Woman's Right: A Social History of Birth Control in America*. New York: Grossman, 1976.

Gore, Tipper. *Raising PG Kids in an X-Rated Society*. Nashville: Abington, 1987.

Graff, Gerald. *Beyond the Culture Wars: How Teaching the Conflicts Can Revitalize American Education*. New York: Norton, 1992.

Grewal, Inderpal, and Caren Kaplan. *Scattered Hegemonies*. Minneapolis: U of Minnesota P, 1994.

Griggers, Cathy. "Lesbian Bodies in the Age of (Post)mechanical Reproduction." *Fear of a Queer Planet: Queer Politics and Social Theory*. Ed. Michael Warner. Minnesota: U of Minnesota P, 1993. 78–192.

Grisham, John. *The Pelican Brief*. New York: Dell, 1992.

Groom, Winston. *Forrest Gump*. New York: Pocket, 1986.

Grossberg, Lawrence. *We Gotta Get Out of This Place: Popular Conservatism and Postmodern Culture*. New York: Routledge, 1992.

Gubar, Susan, and Joan Hoff-Wilson. *For Adult Users Only: The Dilemma of Violent Pornography*. Bloomington: Indiana UP, 1989.

Habermas, Jürgen. *The New Conservatism: Cultural Criticism and the Historians' Debate*. Trans. Shierry Weber Nicholsen. Cambridge: MIT P, 1989.

——. *The Structural Transformation of the Public Sphere: An Inquiry into a Category of Bourgeois Society*. Trans. Thomas Burger. Cambridge: MIT P, 1989.

Hacking, Ian. "Making Up People." *Reconstructing Individualism: Autonomy, Individuality, and the Self in Western Thought*. Ed. T. C. Heller et al. Stanford: Stanford UP, 1986. 222–36.

Halley, Janet E. "The Politics of the Closet: Legal Articulation of Sexual Orientation Identity." *After Identity: A Reader in Law and Culture*. Ed. Dan Danielsen and Karen Engle. New York: Routledge, 1995. 24–38.

Hansen, Miriam. *Babel and Babylon: Spectatorship in American Silent Film*. Cambridge: Harvard UP, 1991.

——. Foreword. *The Public Sphere and Experience: Toward an Analysis of the Bourgeois and Proletarian Public Sphere*. Ed. Oskar Negt and Alexander Kluge. Trans. Peter Labanyi,

Jamie Owen Daniel, and Assenka Oksiloff. Minneapolis: U of Minnesota P, 1993. ix–xli.

Haraway, Donna. "A Manifesto for Cyborgs." *Simians, Cyborgs, and Women: The Reinvention of Nature.* New York: Routledge, 1991. 149–81, 243–48.

Harper, Frances E. W. "Duty to Dependent Races." *Black Women in Nineteenth-Century American Life: Their Words, Their Thoughts, Their Feelings.* Ed. Bert James Loewenberg and Ruth Bogin. 1891. University Park: Pennsylvania State UP, 1976. 245.

———. *Iola Leroy; or, Shadows Uplifted.* 1892. College Park, MD: McGrath, 1969.

Harris, Bertha. "The More Profound Nationality of Their Lesbianism: Lesbian Society in the 1920's." *Amazon Expedition: A Lesbian Feminist Anthology.* Ed. Phillis Birky et al. Washington, NJ: Times Change, 1973. 77–88.

Hartouni, Valerie. "Fetal Exposures: Abortion Politics and the Optics of Illusion." *Camera Obscura* 29 (May 1992): 130–50.

Hawkins, Gordon, and Franklin E. Zimring. *Pornography in a Free Society.* New York: Cambridge UP, 1988.

Heath, Stephen. "Representing Television." *Logics of Television: Essays in Cultural Criticism.* Ed. Patricia Mellencamp. Bloomington: Indiana UP, 1990. 276–302.

Heng, Geraldine, and Janadas Devan. "State Fatherhood: The Politics of Nationalism, Sexuality and Race in Singapore." *Nationalisms and Sexualities.* Ed. Andrew Parker, Doris Sommer, and Patricia Yeager. New York: Routledge, 1992. 343–64.

Hennessy, Rosemary. *Materialist Feminism and the Politics of Discourse.* New York: Routledge, 1993.

———. "Queer Visibility in Commodity Culture." *Social Postmodernism.* Ed. Linda Nicholson and Steven Seidman. Cambridge: Cambridge UP, 1995. 142–83.

Herman, Edward S., and Noam Chomsky. *Manufacturing Consent: The Political Economy of the Mass Media.* New York: Pantheon, 1988.

Herrell, Richard K. "The Symbolic Strategies of Chicago's Gay and Lesbian Pride Day Parade." *Gay Culture in America: Essays from the Field.* Ed. Gilbert Herdt. Boston: Beacon, 1992. 225–52.

Hoberman, J. "Victim Victorious." *Village Voice* 7 March 1995: 31–33.

hooks, bell. "Third World Diva Girls." *Yearning: Race, Gender, and Cultural Politics.* Boston: South End, 1990. 89–102.

Horton, Andrew. *Comedy/Cinema/Theory.* Ed. Andrew Horton. Berkeley: U of California P, 1991.

Hughes, Langston. *The Best of Simple.* New York: Hill, 1961.

———. *The Return of Simple.* Ed. Akiba Sullivan Harper. Introduction by Arnold Rampersad. New York: Hill, 1994.

Itzin, Catherine. *Pornography: Women, Violence, and Civil Liberties.* New York: Oxford UP, 1992.

Jacobs, Harriet. *Incidents in the Life of a Slave Girl: Written by Herself.* Ed. Jean Fagan Yellin. (Orig. ed. Lydia Maria Child.) Cambridge: Harvard UP, 1987.

Jacobus, Mary, Evelyn Fox Keller, and Sally Shuttleworth, eds. *Body/Politics: Women and the Discourses of Science.* New York: Routledge, 1990.

Jacoby, Russell. *Dogmatic Wisdom: How the Culture Wars Divert Education and Distract America.* New York: Doubleday, 1994.

Jameson, Fredric. "Five Theses on Actually Existing Marxism." *Monthly Review* 47, no. 11 (April 1996): 1–10.

——. *The Geopolitical Aesthetic.* Indianapolis: Indiana UP, 1992.

——. "Imaginary and Symbolic in Lacan." *The Ideologies of Theory: Essays 1971–1986.* Vol. 1. Minneapolis: U of Minnesota P, 1988. 75–115.

——. "Postmodernism and Utopia." *Utopia Post-Utopia: Configurations of Nature and Culture in Recent Sculpture and Photography.* Boston, The Institute of Contemporary Art; Cambridge: MIT P, 1988. 11–32.

——. "Reification and Utopia in Mass Culture." *Social Text* 1 (winter 1979): 130–48.

Jeffords, Susan. *Hard Bodies: Hollywood Masculinity in the Reagan Era.* Bloomington: Indiana UP, 1994.

——. *The Remasculinization of America: Gender and the Vietnam War.* Bloomington: Indiana UP, 1989.

Johnson, Barbara. "Apostrophe, Animation, and Abortion." *A World of Difference.* Baltimore: Johns Hopkins UP, 1987. 184–99.

Johnston, Jill. *Lesbian Nation: The Feminist Solution.* New York: Simon, 1973.

Joyrich, Lynne. "Tube Tied: Reproductive Politics and *Moonlighting.*" *Modernity and Mass Culture.* Ed. James Naremore and Patrick Brantlinger. Bloomington: Indiana UP, 1991. 176–202.

Kammen, Michael. *Mystic Chords of Memory: The Transformation of Tradition in Modern American Culture.* New York: Vintage, 1991.

Kaplan, Amy, and Donald Pease. *Cultures of U.S. Imperialism.* Durham: Duke UP, 1993.

Kaplan, E. Ann. *Motherhood and Representation: The Mother in Popular Culture and Melodrama.* New York: Routledge, 1992.

Katz, Jonathan Ned. *The Invention of Heterosexuality.* New York: Dutton, 1995.

Kaufmann, David. "Yuppie Postmodernism." *Arizona Quarterly* 47, no. 2 (summer 1991): 93–116.

Kipnis, Laura. "'The Phantom Twitchings of an Amputated Limb': Colonialism as a Female Disease." *Ecstasy Unlimited: On Sex, Capital, Gender, and Aesthetics.* Minneapolis: U of Minnesota P, 1993. 196–206.

——. "Reading *Hustler:* (Male) Desire and (Female) Disgust." *Cultural Studies.* Ed. Lawrence Grossberg, Cary Nelson, and Paula A. Treichler. Urbana: U of Illinois P, 1992. 373–91.

Kirk, Marshall, and Hunter Madsen. *After the Ball: How America Will Conquer Its Fear and Hatred of Gays in the '90s.* New York: Doubleday, 1989.

Koestenbaum, Wayne. *The Queen's Throat: Opera, Homosexuality, and the Mystery of Desire.* New York: Poseidon, 1993.

Koonz, Claudia. *Mothers in the Fatherland: Women, the Family, and Nazi Politics.* New York: St. Martin's, 1987.

Kosinski, Jerzy. *Being There.* New York: Harcourt, 1970.

Kristeva, Julia. *Powers of Horror: An Essay on Abjection.* Trans. Léon Roudiez. New York: Columbia UP, 1982.

Kuhn, Annette. *Cinema, Censorship, and Sexuality, 1919–1925.* New York: Routledge, 1988.

Landes, Joan B. *Women and the Public Sphere in the Age of the French Revolution.* Ithaca: Cornell UP, 1988.

Laqueur, Thomas. *Making Sex: Body and Gender from the Greeks to Freud.* Cambridge: Harvard UP, 1990.

Lazarus, Neil. "Doubting the New World Order: Marxism, Realism, and the Claims of Postmodernist Social Theory." *differences* 3, no. 3 (fall 1991): 94–138.

Leff, Leonard J., and Jerold L. Simmons. *The Dame in the Kimono: Hollywood, Censorship, and the Production Code from the 1920s to the 1960s.* New York: Grove, 1990.

Lipsitz, George. *Time Passages: Collective Memory and American Culture.* Minneapolis: U of Minnesota P, 1990.

Lloyd, David. "Genet's Genealogy: European Minorities and the Ends of the Canon." *The Nature and Context of Minority Discourse.* Ed. Abdul R. JanMohamed and David Lloyd. New York: Oxford UP, 1990. 369–93.

Lorde, Audre. *Zami: A New Spelling of My Name.* Trumansburg, NY: Crossing, 1982.

Lubiano, Wahneema. "Black Ladies, Welfare Queens, and State Minstrels: Ideological War by Narrative Means." *Race-ing Justice, En-gendering Power: Essays on Anita Hill, Clarence Thomas, and the Construction of Social Reality.* New York: Pantheon, 1992. 323–63.

Luker, Kristen. *Abortion and the Politics of Motherhood.* Berkeley: U of California P, 1984.

Mann, Denise. "The Spectacularization of Everyday Life: Recycling Hollywood Stars and Fans in Early Television Variety Shows." *Star Texts: Image and Performance in Film and Television.* Ed. Jeremy G. Butler. Detroit: Wayne State UP, 1991. 333–60.

——. "Body Narratives, Body Boundaries." *Cultural Studies.* Ed. Lawrence Grossberg, Cary Nelson, and Paula A. Treichler. New York: Routledge, 1992. 409–23.

Martin, Emily. *Flexible Bodies: Tracking Immunity in American Culture from the Days of Polio to the Age of AIDS.* Boston: Beacon, 1994.

——. *The Woman in the Body: A Cultural Analysis of Reproduction.* Boston: Beacon, 1987.

Matsuda, Mari J., Charles R. Lawrence III, Richard Delgado, and Kimberlè Williams Crenshaw. *Words That Wound: Critical Race Theory, Assaultive Speech, and the First Amendment.* Boulder: Westview, 1993.

May, Elaine Tyler. *Homeward Bound: American Families in the Cold War Era.* New York: Basic, 1988.

Mbembe, Achille. "Prosaics of Servitude and Authoritarian Civilities." *Public Culture* 5 (fall 1992): 123–48.

Mbembe, Achille, and Janet Roitman. "Figures of the Subject in Times of Crisis." *Public Culture 7,* no. 2 (winter 1995): 323–52.

McClay, Michael. *"I Love Lucy": The Complete Picture History of the Most Popular TV Show Ever.* New York: Warner, 1995.

McConnell, Robert L. "The Genesis and Ideology of *Gabriel over the White House.*" *Cinema Examined.* Ed. Richard Dyer McCann and Jack C. Ellis. New York: Dutton, 1982. 200–221.

McDonald, Boyd. *Raunch: True Homosexual Experiences.* Boston: Fidelity, 1990.

Mellencamp, Patricia. "Situation Comedy, Feminism, and Freud: The Discourses of Gracie and Lucy." *Studies in Entertainment: Critical Approaches to Mass Culture.* Ed. Tania Modleski. Bloomington: Indiana UP, 1986. 80–95.

Mills, Nicolaus. *Arguing Immigration: The Debate over the Changing Face of America.* New York: Simon, 1993.

Mohanty, Chandra Talpade. "Cartographies of Struggle: Third World Women and the

Politics of Feminism." *Third World Women and the Politics of Feminism*. Ed. Chandra Talpade Mohanty, Ann Russo, and Lourdes Torres. Bloomington: Indiana UP, 1991. 1–47.

Montagu, Frances, and Ashley Montagu. *Life before Birth*. London: Longmans, 1965.

Moon, Michael, and Eve Kosofsky Sedgwick. "Divinity: A Dossier, A Performance Piece, A Little-Understood Emotion." *Tendencies*. By Eve Kosofsky Sedgwick. Durham: Duke UP, 1993. 215–51.

Moore, Stephen, ed. *Restoring the Dream: The Bold New Plan by House Republicans*. New York: Times, 1995.

Morris, Meaghan. "Banality in Cultural Studies." *Logics of Television: Essays in Cultural Criticism*. Ed. Patricia Mellencamp. Bloomington: Indiana UP, 1990. 14–43.

Morrison, Toni, ed. *Race-ing Justice, En-gendering Power: Essays on Anita Hill, Clarence Thomas, and the Construction of Social Reality*. New York: Pantheon, 1992.

Morse, Margaret. "An Ontology of Everyday Distraction." *Logics of Television: Essays in Cultural Criticism*. Ed. Patricia Mellencamp. Bloomington: Indiana UP, 1990. 193–221.

Mosse, George. *Nationalism and Sexuality*. Madison: U of Wisconsin P, 1985.

Mouffe, Chantal. Preface, "Democratic Politics Today"; and "Democratic Citizenship and the Political Community." *Dimensions of Radical Democracy: Pluralism, Citizenship, Community*. New York: Verso, 1992. 1–14, 225–39.

Mowlana, Hamid, George Gerbner, and Herbert I. Schiller. *Triumph of the Image: The Media's War in the Persian Gulf—A Global Perspective*. Boulder: Westview, 1992.

Mullen, Harryette. "Runaway Tongue: Resistant Orality in *Uncle Tom's Cabin, Our Nig, Incidents in the Life of a Slave Girl*, and *Beloved.*" *The Culture of Sentiment: Race, Gender, and Sentimentality in Nineteenth-Century America*. Ed. Shirley Samuels. New York: Oxford UP, 1992. 244–64.

Myerowitz, Joanne, ed. *Not June Cleaver: Women and Gender in Postwar America, 1945–1960*. Philadelphia: Temple UP, 1994.

Neale, Stephen, and Frank Krutnik. *Popular Film and Television Comedy*. New York: Routledge, 1990.

Negt, Oskar, and Alexander Kluge. *Public Sphere and Experience: Toward an Analysis of the Bourgeois and Proletarian Public Sphere*. Foreword by Miriam Hansen. Trans. Peter Labanyi, Jamie Owen Daniel, and Assenka Oksiloff. Minneapolis: U of Minnesota P, 1993.

———. "Selections from *The Proletariat Public Sphere.*" *Social Text* 25/26 (1990): 24–32.

Newton, Esther. *Mother Camp: Female Impersonators in America*. Chicago: U of Chicago P, 1979.

Newton, Esther, and Shirley Walton. "The Misunderstanding: Toward a More Precise Sexual Vocabulary." *Pleasure and Danger*. Ed. Carole Vance. Boston: Routledge, 1984. 242–50.

Nicholson, Linda J., ed. *Feminism/Postmodernism*. New York: Routledge, 1990.

Nsiah-Jefferson, Laurie. "Reproductive Laws, Women of Color, and Low-Income Women." *Feminist Jurisprudence*. Ed. Patricia Smith. New York: Oxford UP, 1993. 322–34.

Oakley, Ann. *The Captured Womb: A History of the Medical Care of Pregnant Women*. Oxford: Blackwell, 1984.

O'Brien, Paddy. *Birth and Our Bodies: Exercises and Meditations for the Childbearing Year and Preparation for Active Birth.* London: Pandora, 1986.

Omi, Michael, and Howard Winant. *Racial Formation in the United States: From the 1960s to the 1990s.* 2nd ed. New York: Routledge, 1994.

Parker, Patricia A. *Literary Fat Ladies: Rhetoric, Gender, Property.* New York: Methuen, 1988.

Patton, Cindy. "Refiguring Social Space." *Social Postmodernism: Beyond Identity Politics.* Ed. Linda Nicholson and Steven Seidman. New York: Cambridge UP, 1995. 216–49.

Penley, Constance, and Andrew Ross, eds. *Technoculture.* Minneapolis: U of Minnesota P, 1991.

Petchesky, Rosalind P. *Abortion and Women's Choice: The State, Sexuality, and Reproductive Freedom.* Rev. ed. Boston: Northeastern UP, 1990.

——. "The Body as Property: A Feminist Re-vision." *Conceiving the New World Order: The Global Politics of Reproduction.* Ed. Faye D. Ginsburg and Rayna Rapp. Berkeley: U of California P, 1995. 387–406.

——. "Fetal Images: The Power of Visual Culture in the Politics of Reproduction." *Feminist Studies* 13, no. 2 (summer 1987): 263–92.

Pfeil, Fred. *White Guys: Studies in Postmodern Domination and Difference.* New York: Verso, 1995.

Pollitt, Katha. *Reasonable Creatures: Essays on Women and Feminism.* New York: Vintage, 1995.

Pollock, Griselda. "Missing Women: Rethinking Early Thoughts on Images of Women." *The Critical Image: Essays on Contemporary Photography.* Ed. Carol Squiers. Seattle: Bay, 1990. 202–19.

Posener, Jill. *Louder Than Words.* New York: Pandora, 1986.

Pourroy, Janine. "Making Gump Happen." *Cinefex* 60 (December 1994): 90–106.

Rapp, Rayna. "Constructing Amniocentesis: Maternal and Medical Discourses." *Uncertain Terms: Negotiating Gender in American Culture.* Boston: Beacon, 1990. 28–42.

Rasula, Jed. "Nietzsche in the Nursery: Naive Classics and Surrogate Parents in Postwar American Cultural Debates." *Representations* 29 (winter 1990): 50–77.

Reagan, Ronald. *Abortion and the Conscience of the Nation.* Afterwords by C. Everett Koop and Malcolm Muggeridge. Nashville: Nelson, 1984.

Robertson, Pamela. "Guilty Pleasures: Camp and the Female Spectator." Unpublished ms., U of Chicago, 1990.

Rogin, Michael Paul. *Ronald Reagan, the Movie: And Other Episodes in Political Demonology.* Berkeley: U of California P, 1987.

Ross, Andrew. *No Respect: Intellectuals and Popular Culture.* New York: Routledge, 1989.

Rouse, Roger. "Questions of Identity: Personhood and Collectivity in Transnational Migration to the United States." *Critique of Anthropology* 15, no. 4 (1995): 353–80.

——. "Thinking through Transnationalism: Notes on the Cultural Politics of Class Relations in the Contemporary United States." *Public Culture 7,* no. 2 (winter 1995): 353–402.

Rubin, Gayle. "Thinking Sex: Notes for a Radical Theory of the Politics of Sexuality." *Pleasure and Danger: Exploring Female Sexuality.* Ed. Carole S. Vance. New York: Routledge, 1984. 267–319.

Samuels, Shirley, ed. *The Culture of Sentiment: Race, Gender, and Sentimentality in Nineteenth-Century America.* New York: Oxford UP, 1992.

Sànchez-Eppler, Karen. "Bodily Bonds: The Intersecting Rhetorics of Feminism and Abolition." *Representations* 24 (fall 1988): 28–59.

Sandage, Scott A. "The Lincoln Memorial, the Civil Rights Movement, and the Politics of Memory, 1939–1963." *Journal of American History* 80, no. 1 (June 1993): 135–67.

Sassen, Saskia. *The Mobility of Capital and Labor.* Cambridge: Cambridge UP, 1988.

Schiller, Herbert I. *Culture, Inc: The Corporate Takeover of Public Expression.* New York: Oxford UP, 1989.

———. *Information and the Crisis Economy.* Norwood, NJ: Ablex, 1984.

Schneider, Cynthia, and Brian Wallis, eds. *Global Television.* Cambridge: MIT P, 1988.

Schwoch, James, Mimi White, and Susan Reilly. *Media Knowledge: Readings in Popular Culture, Pedagogy, and Critical Citizenship.* Albany: SUNY P, 1992.

Scott, Joan W. "The Evidence of Experience." *Critical Inquiry* 17 (summer 1991): 773–97.

Sedgwick, Eve Kosofsky. *Epistemology of the Closet.* Berkeley: U of California P, 1990.

———. "A Poem Is Being Written." *Tendencies.* Durham: Duke UP, 1993. 177–214.

Sennett, Richard. *The Fall of Public Man.* New York: Norton, 1976.

Sewall, May Wright, ed. *The World's Congress of Representative Women.* Chicago and New York: Rand, 1894.

Shilts, Randy. "The Queering of America." *Advocate* 567 (1 January 1991): 32–38.

Shohut, Ella, and Robert Stam. *Unthinking Eurocentrism: Multiculturalism and the Media.* London: Routledge, 1994.

Skocpol, Theda. *Protecting Soldiers and Mothers: The Political Origins of Social Policy in the United States.* Cambridge: Harvard UP, 1992.

Smith, Dorothy E. *The Everyday World As Problematic: A Feminist Sociology.* Boston: Northeastern UP, 1987.

Smith, Neil. "Contours of a Spatialized Politics: Homeless Vehicles and the Production of Geographical Scale." *Social Text* 33 (1992): 54–81.

Smith, Patricia. *Feminist Jurisprudence.* New York: Oxford UP, 1993.

Smith, Valerie. "'Loopholes of Retreat': Architecture and Ideology in Harriet Jacobs's *Incidents in the Life of a Slave Girl.*" *Reading Black, Reading Feminist.* Ed. Henry Louis Gates Jr. New York: Meridian, 1990. 212–26.

Smoodin, Eric. "'Compulsory Viewing for Every Citizen': *Mr. Smith* and the Rhetoric of Reception." *Cinema Journal* 35, no. 2 (winter 1996): 3–23.

Sobchack, Vivian. "Child/Alien/Father: Patriarchal Crisis and Generic Exchange." *Close Encounters: Film, Feminism, and Science Fiction.* Ed. Constance Penley, Elisabeth Lyon, Lynn Spigel, and Janet Bergstrom. Minneapolis: U of Minnesota P, 1991. 3–30.

Sofia, Zoe. "Exterminating Fetuses: Abortion, Disarmament, and the Sexo-Semiotics of Extraterrestrialism." *Diacritics* 14 (summer 1984): 47–59.

Spallone, Patricia. *Beyond Conception: The New Politics of Reproduction.* Granby, MA: Bergin, 1989.

Spigel, Lynn. *Make Room for TV: Television and the Family Ideal in Postwar America.* Chicago: U of Chicago P, 1992.

Spillers, Hortense. "Mama's Baby, Papa's Maybe: An American Grammar Book." *Diacritics* 17, no. 2 (summer 1987): 65–81.

———. "Notes on an Alternative Model — Neither/Nor." *The Difference Within: Feminism and Critical Theory.* Ed. Elizabeth Meese and Alice Parker. Philadelphia: Benjamins, 1989. 165–87.

Spivak, Gayatri Chakravorty. "Draupadi" and "Breast-Giver." *In Other Worlds: Essays in Cultural Politics.* New York: Methuen, 1987. 179–96, 222–40.

———. "Acting Bits/Identity Talk." *Critical Inquiry* 18 (summer 1992): 770–803.

———. "Can the Subaltern Speak?" *Marxism and the Interpretation of Culture.* Ed. Cary Nelson and Lawrence Grossberg. Urbana: U of Illinois P, 1988. 271–313.

———. "In a Word. *Interview.*" *differences* 1 (summer 1989): 124–56.

———. "The Politics of Translation." *Destabilizing Theory: Contemporary Feminist Debates.* Ed. Michèle Barrett and Anne Phillips. Cambridge, MA: Polity, 1992. 177–200.

———. *Outside in the Teaching Machine.* New York: Routledge, 1993.

———. "Woman in Difference." *Outside in the Teaching Machine.* New York: Routledge, 1993. 77–95.

Stabile, Carole. *Feminism and the Technological Fix.* Manchester: Manchester UP, 1994.

Stallybrass, Peter, and Allon White. *The Politics and Poetics of Transgression.* Ithaca: Cornell UP, 1986.

Stamworth, Michelle. "Birth Pangs: Conceptive Technologies and the Threat to Motherhood." *Conflicts in Feminism.* Ed. Marianne Hirsch and Evelyn Fox Keller. New York: Routledge. 288–304.

Stanton, Elizabeth Cady, and the Revising Committee. *The Woman's Bible.* 1898. Seattle: Coalition Task Force on Women and Religion, 1974.

Stephens, Sharon, ed. *Children and the Politics of Culture: Risks, Rights and Reconstructions.* Princeton: Princeton UP, 1995.

Stewart, Susan. *On Longing: Narratives of the Miniature, the Gigantic, the Souvenir, the Collection.* Baltimore: Johns Hopkins UP, 1984.

Strathern, Marilyn. *Reproducing the Future: Essays on Anthropology, Kinship, and the New Reproductive Technologies.* New York: Routledge, 1992.

Taussig, Michael. *The Nervous System.* New York: Routledge, 1992.

———. *Shamanism, Colonialism, and the Wild Man: A Study in Terror and Healing.* Chicago: U of Chicago P, 1987.

Taylor, Janelle Sue. "The Public Fetus and the Family Car: From Abortion Politics to a Volvo Advertisement." *Public Culture* 4, no. 2 (spring 1992): 67–80.

Terkel, Studs. *Working: People Talk About What They Do All Day and How They Feel About What They Do.* New York: Pantheon, 1974.

Tocqueville, Alexis de. *Democracy in America.* Vol. 1. Trans. Henry Reeve. Ed. Philips Bradley. New York: Vintage, 1945.

Trebay, Guy. "In Your Face." *Village Voice* 14 August 1990: 35–39.

Treichler, Paula A. "Feminism, Medicine, and the Meaning of Childbirth." *Body/Politics: Women and the Discourses of Science.* Ed. Mary Jacobus, Evelyn Fox Keller, and Sally Shuttleworth. New York: Routledge, 1990.

Treichler, Paula A., and Lisa Cartwright, eds. *Imaging Technologies, Inscribing Science.* Spec. issue of *Camera Obscura* 28 (January 1992) and 29 (May 1992).

Tribe, Laurence H. *Abortion: The Clash of Absolutes.* New York: Norton, 1990.

Tsing, Anna Lowenhaupt. "Monster Stories: Women Charged with Perinatal Endangerment." *Uncertain Terms: Negotiating Gender in American Culture.* Boston: Beacon, 1990. 113–38.

Tucker, Scott. "Gender, Fucking, and Utopia: An Essay in Response to John Stoltenberg's *Refusing to Be a Man.*" *Social Text* 27 (1991): 3–34.

302

Tyler, Carole-Anne. "Boys Will Be Girls: The Politics of Gay Drag." *Inside/Out: Lesbian Theories, Gay Theories.* Ed. Diana Fuss. New York: Routledge, 1991. 32–70.

Ungar, Roberto. *Passion: An Essay on Personality.* New York: Free, 1984.

Vance, Carole S. "The Pleasures of Looking: The Attorney General's Commission on Pornography versus Visual Images." *The Critical Image: Essays on Contemporary Photography.* Ed. Carol Squiers. Seattle: Bay, 1990. 38–58.

Verrilli, George E., and Anne Marie Mueser. *While Waiting: A Prenatal Guidebook.* New York: St. Martin's, 1989.

Warner, Michael. Introduction. *Fear of a Queer Planet.* Minneapolis: U of Minnesota P, 1993. vii–xxxi.

———. "The Mass Public and the Mass Subject." *Habermas and the Public Sphere.* Ed. Craig Calhoun. Cambridge: MIT P, 1992. 377–401.

Weller, Barry. "The Royal Slave and the Prestige of Origins." *Kenyon Review* 14 (summer 1992): 65–78.

West, Cornel. "The New Cultural Politics of Difference." *Out There: Marginalization and Contemporary Cultures.* Ed. Russell Ferguson, Martha Gever, Trinh T. Min-ha, and Cornel West. Cambridge: MIT P, 1990. 19–36.

Williams, Patricia J. *The Alchemy of Race and Rights.* Cambridge: Harvard UP, 1991.

———. "Law and Everyday Life." *Law and Everyday Life.* Ed. Austin Sarat and Thomas K. Kearns. Ann Arbor: U of Michigan P, 1995. 171–90.

———. "A Rare Case Study of Muleheadedness and Men." *Race-ing Justice, En-gendering Power: Essays on Anita Hill, Clarence Thomas, and the Construction of Social Reality.* Ed. Toni Morrison. New York: Pantheon, 1992. 159–71.

Williams, Phyllis S. *Nourishing Your Unborn Child.* New York: Avon, 1974.

Wittig, Monique. *The Lesbian Body.* Trans. David Le Vay. Boston: Beacon, 1986.

———. "The Straight Mind." *Out There: Marginalization and Contemporary Cultures.* Ed. Russell Ferguson et al. Cambridge: MIT P, 1990. 51–57.

Wolfe, Charles. "*Mr. Smith Goes to Washington:* Democratic Forums and Representational Forms." *Closed Viewings: An Anthology of New Film Criticism.* Ed. Peter Lehman. Tallahassee: Florida State UP, 1990. 300–331.

Yellin, Jean Fagan. "*Written by Herself:* Harriet Jacobs's Slave Narrative." *American Literature* 53 (November 1981): 479–86.

Young, Iris Marion. "Polity and Group Difference: A Critique of the Ideal of Universal Citizenship." *Ethics* 99 (January 1989): 250–74.

———. *Throwing Like a Girl and Other Essays in Feminist Philosophy and Social Theory.* Bloomington: Indiana UP, 1990.

Zavarzadeh, Mas'ud, and Donald Morton. *Theory/Pedagogy/Politics: Texts for Change.* Urbana: U of Illinois P, 1991.

Žižek, Slavoj. *The Sublime Object of Ideology.* New York: Verso, 1989.

Index